Relational Poverty Politics

Relational Poverty Politics

FORMS, STRUGGLES, AND POSSIBILITIES

EDITED BY
VICTORIA LAWSON
AND SARAH ELWOOD

THE UNIVERSITY OF GEORGIA PRESS
Athens

© 2018 by the University of Georgia Press
Athens, Georgia 30602
www.ugapress.org
All rights reserved
Set in 10/12.5 Minion Pro by Graphic Composition, Inc., Bogart, GA

Most University of Georgia Press titles are
available from popular e-book vendors.

Printed digitally

Library of Congress Cataloging-in-Publication Data
Names: Lawson, Victoria A., editor. | Elwood, Sarah, editor.
Title: Relational poverty politics : forms, struggles, and possibilities / edited by Victoria Lawson
and Sarah Elwood.
Description: Athens : The University of Georgia Press, 2018. | Series: Geographies of justice and
social transformation ; 39 | Includes bibliographical references and index.
Identifiers: LCCN 2017048365| ISBN 9780820353135 (hbk : alk. paper) | ISBN 9780820353142 (pbk :
alk. paper) | ISBN 9780820353128 (ebk)
Subjects: LCSH: Poverty—Government policy. | Poverty.
Classification: LCC HC79.P6 R45 2018 | DDC 362.5/561—dc23
LC record available at https://lccn.loc.gov/2017048365

For Frances Fox Piven,
who continues to inspire and teach us,
and for Vicky's brother Richard.

CONTENTS

FOREWORD

FRANCES FOX PIVEN

The concept of "relational poverty" implies a theory or theories about causality. In contrast to prevalent understandings that root economic hardship in the deficits of individuals or families or subcultures, the theory asserts that poverty is best explained by patterns of human relationships, and by the social institutions that organize those relationships. And in contrast to understandings that ascribe hardship to the consequences of social exclusion or isolation, it asserts that poverty is importantly the result of the different terms and conditions on which people are included in social life.

To state this idea baldly is immediately illuminating because it directs our attention to the patterns of social relationship in which some people dominate and even crush others in order to dispossess or expropriate the life-giving resources that these people would otherwise control, whether through enclosure of the commons, or the imposition of confiscatory taxes, or by foreclosing on their farms or homes. It also directs our attention to exploitation, to the many ways that some people extract profit from the labor of others, whether through slavery or debt peonage or forced labor or wage labor. Then there are also the multiple relations with kin, community, church, and party that most of the time reinforce the relations of domination that underlie poverty, whether by invoking theories of God's will or by drawing on attachments to family, tribe, or community or by invoking the authority of tradition. These processes lead to what the contributors to this volume rightly call *differential inclusion*. (Although I should note that under some conditions these multiple relations can also become the nodes that encourage defiance, as when a dissident church legitimates discontent from below, or when insurgency among one group encourages uprisings among other similarly situated people.)

To be sure, the view that the reasons for poverty are in individual or family or community traits is not totally wrong. There are of course instances where individual or family circumstances do partially explain poverty, but even then the social institutions in which people are embedded matter greatly. Whether these are kinship networks or social welfare programs, they can work to help sustain those without the capacities to function on the prevailing terms, although they can also extract in exchange terrible costs in social degradation. Similarly, while remote villages in barren climes may indeed be physically isolated, there are in fact fewer and fewer places that are so remote that they are beyond the influence of worldwide capitalism, and now, in the age of the Anthropocene, even isolated settlements are increasingly at the mercy of climate change set in motion by capitalist practices and relations. However indirectly, even the hardship produced by the droughts and floods brought on by global warming can also be understood in the framework of relational poverty.

To posit that most of the world's poverty has to be understood in relational terms is, I think, a very promising perspective because it opens up large possibilities for change. For one thing, unlike climatic conditions or genetic disposition or family dysfunctions, social relations are malleable, and indeed they do change and change continuously, and it is people who change them. By contrast, diagnoses that attribute poverty to the nature or nurture of those afflicted, while they lead to all sorts of individual, family, and community therapeutic interventions, and also support the professionals who implement them, have generally uncertain effects on poverty. (Direct provision of resources is another matter. There is no gainsaying that the straightforward provision of cash or food or shelter, can ease poverty!)

More important, once attention is directed to the social interactions that lead to dispossession or exploitation, and then to poverty, this way of understanding poverty opens the possibility that the poor themselves can become actors in the chain of events that can produce some relief of hardship. The idea of relational poverty directs us to attend to the potential power of the poor themselves. This is a big claim, and I have to explain.

We usually think of power as the ability of one actor or group of actors to dominate others as a result of the resources they bring to bear in social interactions. This Weberian idea has led analysts to develop lists of "power resources" that can be used to sway people in social interaction, from personal attributes to wealth, weapons, and positions of authority in major institutions. This view is handy enough because much of the time it explains what we regularly observe, that the rich and well-placed are on top, and the poor and degraded are on the bottom of social hierarchies. Power resources are fungible, and those who have riches also can buy armies, and armies in turn can be deployed to increase stores of riches. Although much of our experience fits this model, some of it doesn't.

Workers do sometimes prevail in contests with employers, the poor sometimes win measures that ease their condition, and even the slave can influence the master as in Hegel's master slave dialectic. There is in short another kind of power that does not rest on the unequally distributed attributes and assets usually named by power analysts. It is the power inherent in the interdependence entailed by cooperative social relationships themselves. Workers depend on employers, but employers also depend on workers, the rich also depend on the poor if only for their quiescence, parents on their children's affection and obedience, teachers on their students for respect, and so on.

While we can spin out the implications of this kind of interdependent power so as to cast light on manifold social relations—doctors and their patients, beauticians and their clients, landlords and their tenants—clearly some kinds of interdependence are more important than others in generating and sustaining the processes of expropriation and exploitation that lead to large-scale poverty. These interdependencies are also more important in collective efforts from the bottom to resist those processes by refusing the cooperation implied by interdependence. Because the relationships that are the axes of expropriation and exploitation have widespread ramifications, they are also the focus of a good deal of political work by influential actors, work that draws on a wide range of political resources beyond interdependence. Much of that work is directed to restraining and obscuring the possibility of the exercise of interdependent power from below.

One way to inhibit power from below is by rule making. The social relations that generate and sustain poverty, and which also create the potential for interdependent power, are institutionalized. And that means they are embedded in rules, as well as ideas and practices, that are also institutionalized. The rules, whatever other functions they may serve in facilitating the complex forms of cooperation we call society, are also power strategies by which dominant groups, drawing not only on interdependent power but on the full range of other power resources they control, inhibit or prevent the actualization of interdependent power from below. The examples are manifold, from feudal laws that bound workers to their employers to laws against vagrancy and begging that foreclosed the exit options of workers, laws against theft or poaching that upheld the expropriation of the commons, laws against worker strikes, and laws against the worker "combinations" or unions that facilitated strikes. Moreover, important rules also become laws, which means that they are backed not only by custom and ingrained social deference but by the majesty and coercive force of the state. Rules, in other words, stabilize domination.

Rules are not simply proclamations, and they are not simply state edicts. Over time they also come to be legitimated by thick interpretations of social life that justify conformity, indeed make conformity seem inevitable. These interpretations and the culture of domination they constitute function to obscure the very possibility of power from below. Importantly, this culture obscures the relational sources of poverty and the actuality of interdependence that this implies, and therefore the possibility of interdependent power from below. If the power of the poor depends on the reality of interdependent social relations, its actualization depends on the development of ideas, of mental constructs that expose that interdependence. In other words, it depends on the development of insurgent interpretations or insurgent subcultures.

It is not only elites who do political work. When socially ingrained expectations are disappointed, when the promises a society and its elites make are dashed, ordinary people may be propelled to engage in collective refusal, to walk out or sit down or strike or boycott or simply refuse to obey the rules of civic life by rioting. But collective defiance from below is hard. Unless people are already bound together in cohesive social groups, insurgency requires what some people call *organizing*. This is the work of bringing people together and committing them to a collective endeavor, maybe a dangerous collective endeavor, so that the insurgents have the capacity to act in concert, at least to the extent necessary to take advantage of interdependence. Also the insurgents must be able to withstand the countervailing pressures that are likely to be exerted by family or church or party. They must be able to endure the interruption of the relations on which they also depend. And they must be able to withstand the deployment of force and violence that is always an aspect of relations of domination and of the poverty they produce—think of layoffs, evictions, incarceration, hunger—but the force that can be deployed against rule breakers is often especially virulent and fearsome. In sum, while interdependence and the potential for power it suggests is widespread, and arguably actually increases as neoliberal capitalism spreads its complex networks of communication and transportation across the globe, much of social life works against the ability of people to activate that latent power.

Before any of that can happen, the thick weight of dominant interpretations of social life that legitimate extreme inequality must begin to weaken. People must begin to think that the prevailing order is neither just nor inevitable. More important, they must begin to imagine that they themselves can play a role in changing that order.

One key element in the development of such an insurgent subculture is the recognition by ordinary people that those who dominate them also depend on them. They have to recognize interdependence. Think only of the obstacles to recognizing interdependence in the face of prevailing understandings that privilege the contributions of elites to social life, and even erase the contributions of lower status groups. In the traditional family, the earnings of men were given much more weight than the domestic and emotional services of women, just as the contributions of investors are now privileged over productive labor. Insurgents have to do heavy cultural work to lift the weight of these definitions, as labor insurgents have tried to do throughout the history of the labor movement. But think today even of the lowly nannies and domestics who mind the children and clean the homes of the bankers who sit at the top of the American economy. Everything in our contemporary political culture reminds us of the critical role of the bankers. But what if the nannies went on a well-organized strike?

A world dominated by international networks of capitalists and the state power they control desperately needs the tempering influence of popular insurgency, not only by nannies but by the masses of displaced migrants trudging across the globe and by the growing numbers of precarious workers in the informal sectors everywhere. We social scientists often like to think we can play a role in solving social problems. Maybe, just maybe, we can, if we direct our skills to tracing the contemporary patterns of interdependence that weave the world together, measure the costs of ongoing arrangements that produce widespread poverty through exploitation and expropriation, and illuminate the ways that the poor themselves can upset those patterns.

ACKNOWLEDGMENTS

This book is rooted in feminist inspirations. We are constantly inspired by those who insist on thinking and acting in boundary-crossing ways to connect people in order to challenge impoverishment. To call out some of our greatest inspirations: Ananya Roy's call for transnational analysis led us to create the Relational Poverty Network (RPN) at the outset, Richa Nagar's collaborative feminist knowledge-making project inspired our approach to building this volume, and Frances Fox Piven's insistence on a fierce political project around poverty moves us forward.

We are grateful to all chapter authors for going with us on this journey. You were creative, collaborative, and always responsive thought partners, and this book is better for your collaboration with us. Thank you. Our collective work is much improved by the dedicated and timely work of all chapter reviewers, as well as the anonymous reviewers. We owe them all a debt of gratitude for engaging with and improving the project. We thank Darin Rogers and Andre Ortega for sharing their photo for the book cover.

This book would never have materialized without the dedicated work of Austin Crane, who is a brilliant, patient, and consistently supportive presence in our bookmaking. Monica Farías was there from the very beginning, organizing and participating in the foundational seminar that imagined the RPN into being. Magie Ramirez got the network off the ground from day one, working to materialize the ideas into an actual network. Elyse Gordon worked tirelessly to mount the opening conference of the RPN and helped us imagine many other network activities. Amy Piedalue organized the writing retreat that began this volume. Jordyn Vandeleur, Stella Jones, Koji Pingry, Sam Nowak, and Helen Olsen have all supported the work of the network as research assistants, and we are grateful for their wonderful contributions. All of our research assistants are creative intellectual partners who play essential, generative, collaborative, always patient, and good-humored roles in the work of the RPN.

We are deeply grateful to our graduate and undergraduate students who have engaged with us and pushed us to write, teach, and act beyond our own theoretical and political "homes." In particular, we are deeply indebted to Edgar Sandoval, Elizabeth Shoffner, Magie Ramirez, Monica Farías, Emma Slager, Elyse Gordon, Austin Crane, Yolanda Valencia, Katie Gillespie, Michelle Daigle, and

Tish Lopez. All of them have been generous with their intellectual and caring support of our work and our community. Their engagements with us have created the conditions for learning, and as a result we have grown as scholars and as people.

We are fortunate to work with, be inspired by, and learn from a wonderful community of scholars, teachers, and activists. Listing is always a dangerous enterprise! This said, we are particularly thankful to Lisa Elwood-Faustino, Lucy Jarosz, Ananya Roy, Eric Sheppard, Helga Leitner, Ezequiel Adamovsky, Stephen Healy, Santiago Canevaro, Nicolás Viotti, Anne Bonds, Richard Ballard, Tony Sparks, David Giles, Frances Fox Piven, Carolyn Pinedo Turnovsky, Tim Harris, Tony Lucero, and Emma Shaw Crane. These wonderful people have talked out ideas endlessly, they have supported us and the work in every way, and they have sustained us with care, love, and humor at every turn.

We also thank a broader network of fellow thinkers who have supported both the network and the project of thinking poverty in new ways. In particular we thank Eugene McCann, Ruthie Wilson Gilmore, Laura Pulido, Megan Ybarra, Luke Bergmann, Resat Kasaba, Doreen Massey, Kathie Gibson, Mona Atia, Nick Schuermans, Kristy Copeland, Dena Aufseeser, Anisa Jackson, Allison Chan, Rhoda Rosen, Gillian Rose, Natasha Marin, all members of our 2014 and 2016 relational poverty seminars, all participants in the 2017 RPN Summer Institute, and all RPN members for signing onto this project!

Place matters, and the Helen Riaboff Whiteley Center matters more than most, providing us a tranquil and beautiful space to create the network and this book. All the staff, and especially Kathy Cowell, are always welcoming, supportive, and genuinely interested in the work we are doing.

Projects of this kind don't come to fruition without funding support. We are grateful for NSF grant BCS-1852810 and to the University of Washington Department of Geography and College of Arts & Sciences for providing all kinds of support to our work. In particular, Lucy Jarosz and Judy Howard have provided us with support at key moments on this journey.

Finally and most importantly, we would not have been able to do this work without love and friendship. Vicky is so thankful for her deep friendship with Sarah Elwood, who has been the most inspiring, generous, and loving person with whom I could have done this work. Vicky also calls out her partner Dean Odegard and all the furry members of our immediate family who supported her and kept her close to sane (!) throughout these last years. Sarah is grateful for all that two decades of friendship and collaborative thinking with Vicky Lawson has brought. The chance to think, work, laugh, learn, and grow together is precious to me. Sarah also thanks her spouse, Lisa Elwood-Faustino: Your love, inspiration, politics, and smart remarks are woven into everything I do.

Relational Poverty Politics

(Un)Thinkable Poverty Politics

SARAH ELWOOD AND VICTORIA LAWSON

Since we are an agricultural family, there is always that quick money for those three months when cherries are in season. . . . There was one semester where I wasn't going to work but money was tight so I had to, and then I started working in the fields, and I flunked my classes. Because it was just too much. . . . I can't even apply for the California DREAM Act because it's GPA-based so I don't have that chance until I clean up my GPA, which is still messed up from when I had to work in the fields.

> —Alejandra, in Negrón-Gonzales (this volume)

Yes I can earn more but, in life, I am not pursuing money alone. I like this [theater] work. I have other hungers than money. . . . I want to . . . create more people who will think of people.

> —Pradeep Sardar, in Da Costa and Nagar (this volume)

Another world is possible, and exists in the shadows of this one.

> —David Boarder Giles (this volume)

Relational Poverty Politics interrogates the breadth of forms, struggles, and possibilities of poverty politics that are constituted across differences of race, gender, nationality, ability, religion, and class. The passages above push the boundaries of what is "thinkable" as poverty politics and invite new ways of understanding and challenging impoverishment. Alejandra, a community college student and low-wage agricultural worker in California, describes interlocking systems of impoverishment in low-wage work and policy rules. Her words challenge representations of the U.S. DREAM Act as an "opportunity" for undocumented youth, revealing it instead as a structure of discipline and adverse incorporation. Pradeep, a rural activist performer in political theater in India, formerly a landless agricultural worker, casts as commensurate the need for money and the need for the creative and socially transformative work of doing theater—an articulation of multiple urgent hungers that rethinks how we understand "poverty." Contributing author David Giles references new political horizons in the work of Food Not Bombs, a global movement of anarchist groups that reappropriate, consume, and share "waste" food, creating abject economies that at once connect to (the margins of) liberal economies and remain unthinkable/illegible to them. These stories pose questions about how people mobilize against impoverishment today.

Relational Poverty Politics expands poverty analysis by attending to the complex articulations of political-economic, representational, sociocultural, embodied, and affective processes of impoverishment that mobilize a range of poverty politics. We open the field for new ways of understanding poverty, beyond reductive economism, by theorizing a diverse range of "thinkable" and "unthinkable" poverty politics and their interrelations. We are inspired by Marxian, poststructural, feminist, and black political thought that conceives of politics as struggles to uphold or disrupt existing political-economic and social orders that delimit the kinds of subjects, meanings, claims, and, ultimately, material relations that can exist, be perceived, and be demanded (Rancière 2004; McKittrick and Woods 2007; Hall and Massey 2010; Cacho 2012; Pulido 2017). This formulation of politics holds a generative paradox that we use to extend theoretical and political imaginaries around poverty: For Cacho (2012) and McKittrick and Woods (2007), "thinkable politics" always coexist with "unthinkable politics"— subjects, meanings, claims, relations, and actions formed *outside the terms of what can be* under existing racial capitalist social orders. Unthinkable politics cannot exist and yet nonetheless they do. From this foundation, we develop a framework for theorizing thinkable and unthinkable poverty politics that expands concepts of poverty and poverty politics, bringing to light previously overlooked processes of impoverishment and mobilizations against poverty.[1] To be clear, we conceptualize thinkability and unthinkability not as distinct, closed categories, but rather as dialectically related analytics that reveal distinct power relations, legibilities, and framings of poverty politics. We employ this framework for theorizing, understanding, and opening space for new imaginations and actions that have been foreclosed in much poverty research.

We conceive of thinkable poverty politics as projects of government (broadly written) that identify problems, justify interventions, and inaugurate solutions that stabilize dominant forms of economic and political power (Rose and Miller 1992; Roy and Shaw Crane 2015). Thinkable projects of government that define poverty politics arise in relation to the current conjuncture of globalized and financialized capitalism, secured by ideological projects in particular places that secure "common sense" ways of thinking and doing everyday life (Hall and Massey 2010). Poverty has always been a problem of government in capitalist states because its persistence belies narratives of progress and fairness. Persistent poverty is a contradiction that must be depoliticized in order to stabilize political-economic orders and power hierarchies. Writing about the United Kingdom, but with arguments also deeply resonant in the United States today,

Hall and Massey discuss how market fundamentalism and individualism have been installed as the hegemonic "common sense" of contemporary neoliberal political and cultural discourse. Material practices of everyday life (re)produce this ideology through constant associations between the market and claims of efficiency, fairness, freedom, and choice in media, political discourse, consumerist culture, education, and research. In addition to thoroughly naturalizing economic forces and markets as both inevitable and good, this discourse excises a critical analysis of capitalism concerned with the redistribution of wealth and collective public responsibility for the vulnerable such that "the stubborn facts about poverty, inequality . . . all became 'unspeakable'" (Hall and Massey 2010, 61). As such, broad consent to these particular "truths" and erasures secures hegemonic understandings of what sorts of poverty politics are thinkable in particular times and places.

The production of material and social difference and value is fundamental to ideological projects under capitalism (Gramsci 1929–35; Laclau and Mouffe 1985; Diez 2013). Contemporary ideologies built around market fundamentalism and individualism stabilize capitalist power-knowledge orders through categorizing and disciplining "deserving" subjects, as well as by excluding and/or enacting violence upon those deemed undeserving (Schram 2000; Goode and Maskovsky 2001; Lawson 2012). Racism is a structuring force within capitalism, and we employ "racial capitalism" to signal the centrality of racism to "common sense" projects of governance and poverty politics (Robinson 1983; Melamed 2015; Gilmore 2002; Pulido 2017). For example, racial capitalism is secured by dividing groups who have common interests (i.e., in-common critiques of inequality and individualism) through a racialized politics of fear and exclusion. The production of divisions between people on the basis of class, race, gender, citizenship, sexuality (and more), and the ways that processes of social differentiation obscure in-common exploitation and marginalization are essential mechanisms in stabilizing consensus around ever more concentrated political-economic power and the ideologies that support it (e.g., market fundamentalism). *Relational Poverty Politics* analyzes how these contemporary articulations of economic, political, cultural, and discursive projects animate thinkable poverty politics across diverse places. But beyond this, we also explore unthinkable (unspeakable) poverty politics existing outside of hegemonic common sense. How, we ask, are ideological projects around poverty and the current social order unsettled, undone, even exploded? By bringing together scholarship across different countries, sites of mobilization, and subject positions—and by analyzing the dialectical interrelation of thinkable and unthinkable poverty politics—the collection illuminates fissures and gaps in hegemonic framings of impoverishment and identifies resources for thinking and doing otherwise.

Much contemporary critical poverty scholarship has focused on thinkable poverty politics including the regulation, territoriality, and governance of poverty, bureaucracies of poverty management, and the financialization of poverty. These forms of governance, surveillance, and control are poverty politics that reproduce the "poor other," make certain subjects legible as deserving/legitimate and others as flawed and in need of reform and control in ways that limit imaginations about how impoverishment can be challenged (Schram 2000; Goode and Maskovsky 2001; O'Connor 2001; Lyon-Callo 2008; Roy 2010, 2015; Roy and Shaw Crane 2015). *Relational Poverty Politics* joins with this critical literature to examine the ways in which poverty is an always-already political project: from its problematization within the development industry grounding a Cold War project of capitalist economic development to a neoliberal politics of North Atlantic antiwelfarism that stabilizes liberal democracies by locating poverty in flawed individuals (Escobar 1995; Ferguson 1994; Schram 2000; Roy and Shaw Crane 2015). We extend this emphasis on governmental projects of thinkable poverty politics to trace the ways in which poverty activists themselves often demand forms of access and inclusion into existing social, economic, and cultural projects. For example, Maskovsky (this volume) analyzes struggles in which impoverished people with HIV/AIDS claim access to subsidized housing on the basis of their health status. These activists seek inclusion under the terms of safety net policies that prioritize homeless individuals with HIV/AIDS over those without, and situate themselves as legitimate claimants through reference to biomedical framings of "ill and vulnerable subjects."

This volume explores the thinkable poverty politics constituted through insistent exercises of power over those named as poor via state-sanctioned violence, border management, workfare, as well as land, housing, and healthcare policies that frame who is poor, why, and what should be done. We contribute to understandings of the political work done by poverty management machineries by attending to the ways that thinkable poverty politics entail *modes of differential incorporation*. Chapter authors engage poverty management as a politics that not only excludes (e.g., by rendering some subjects undeserving) but also includes under adverse conditions or incorporates only those poor subjects able to conform to normative ideals. This book reveals a range of politics of differential incorporation, such as unequal access to social assistance or higher education benefits along lines of race and/or citizenship, whether directly through state welfare policy (Ye, this volume) or de facto through racialized incorporation into low-wage exploitative work (Negrón-Gonzales, this volume). Diagnosing processes of differential incorporation is a crucial step in understanding how the normative consensus around poverty is secured in particular conjunctures and then how it can be transformed. Contributors to this book show that processes of differential incorporation are strategies for gaining (limited) access to housing, income, and/or healthcare, yet do so upon existing terms of differential social and material valuation. Consent to the existing order is ensured through distribution of limited gains, while the underlying structures (e.g., capitalist labor exploitation, racialized bordering, privatization of care) remain in place. For example, the U.S. DREAM Act can be scripted and widely understood as an "opportunity" for undocumented students to access higher education, and yet it is off-limits to many undocumented students because of their poverty and precarious position in labor markets (Negrón-Gonzales, this volume).

Pushing beyond a thinkable poverty politics of differential incorporation, *Relational Poverty Politics* is also inspired by diverse mobilizations around the globe, such as the World Social Forum, Arab Spring, Podemos, June 2013 movements in Brazil, Occupy, Food Not Bombs, Black Lives Matter, and countless small struggles that are not widely recognized nor typically understood as poverty politics.[2] These mobilizations reveal vital repertoires of poverty politics outside thinkable orders: anarchist formulations of diverse economies that run on the "waste" of capitalist systems, unexpected alliances across lines of power and privilege, refusals of conventional understandings of poverty, and hopeful practices in the face of extreme suffering. Conceptualizing these as unthinkable poverty politics, we examine meanings, claims, actions, and relations that form a constitutive outside to poverty management, governance, and differential incorporation and, as such, challenge material and discursive constructions of impoverishment in new ways. Theorizing *unthinkable poverty politics of refusal, hope, and possibility* makes visible subjects, forms of agency, alliances, tactics, and meanings that have been unrecognizable within poverty studies and the regimes of discourse and intervention discussed above.

The contributors' attention to unthinkable politics illuminates poverty politics beyond imaginaries and practices typically recognized as political and transformative. For instance, Pradeep Sardar (above) chooses to work less for pay to feed his creative hunger for theater. This is a transformative politics that rejects the normed "common sense" about the primacy of economic security, focusing instead on building personhood and alliances across seemingly impossible caste/religious divides (Da Costa and Nagar, this volume). *Relational Poverty Politics* traces unthinkable poverty politics that refuse normative categories (e.g., deservingness, worker or student, caste, etc.) around which poverty is produced, including creative survival strategies enacted in spite of violent oppression and hopeful alliances across racialized, gendered, classed, and other forms of difference and privilege. The exercises of hope, refusal, and possibility unfolded in this volume open political horizons of thought and action that lie beyond the seemingly inevitable limits defined by the existing order on its own terms. Recognizing unthinkable poverty politics stands as a critically important way to imagine and fight for solidarities that build transgressive politics.

The chapters in *Relational Poverty Politics* engage in transnational theorizing to carry out a relational analysis of diverse mobilizations against poverty in India, Brazil, the United States, Thailand, and South Africa. This relational analytic approach entails antiessentialist theorization, recognizing multiple causal processes of impoverishment, and a humble epistemological stance toward knowledge making that relies on localized forms of analysis and attends to diverse geohistorical relations producing/resisting impoverishment (Elwood, Lawson, and Sheppard 2016). The authors write against a coherent and settled concept of "poverty," deconstructing this category by theorizing with those named as poor. The authors themselves engage in unthinkable poverty politics by refusing "poverty" as a universal and economistic category—instead attending to historical and contemporary differences in how poverty is articulated and produced in diverse sites. They also examine how mobilizations against poverty may be limited by universal claims (rooted in European geohistory) that afford power and privilege to certain groups and identities. These analytical moves bring feminist and postcolonial theory to bear on Western "Truth" that poverty is an economic and individualized condition of persons who lack ethics or "modern attributes" such as personal responsibility, docility, ambition, education, jobs, or capital. In contrast, the contributors' relational analyses illuminate structural, discursive, violent, and governmentalizing processes that continually produce impoverishment. *Relational Poverty Politics* opens analytical space for concepts and practices ignored in much poverty research, such as state-sanctioned violence, the reappropriation of "waste" as valuable, performative encounters with assertions of privilege(s), and combative ontologies that refuse "development." By drawing together relational analyses of diverse mobilizations, this collection makes visible constellations of relations, ideas, and practices that remain unthinkable in much of poverty studies.

Thinking Poverty Relationally

Our analysis is rooted in relational theorizations of poverty, which treat poverty and privilege as mutually constituted, examining poverty not as a category or material position, but as a relationship and a site of conflict, crisis, and contestation (Goode and Maskovsky 2001; Green 2006; Hickey 2009; Mosse 2010; Elwood, Lawson, and Sheppard 2016). This approach emerges from relational poverty studies, a field that coalesced from critical development and cultural studies in the 2000s (Watkins 1994; Schram 2000; O'Connor 2001; Hickey 2009; Mosse 2010).[3] Relational poverty scholars counter poverty studies' predominant emphasis on measuring, benchmarking, and individualizing poverty through structural analyses of the constitution and reproduction of poverty (Addison, Hulme, and Kanbur 2009; du Toit 2009; Hickey 2009; Mosse 2010).

Relational theorizations of poverty conceptualize impoverishment as produced through multidimensional economic, political, and cultural processes, and through social relations. Scholars trace, for example, how land dispossession or adverse incorporation into capitalist economies intersects with racialization, gendering, and other processes of social categorization and exclusion, sustaining and amplifying the marginalization of impoverished people and places (Wood 2003; Green 2005, 2006; Kaplinsky 2005; du Toit and Hickey 2007; De Herdt and Bastiaensen 2008). From these foundations, relational poverty analyses explore how poverty is produced by capitalist, white supremacist, sexist, and heteronormative institutions and rules; by political-economic processes and through identity making (by middle classes, elites, policy makers, religious or sectarian nationalists). Theorizing impoverishment as produced through intersecting power relations of race, caste, class, identity, coloniality, ability, and gender counters theoretical closures in much poverty knowledge. In particular, relational theorizations illuminate geohistorical interconnections in poverty processes around the globe, and highlight asymmetrical circulations of poverty theory and "expertise" between majority and minority worlds (Roy 2003, 2012; Lawson 2012; Leitner and Sheppard 2015; Elwood, Lawson, and Sheppard 2016).

Relational poverty theory attends not just to structural processes of impoverishment but also to the formation of social subjects in relation to poverty and privilege, conceptualizing social subjects as emergent and coproduced, rather than as distinct categories (e.g., "middle class," "poor," etc.) from which identities arise (Somers 1998; Adamovsky 2009; Mosse 2010). This theorization of subjects is foundational to illuminating "poverty difference" as produced through discourses that separate impoverished people and places as "other" from a normative group, that name and categorize them as poor, and that signify this poor other as deficient, criminal, backward, and/or lazy (Newman 1999; Guano 2004; Green 2006). These relational accounts further illustrate how discourses of poverty difference always also produce (and govern) more privileged class subjects, particularly the normative middle-class subject against whom poor others are framed (Goode and Maskovsky 2001; Fernandes and Heller 2006; Blokland 2012). Relational poverty thought emphasizes the intersectionality of poverty discourses, showing how constructions of class difference and subordination become harnessed to gendered or racialized representations (Watkins 1994; hooks 2000; Schram 2000). Processes of sociocultural categorization and differentiation are seen as intertwined with political economic structures and relations, as for instance when impoverishment driven by labor market changes and diminished welfare assistance is obscured by a cultural politics of "personal responsibility" that blames poverty on individuals' poor choices (Schram 2015; Elwood, Lawson, and Sheppard 2016).

Relational poverty theory has made critical inroads in understanding interrelated processes that give rise to poverty and privilege in different times and places, yet this body of work has directed comparatively little attention to theorizing poverty *politics*. The projects of governance, poverty management, and (re)production of social boundaries at the center of relational poverty studies are indeed all forms of poverty politics, yet are not explicitly theorized as such.

Relational Poverty Politics centers poverty politics, attending to questions of power that are as yet unanswered (and often unasked). We build upon theorizations of the coproduction of poverty and privilege to illuminate forms of poverty politics that make unequal power relations unremarkable and even acceptable in particular conjunctures. Theorizing poverty politics broadly allows researchers to trace how hegemonic consensus is secured around the relational systems of material and social (de)valuation that produce impoverishment. We extend relational poverty studies' focus on processes of exclusion and social difference to ask what other kinds of poverty politics are possible and might already exist. This open theorization of poverty politics thinks beyond the limits of existing structures (in theory and in the world) to illuminate other kinds of social subjects, vocabularies, and actions. *Relational Poverty Politics* extends relational poverty studies by centering poverty politics and theorizing both politics that reproduce existing processes of impoverishment and their social arrangements (thinkable poverty politics), and those that frame an outside to the existing social order or are unrecognizable under its ideologies and norms (unthinkable by dominant projects of government, social regulation, and thought).

Theorizing Poverty Politics

Poverty research has long identified the separation of deserving/undeserving that divides purportedly reformable subjects from excluded and supposedly unredeemable others. This binary does vital political work, upholding a framing of "thinkable" subjects and politics that refuses its other: subjects and practices framed as "unthinkable" poverty politics. As we elaborate below, thinkable poverty politics refers to projects of government, discourses, actions, programs, and tactics that make impoverished subjects legible, and define the terms upon which they may access or claim resources, in ways that lead to their differential incorporation into existing sociopolitical and economic orders. By contrast, unthinkable poverty politics are those articulated in contradiction to "common sense" subject positions, discourses, and projects of government that sustain this order and consent to it, producing politics and subjects illegible to existing hierarchies of power/knowledge. Our book interrogates a wide repertoire of subjects, spaces, and practices that reproduce or refuse thinkability and that may contribute to a transgressive project of unthinkable poverty politics.

Poverty is a unique site from which to theorize these forms of politics because it is simultaneously produced through normative ideologies while simultaneously remaining Other to them. Critical race feminism, relational poverty theory, and black geographies scholars argue that hegemonic notions of liberal democratic life rest on theorizations of a Universal subject, a normative ideal citizen who can choose full participation in social and political life (McKittrick and Woods 2007; Cacho 2012; Elwood, Lawson, and Sheppard 2016). Yet daily struggles for survival by impoverished (often racialized) people experiencing multiple forms of violence and exclusion make full participation impossible for many, as do de jure exclusions like criminalization and denial of voting rights. Furthermore, assertions of universality obscure the impossibility of full subjecthood under dominant frames that make certain subjects and their politics illegible (Schram 2000; McKittrick and Woods 2007; Cacho 2012; Spade and Willse 2015; Elwood, Lawson, and Sheppard 2016). The lives of impoverished racialized subjects reveal sociospatial processes of exclusion *and* allow us to see how impoverishment is always also challenged, sometimes on terms outside dominant projects of government and normalization.

Below we discuss the concept of thinkable poverty politics and the deserving (or reformable) subjects these poverty politics both necessitate and produce. We then turn to a discussion of politics enacted by those framed as undeserving, other, killable, and subject to social death. For these subjects unthinkable politics are essential forms of voice and agency that resist their outsider position of illegibility. Undergirding this discussion is the crucial understanding that poverty politics are neither predictable nor unitary. We argue that framing thinkable and unthinkable as dialectically related analytics can untangle the range of contradictory and complex relations and possibilities that a detailed engagement with poverty politics allows.

THINKABLE POVERTY POLITICS

Thinkable poverty politics grow from and (re)produce hegemonies. That is, they are imaginable and legitimate within existing projects of government and "common sense" ideology that normalize certain subjects, programs of action, and forms of economic and social relations in particular times and places (Laclau and Mouffe 1985; Rose and Miller 1992; Hall and Massey 2010; Roy and Shaw Crane 2015). Realms of governability frame embodiment, behavior, morality, and legitimate political speech and action by exercising biopolitical and disciplinary power to define "proper and improper" categories of subjects: those who can take part and those who are excluded (Foucault 1990; Cruikshank 1999; Spade and Willse 2015). Drawing on Rancière's (2004) ideas about sensible politics, we conceptualize "thinkable politics" as programs, policies, or actions conducted upon, or argued for, by subjects who are (or are potentially) audible and legible within existing governmental and normative socioeconomic orders. These programs of action and subjects are legible because they conform with taken-for-granted understandings about who is poor and why within the current conjuncture (Hall and Massey 2010). Societal norms (about class, race, democratic practice, sexuality, gender, and so on) circulate as systems of control that define which subjects can be incorporated into existing racial capitalist economies (Gilmore 2002; McKittrick 2016; Pulido 2017). To be sure, the enactment of thinkable politics does not ensure uncomplicated or uncontested outcomes. However, thinkable politics entail and are framed by the "constitutive discourses that contribute to solidifying what is possible to think, say, do and be" (Cruikshank 1999, 2).

Distinctions between "deserving" and "undeserving" people mark the limits of thinkable poverty politics in specific conjunctures. In the United States (and other North Atlantic welfare states to varying extents), thinkable politics frames deserving impoverished people as flawed but reformable, and poverty as a technical and apolitical problem that is solved by incorporating people into existing structures of economy and government (Schram 2000; O'Connor 2001). In international development projects, thinkable politics often construct entrepreneurial subjects deserving of interventions such as micro loans, education, land reforms, and the like (Escobar 1995; Roy 2010; Maurer 2015; Borges, this volume; Sampat, this volume). Thinkable poverty politics in many places involve processes of differential incorporation wherein those framed as "deserving poor" are not fully excluded from social and economic life but rather are incorporated, or demand incorporation, under adverse conditions (du Toit and Hickey 2007; Maskovsky, this volume; Negrón-Gonzales, this volume; Pittman, this volume). Much poverty action is thinkable in the sense that policy and political responses to impoverishment maintain existing racial capitalist relations of accumulation, dispossession, and privilege by constructing poverty as a problem of individual subjects who have personal deficiencies, behave inappropriately or immorally, or do not engage sufficiently with market incentives (Lawson 2012). Consensus around such liberal framings of individual subjects fully responsible for their own poverty produces particular responses to poverty and situates them as commonsensical and necessary: including reformist remedies such as training/education and workfare policies, and discipline and control for unruly subjects (Cruikshank 1999; Schram 2000; Cope and Gilbert 2001; DeVerteuil 2003; Wilson and Grammenos 2005; Watkins-Hayes 2009; Roy 2010; Sparks 2010; Miewald and McCann 2014; Lawson et al. 2015).

Our approach is deeply indebted to critical poverty scholars' analyses of differential incorporation, which we conceptualize as thinkable politics that obscure systemic social injustice. Prior critical poverty research is extremely broad and nuanced, analyzing projects of government, policy, and knowledge making that target impoverished people through their adverse inclusion via labor market segmentation and the normalization of subjects and behaviors through mechanisms of discipline and control enacted in policy and discourse. These politics are not stable but are reframed from place to place, changing the terms and outcomes but not the pacifying/normalizing intentions, of differential incorporation (Schram 2000; Goode and Maskovsky 2001; O'Connor 2001;

Roy 2010). Three recent examples from critical poverty studies illustrate the ways that thinkable poverty politics of differential incorporation circulate and are enacted in international development circles, in government policy, and by charitable foundations. Across spacetimes, these projects of differential incorporation governmentalize those named as poor and incorporate them into existing socioeconomic orders in ways that limit the language, meaning, and repertoire of poverty politics to the thinkable.

First, Peck and Theodore (2015a) explore the globalized flow of conditional cash transfer (CCT) policies that provide payments to impoverished households, conditional upon compliance with rules designed to build "human capital." Heavily promoted by the World Bank, these programs have become "the [contemporary] default setting for anti-poverty reform" (Peck and Theodore 2015b, 103) in the international development community based on the claim that "correction" and "improvement" of impoverished people are essential for development. The specifics vary by country, but CCT conditionalities typically focus on school attendance and family health and nutrition to ensure productive, healthy, and well-trained people ready for incorporation into low-wage work and/or to render them politically pacified despite their marginal situations. As such, CCTs consolidate a postwelfare world in which a redistributive politics of *unconditional* cash transfers are largely silenced as a viable alternative in global development debates.

Second, Roy, Schrader, and Shaw Crane (2015, 290) examine a historical politics of differential incorporation that anticipates the CCT logics described above, tracing how the 1960s Gray Areas program linked poverty to concerns about racialized violence in American cities. This program of community interventions was designed to pacify impoverished inner-city neighborhoods by framing widespread civil rights protests as problems of "juvenile delinquency" and "gang violence." The remedies included public works projects to improve health and sanitation, coupled with youth vocational training and induction into the military. Here again, a poverty politics of incorporation and pacification of marginalized people is achieved through projects "founded on the belief that if people living in poverty in neighborhoods of transition could be given the skills to participate in middle class life, they too could have access to boundless opportunity" (Roy, Schrader, and Shaw Crane 2015, 300).

Third, Kohl-Arenas (2015) interrogates the ways in which mainstream philanthropic foundations perpetuate impoverishment and maintain elite privilege.[4] Focusing on charitable "antipoverty" programming in California's Central Valley, Kohl-Arenas illustrates a poverty politics of adverse incorporation of Latino farmworkers into agribusiness and immigration politics that leaves white class privilege unquestioned and depoliticized. Foundation staffers roll out this poverty politics via "self-help" programs of education, "training" for grant getting, and provision of basic services to incorporate farmworker leadership and community members into existing economic and political structures while leaving their exploitative work conditions unchanged. Echoing the 1960s Gray Areas program, these foundations in the 2010s fund civic initiatives where immigrant families "participate" in public life and community organizers are "trained" in program evaluation metrics and budgeting, while simultaneously foundations refuse to fund a radical politics of labor organizing. This poverty politics of differential incorporation does crucial work in generating consensus around the socioeconomic orders of racial capitalism by incorporating Latino workers into agribusiness while shifting attention away from the racialized structures and relations that produce their impoverishment.

Relational Poverty Politics builds on this work by theorizing these forms of differential incorporation as thinkable poverty politics. It is the very thinkability of these interventions that sustains dominant ideologies that frame who is poor, why, and what should be done about it, thus reinforcing hierarchies of elite power and securing consent to them. Furthermore, by treating differential incorporation as an always-intersectional process (drawing on critical race feminists' theorizations of the interoperation of race, citizenship, gender, sexuality, and other systems of social valuation), this book expands the realms through which poverty is made thinkable to sustain power hierarchies. Espiritu (2003, 47) argues that the marginality of racialized immigrant groups is constituted through their "differential inclusion," a position in which they are "deemed integral to the nation's economy, culture, identity and power—but integral only or precisely because of, their designated subordinate standing." This collection demonstrates that in addition to sustaining existing governmental and economic orders, thinkable poverty politics also sustain power hierarchies through gender and sexuality, citizenship and bordering, racialization and criminalization. For example, impoverished persons are incorporated into insecure and low-wage labor through intersecting processes of class, race, gender, and citizenship. Pittman (this volume) analyzes how suburban, white, middle-class nuclear family norms about parental rights shape safety net programs, denying parental rights to low-income African American grandmothers who care for grandchildren and pushing them into marginalized work. These limited framings of "parent" render grandmothers ineligible for supports such as child-only TANF grants (cash welfare payments) and childcare subsidies, forcing them into low-wage work and reproducing their experiences of severe deprivation. Ye (this volume) investigates relations between low-wage work and citizenship in rapidly diversifying Singapore, exploring how marginalized people are incorporated through uneven modes of governance, ordering, and management in social assistance programs. She shows how race, class, and citizenship norms established through state policies are brought to bear in community-provided assistance spaces and how these ultimately reproduce precarity (simultaneously poverty and undocumented status) for immigrant workers.

We also explore the extent to which thinkable politics return a subordinated group to a position of supposed social value, defined in terms of structures of differential incorporation. For instance, revaluation of undocumented Latinos through assertions that they are law-abiding "good" families reinforces long-standing discourses of criminality and immorality used to produce poverty difference and uphold racial capitalism (Cacho 2012; Swerts, this volume). These politics secure systems of subordination, cement differences between marginalized groups, and preclude the possibility of forming of social alliances across difference. Yet rejecting them is inconceivable because they arise from the dominant terms on which social value is defined. Negrón-Gonzales (this volume) reveals the inextricable and contradictory relation of the student "DREAMer" and the undocumented worker. She argues that even for those who are granted access to education through the U.S. DREAM Act, their futures are limited by both the terms of the law itself and their complex positionalities as low-wage workers and members of vulnerable families (in both economic and citizenship terms). Maskovsky (this volume) reveals the intersections of homelessness, race, and health vulnerability through his analysis of ACT UP politics in Philadelphia. He analyzes a city politics that renders homeless people a low priority for assistance within its budget calculus, such that diverse activists with HIV/AIDS build identities and tactics around having a life-threatening illness and urgent needs for shelter. To be viewed as making legitimate claims for shelter within this context, homeless people with HIV/AIDS construct themselves as particularly vulnerable and needy, reinforcing dominant narratives of deservingness and poverty difference.

In these cases, differential inclusion cements multiple relations of subordination through which marginalized groups are adversely positioned, while the circulation of norms about ideal subjects (law-abiding, moral, autonomous) masks this subordination by suggesting (falsely) that they can achieve inclusion by performing normative ideals. In so doing, differential incorporation reproduces thinkable poverty politics that both structure relations between poverty and privilege and frame the kinds of claims that impoverished subjects and mobilizations against poverty can imagine, articulate, and enact, in ways that ultimately shore up hegemonic systems of social (de)valuation and capitalist accumulation.

UNTHINKABLE POVERTY POLITICS

Relational Poverty Politics also reads beyond racial capitalist structures of incorporation to theorize poverty politics created by devalued subjects enacting meanings and actions that transform fields of political possibility (Rancière 2004).[5] We are inspired by Rancière's (2004) formulation of politics as existing in the disruption of meanings and existing power orders by those who have no part in hegemonic definitions of community. As Massey (2014, 2041) argues, "hegemonies are not totalities."[6] Therefore it is vital to trace a range of "unthinkable [poverty] politics" (Cacho 2012, 31) of refusal, rebellion, creativity, hope, and alliance making. These politics emerge in opposition to a politics of incorporation that rests on relational processes of social devaluation (see also McKittrick and Woods 2007; Pulido 2017). Cacho (2012, 31) argues for a politics of "dismembering social value" that enters the space of "social death."[7] In this space, unthinkability involves refusing existing political-economic hierarchies, racist norms, and social systems of valuation to instead imagine life otherwise and to struggle for meaning and value beyond that defined by existing power/ knowledge orders. Politics are unthinkable not merely because they are difficult or unlikely to succeed "but because [enacting them arouses] the threat or promise of state violence" (Cacho 2012, 145).

In the face of hegemonic consensus and its thinkable poverty politics, counterpolitics by those named as poor should not exist—and yet they not only exist, they also are rebelliously creative, offering openings toward transgressive politics (Woods 1998; McKittrick 2016). Poverty scholars tend to reproduce economism (even on the left). Much poverty work has not engaged robustly with intersectional theorizations of unthinkability and yet racialization, sexuality, citizenship, gender, caste, and religion are central to the construction of disposable, forgettable or unseeable, impoverished subjects. Our theorization of "unthinkable" poverty politics is deepened by McKittrick and Woods's (2007) analysis of the paradoxical sociospatial relations of black geographies in which the reinscription of dominant power hierarchies rests upon making black bodies/spaces invisible, forgettable, outside the norm; and yet that which is framed as invisible and forgettable is always producing politics. Despite a constellation of forces aligned toward their erasure, exclusion, and death, the lived presence of racialized communities and their agency in making material and imagined worlds are deeply political on many levels. Impoverished neighborhoods and households live in spite of structural, discursive, and embodied violence; some refuse universal liberal subjecthood, revealing it to be an impossible fiction; and others act within contexts that render action impossible or respond to it with violence and expulsion. Our contributors illuminate the creative presence of "unthinkable politics" that exist outside dominant systems of recognition, ordering, and social (de)valuation in (1) refusals of existing political and economic orders, (2) the redefinition of meaningful lives, and (3) efforts to build political solidarities across projects of difference and devaluation that produce unthinkability (race, class, caste, citizenship, gender, sexuality, and more). In framing these poverty politics as unthinkable, we do not suggest that the people practicing them are powerless or lack agency and capacity. Rather, unthinkability as an analytic opens the possibility of recognizing forms of agency that are profoundly challenging to the status quo of who are legitimate subjects, what are legitimate actions, and what can push on normative, liberal framings of legibility. As our contributors show, in some instances, these politics may indeed remain marginalized and repressed (yet nonetheless vital to understand), but in other instances, their political repertoires open up new horizons in understanding and acting on poverty. The lens of unthinkability brings into view and insists on making heard that which thinkable poverty politics would prefer not to see or hear.

Unthinkable poverty politics entail refusals of existing political and economic orders. For example, Giles (this volume) works with Food Not Bombs (FNB), a globalized movement of anarchist soup kitchens that reappropriate and revalorize capitalist (waste) surpluses. FNB is a loose coalition of actors excluded from meaningful political representation including people who are homeless, indigenous, undocumented, queer, and more. They dumpster-dive, prepare food, and distribute it to impoverished persons in public places in deliberate contravention of city ordinances against public feeding. These activists reject disciplining governmental projects, refusing prevailing liberal and capitalist norms and legal structures. Instead, FNB's unthinkable politics insist on embodiments that are illegible to dominant orders and survive in wasted spaces and food supplies where they are free to convene and enact alternative worlds. Unthinkable poverty politics also come into being through mobilizations against poverty that coalesce despite militarized violence. Glassman (this volume) analyzes the Thai Red Shirt movement, a coalition of farmers, workers, and provincial leaders who engage in street protests in the face of the 2014 military coup and rising authoritarianism. The Red Shirt activists endure violent clashes with police and military in order to support the ousted Thaksin government and more broadly redistributive policies to address their long-standing impoverishment, politics that are unthinkable in their refusal of the current authoritarian political order and because the protests arouse inevitable state violence. Furthermore, the Red Shirts challenge the very reproduction of capitalist relations through violence. By protesting after the military coup and prior rounds of violent repression, Red Shirt politics reveal the unthinkable: that policing and militarized killing are central to the securing of capitalist class relations in Thailand (and indeed, Glassman argues, everywhere).

Unthinkable poverty politics are made when impoverished people fight for more than just a life—bodily survival—but a *meaningful* life, and in so doing, rework the meaning of "poverty" itself. Borges (this volume) collaborates with her South African hosts to understand their autonomous meanings and desires, their struggles to be alive on their own terms and to produce knowledge that challenges the limits of thought and action under dominant ideologies and the structures/relations they uphold. For instance, the family Borges worked with received a farm as part of land reform as reparations for their prior dispossession. In dominant terms (defined by the state) their farm failed because of their indebtedness when the sheep flock died. However, in spite of this "failure" and its deepening of their material hardships, family members construct a politics of hope that refuses dominant definitions of "success." Acquiring the farm and completing wedding rites for now deceased grandparents are parts of their on-going and incommensurable struggles for meaningful lives. These politics lie outside the "thinkable" finite solution to an objective, material poverty (e.g., a farm, a legal inheritance). Instead, their lives teach us about intangible and il-legible politics that resist silencing approaches "that reduce the meaning of their lives to what is known (lack of wealth) instead of acknowledging what inspires them: an unbreakable engagement in producing knowledge and hope that goes beyond the modern and colonial hegemonic stranglehold on their thoughts and actions" (Borges, this volume). Da Costa and Nagar (this volume) also explore unthinkable poverty politics arising as people insist that lives that are meaning-ful on terms illegible to hegemonic orders. They consider the "hunger for the-ater" expressed by impoverished performers in political theater in India. Their collaborators refuse a modernist framing of hunger resulting from poverty: a lack of income to buy food. Instead the authors reframe hunger as multidimen-sional, entailing the building of personhoods and alliances that courageously resist structural impediments, and refuse statist categorizations and frameworks that hierarchize, segregate, and kill. Their collaborators in India build a politics through theater that rethinks marginality, refuses familiar divisions of caste, class, and religion, and articulates solidarities across lines of social devaluation.

Unthinkable poverty politics also arise through efforts to create political sol-idarities across the axes of social devaluation and long-standing relations of violence and dispossession. Unthinkability is produced and maintained through "social death": extreme forms of intersectional outsiderness. In this context, ef-forts to forge mutuality or common cause across these lines of power and priv-ilege are themselves an unthinkable politics. So too are efforts to forge political solidarities among differently marginalized unthinkable groups, given that their struggles for legitimacy often set these groups against one another. Contributors examine the kinds of reworked relational subjects that emerge through these unthinkable politics and the kinds of challenges they can (and cannot) mount to systems of thinkability.

Swerts (this volume) examines the forging of cross-status allyship between citizens and noncitizens in the DREAM movement, despite state-sanctioned violence aimed at shoring up this very distinction (deportation, arrest, incarcer-ation). He shows how boundary-bridging work by activists defies the privileging of citizens in broader U.S. society, as DREAMers engage instead in practices that rework power differentials. This process of intersubjective exchange across power lines produces critically reflexive ally subjects who step back from their privilege in key ways and step up to materially support the unthinkable poli-tics of their partners, who risk deportation by coming out publicly as undoc-umented. Magalhães (this volume) explores the unlikely political partnerships that arose in Brazil in June 2013 street protests among middle-class and impoverished people, LGBT activists and unionists, anarchists and media activists. These diverse protesters articulated broad claims for redistribution and against poverty and had some localized successes. Yet they were swiftly overtaken by other cross-difference coalitions seeking to reinscribe dominant socioeconomic orders, underscoring the need to theorize how unthinkable politics become reincorporated to the realms of thinkability. Sampat's analysis goes directly to this point, as she explores how the redistributive claims made by allied activists in India against growth infrastructure development generate some "wins" but ultimately remain inscribed within thinkability. In her case, activists with vastly different social, political, and economic power come together across caste, gender, and class to fight dispossession driven by the rentier economy and call for more egalitarian and environmentally sustainable initiatives. Sampat's analysis reveals that forms of privilege rooted in India's historical land impasse position ally subjects differently in terms of how they stand to benefit from potential outcomes of their activism. She argues that such an alliance may successfully fight an immediate threat, but contains forms of differential incorporation that reproduce long-standing relations of inequality and preclude more radically transformative poverty politics.

Thinkable and unthinkable politics are theoretically distinct and incommensurable—an idea we take up in more detail in the concluding chapter. Yet the complex grounded struggles in the contributed chapters often contain elements of both a poverty politics of differential incorporation and unthinkable poverty politics of refusal, hope, and allyship. Individually and as a collection, the chapters reveal thinkable and unthinkable poverty politics in dynamic relation. Weaving together these analyses within a single volume illustrates complexities and contestations in poverty politics, ultimately revealing how a relational analysis theorizes a range of poverty processes and politics and suggests new trajectories of thought and action.

Building Relational Analyses of Poverty Politics

Relational Poverty Politics builds relational analysis in two registers: (1) antiessentialist theorizations of poverty that interrelate multiple causal processes (Elwood, Lawson, and Sheppard 2016) and (2) a relational epistemological stance: open to surprise, engaged in situated dialogue, and employing methodologies of collaboration open to new ethnographic subjects and theoretical circulations (Roy 2015; Borges, this volume; Da Costa and Nagar, this volume). Our approach is firmly grounded in feminist and postcolonial theory, in conversation with Marxian poverty research. We innovate through relational epistemologies rooted in feminist and postcolonial theorizations that understand theory as always situated, partial, and produced through relations of power (Haraway 1988; Rose 1994), and ways of knowing as always conditioned by asymmetrical geohistorical relations (Said 1979; Chakrabarty 2000; Mbembe 2001; Roy 2015).

The first register of our relational poverty analysis is an antiessentialist approach that refuses singular and universalizing theoretical claims about impoverishment, instead investigating multiple interrelating processes. This mode of explanation accounts for impoverishment as constituted through multiple processes (e.g., governmentalizing practices, capitalist accumulation/dispossession, representational and discursive practices, cultural politics of identity, making lives, and so on) interrelating with one another differently across spacetimes (Elwood, Lawson, and Sheppard 2016). It also entails an engaged pluralism in which explanations of poverty themselves are opened up to different theoretical claims (Longino 2002; Barnes and Sheppard 2010). This orientation guides *Relational Poverty Politics* in multiple ways. Some authors engage a theoretical pluralism that pushes poverty theory to include not-yet-recognized concepts and processes. For example, Giles (this volume) theorizes illiberal embodiment by FNB activists to explore unthinkable politics that challenge capitalist norms and legal frameworks, and Swerts (this volume) identifies boundary-bridging practices that disrupt the privilege of citizenship and enable alliances within the DREAM movement. Other contributors rely on a single theoretical framework but extend its reach to consider processes previously unconsidered or thought to be external (epiphenomenal). For example, Glassman (this volume) extends Marxian analyses of capitalism and inequality by insisting that militarized violence is central to the securing of capitalist class relations and elite privilege. The collection as a whole constitutes an engagement among plural theoretical approaches by including interventions that understand impoverishment and poverty politics through different sites, processes, spaces, ontologies, and epistemologies. The authors do not all draw from the same theoretical frameworks. Some draw more strongly on Marxian political economy, others lean more toward cultural analyses, and some are much more pluralist in orientation. As such, *Relational Poverty Politics* opens new theoretical and political horizons that extend poverty scholarship.

The antiessentialist, pluralist modes of explanation that are a hallmark of the relational analyses in this collection build new insights by remaining open to unseen possibilities. This stance treats economistic explanations of impoverishment as partial and in need of richer theorization, and looks for already-present counterformations that could produce other possible politics (Gibson-Graham 2006, 2008; McKinnon 2013). An epistemological openness to unseen possibilities of thinkable poverty politics of exclusion, boundary making, and differential incorporation does not mean that these are necessarily reproduced in all spacetimes or that they exclude other poverty politics. Rather, we argue that multiple forms of poverty politics always coexist. Our contributors illuminate not only the anticipated forms of oppression, disciplining, and silencing so common in critical poverty analysis but also and very importantly unthinkable poverty politics including hopeful practices that refuse to define a meaningful life in terms of wealth or development or that involve the formation of ally subjects across difference (Borges, this volume; Da Costa and Nagar, this volume; Swerts, this volume).

The second register of our relational poverty analysis is an epistemological commitment to making poverty knowledge differently: challenging a divisive geopolitics of knowledge through transnational theorizing *from* (rather than *about*) postcolonial settings; taking apart elite notions of expertise by learning from actions and voices of those subjected to impoverishment; centering poor people's own creative analyses and actions as a way to rethink who is knowledgeable and who can make change; and boundary-crossing processes of mutual learning in the creation of this collection. This book traces *how* poverty knowledge can be made in ways that challenge long-standing boundaries and power hierarchies of knowledge production. We take seriously postcolonial arguments that the place of theorizing conditions what can be known and what can be said (Esteva 1987; Spivak 1990; Escobar 1995; Chakrabarty 2000). This collection builds a "relationality of theory" (Roy 2015, 207) through analysis across, and dialogue among, scholars living and working in places differently positioned within global circuits of knowledge and power. Following Chakrabarty (2000) we provincialize authoritative poverty knowledge through a double move: (1) deconstructing Eurocentric "Truth" about poverty and (2) analyzing the forms, challenges, and possibilities of alternative knowledges, politics, and practices arising outside North Atlantic states (Said 1979; Roy 2010; Roy and Crane 2015).

Building new geographies of theory entails opening up "the relationship between thought and place . . . to rethink the territory of thought itself" (Roy and Shaw Crane 2015, 16). Taking seriously the creative potentials of transnational circulation of ideas, in 2015 we brought an interdisciplinary group of scholars living and working in Asia, North America, South America, and Europe together for extended discussions of draft chapters and to frame the overall project. Across different national contexts, disciplinary backgrounds, theoretical orientations, epistemologies, and methodologies, we discussed what constitutes poverty politics, how a relational poverty analysis is enacted, what relational poverty politics are illuminated and theorized, and how these insights complement and extend each other's chapters. This process of relational knowledge making across multiple differences of language, theory, discipline, place of origin, identity, and position in geohistories of the academy was challenging. We did not always understand or share one another's theoretical and epistemological priorities, or agree on how they should shape the collection as a whole. Yet this engaged process of relational knowledge making invites our readers to open up poverty politics as epistemological questions: What counts as poverty politics in different chapters? What kinds of learning go on across these sites and forms of poverty politics? How does our own work inform understandings in other places, and what new insights arise when we read our own cases through theory that "travels" from elsewhere? How do dialogic processes of making poverty knowledge differently in our everyday emplaced lives transform how we know poverty politics in these and other places? We build a different relationality of theory in *Relational Poverty Politics* through our collective engagement with these questions in the process of making this collection.

NOTES

1. We are indebted to Lisa Marie Cacho, whose book *Social Death: Racialized Rightlessness and the Criminalization of the Unprotected* (2012) has been a crucial catalyst in our formulation of unthinkable poverty politics.

2. We are also inspired by Piven and Cloward's influential book *Poor People's Movements* (1978), which focuses attention on "lower-class [*sic*]" class movements to understand their disruptive effects on powerful institutions addressing poverty and to consider the limits of popular protest. Little work has focused as centrally on poverty politics since this volume.

3. Earlier structural analyses of poverty and privilege that dealt with material, political, and race relations (Marx 1861; Polanyi 1944; Piven and Cloward 1978) have a strong affinity with relational poverty scholarship but without the integration of cultural politics, discourse and representation, critical development studies, and postcolonial theory that defines the current trajectory.

4. Adams (2013) traces similar effects produced through discourses and practices of charitable giving in the rebuilding of New Orleans after Hurricane Katrina.

5. We are also influenced by Gibson-Graham's (2008) call to "read for difference" and in so doing find actually existing politics of possibility—the "other worlds" that David Giles reminds us exist already in the shadows of this one.

6. See also Žižek (1989) on the ways that realities are held together by hegemonic systems yet are not ever fully contained by them, leaving openings for counterhegemonic politics.

7. Social death is to be ineligible for personhood, to be denied the right to have rights under existing social and political arrangements. As Cacho (2012, 6) argues, "to be ineligible for personhood is a form of social death; it not only defines who does not matter, it also makes mattering meaningful." As such, social death reflects the reinscription of existing racial, class, and gender hierarchies, making a politics of incorporation (a thinkable politics) a form of revalorizing those very violent hierarchies.

REFERENCES

Adamovsky, Ezequiel. 2009. "Historia de la clase media argentina: apogeo y decadencia de una ilusión, 1919–2003." Buenos Aires: Planeta.

Adams, Vincanne. 2013. *Markets of Sorrow, Labors of Faith: New Orleans in the Wake of Katrina*. Durham, N.C.: Duke University Press.

Addison, Tony, David Hulme, and Ravi Kanbur, eds. 2009. *Poverty Dynamics: Interdisciplinary Perspectives*. Oxford: Oxford University Press.

Barnes, Trevor J., and Eric Sheppard. 2010. "'Nothing Includes Everything': Towards Engaged Pluralism in Anglophone Economic Geography." *Progress in Human Geography* 34, no. 2: 193–214. doi:10.1177/0309132509343728.

Blokland, Talja. 2012. "Blaming Neither the Undeserving Poor nor the Revanchist Middle Classes: A Relational Approach to Marginalization." *Urban Geography* 33, no. 4: 488–507. doi:10.2747/0272-3638.33.4.488.

Cacho, Lisa Marie. 2012. *Social Death: Racialized Rightlessness and the Criminalization of the Unprotected*. New York: New York University Press.

Chakrabarty, Dipesh. 2000. *Provincializing Europe: Postcolonial Thought and Historical Difference*. Princeton, N.J.: Princeton University Press.

Cope, Meghan, and Melissa R. Gilbert. 2001. "Geographies of Welfare Reform." *Urban Geography* 22, no. 5: 385–90. doi:10.2747/0272-3638.22.5.385.

Cruikshank, Barbara. 1999. *The Will to Empower: Democratic Citizens and Other Subjects*. Ithaca, N.Y.: Cornell University Press.

De Herdt, Tom, and Johan Bastiaensen. 2008. "The Circumstances of Agency: A Relational View of Poverty." *International Development Planning Review* 30, no. 4: 339–57. doi:10.3828/idpr.30.4.2.

DeVerteuil, Geoffrey. 2003. "Homeless Mobility, Institutional Settings, and the New Poverty Management." *Environment and Planning A* 35, no. 2: 361–79. doi:10.1068/a35205.

Diez, Thomas. 2013. "Normative Power as Hegemony." *Cooperation and Conflict* 48, no. 2: 194–210. doi:10.1177/0010836713485387.

du Toit, Andries. 2009. "Poverty Measurement Blues: Beyond 'Q Squared' Approaches to Understanding Chronic Poverty in South Africa." In *Poverty Dynamics: Interdisciplinary Perspectives*, edited by Tony Addison, David Hulme, and Ravi Kanbur, 225–46. Oxford: Oxford University Press.

du Toit, Andries, and Sam Hickey. 2007. "Adverse Incorporation, Social Exclusion, and Chronic Poverty." Chronic Poverty Research Centre Working Paper No. 81, University of Manchester. http://www.gsdrc.org/go/display&type=Document&id=3214 (accessed July 20, 2016).

Elwood, Sarah, Victoria Lawson, and Eric Sheppard. 2016. "Geographical Relational Poverty Studies." *Progress in Human Geography*. Advance online publication. doi:10.1177/0309132516659706.

Escobar, Arturo. 1995. *Encountering Development: The Making and Unmaking of the Third World*. Princeton, N.J.: Princeton University Press.

Espiritu, Yen Le. 2003. *Home Bound: Filipino American Lives across Cultures, Communities, and Countries*. Berkeley: University of California Press.

Esteva, Gustavo. 1987. "Regenerating People's Space." *Alternatives: Global, Local, Political* 12, no. 1: 125–52. doi:10.1177/030437548701200106.

Ferguson, James. 1994. *The Anti-politics Machine: "Development," Depoliticization, and Bureaucratic Power in Lesotho*. Minneapolis: University of Minnesota Press.

Fernandes, Leela, and Patrick Heller. 2006. "Hegemonic Aspirations." *Critical Asian Studies* 38, no. 4: 495–522. doi:10.1080/14672710601073028.

Foucault, Michel. 1990. *The History of Sexuality, Volume 1: An Introduction*. New York: Vintage.

Gibson-Graham, J. K. 2006. *A Postcapitalist Politics*. Minneapolis: University of Minnesota Press.

———. 2008. "Diverse Economies: Performative Practices for Other Worlds." *Progress in Human Geography* 32, no. 5: 613–32. doi:10.1177/0309132508090821.

Gilmore, Ruth Wilson. 2002. "Fatal Couplings of Power and Difference: Notes on Racism and Geography." *Professional Geographer* 54, no. 1: 15–24. doi:10.1111/0033-0124.00310.

Goode, Judith, and Jeff Maskovsky. 2001. *The New Poverty Studies: The Ethnography of Power, Politics, and Impoverished People in the United States*. New York: New York University Press.

Gramsci, Antonio. 1929–35. *Prison Notebooks*. New York: Columbia University Press.

Green, Maia. 2005. "Discourses on Inequality: Poverty, Public Bads and Entrenching Witchcraft in Post-adjustment Tanzania." *Anthropological Theory* 5, no. 3: 247–66. doi:10.1177/1463499605055959.

———. 2006. "Representing Poverty and Attacking Representations: Perspectives on Poverty from Social Anthropology." *Journal of Development Studies* 42, no. 7: 1108–29. doi:10.1080/00220380600884068.

Guano, Emanuela. 2004. "The Denial of Citizenship: 'Barbaric' Buenos Aires and the Middle-Class Imaginary." *City Society* 16, no. 1: 69–97. doi:10.1525/city.2004.16.1.69.

Hall, Stuart, and Doreen Massey. 2010. "Interpreting the Crisis." *Soundings* 44, no. 1: 57–71. doi:10.3898/136266210791036791.

Haraway, Donna. 1988. "Situated Knowledges: The Science Question in Feminism and the Privilege of Partial Perspective." *Feminist Studies* 14, no. 3: 575–99. doi:10.2307/3178066.

Hickey, Sam. 2009. "Rethinking Poverty Analysis from the Margins: Insights from Northern Uganda." *Afriche e Orienti* 11, no 2: 119–36.

hooks, bell. 2000. *Where We Stand: Class Matters*. New York: Routledge.

Kaplinsky, Raphael. 2005. *Globalization, Poverty and Inequality: Between a Rock and a Hard Place*. Cambridge: Polity.

Kohl-Arenas, Erica. 2015. *The Self-Help Myth: How Philanthropy Fails to Alleviate Poverty*. Oakland: University of California Press.

Laclau, Ernesto, and Chantal Mouffe. 1985. *Hegemony and Socialist Strategy: Towards a Radical Democratic Politics*. London: Verso.

Lawson, Victoria. 2012. "Decentring Poverty Studies: Middle Class Alliances and the Social Construction of Poverty." *Singapore Journal of Tropical Geography* 33, no. 1: 1–19. doi:10.1111/j.1467-9493.2012.00443.x.

Lawson, Victoria, Sarah Elwood, Santiago Canevaro, and Nicolas Viotti. 2015. "'The Poor Are Us': Middle-Class Poverty Politics in Buenos Aires and Seattle." *Environment and Planning A* 47, no. 9: 1873–91. doi:10.1177/0308518X15597150.

Leitner, Helga, and Eric Sheppard. 2015. "Provincializing Critical Urban Theory: Extending the Ecosystem of Possibilities." *International Journal of Urban and Regional Research* 40, no. 1: 228–35. doi:10.1111/1468-2427.12277.

Longino, Helen E. 2002. *The Fate of Knowledge*. Princeton, N.J.: Princeton University Press.

Lyon-Callo, Vincent. 2008. *Inequality, Poverty, and Neoliberal Governance: Activist Ethnography in the Homeless Sheltering Industry*. Toronto: University of Toronto Press.

Marx, Karl. 1861. *Capital: A Critique of Political Economy*. Vol. 1. Moscow: Progress Publishers.

Massey, Doreen. 2014. "The Kilburn Manifesto: After Neoliberalism?" *Environment and Planning A* 46, no. 9: 2033–49. doi:10.1068/akilburn.

Maurer, Bill. 2015. "Data Mining for Development: Poverty, Payment, and Platform." In *Territories of Poverty: Rethinking North and South*, edited by Ananya Roy and Emma Shaw Crane, 126–43. Athens: University of Georgia Press.

Mbembe, Achille. 2001. *On the Postcolony*. Berkeley: University of California Press.

McKinnon, Katherine. 2013. "A Different Kind of Difference: Knowledge, Politics and Being Antipodean." *Dialogues in Human Geography* 3, no. 2: 213–16. doi:10.1177/2043820613493156.

McKittrick, Katherine. 2016. "Rebellion/Invention/Groove." *Small Axe: A Caribbean Platform for Criticism* 20, no. 49: 79–91.

McKittrick, Katherine, and Clyde Adrian Woods. 2007. *Black Geographies and the Politics of Place*. Toronto: Between the Lines.

Melamed, Jodi. 2015. "Racial Capitalism." *Critical Ethnic Studies* 1, no. 1: 76–85. doi:10.5749/jcritethnstud.1.1.0076.

Miewald, Christiana, and Eugene McCann. 2014. "Foodscapes and the Geographies of Poverty: Sustenance, Strategy, and Politics in an Urban Neighborhood." *Antipode* 46, no. 2: 537–56. doi:10.1111/anti.12057.

Mosse, David. 2010. "A Relational Approach to Durable Poverty, Inequality and Power." *Journal of Development Studies* 46, no. 7: 1156–78. doi:10.1080/00220388.2010.487095.

Newman, Katherine S. 1999. *Falling from Grace: Downward Mobility in the Age of Affluence*. Berkeley: University of California Press.

O'Connor, Alice. 2001. *Poverty Knowledge: Social Science, Social Policy, and the Poor in Twentieth-Century U.S. History*. Princeton, N.J.: Princeton University Press.

Peck, Jamie, and Nikolas Theodore. 2015a. *Fast Policy: Experimental Statecraft at the Thresholds of Neoliberalism*. Minneapolis: University of Minnesota Press.

———. 2015b. "Paying for Good Behavior: Cash Transfer Policies in the Wild." In *Territories of Poverty: Rethinking North and South*, edited by Ananya Roy and Emma Shaw Crane, 103–25. Athens: University of Georgia Press.

Piven, Frances Fox, and Richard A. Cloward. 1977. *Poor People's Movements: Why They Succeed, How They Fail*. New York: Vintage.

Polanyi, Karl. 1944. *The Great Transformation*. New York: Farrar & Rinehart.

Pulido, Laura. 2017. "Geographies of Race and Ethnicity II." *Progress in Human Geography* 41, no. 4: 524–33. doi:10.1177/0309132516646495.

Rancière, Jacques. 2004. *The Philosopher and His Poor*. Durham, N.C.: Duke University Press.

Robinson, Cedric J. 1983. *Black Marxism: The Making of the Black Radical Tradition*. Chapel Hill: University of North Carolina Press.

Rose, Gillian. 1994. *Feminism and Geography: The Limits of Geographical Knowledge*. Oxford: Blackwell.

Rose, Nikolas, and Peter Miller. 1992. "Political Power beyond the State: Problematics of Government." *British Journal of Sociology* 43, no 2: 173–205. doi:10.1111/j.1468--4446.2009.01247.x.

Roy, Ananya. 2003. "Paradigms of Propertied Citizenship: Transnational Techniques of Analysis." *Urban Affairs Review* 38, no. 4: 463–91. doi:10.1177/1078087402250356.

———. 2010. *Poverty Capital: Microfinance and the Making of Development*. New York: Routledge.

———. 2012. "Why the Middle Class Matters." *Singapore Journal of Tropical Geography* 33, no. 1: 25–28. doi:10.1111/j.1467-9493.2012.00445.x.

———. 2015. "Who Is Afraid of Postcolonial Theory?" *International Journal of Urban and Regional Research* 40, no. 1: 200–209. doi:10.1111/1468-2427.12274.

Roy, Ananya, and Emma Shaw Crane. 2015. *Territories of Poverty: Rethinking North and South.* Athens, Ga.: The University of Georgia Press.

Roy, Ananya, Stuart Schrader, and Emma Shaw Crane. 2015. "Gray Areas: The War on Poverty at Home and Abroad." In *Territories of Poverty: Rethinking North and South*, edited by Ananya Roy and Emma Shaw Crane, 289–314. Athens: University of Georgia Press.

Said, Edward W. 1979. *Orientalism.* New York: Vintage.

Schram, Sanford. 2000. *After Welfare: The Culture of Postindustrial Social Policy.* New York: New York University Press.

———. 2015. *The Return of Ordinary Capitalism: Neoliberalism, Precarity, Occupy.* Oxford: Oxford University Press.

Somers, Margaret R. 1998. "'We're No Angels': Realism, Rational Choice, and Relationality in Social Science." *American Journal of Sociology* 104, no. 3: 722–84. doi:10.1086/210085.

Spade, Dean, and Craig Willse. 2015. "Norms and Normalization." In *The Oxford Handbook of Feminist Theory*, edited by Lisa Jane Disch and Mary Hawkesworth, 551–71. Oxford: Oxford University Press.

Sparks, Tony. 2010. "Broke Not Broken: Rights, Privacy, and Homelessness in Seattle." *Urban Geography* 31, no. 6: 842–62. doi:10.2747/0272-3638.31.6.842.

Spivak, Gayatri Chakravorty. 1999. *A Critique of Postcolonial Reason: Toward a History of the Vanishing Present.* Cambridge, Mass.: Harvard University Press.

Watkins, Evan. 1994. *Throwaways: Work, Culture and Consumer Education.* Stanford, Calif.: Stanford University Press.

Watkins-Hayes, Celeste. 2009. *The New Welfare Bureaucrats: Entanglements of Race, Class, and Policy Reform.* Chicago: University of Chicago Press.

Wilson, David, and Dennis Grammenos. 2005. "Gentrification, Discourse, and the Body: Chicago's Humboldt Park." *Environment and Planning D: Society and Space* 23, no. 2: 295–312. doi:10.1068/d0203.

Wood, Geof. 2003. "Staying Secure, Staying Poor: The 'Faustian Bargain.'" *World Development* 31, no. 3: 455–71. doi:10.1016/s0305-750x(02)00213-9.

Woods, Clyde. 1998. *Development Arrested: The Blues and Plantation Power in the Mississippi Delta.* London: Verso.

Žižek, Slavoj. 1989. *The Sublime Object of Ideology.* New York: Verso.

CHAPTER 1

Safety Net Politics

Economic Survival among Impoverished
Grandmother Caregivers

LASHAWNDA PITTMAN

How do grandparents faced with the unexpected and sudden assumption of primary caregiving responsibility for their grandchildren cope with this situation? How do they make room for their grandchildren, as renters, subsidized housing recipients, or home owners anxious to relocate to publicly subsidized senior housing? What factors contribute to their underutilization of public assistance despite high levels of poverty? Finally, and most important, how do low-income African American custodial grandmothers overcome barriers to public support, and what are the economic implications of their caregiving?

Scholars and policy makers are increasingly considering these questions as the number of grandparent-headed households (GPHHs) in the United States continues to reach historic highs. Previous research has shown that, despite the fragile economic status of grandparents, current child welfare and kinship care policies and practices make them the primary safety net for children in need of out-of-home care. This trend, combined with insufficient government supports, has profound implications for the economic welfare of GPHHs (Baker, Silverstein, and Putney 2008; Copen 2006; Pittman 2015). I suggest that, as grandparent caregivers in skipped-generation households (SGHs, defined as GPHHs with no parents present) navigate the safety net, they are challenged by family dynamics, social welfare policy eligibility criteria, and street-level implementation.

My study of the survival strategies of low-income African American custodial grandmothers providing care in informal kinship arrangements (children not involved with the public child welfare system) reveals the structural vulnerability of families that experience multiple and intersecting disadvantages compounded by non-heteronormative family forms, lacking legal protections and publicly recognized authority as parents. Relational poverty (relpov) and intersectional frameworks help make sense of *who* provides care, *what* resources they have available to do so, and *how* accessible they are.

A relpov analysis calls attention to the ways in which poverty and privilege are mutually constituted, the structures that produce poverty (e.g., global political economy, diminished welfare state, etc.), and the unequal power "wielded through the political, institutional and cultural relations between subjects, social groups and governments" that impoverishment entails (Elwood, Lawson, and Sheppard 2016). Furthermore, from a relpov perspective, race and gender are constitutive of poverty alongside the political economy, not secondary to it. African American grandmothers' caregiving history shows the ways in which impoverishment is produced through intersecting power relations, as well as the forms of agency used by the poor. The coercion of free labor under slavery, exploitation of labor in the postslavery debt peonage system, exclusion of blacks from most of the formal sector prior to the civil rights era, and their disproportionality in the expanded informal, contingent, and low-wage service economies of the postindustrial era have necessitated black grandmothers' greater involvement in the parenting of their grandchildren and have contributed to their poverty rates.

An intersectional perspective establishes that structures of inequality are mutually constituted with respect to not only poverty but also race, gender, and age. From this standpoint, these systems of oppression are conceptualized as an interlocking matrix of power relations. Not only are naturalized assumptions about "race" and sex part of the processes of capitalism, colonialism, and structuring of the welfare state, but so too are notions of what constitutes a family (Gilbert 1997). As a result, African Americans and non-heteronormative families have been differentially incorporated into American society. Differential incorporation refers to the "unequal treatment and differential access of ethnic and racial minorities to the economic, social, political and cultural rewards in a plural society" (Henry 1994, 16–17).

The grandmothers I study experience differential incorporation owing to their race, gender, age, and family forms. I argue that as they creatively remake family, grandmothers subvert normative assumptions of family, resist the devaluation of their caring labor, and devise strategies to allow for the fluidity and complexity of GPHHs. In remaking family they prioritize caregiving and negotiate risks in pursuit of resources. I consider these forms of poverty politics in three policy settings critical to GPHHs and low-income households broadly: subsidized housing, subsidized childcare, and cash assistance. Broadly, poverty politics are "struggles around who is poor, what it means to be poor, what should be done (or not) and who should do it" (Elwood, Lawson, and Sheppard 2016).

Impoverishment of Grandparent-Headed Households

Grandparents are primarily responsible for over 2.9 million children in the United States today. Roughly two-thirds of these grandparents are custodial grandmothers. One-third (32 percent) of SGHs live below the federal poverty level (FPL), which is nearly double the rates among parent–child families. SGHs headed by custodial grandmothers fare the worst, with two-thirds living at or below the FPL (U.S. Census Bureau 2010).

African Americans make up a disproportionate share of GPHHs, accounting for 24 percent of these households even though they are only 13 percent of the U.S. population. Moreover, African Americans are nearly twice as likely to live in SGHs as their white counterparts (13 versus 7 percent) (Livingston and Parker 2010). While the number of these households has risen among all racial-ethnic groups, the overrepresentation of African Americans in the child welfare and criminal justice systems, coupled with changing welfare policies, has dramatically altered black parents' ability to care for their children, the demands placed on caregivers, and the availability of needed resources. In contrast to dominant arguments that individual failings and poor choices are the cause of African Americans' high poverty rates, the highly racialized, gendered, and tightly interwoven nature of these structural causes of poverty have been well documented (Alexander 2010; Gustafson 2009; Roberts 2003).

Previous research has found that increased female incarceration, reduced cash welfare benefits, and other state-specific characteristics and policies drove the growth in foster care caseloads from 1985 to 2000. As the number of incarcerated mothers more than tripled (Swann and Sylvester 2006, 311), caseloads more than doubled, compelling grandparents to care for as many as two-thirds of their children (Johnson and Waldfogel 2002). As black children went from being excluded to disproportionately included in the child welfare system, a growing number of African American grandparents provided care in order to keep them from "going into the system" and under the auspices of the child welfare system (Murphy, Hunter, and Johnson 2008).

Even as punitive law enforcement policies increased African American incarcerations and lengths of stay, child welfare policy reduced the time children spend in foster care. The Adoption Assistance and Child Welfare Act of 1980 and the 1997 Adoption and Safe Families Act were passed to reduce foster care drift and to make placement with relatives a viable option for out-of-home care (Murphy, Hunter, and Johnson 2008). As a result, the number of children being raised by a grandparent more than doubled from 3 percent in 1970 to 7 percent in 2010. The most significant increase occurred among SGHs, rising more than 50 percent between 1990 and 2005 (Scommegna 2012).

The interrelationship between the cash welfare and foster care systems also contributes to the rise in GPHHs. Children who receive or have received public assistance are overrepresented in state custody. In fact, the falling values of welfare benefits were the second largest contributor to the growth in foster care caseloads (15 percent) (Swann and Sylvester 2006). Without the resources they need to provide for their families, low-income African American parents have relied on their children's grandparents to absorb caregiving responsibilities.

As certain public policies have led to higher rates of GPHHs, others affected supports available to GPHHs. Most legislation in the last twenty years has focused on GPHHs *within* the child welfare system (Beltran 2014a). While federal and state legislation on behalf of relatives providing care *outside* of the child welfare system has consisted largely of budget-neutral policies, like educational and healthcare consent laws that enable caregivers in seventeen and twenty-five states to access education and healthcare for children in their care without the need for legal custody or guardianship, respectively (Beltran 2014a).

These interrelated factors both increase the number of GPHHs among African Americans and exacerbate their impoverishment. By almost every available measure, the level of need experienced by GPHHs is not reflected in their overall benefit receipt patterns (Baker, Silverstein, and Putney 2008; Copen 2006). Grandmothers participating in this study identify stigmatization, family dynamics, punitive social welfare policies, and a structural lag between antipoverty programs and GPHHs as chief deterrents to accessing formal resources. Given these intersecting factors, it isn't surprising that fewer than 12 percent of kinship families receive Temporary Assistance for Needy Families (TANF) assistance, and only 6 percent of children living with relatives receive TANF child-only payments, even though nearly all are eligible (Beltran 2014b). Moreover, because most kinship caregivers fail to receive TANF, they miss opportunities to connect to other critical safety net programs. TANF can be an important gateway program for low-income households because it often entails categorical eligibility for other programs. For example, only 17 percent of low-income working kinship caregivers receive childcare assistance and only 15 percent receive housing assistance. Fewer than half (42 percent) receive assistance from the Supplemental Nutrition Assistance Program, although most report food insecurity (Annie E. Casey Foundation 2012).

State-to-state discretion in designing welfare programs shapes caregivers' public assistance experiences.[1] Grandparent caregivers applying for TANF family grants must participate in work activities no later than twenty-four months after receiving assistance (Smith and Beltran 2003). Under Aid to Families with Dependent Children (AFDC), older grandparents benefited from federally mandated age exemptions, but with TANF, states now have discretion regarding these exemptions. Most GPHHs are eligible to receive the TANF child-only grant. Adult income and assets are excluded from TANF child-only grants, and most states impose no work, income, or benefit time limits. Child-only cases have increased dramatically since the passage of welfare reform, rising from only 10 percent of the overall caseload in 1988 to 41 percent in 2009 (Falk 2014). On top of formal policy restrictions, studies identify four main reasons for the lack of program participation among GPHHs: (1) a structural gap between non-heteronormative family forms and social welfare policies (Baker, Silverstein, and Putney 2008), (2) lack of awareness of available rights and resources (Fuller-Thomson and Minkler 2003),

(3) misinformation about eligibility criteria, and (4) fear of drawing attention to their caregiving circumstances, including the severity of their poverty and material hardship, poor health, and family instability (Cox 2003; Pittman 2014, 2015).

African American grandparents who are most economically disadvantaged and have the fewest resources to draw upon are most likely to assume the primary caregiving role. Not surprisingly, the highest poverty rates among GPHHs occur among African American grandparents (Minkler and Fuller-Thomson 2005). These grandparents are also more likely than grandparents from other racial-ethnic groups to be caring for more grandchildren, for longer periods of time and to be managing additional caregiving responsibilities. Low-income black grandmothers contend not only with the economic burdens of primary caregiving but also with integrating the sudden and unexpected onset of caregiving responsibilities into an array of competing demands, without adequate resources. They also do so in the context of a punitive and minimal safety net that devalues care work and that is designed to reinscribe nuclear family forms.

This being the case for so many GPHHs, we should conceptualize their safety net experiences more broadly—beyond grandmothers' caregiving for their grandchildren—to add greater complexity to our understanding of their economic survival strategies and outcomes, and to how we think about agency and politics devised to respond to punitive and excluding systems. While African Americans have gone from being excluded for much of the history of the welfare state to welfare dependency being viewed by the American public as a black cultural trait, it has not been without resistance on their part (Roberts 1996). Ranging from collective mobilization to individual forms of resistance, African Americans have challenged the stratification of the welfare state and differential treatment of its recipients based on discourses about earned entitlements and undeserved handouts.

Early on, black reformers pushed to expand welfare's cultural meaning beyond its definition as a public handout to the poor. Where white reformers focused on moral motherhood (which excluded black women and non-heteronormative families), black women's organizations stressed the value of women's work in the home. They also linked welfare to citizenship. "For these advocates, race issues were poverty issues, and women's issues were race issues. Race uplift work was usually welfare work by definition, conceived as a path to racial equality. And black poverty could not be ameliorated without challenges to white domination" (Roberts 1996, 1585). Black organizing prior to welfare reform combined civil rights and welfare activism that encompassed a wide range of programs, including fair housing policy, political empowerment, and affirmative action in Social Security and AFDC. The fight for African Americans' equal incorporation was about interrelated systems. Black people's organizing during the post-welfare-reform era has focused on increasing jobs and living wages, access to universal, quality childcare, government support for care work, family-friendly employment policies, and affordable housing and healthcare, as well as opposing marriage promotion (Hays 2004). Individual resistance includes supplementing welfare benefits with monetary support from intimate partners and informal and off-the-books work, developing a range of responses to dominant constructions of the welfare mother (e.g., distancing, rejecting, accommodating), practicing everyday forms of resistance, and engaging in discursive and instrumental tactics, to name a few (McCormack 2004).

While previous research has examined how the gendered nature of state policies affects women's mobility differentially across the life course (Gilbert 1997), the assumption is that women will be accessing distinct systems—Social Security *or* TANF, not both—based on age. Less is known about the ways in which African American grandmothers parenting their grandchildren obtain or maintain access to safety net programs designed for nuclear and single-parent-headed families *or* the elderly—not intergenerational families of varying ages.

I examine the coping strategies of low-income African American grandmothers raising grandchildren in Chicago in a qualitative study that I conducted from 2007 to 2011. Data were collected through in-depth, semistructured interviews and participant observation sessions with seventy-seven custodial grandmothers between the ages of thirty-eight and eighty-three living in the greater Chicago metropolitan area. All seventy-seven participants self-identified as U.S.-born black women with an average age of fifty-four years. All study participants were primary caregivers to at least one grandchild or great-grandchild under the age of eighteen with no parents living in the home. Study participants had 3.2 children on average. Seventeen were married, twelve were divorced, three were engaged, and eight were widows. (The rest were single.) All but twenty reported yearly household incomes of less than fifteen thousand dollars.[2] Of the twenty women who reported household incomes greater than fifteen thousand, seventeen had incomes approximately 1.5 times the FPL and three had income twice the FPL. Twenty-eight of the women were working at the time of recruitment, twelve were retired, and thirty-seven were unemployed.

Study participants were raising an average of 2.37 grandchildren for an average of 5.25 years. Twenty-five grandmothers provided care informally, thirty-three were legal guardians, twelve were kinship foster care providers, three were subsidized guardians, and four had adopted their grandchildren. This chapter focuses on fifty-eight of the seventy-seven caregivers who were *not* providing care under the auspices of the child welfare system (which provides higher levels of assistance).

Remaking Families and the Safety Net

At the outset of the assumption of primary caregiving responsibilities, grandparents must remake family, meaning they must establish continuity and stability for their grandchildren, integrate SGHs into their lives, and devise strategies to deal with their family's differential incorporation into antipoverty programs designed to support families (Pittman 2014, 2015). When remaking family intersects with their pursuit of resources, grandparent caregivers must negotiate both real and perceived risks. These caregivers must try to maintain their own public assistance even as their grandparent caregiving roles undermine their efforts and eligibility. They must gauge whether they can obtain public support for grandchildren in their care without losing custody or jeopardizing their own fragile financial status owing to their impoverishment, poor health, and/ or family instability. GPHHs develop several risk negotiation strategies to compensate for their lack of legal protections and limited parental authority within their non-heteronormative family form. At the heart of resistance strategies enacted in the face of impoverishment was grandmothers' prioritization of their caregiving. As such, they allowed parents to maintain control over scarce resources, brokered deals with parents to share resources intended for children, or sidestepped parental authority by becoming legal guardians. Grandmothers also accepted the stigma and misinformation they received from institutional agents. Last, while most struggled to satisfy eligibility criteria, others bypassed bureaucratic regulations.

SUBSIDIZED HOUSING

In the process of remaking family some grandparents began by determining whether their housing adequately accommodates their grandchildren. Nineteen of the fifty-eight grandmothers in the study already received some form of housing assistance, which speaks to their fragile financial status at the time care shifted to them and to their prioritization of caregiving despite their financial circumstances. When forty-one-year-old Ms. Boyd's twenty-one-year-old daughter left her to raise her two-year-old daughter, Ms. Boyd was using a housing choice voucher (HCV) after being displaced from Robert Taylor Homes. Ms. Francois, who'd been displaced from Cabrini-Green Homes, also relied on an HCV. Ms. Randolph and her husband were HCV recipients as well. Although both were disabled, they cared for their five teenage grandchildren when the mother would not.

Study participants also included Section 8 and public housing recipients. Subsidized housing regulations prevent the housing expenditures of recipients from exceeding 30 percent of household income; unfortunately, few of the participants were employed. Although most lived on Supplemental Security Income (SSI), some, like Ms. Boyd, had no income. Ms. Cooper, a thirty-eight-year-old mother of three, cared for her two teenage daughters and her infant granddaughter while living in public housing. Both grandmother and mother were battling recent HIV/AIDS diagnoses. Forty-nine-year-old Ms. Alston "inherited" her mother's Chicago Housing Authority (CHA) subsidized apartment after her death and lived in it with the grandson she'd raised since he was a newborn when his mother spiraled into depression after the murder of his father.

Because it was not uncommon for children to leave study participants' homes to reunite temporarily with parents and then return (Letiecq, Bailey, and Porterfield 2008), most study participants simply refused to divulge their housing composition. Ms. Jean's response when I asked whether her grandson lived with her represents the use of this risk negotiation strategy: "Uh, yes. Technically he don't but he came back in. He's not on the lease." Ms. Jean had lived in subsidized housing for eleven years, but she'd been caring for her grandson for only four. When she assumed care, the relationship between Ms. Jean and her daughter was tenuous. Although she had nowhere to go, her daughter would take her baby when Ms. Jean forced her to leave their home. When the grandson told his grandmother that he and his mother had slept on a train one night, Ms. Jean called child protective services and arranged to assume legal guardianship. Although she did not add him to her lease—so as not to jeopardize her subsidized housing—the once unemployed grandmother got a full-time job so that she could provide for him.

The grandmothers I interviewed struggled not only with family dynamics but also with the housing authority requiring legal guardianship before they could add children to their leases or apply for subsidized housing—despite a Fair Housing Act (FHA) mandate that protects them from such action. According to the FHA, "familial status" includes grandparents and other relatives who lack legal custody of the children they care for, if a parent or other custodial individual so designates them (Fuller-Thomson and Minkler 2003). Yet some housing authorities unlawfully require relatives to have legal custody or guardianship of grandchildren to qualify as "families" living in assisted housing. Again, this demonstrates the differential incorporation of GPHHs in social welfare programs. Study participants weighed the fluidity and uncertainty that came with grandparent caregiving against a tightly subsidized housing market. As such, some would not divulge their household composition for fear of losing their housing subsidies. Others assumed guardianship to keep children in their care, add them to their leases, or apply for Section 8 status.

When some housing authority officials and landlords of privately operated subsidized housing required grandparent caregivers to demonstrate proof of guardianship or custody, it often led to family conflict. For instance, the daughter of fifty-eight-year-old Ms. Price lived with her mother in a multigenerational household when she became pregnant with her first child. According to Ms. Price, when she met the father of her second child, she then "started just having kids, having kids, having kids, having kids." When her daughter would not enroll the children in school or give Ms. Price guardianship so that she could do so, Ms. Price was clear—the children could stay, but her daughter and her new beau had to go. Unfortunately, she was told by housing authority officials that she had to have legal guardianship to add her grandchildren to her lease: "You have to put them on your lease that they actually stay here. . . . You have to legally have them." Her process of remaking family was complicated by policies and practices that reinscribed normative nuclear family forms. Ms. Price sidestepped parental authority by devising a plan to get legal guardianship of her grandchildren without her daughter's consent. Providing proof of legal guardianship enabled her, like other study participants, to both keep her grandchildren in her care and maintain her housing subsidy.

Misinformation about the issue of legal guardianship or custody resulted from differential incorporation of GPHHs and was a barrier to grandmothers trying to both utilize and access subsidized housing. In spite of these struggles with misinformation about legal guardianship, many caseworkers, housing authority officials, and landlords not only adhered correctly to the federal statute but also advocated for these vulnerable families. Grandmothers lacking institutional support devised other strategies to keep their grandchildren and also access and utilize subsidized housing. While most adhered to CHA rules and regulations, some ignored bureaucratic strictures.

Grandmothers' strategies to obtain public assistance or to make the most of a housing subsidy also included applying for subsidized housing outside of the city during the Chicago freeze on Section 8 and contemplating moving to a shelter in lieu of other options. Previous studies indicate that some grandparents in similar situations lived in senior housing with their grandchildren anyway, risking eviction, the loss of housing subsidies, and the loss of their grandchildren (Fuller-Thomson and Minkler 2003). Senior housing that did not permit children was an issue for renters *and* home owners participating in this study who qualified for and wanted to take advantage of publicly subsidized senior housing. They all wanted to give up the homes in which they had raised their children and retire to senior housing to accommodate changes in their economic and health status.

SUBSIDIZED CHILDCARE

Although maintaining or securing housing was critical to these grandmothers thrust into the primary caregiving role, so too was maintaining or securing employment. Caregiving for their grandchildren could push economically vulnerable caregivers into acute poverty by preventing them from participating in the labor market. Most of the employed grandmothers I studied combined paid work and care work by decreasing or increasing their work hours, changing occupations, or altering their work schedules. However, grandmothers caring for non-school-age children faced unique challenges, and some were forced either to quit their job or to forgo seeking employment.

Family dynamics as well as programmatic barriers impeded grandmothers seeking subsidized childcare. The complexity of their family lives required complex and varied strategies. Some grandmothers were forced to quit their jobs or to forgo seeking unemployment because they were unable to afford formal childcare, qualify for subsidized childcare, or find reliable informal childcare. Ms. Boyd shared, "I need to get a job. Then that's another thing, how can I get a job with *her* [granddaughter]? . . . I will need to go through the proper thing because I can't afford daycare. Because you know they will pay childcare. . . . But then it'd have to be in her momma name. So, then I'm dealing with that!"

What Ms. Boyd and others in her predicament meant by "that" was the tug-of-war between parents and grandparents over legal guardianship. To apply for subsidized childcare Ms. Boyd would have had to be the representative payee for her granddaughter's TANF assistance. Yet this would have risked losing the child and jeopardizing her safety because the child's mother could have taken the child from Ms. Boyd to keep her public aid benefits. So Ms. Boyd allowed the mother to maintain control over the child's public assistance, forgoing childcare assistance and her own employment opportunities in the process. As parents struggled with the intersecting structures and processes contributing to their poverty and vulnerability, grandmothers had to decide whether to prioritize their poverty or relieve their own. Ultimately, this decision hinged on whether or not its consequences would ensure the safety and welfare of their grandchildren.

Family dynamics was not the only impediment study participants faced in applying for subsidized childcare. Most of them also found the Illinois Childcare Assistance Program (ICCAP) difficult to access owing to work, education or training, and income eligibility criteria. The ICCAP work and school requirements were especially difficult for low-income families (Butts, Thang, and Hatton-Yeo, 2014). They collectively questioned the logic of the program by asking, "How do I find or keep a job if I have no childcare so that I can find or keep a job?"

Ms. King had difficulty finding work because of her inability to afford formal childcare or qualify for subsidies. When her twenty-four-year-old daughter died of childbirth complications, Ms. King was left to care for a newborn and a toddler. Shortly thereafter, she lost her high-earning job. "I worked all my life. So, I have never been in the system and never had to have any public assistance or anything." She needed a job to pay for childcare and yet she needed childcare in order to work, but when she turned to public aid, she was faced with policies that were ill suited to her circumstances. "You cry, 'Oh why should I need childcare?' [*laughs*] Because you're not working or you ain't in school. I said, 'Well how do you think I'm gonna get a job if I don't have any childcare? I can't go for a job interview'. . . . I got infants. I can't go anywhere, and I can't leave them and no one can babysit because everybody else works." She also had difficulty meeting the

ICCAP school requirement. She had a bachelor's degree, and advanced degrees did not fall under the program's eligibility criteria.

The income eligibility requirement also confounded some study participants. Although many worked in low-wage jobs, they had done so long enough to earn somewhat more than was allowed by this means-tested program. Yet, few earned enough to pay directly for childcare. When grandmothers are the principal childcare providers, their role as childcare consumers and the unaffordability of childcare in the private, unsubsidized market are largely ignored in current policy, even though most grandmothers remain in the labor market. While most study participants who failed to satisfy eligibility criteria either paid for or forswore formal childcare, some responded by trying to bypass bureaucratic regulations.

Lacking access to childcare challenged custodial grandmothers' efforts to achieve economic self-sufficiency or to escape impoverishment. Paying for childcare made it difficult to pay for health insurance, rent, and utilities because safe, reliable childcare is expensive. Study participants understood why some grandparent caregivers decline to report their full income or devise other strategies to qualify for childcare subsidies. The ICCAP was designed with low-income parent-headed and nuclear families in mind. As a result, GPHHs experienced differential incorporation owing to their nonnormative family form. Some who were unable to pay for childcare were compelled to quit their jobs or were unable to secure employment. Paradoxically, grandmothers' ability to parent was compromised in much the same way that racial discrimination experienced by their children in the criminal justice, child welfare, and welfare systems compromised the children's ability to parent.

TANF

Although this research focuses on SGHs in which parents aren't living in the homes with grandmothers and grandchildren, many parents were peripherally involved in their children's lives (Baker, Silverstein, and Putney 2008). Nevertheless, in spite of a wide range of peripheral parental involvement, grandmothers excluded certain parents from assisting them, especially those who were addicted to drugs and alcohol or who had more children and were trying to maintain their own households.

Grandmothers asked drug-free parents with no economic responsibilities beyond caring for themselves to make regular financial contributions, to fill certain specific needs, and to step in when grandmothers and their charges needed them urgently. Parents contributed financially by paying utility bills, purchasing food, or handing over a portion of the child's monthly public assistance, such as Food Stamps, TANF, or Social Security payments. Yet even though grandmothers insisted that parents who were able to contribute financially do so, the majority did not. Thus, parental contact often failed to translate into shared parental responsibility.

When a parent received TANF benefits for a child, the grandparent would be disqualified from receiving such public assistance. When Ms. Boyd's daughter left her with a two-year-old daughter *without* the child's public assistance, Ms. Boyd ended up caring for her granddaughter without either formal support or an income rather than risk her granddaughter's safety by demanding that the mother relinquish TANF payments or take care of her own child: "A lot of people say, 'You let her do it, you ain't saying nothing.' They don't understand! I'm not gonna make her take my grandbaby nowhere that it ain't safe at just so I can say she with her mommy."

Several grandmothers who were eligible for TANF child-only grants did not receive them because they let parents receive the public assistance rather than risk parents retaliating by taking the child (Letiecq, Bailey, and Porterfield 2008). Away from the grandmother, the child might be subjected to abuse, neglect, homelessness, a dangerous environment, or abusive or negligent partners (Pittman 2014). The complexity of the poverty politics at work in their lives meant that some grandmothers were prevented from receiving the only form of cash assistance for which they were eligible when they made the complicated and often coercive decision to forgo resources to protect their grandchildren. Competition over scarce resources within marginalized families and communities is but one consequence of a poverty politics that excludes and penalizes the impoverished more than it provides incentives for advancement.

Forty-seven-year-old Ms. Martin had been caring for her son's child, seven-year-old Kwan Jr., known as KJ, off and on since he was three months old. His mother Tonya, age sixteen when he was born, had proved unreliable as a parent. When asked how she ultimately ended up with KJ in an SGH, Ms. Martin replied, "I had lost my job so I had to give up my place and I was living with my sister. . . . Kwan [child's father] was living there with me and a couple of my other children. And she [Tonya] just . . . told me she didn't want him anymore. . . . Then my son, he took the baby. . . . But he was only seventeen."

Parents could apply their parental rights to take children from grandmothers who lacked custody or legal guardianship (Perez-Porter and Flint 2000). Parents often removed or tried to remove children from a grandmother's care to receive the resources the child received or could potentially receive. Ms. Martin could not stop KJ's mother from using him to try to get Section 8 status. She could not prevent Tonya from resuming parenting even though "she didn't want him." So she continued to say no when Tonya attempted to resume parenting to access resources for herself: "She trying to get Section 8. . . . But like I told her, 'I don't care about you putting him on the lease because they ain't gonna do nothing to me. . . . He gonna stay right here where he is, and he's gonna stay in the school he's at.'"

While some grandmothers wanted public assistance to buttress their fragile financial status, others were willing to forgo these resources so that their financially struggling daughters could keep them. For example, Ms. Cooper allowed her daughter to receive the child's public assistance in the hope that it would help her get on the right track; she asked her daughter only to keep her granddaughter clothed, which for the most part she did. She and others expressed that this risk negotiation strategy was a small price to pay for ensuring the safety and well-being of their grandchildren. Some grandmothers in the study strategized to procure public assistance received by parents intended for their grandchildren rather than accommodate or negotiate with the parents.

While family dynamics can be a barrier to receiving public assistance, so too are social welfare policies and program implementation. Three such barriers to TANF receipt were identified: stigma and discrimination, misinformation, and an inability to meet eligibility criteria owing to aging and health-related issues. To minimize the risk of losing their grandchildren and maximize the likelihood of receiving public assistance, study participants acquiesced when confronted with bias or misinformation, satisfied eligibility criteria when possible, bypassed bureaucratic regulations when impossible, and did without when all else failed.

Study participants were commonly misinformed about the TANF eligibility criteria. In fact, next to parental receipt of public assistance, misinformation about the TANF requirement of legal guardianship was a chief barrier to TANF access. Misinformation stemmed from GPHHs differential incorporation into safety net programs designed with nuclear families in mind. As such, street-level bureaucrats had difficulty translating program policies into practices appropriate to GPHHs. For example, fifty-eight-year-old Ms. Toering had cared for seven-year-old Cambria, her youngest son's only daughter, off and on since her birth. Ms. Toering felt that Cambria's mother's care was inadequate and unsafe. Initially, Ms. Toering was not sure whether she should "take" Cambria from her mother. "But this last year I just really—I couldn't take it." After a series of incidents, she contacted the Department of Children and Family Services (DCFS) three times—to no avail, because she lacked legal guardianship.

Ineligibility for ongoing public assistance, inaction on the part of the state, and fear that the child's mother would remove her from Ms. Toering's care all contributed to Ms. Toering's pursuit of legal guardianship—without the mother's consent and with little assistance from state agents. Ms. Toering told me, "because I went through the guardianship on my own, it's nothing they can do about it as far as helping me out." Although relative caregivers are eligible for TANF child-only grants without being legal guardians of the children in their care, Ms. Toering and others reported that they were told otherwise. Owing to such barriers, fewer than one-fourth of eligible study participants received the $107 monthly stipends.

To pursue the option of applying for TANF family grants for themselves and the child, the grandmothers' incomes had to be included in the benefit calculation. Kinship caregivers in family TANF cases are also subject to time limits and employment and training requirements, and so aging and health-related issues often complicated these applications. For instance, although she desperately needed the medical card that came with public assistance, fifty-nine-year-old Ms. Jena found it difficult to sustain her participation. Care of her grandchildren was transferred to her when her developmentally disabled daughter "had kids too young, when she was still my dependent." When Ms. Jena sought mental health services for herself and her children because they were the offspring of sexual abuse by her stepfather, the family experienced a downward spiral. When she was awarded workfare, she fulfilled the TANF family grant work and training requirement by working a volunteer assignment at a social service organization for thirty hours a week.[3] Ms. Jena explains why her participation in the program was short-lived: "I guess it became a little bit difficult for me. Again, when I have family problems or whatnot, it's hard on me. And with the osteoarthritis the pain that sometimes I get. And dealin' with the issues of my family . . . weighs me down." When Ms. Jena could no longer participate in the program, her resources were cut off, including her access to medical coverage and the $292-per-month cash assistance she received for herself and her fifteen-year-old grandson. Only two grandmothers participating in this study who applied for a TANF family grant qualified for the program.

The Compulsion and Cost of Remaking Family

Relpov and intersectional frameworks extend and deepen existing knowledge about *who* provides care for children in need of out-of-home care, *what* resources they have available to do so, and *how* they access those resources. African Americans' history of marginalization and differential incorporation is as long as their time in this country. Contemporary African Americans live in a postracial and neoliberal society. In this culture, the illusion of equality makes it easy to blame racialized individuals for their impoverishment and other poor outcomes. A poverty politics of differential incorporation undermines African Americans' parenting, including the racial discrimination they experience at every stage of the criminal (in)justice system, their increased likelihood of being sanctioned and of losing (insufficient) welfare benefits, and the racism they experience in a child welfare system that removes black children from their homes more than any other racial-ethnic group, largely owing to poverty-related neglect (Alexander 2010; Gustafson 2009; Roberts 2003).

Current criminal justice, welfare, and child welfare system policies serve neoliberal governmental aims of reducing the cost of labor to businesses and industry, shrinking the welfare state, fighting for family values that reinscribe heteronormative nuclear family forms, and pushing for "race-neutral" social policies that reinforce white privilege. The poverty politics that produce the rise in GPHHs among the most vulnerable populations also benefit the private sector, which profits from cheap labor, government contracts granted to manage families involved in the child welfare system, prison contracts, and coerced prison labor. All of these systems and relations of power perpetuate differential incorporation. Sadly, the same systems of power that threaten the economic, political, and social well-being of African Americans also threaten their ability to parent.

When grandmothers step in to care for their grandchildren they are deeply familiar with the differential incorporation experienced by African Americans. They've dealt with interlocking systems of oppression longer than their children, and are motivated to assume primary caregiving responsibilities to shore up and improve the life chances of their grandchildren. Yet, they do so not only at a vulnerable stage of their life course but also from a position of vulnerability with respect to judicially favored parents and the state. Their nonnormative family form requires continuous legitimation in an era in which bureaucratization is used as a tool to marginalize certain populations. And yet grandmothers also exercise forms of resistance and agency, using multiple strategies appropriate for their unique circumstances to mitigate the negative impact of structural vulnerabilities on their access to the safety net.

Nonetheless, grandmothers' resistance strategies are no match for safety net policies and practices geared toward reforming and disciplining the poor. As a result, although thirteen study participants were income-eligible to receive the TANF family grant, only two were able to satisfy the entitlement program's eligibility criteria. Only five grandmothers were able to satisfy the eligibility criteria for subsidized childcare. Grandmothers unable to qualify for safety net programs are disconcerted because the official poverty measure (OPM) fails to adequately capture the actual income needed to support a basic standard of living for GPHHs.

The structural lag between GPHHs and safety net programs is compounded by inadequate and punitive welfare policies that engender competition over scarce resources. Without legal protections or publicly recognized authority as parents, grandmothers found it difficult to access safety net programs, including TANF child-only grants. While some grandmothers devised strategies to take legal guardianship from parents, others struck deals with parents to share resources. Still others simply did without. The risk of doing without grandchildren—safe and sound in their care—wasn't an option. This politics of remaking family enabled them to prioritize caregiving, and to survive poverty at the intersections of governmental, racialized, classed, and gendered power relations that contribute to their differential incorporation into U.S. society.

NOTES

I am especially grateful to the study's interviewees for their participation and candor. Support was graciously provided by the National Science Foundation (Award No. 1004123) and the Office of Planning, Research and Evaluation, Administration for Children and Families, U.S. Department of Health and Human Services (Grant No. 90YE0112). Research support was provided by the West Coast Poverty Center, Center for Studies in Demography and Ecology, and Women Investigating Race, Ethnicity and Difference (WIRED). I thank coeditors Vicky Lawson and Sarah Elwood for the opportunity to deepen my perspective of this work and anonymous reviewers for their comments and criticisms.

An earlier version of this chapter was published in the *Russell Sage Foundation Journal of the Social Sciences,* http://www.rsfjournal.org/doi/full/10.7758/RSF.2015.1.1.05.

1. "Under AFDC all relatives caring for a child could receive child-only payments, but under TANF such entitlement no longer exists, although states may provide cash assistance to kinship caregivers. Currently all states except Alabama provide TANF child-only payments to kinship caregivers who seek assistance" (Park 2006).

2. The federal poverty level during the years of data collection for families of two, three, four, and eight was $13,690, $17,170, $20,650, and $34,570, respectively.

3. Workfare programs assign recipients of public assistance to employment without compensation. Workfare is required for persons who do not participate in job search training and work programs but who are not exempt from registration with the Job Service.

REFERENCES

Alexander, Michelle. 2010. *The New Jim Crow: Mass Incarceration in the Age of Colorblindness.* New York: New Press.

Annie E. Casey Foundation. 2012. *Stepping Up for Kids: What Government and Communities Should Do to Support Kinship Families.* Kids Count Policy Report. http://www.aecf.org/resources/stepping-up-for-kids.

Baker, Lindsey, Merril Silverstein, and Norella Putney. 2008. "Grandparents Raising Grandchildren in the United States: Changing Family Forms, Stagnant Social Policies." *Journal of Societal and Social Policy* 7: 53–69.

Beltran, Ana. 2014a. "Grandfamilies: The Contemporary Journal of Research, Practice and Policy." *Contemporary Journal of Research, Practice and Policy* 1: 56–73.

———. 2014b. "Improving Grandfamilies' Access to Temporary Assistance for Needy Families." Policy Brief. Washington, D.C.: Generations United.

Butts, Donna M., Leng Leng Thang, and Alan Hatton-Yeo. 2014. *Policies and Programmes Supporting Intergenerational Relations: Background Paper.* New York: Division for Social Policy and Development, United Nations Department of Economic and Social Affairs.

Copen, Casey. 2006. "Welfare Reform: Challenges for Grandparents Raising Grandchildren." *Journal of Aging & Social Policy* 18, nos. 3/4: 193–208. doi:10.1300/j038v18n03_13.

Cox, Carole. 2003. "Designing Interventions for Grandparent Caregivers: The Need for an Ecological Perspective for Practice." *Families in Society* 84, no. 1: 127–34. doi:10.1606/1044-3894.76.

Elwood, Sarah, Victoria Lawson, and Eric Sheppard. 2016. "Geographical Relational Poverty Studies." *Progress in Human Geography*. Advance online publication. doi:10.1177/0309132516659706.

Falk, Gene. 2014. *Temporary Assistance for Needy Families (TANF): Size and Characteristics of the Cash Assistance Caseload*. Congressional Research Service Report R43187. Washington, D.C.: U.S. Congress.

Fuller-Thomson, Esme, and Meredith Minkler. 2003. "Housing Issues and Realities Facing Grandparent Caregivers Who Are Renters." *The Gerontologist* 43, no. 1: 92–98. doi:10.1093/geront/43.1.92.

Gilbert, Melissa R. 1997. "Feminism and Difference in Urban Geography." *Urban Geography* 18, no. 2: 166–79. doi:10.2747/0272-3638.18.2.166.

Gustafson, Kaaryn. 2009. "The Criminalization of Poverty." *Journal of Criminal Law and Criminology* 99, no. 3: 643–716.

Hays, Sharon. 2004. *Flat Broke with Children: Women in the Age of Welfare Reform*. Oxford: Oxford University Press.

Henry, Frances. 1994. *The Caribbean Diaspora in Toronto: Learning to Live with Racism*. Toronto: University of Toronto Press.

Johnson, Elizabeth I., and Jane Waldfogel. 2002. "Parental Incarceration: Recent Trends and Implications for Child Welfare." *Social Service Review* 76, no. 3: 460–79. doi:10.1086/341184.

Letiecq, Bethany L., Sandra J. Bailey, and Fonda Porterfield. 2008. "We Have No Rights, We Get No Help." *Journal of Family Issues* 29, no. 8: 995–1012. doi:10.1177/0192513X08316545.

Livingston, Gretchen, and Kim Parker. 2010. "Since the Start of the Great Recession, More Children Raised by Grandparents." Social and Demographic Trends Report. Washington, D.C.: Pew Research Center.

McCormack, Karen. 2004. "Resisting the Welfare Mother: The Power of Welfare Discourse and Tactics of Resistance." *Critical Sociology* 30, no. 2: 355–83. doi:10.1163/156916304323072143.

Minkler, Meredith, and Esme Fuller-Thomson. 2005. "African American Grandparents Raising Grandchildren: A National Study Using the Census 2000 American Community Survey." *Journals of Gerontology Series B: Psychological Sciences and Social Sciences* 60, no. 2: S82–92. doi:10.1093/geronb/60.2.s82.

Murphy, Yvette, Andrea Hunter, and Deborah Johnson. 2008. "Transforming Caregiving: African American Custodial Grandmothers and the Child Welfare System." *Journal of Sociology and Social Welfare* 35, no. 2: 67–89.

Park, Hwa-Ok Hannah. 2006. "The Economic Well-Being of Households Headed by a Grandmother as Caregiver." *Social Service Review* 80, no. 2: 264–96.

Perez-Porter, Melinda, and Margaret M. Flint. 2000. "Grandparent Caregiving: Legal Status Issues and State Policy." In *To Grandmother's House We Go and Stay: Perspectives on Custodial Grandparents*, edited by Carol B. Cox, 132–48. New York: Springer.

Pittman, LaShawnDa. 2014. "Doing What's Right for the Baby: Parental Responses and Institutional Decision-Making of Custodial Grandmothers." *Women, Gender, & Families of Color* 2, no 1: 32–56.

———. 2015. "How Well Does the 'Safety Net' Work for Family Safety Nets? Economic Survival Strategies among Grandmother Caregivers in Severe Deprivation." *Russell Sage Foundation Journal of the Social Sciences* 1, no 1: 78–97.

Roberts, Dorothy E. 1996. "Welfare and the Problem of Black Citizenship." Faculty Scholarship Paper 1283. Philadelphia: University of Pennsylvania Law School.

———. 2003. *Shattered Bonds: The Color of Child Welfare*. New York: Basic Books.

Scommegna, Paola. 2012. "More U.S. Children Raised by Grandparents." Washington, D.C.: Population Reference Bureau.

Smith, Carrie Jefferson, and Ana Beltran. 2003. "The Role of Federal Policies in Supporting Grandparents Raising Grandchildren Families." *Journal of Intergenerational Relationships* 1, no. 2: 5–20. doi:10.1300/j194v01n02_02.

Swann, Christopher A., and Michelle Sheran Sylvester. 2006. "The Foster Care Crisis: What Caused Caseloads to Grow?" *Demography* 43, no. 2: 309–35. doi:10.1353/dem.2006.0019.

U.S. Census Bureau. 2010. "Current Population Survey, America's Families and Living Arrangements." Washington, D.C.: Government Printing Office.

CHAPTER 2

Differential Inclusion through Social Assistance

Migration, Precarity, and Diversity in Singapore

JUNJIA YE

The challenge of poverty in Southeast Asia is often assumed to be located in the region's poorest, least developed countries. Recent work, however, has shown that by 2008 over 80 percent of Asia's poor were living in rapidly growing countries (Wan and Sebastian 2011, 29). Much of this regional incarnation of the "new geography of global poverty" points to the urgent need to uncover the partially obscured poor in "successful" countries (Rigg 2016, 4). The recent movement of new migrants of various backgrounds into certain ever-growing cities is raising new questions about the study of sociospatial difference in urban life. Neoliberal processes that drive migrant-led diversification in these cities are also contouring the growing inequality and precarity in populations composed of long-term residents, altering the ways in which difference is envisaged and experienced. The ways in which these configurations of difference, in turn, are producing new and more nuanced forms of sociospatial inequalities in the global city, however, have largely remained obscured in the growing literature on diversity.

In short, the diversification of people in the city is also paralleled by the diversification of precarity. Difference, in this chapter, is hence framed in terms of poverty expressed as precarity. In other words, I illustrate the sociopolitical relations that generate precarity as a key axis of differentiation. This chapter demonstrates that diverse peoples are incorporated through uneven modes of governance, ordering, and management, rather than social and political exclusion. My work on poverty politics speaks against more conventional and monetary ways of understanding how the poor are constituted. I analyze relational poverty as precarity sustained through differential inclusion through the realm of public assistance. While much has been written on the management of migrants into receiving societies, far less has been documented on the management of precarity in those places. The sociopolitical relations that generate and govern precarity and precarious subjects in conditions of migrant-led diversification have thus far remained obscure.

This chapter deconstructs "poverty" as a universal truth. I move away from economistic constructions of poverty that tend to obscure governmentalizing processes that are contingent and structural. Specifically, I interrogate how citizenship and race are deployed in the context of rapidly diversifying Singapore through the analysis of organized social assistance for both migrants and locals by state organizations as well as by NGOs. I contend that the same processes that are driving migration and diversification such as urban transformation, economic restructuring, flexibilization of the labor force, and depression of wages are generating precarious livelihoods for both migrants and locals. I draw upon empirical data from Singapore to identify how public assistance and consequently its beneficiaries are administered. My argument is developed from analysis of policy documents and ministerial speeches from relevant websites, and interviews conducted with staff and volunteers of state-linked organizations and NGOs in Singapore from November 2011 to December 2012 and from December 2014 to February 2015. Examining both state-provided and community-run spaces of assistance, this analysis provides insight into how race, class, citizenship, and ethnicity interact in aggregate ways to contour access to assistance.

I rearticulate the meaning of poverty as precarity, as experienced through normativities of deservingness and nonbelonging. I not only situate precarity, an enduring feature of the human condition, in the microspaces of encounters but also, more generally, view it as a relationship conditioned by measures that organize and manage diversification. The spatialization of precarity is enacted through the spaces in which social assistance takes place, where middle-class actors encounter precarious subjects by providing assistance. As analyzed here, precarity is not a settled or static position but rather is generated through relationships of race, class, and citizenship channeled through the distribution of public assistance via state- and community-based structures. The first part of the chapter illustrates how state-provided assistance, inflected by constructions of citizenship and race, produces a migrant-local divide in who is rendered precarious/impoverished. The second part of the chapter highlights encounters between middle-class staff and/or volunteers at community-based social support organizations and their clientele living on the socioeconomic margins in the city, focusing on the politics of help and precarity through dynamic class-based encounters in these spaces. This second section demonstrates how race, class, and citizenship norms set in play through state-provided assistance are brought to bear through cross-class encounters in community-provided assistance spaces, forming the social relations that ultimately shape the experience of precarity and precarious subjects. Through these two interrelated sets of processes, I trace change and continuity in the construction of precariousness in the city. I demonstrate that public assistance shapes the experience of precarity along lines of race and citizenship and furthermore that the poor are expected to behave in ways that are deemed deserving of help and inclusion. Within these politicized configurations of assistance, ultimately migrants are excluded from public assistance. Through the analysis of state- and community-provided spaces of assistance, I show that race, class, ethnicity, and citizenship become the filters of inclusion, differentiating access to assistance. I demonstrate that citizenship is intimately implicated in the representational politics of poverty via processes of differential inclusion and boundary making as well as through the politics of class, race, and immigrant identities. Through these processes of differential inclusion, citizen-subjects are rendered "thinkable" to poverty management.

This chapter locates the analysis of relational precarity in Singapore, which not only is an example of a Southeast Asian country that has been successful in alleviating absolute poverty but also, by many accounts, exemplifies what *a successful city is*.[1] The city-state's aspirations as a global financial center are focused on expanding its influence over the organization and management of global capital flows. Singapore's development toward becoming a livable and sustainable city with a high-quality environment for living, working, and playing has been enviously studied by different city planners around the world. The Fraser Institute lists Singapore, with an annual GDP per capita of $54,101 in 2013, as the second freest economy in the world, behind Hong Kong (Gwartney, Lawson, and Hall 2014, 148; World Bank 2017). As such, poverty and how the poor are managed acquire a different dimension. Besides having neither a minimum wage nor an official poverty line, Singapore has one of the world's highest Gini coefficients—a measure of the income distribution of a nation's residents, where zero reflects complete equality and 1 indicates complete inequality. It was logged at 0.478 in 2014 (Chan 2014). For all of its successes, Singapore contains staggering contrasts of wealth, poverty, and power. The city-state also relies on increasing numbers of low-wage, foreign-born workers to do the jobs that locals cannot be persuaded to do. In this sense, the Singapore case demonstrates the need to reconceptualize poverty as relative rather than absolute. The form of relational poverty politics unfolding in Singapore includes thousands of transnational migrant workers who service and support the needs of the emerging middle classes, in the increasing urban expansion of the city. This group of the poor are strategically included in the economy yet lack significant ability to shape political debate and they are, by and large, depoliticized: denied citizenship. In this sense, their experience of being poor in Singapore, being vulnerable to exploitation by middle-class employers and being on the margins of representation, is reflected in their lack of access to public assistance, which reinforces their precarity.

Differential Inclusions into Public Assistance

The concept of differential inclusion has traveled widely to theorize various strategic forms and permutations of citizenship. Although it has assumed many names, this concept has long provided a means for describing and analyzing how inclusion in a sphere or realm can be subject to varying degrees of subordination, rule, discrimination, and segmentation (Espiritu 2003; Ong 2000; Cacho 2012). More recently, the concept of differential inclusion has been deployed to draw attention to the prodigious and increasing presence of migrants in the European space that belies the widespread notion of Fortress Europe (Mezzadra 2011; Mezzadra and Neilson 2012). Attention to differential incorporation (rather than outright exclusion/deportation/removal) provides an opportunity both empirically and theoretically to conceptualize the relational and changing politics of precarity situated within broader dynamics of citizenship, migration, race, and class.

One of the key theoretical strengths of differential inclusion lies in demonstrating how its deployment through both state and everyday practices situates and flexibilizes the experience of belonging through *calculations of inclusion*. Aihwa Ong's notion of graduated sovereignty is helpful in developing a more nuanced understanding of citizenship and belonging in her conceptualization of neoliberalism and neoliberalism as exception (2000). According to Ong, graduated sovereignty refers to "the differential treatment of a populations in relation to ethno-racial differences, and the dictates of development programs" (2006, 88). Ong is applying graduated sovereignty to the differences of privilege and power between *bumiputera* Malays and the non-Malays and indigenous populations within Malaysia. While her definition is still confined to variegated citizenship, it can be expanded to talk about the selective incorporation of diversity where diversity is subjected to situated and predominant notions of difference where poverty as precarity is a key axis of differentiation. As Espiritu (2003, 56) discusses in *Home Bound*, the differential inclusion of Filipino Americans serves political, economic, and cultural purposes "because they were absolutely critical to American economic development, to the reconstruction of white American manhood, and to the larger project of nation building." Differential inclusion allows us to see the nonlinear, uneven ways in which structural constructions of citizenship shape norms and values that are crucial to belonging. People who occupy legally vulnerable and criminalized statuses are excluded from the law's protection but continue to exist within its folds of regulation and discipline (Espiritu 2003).

Neoliberal discursive practices of value are imposed onto lives when they are assessed comparatively and relationally within economic, legal, and political contexts and discourses. In this regard, the relational poverty politics expressed through precarity co-constitutes insiders via the framing of outsiders who can never fully belong but who, at the same time, are managed through the normative inside. As Cacho demonstrates, this is framed by "a culture of punishment according to the market logic of supply and demand" (2012, 33). The power nexus of citizenship and race can be seen through the realm of assistance where, in the present case, "punishment" manifests as how assistance is distributed. Many feminist scholars have shown how being included within the narrative of value is contoured through welfare policies, that, in turn, shape the norms and values of society and are important sites of governance processes (Lawson and Elwood 2014; Teo 2014). Crucially, the definition and implementation of welfare regimes define and limit citizens' sense of their relationship to the state and to others in society (Somers 2008). Furthermore, it is important to examine not just how much is spent, absolutely and relatively, but also how spending on support is oriented and the principles around which reforms are designed (Teo 2014). Indeed, as Sennett points out, the "act of giving needn't in itself carry the positive charge of a cooperative act. Giving to others can be a way of manipulating them, or it can serve the more personal need to affirm something in ourselves" (2003, 136). Problematizing apparent generosity, or largesse, Sennett goes on to argue that at the core of any form of welfare is the double-edged gift. At "one extreme is a gift freely given, at the other is the manipulative gift. The first embodies that aspect of character focused on the sheer fact that others lack something, that they are in need; the other act of giving uses it only as a means to gain power over them" (2003, 137–38). To be included within welfare often requires that one be subjected to particular conditions or fit into preexisting normativities (in this case racialized categories). I argue that connectedness and disconnection must be understood as co-constituted to gain an accurate picture of migrant-led urban precarity.

To understand how the processes of citizenship and race work together to manage identities and boundary making, I consider the city-state's organization of difference in its historical context. Singapore's diversity was present even during precolonial times, when it was already a bustling trade emporium (Chew and Lee 1991). Following independence in 1965, the governing body faced the challenge of imagining a common objective as a nucleus of nationhood for the city-state. Socially and politically, building a nation-state out of an ethnically diverse population with a complex background of economic, political, social, and cultural differences has resulted in the attempt of the ruling party, the People's Action Party, to produce an overarching national identity and an ideology of "multiracialism" (Lai 1995, 17). This measure officially gives separate but equal status to the Chinese, Malays, Indians, and "Others" (or CMIO, for short) and informs official policies on various issues related to the economy, language, culture, religion, and community life (Lai 1995; Perry, Kong, and Yeoh 1997) and indeed welfare.[2] This framework of race became part of the national imagination such that Singaporeans of various backgrounds could imagine themselves as a multiracial people. English was adopted as a convenient language of trade and is the first language of the country, tying the different ethnic groups together.

The insecurity of Singapore's regional geopolitics was, and often continues to be, an active dimension affecting ethnic relations and management in the city-state. Situated in the Malay Archipelago that has a large "indigenous" Malay population and an "immigrant" Chinese minority, Singapore's ethnic composition created an arguably disadvantageous fit to its surrounding region. Because of its ethnic differentiation and dominance of its Chinese people, many view Singapore as a Chinese place, or even state (Lai 1995). To some extent, the ethnic identities of the Chinese and Malays in Singapore are shaped by the comparison of their economic and political positions with those of the Chinese and Malays in Malaysia. The position of Chinese in Singapore is further structured by the historical experiences of the Chinese immigrant minorities in Southeast Asia. Conversely, however, others view the Malays' social position in Singapore as a disadvantaged indigenous minority (Lai 1995). Finally, the ethnically differentiated development during the colonial period has resulted in limited interaction, the maintenance of rigid ethnic boundaries, strong stereotyping, and an underlying sense of insecurity and fear of dominance by Chinese and Malays of each other. These fears culminated in three violent riots prior to Singapore's independence (Lai 1995).

The construction of Singaporean multiracialism must be understood against this background. Until the 1960s, Singapore's population mostly lived in separate ethnic settlements established by the colonial administration. Large-scale resettlement into self-contained public housing estates, implemented through the Housing and Development Board (HDB), was one of the ways in which the ideology of multiracialism materialized spatially. Through the construction of publicly administered, largely ownership-based, housing projects, the HDB has been able to provide Singaporeans with affordable shelter and spaces to facilitate interaction among different ethnicities (Goh 2005). These include neighborhood schools, markets, community centers, playgrounds, void decks, and walkways that link one block of flats to another (Chua 1995; Lai 1995; Perry, Kong, and Yeoh 1997). Ethnic quotas are enforced to ensure each housing block reflects Singapore's ethnic composition. The state's sociospatial engineering of diversity in HDB estates precludes ethnic segregation. People are not just thrown into contact, but through state practice are forced into contact. From a strategic level, then, public housing in Singapore is a powerful tool in managing ethnic diversity and relations. The state also manages race and ethnic relations via the school curriculum, where the ethnicity of the student determines his or her "mother tongue"—for example, a Malay student must study Malay, an Indian student must study Tamil. The management of citizenship through multiculturalism in the Singapore context relies on the simplification and essentialism of race. Race and ethnic identity are also clearly denoted on every Singaporean's identity card. This particular vernacular of multiracialism is conveyed, experienced, and spatialized as commonplace in the everyday lives of Singaporeans.

To address rising tensions that have come with the increasing numbers of newcomers, state agencies have developed myriad campaigns, councils, and discursive measures. The National Integration Council, for example, was set up in 2009 for "new immigrants, foreigners and locals to interact and communicate with one another" (National Integration Council 2010). This council also funds community integration projects that promote volunteerism, enhance interactions between foreigners and locals, and teach norms and values of Singapore to new-comers as part of their "learning journey" (National Integration Council 2010).

> We can leaven our staid society with the zest from the large numbers of foreigners in our midst: Interweave our complaining culture with the immigrant's gratitude for efficiency, for peace and security; inject third-generation Singaporean compla-cency with the DNA of the immigrant drive to succeed; overcome being kiasu (fear of losing) with newcomers' courage to embrace change; and rekindle love for our nation through the fervour of immigrants who forge new ties with the adopted land of their choice. (Hoong 2015)

Aside from such discourses and social measures that situate diversity through the lens of Singapore-style integration, the ways in which migrants are incorpo-rated economically must also be acknowledged. We see later on, however, that low-wage migrants continue to be left out of state-provided assistance while also being subjected to normativities of inclusion and community-based aid.

Differential Incorporation of New Migrants

The integrated development processes of state-led export orientation and for-eign investment driven developmental strategies perceived to attract desirable "global capital" require the import of human capital, both high- and low-wage labor. Economic restructuring measures since the early 1970s have illustrated configurations of state, capital, labor, and commodity production within a changing international division of labor of which Singapore has always been keen to be a part. While these measures are by no means limited to practices of the state and are instead conditioned by the dynamics of global restructuring, the Singaporean state has particularly strong control over its strategies of de-velopment through its purposeful processes of diversification (Olds and Yeung 2004). While many of the measures adopted are consistent with neoliberal models found elsewhere, the distinctiveness of the Singaporean case lies in the explicit and strong role of the state in shaping economic, political, and social life in the city-state.

While other transnational sojourners, such as marriage and student mi-grants, also contribute to growing social diversity, the sharp increase in immi-gration to Singapore in the past two decades has been propelled by the urgent economic need to fortify Singapore's labor force. The turn of the century saw an increasing share of the noncitizen population resulting from the city-state's restructuring of policies to attract and rely on foreign labor. The deliberate and strategic reliance on "foreign workers" is part and parcel of the dominant neoliberal discourse of globalization as an "inevitable and virtuous growth dynamic" (Coe and Kelly 2002, 348).

The calculated integration of foreigners reproduces a relational and graduated continuum of laboring bodies in Singapore. Today, foreigners make up 30 percent of the total workforce in Singapore (Population.sg Team 2016). As elsewhere, the transnational migrant population grows in tandem with restructuring processes to render labor more "flexible" in relation to capital. The workforce was strategically and rigorously configured to incorporate a significantly large foreign labor pool that can be broadly divided into two strands: "foreign talent" and "foreign workers." Both strands of workers are brought into Singaporean space strategically and are administered very differently (Yeoh 2006). In a broad Foucauldian sense, these new arrivals are brought into the fold of governance and discipline, even those groups of workers that do not hold citizenship rights. Foreigners' access to rights and privileges is mainly differentiated by skills status and by the perceived desirability of these skills to the achievement of national goals. Differentiated access is institutionalized by the issuance of a range of work passes and permits that fall broadly into the employment pass and the work permit categories.

Building a nation through an outward-looking and flexibilized development model also requires selectively inclusionary projects to entice "foreign talent"— highly skilled professional workers, entrepreneurs, and investors who are part of the face of cosmopolitanism in Singapore (Ye 2016). This group of migrants holds a form of the employment pass that enables them to apply for dependents' passes and access to greater job mobility (National Integration Council 2010). Far greater in number, however, are work permit holders, most of whom are concentrated in the manufacturing, construction, shipbuilding, and domestic industries. This pool is also broken down further by nationality, with rules and regulations set by the Ministry of Manpower (MOM), permitting only certain nationalities to access work in particular industries (Ye 2013).

The bulk of the increase in foreigners comes from the increase of male and female low-wage temporary migrant labor in the city-state who hold work permits and who are ineligible to bring their dependents or hold citizenship (Ye 2013, 2014). Of this group that hold work permits, the largest percentage of increase comes from foreign construction workers, many of whom are men from Bangladesh, China, India, and Myanmar (Ye 2016). A large number of workers from the Philippines also take on low-paying service sector work outside of domestic work. These socioeconomic divisions manifest tangibly in the segregated landscapes inhabited by temporary migrant workers compared to other populations in Singapore. Shipyard and construction jobs entailing shift work mean that the majority of male migrants may work in the day or at night, and they generally work at sites separated from interactions with the public. There is also a high degree of spatial constraint in the daily lives of the Bangladeshi workers as the everyday lives of migrant workers are highly reliant upon their employers. Institutionalized within MOM guidelines for employers who hire foreign workers is the policy that mandates low-wage male migrant workers in Singapore be housed in state-approved, employer-provided accommodation. These come in the form of purpose-built dormitories that are commercially run industrial and/or warehouse premises that have been partly converted to house workers, temporary quarters on work sites, harbor crafts (such as ships and marine vessels), and, to a smaller extent, HDB flats (Ministry of Manpower, n.d.). The majority of such accommodations are segregated from residential areas where locals live. Their circumscribed positions in Singapore are further reinforced by their highly limited access to state-organized social support, as discussed below.

Situating Economic and Social Support in Singapore

As many feminist scholars have shown, welfare policies situate and shape needs and degrees of deservedness (Fraser 1994; Lawson and Elwood 2014; Schram 2000). These in turn shape the norms and values of society and are important sites of governance processes (Lawson and Elwood 2014; Teo 2014). Crucially, welfare regimes define and limit citizens' sense of their relationship to the state and to others in society (Somers 2008). Furthermore, it is not just how much is spent, absolutely and relatively, but also how spending on support is oriented and the rationalities around which reforms are designed (Teo 2014). Even as public spending increases to fund a growing range of welfare services, particularly in response to growing inequality or in times of a recession, specific programs, campaigns, measures, and policies operate in ways that mask certain constraints on the vulnerable. Welfare, even with diversification, can continue to filter out different groups of people. Even as there is continuity in various forms of state-led social assistance, the ways in which these are mobilized also account for partition, filtering, and hierarchization.

Economic and social assistance in Singapore is shaped not only by state-led management of difference and diversity through race and citizenship but also by the city-state's emphasis on values of meritocracy and self-reliance and aspirations of social mobility. As Prime Minister Lee Hsien Loong said during the National Day Rally in 2014: "[Singapore's first president] Encik Yusof showed that in Singapore, you can rise to the top if you work hard. He stood for enduring values that underpin Singapore's success—meritocracy, multiracialism, modernization" (Loong 2014). Within this context of meritocracy and a multiracial citizenry imagined as "separate but equal," there are a variety of state-led social and economic support services for Singaporean citizens. Social support is inflected by both citizenship as well as race and class through the national narrative of multiculturalism, migration and labor policies.[3] The principles embedded within the Singapore state's approach toward issues of state support include an emphasis on the importance of self-reliance through formal employment; reliance on family members before non–family members; the significant role of nongovernmental organizations known as voluntary welfare organizations; and the state as supporter of last resort (Teo 2014, 100). It bears pointing out that state support programs in Singapore target not just the poor. Middle-class Singaporeans are also recipients of economic help from state agencies in the form of monetary incentives and grants in buying flats, in school fees, and in childcare (it should be noted these are given only to heterosexual, married couples).

Many of the state's assistance measures also come in the form of labor market interventions. Most of these schemes are run by the Ministry of Manpower, the Workforce Development Agency, and the Inland Revenue Authority and include programs such as the Skills Programme for Upgrading and Resilience (Ministry of Manpower 2009), which subsidizes *employers* for their employee training courses to increase productivity, and the Wage Credit Scheme (Inland Revenue Authority of Singapore 2017), where the government will cofund 40 percent of salary increases for Singaporean employees over the next three years. The Progressive Wage Model was introduced to landscaping and cleaning sectors of the labor market in mid-2015 to prevent employers from outsourcing. As National Trade Union Center Assistant Secretary-General Zainal Sapari said,

> With the Progressive Wage Model, we are hoping that we level the playing field in terms of the wages paid to the workers and if they have to compete, they really have to compete based on their productivity, based on their track record. We want to give the assurance to the service buyers that the Progressive Wage Model is not about increasing salaries, it's about ensuring that the workers are properly skilled, about ensuring that there will be higher level of productivity and hopefully they will get a better service out of it. (Saad 2015)

Productivity, in this sense, forms the normative criterion that naturalizes a hierarchy of value. Through these programs of upgrading people's skills and service provision and staggering wages alongside economic output, the increase of state support has, in effect, rationalized economic productivity as part of a gradation of worthiness and deservingness. Having said this, there has been greater attention paid to aiding the poor. Comcare Long Term Assistance, run by the Ministry of Social and Family Development, is a scheme that provides cash assistance to low-income households who have no access to stable sources of income (Ministry of Social and Family Development 2017). Childcare subsidies are also dependent upon income, with the lowest 20 percent of household income receiving about 90 percent of the subsidies (Ministry of Social and Family Development 2016). These forms of assistance from the state are available only to Singaporean citizens, with permanent residents eligible for only some of them.

As we can see, assistance is shaped by labor market changes. The way these intersect with citizenship demonstrates that access to assistance both is predicated upon and reinforces what it means to be a citizen. Furthermore, the majority of these forms of support are also, in practice, cost-cutting measures more directly beneficial to companies rather than to workers. This is coherent with the state's principles of self-reliance through formal, paid employment. The people who are eligible to receive aid on these terms are valued because they fit within the normative terms of citizenship. Assistance, hence, becomes the zone that reestablishes these terms where a growing number of workers in Singapore's workforce are not included.

A form of assistance that is also consistent with the state's social management is the community self-help groups organized around the national multiracialism schema. The sociopolitical salience of meritocracy and multiracialism, in essence, precludes the questioning of race and vulnerability in the provision of assistance. Precarity is therefore very much structured against the normativity of productivity. Strikingly, low-wage migrants are not recognized as poor within this dominant frame of assistance. These ongoing reinforcements of race, class, and citizenship entrench commonly held beliefs and norms about who constitute poor others and how they need to be managed.

Class, Race, and Citizenship along Assistance Trajectories

The importance of race-based self-help groups, formed in the early 1990s, is evident in the steady increase of funding they have received from the government. In 2014, the Singapore Indian Development Association received up to $3.4 million, up from $1.7 million previously, and the Eurasian Association received up to $400,000, up from $200,000. The Malay self-help groups of MENDAKI and Association of Muslim professionals received grants of $5 million, up from previous $4 million, while the Chinese Development Assistance Council (CDAC) received a one-time sum of $10,000 for a four-year period beginning 2014 (Chuan 2014). While each group caters to its corresponding ethnic community, common among them is their approach to welfare through emphases on education, strengthening family ties (in the Singaporean context, this means a heterosexual family unit) and employability. The beneficiaries of these self-help groups are mainly lower-income citizens. For example, MENDAKI's programs largely cater to the lower 30 percent of the Malay/Muslim population (Yayasan Mendaki 2016).

While each of these self-help groups adheres closely to the ideology of multiracialism, it must be remembered that race is deployed very strategically here. Help is accessible only to Singaporeans and, to an extent, permanent residents who fall within the state's CMIO ethnic/racial organization of society (despite the fact that there are now large numbers of especially low-wage migrants from China and India within the country's borders). As the following quotes demonstrate, the politics of welfare inclusion is strongly contingent upon citizenship and race.

> Because we want to help our local Singaporeans first. . . . Because some of the funding that we get are from the government, so we have to be sure that we have the right target. (Respondent A, from a government-linked group)

> When we say Singaporeans and PRs [permanent residents], and we are talking about Singaporean Indian and Indian PRs, for us, it's the government's interpretation of "Indian" which is anyone from the subcontinent. (Respondent B, from a government-linked group)

Precarity management is strongly informed by the management of race. These raced and classed politics of boundary making within social assistance produce modes of differential inclusion that situate relational precarity politics in Singapore. This powerful imagination of who constitutes the precarious is materially consequential as only those recognized as citizens qualify for assistance. The above quotes illustrate that the increased diversity of people leading precarious lives is not reflected in the provision of organized help toward legal labor migrants to Singapore. Paradoxically then, the ethos of self-reliance through formal employment in the realm of assistance excludes a growing number of migrant workers. The myth of productivity as a proxy for assistance is situated within a particular framework of race and citizenship.

As Respondent C, who is currently working for a community development center (CDC) for Singaporeans but who used to work for a migrant NGO, says, "[The migrant workers] don't have any help services. Actually for Singaporeans they can go to CDC, FSCs [family service centers], religious organizations, self-help group like CDAC, MENDAKI, whereas the migrants will just go to NGOs. I don't think (any of these) will help [migrants]." This section has demonstrated how economic growth and the absolute increase in funds for public assistance constitute the very forms of differential inclusion that render certain people much more precarious than others. I locate the relational politics of precarity within differential incorporation rather than exclusion to disrupt the narrative of meritocracy and multiculturalism. My analysis of how assistance is organized and distributed shows that race is intimately tied to and plays crucial roles within the imagination and making of citizenship and precarity.

Disciplining Norms through Assistance

Social support is inflected by citizenship as well as race, through the national narratives of multiculturalism, migration, and labor policies, and cross-class encounters. Where newcomers do receive assistance from state-linked organizations, this appears to be more focused on the issue of social integration, rather than economic redistribution. This part of the chapter also highlights encounters between middle-class staff and/or volunteers at social support organizations and their clientele, who are living on the socioeconomic margins in the city. This section further illustrates the politics of help and precarity through dynamic cross-class encounters that reinforce rather than challenge middle-class norms. This section also demonstrates how the contours of the "thinkable" are sustained. I show how existing governmental and economic orders are reinforced through encounters that order, frame, and produce the precarious subject. These encounters are embedded with the multidimensional processes of incorporation that produce impoverishment through assistance.

The state's integration efforts and citizenship norms of multiracialism and diversity appear to have been internalized within some welfare organizations.

> Then we bring them out for this learning journey, where we get them actively involved through participating and bonding with the locals through local events: lantern festival, Chinese new year celebration, Hari Raya and all that. And of course, our ultimate aim is to get them involved in volunteerism. No point getting a pink IC [identity card] and be part of Singaporean. But most important, you must get yourself emotionally involved, because this is your country and no better way than volunteerism. (Respondent D, volunteer with a local CDC)

> For me, my friends are all quite—the normal issue is integration. Not only back home, in the office they integrate with locals. Most time is spent with colleagues. They come home and have little time to talk to the rest of the laborers. (Respondent E, new migrant to Singapore who is volunteering with a local community development group)

The explicit tutelage of integration by the state is driven through assistance organizations and their volunteers. This reflects a centralized response to ongoing diversification that addresses national interests rather than improved labor standards and greater equality for all newcomers. As such, new arrivals become subject to governmental reform. Assistance becomes a set of relations of power, practices, technologies, and rationalities that regulate subjectivities involved in both the government of others and self-government. The affect of integration also becomes part of the grammar of inclusion where a new migrant may have gained official citizenship (the pink identity card that all Singaporean citizens carry) but whose integration is incomplete without putting emotional inclusion into practice. "I guess I really note the value of your family context. I think it's what is caught and not necessarily taught. Even in school, I had really great role models for teachers who were incredibly civic-minded, and all this kind of stuff" (Respondent F, CEO of a Singapore-based NGO). Many of the staff and volunteers I interviewed shared similar narratives of what motivated them toward volunteering in the first place. Most are from middle-class families and are well educated. Their frequent engagements with the poor predominantly occur in welfare offices where their relationships are situated in skewed ways (i.e., volunteer/staff serving beneficiaries who are poor).

> It is very difficult to really say whether we are helping them or not. Because I see so many of them come all the time to ask for [supermarket] vouchers. I know some of them take the vouchers and go buy beer. Ten dollars, twenty dollars, sometimes its up to thirty dollars but nowadays very rare because we know their tricks. Obviously vouchers alone will not solve their problems. They also have to learn how to manage their money, save money, don't have so many kids if they cannot afford, don't gamble or sometimes just work. Don't know why they are so free. Sometimes there are contractors in the neighborhood who ask if there are people who want to work for one day but they don't want! Sometimes they don't think the pay is enough or maybe they are just lazy? I think it's hard. It's really their attitude sometimes. (Respondent G, a volunteer with a government-linked organization)

According to Respondent G, the deeper underlying reasons why some of the Singaporean citizens he meets need help stem from their own laziness, their trickster attitude, and their lack of family planning. While it is true that supermarket vouchers alone are inadequate in addressing the needs of the poor, the judgment and distance from Respondent G reproduce middle-class framings of how one should discipline oneself in order to lead a non-poor life. Precarity and the precarious subject are therefore represented through the middle-class gaze within the context of "assistance." This is also a poverty politics that is distinctly racialized in the Singaporean context. "I know they are nice guys. And I just hope that they are sensible—don't spend so much money on unnecessary things and send more money home. I try to remind them when I can" (Respondent H, a volunteer with a church group). As argued by Lawson and Elwood (2014), there is nothing wrong with talking about finances with clients, but the politics of this exchange emerge through the iteration of norms from a middle-class person to unemployed men who are presumed to be susceptible to reckless spending. Such middle-class attitudes toward how the poor ought to behave or must change in order to succeed serve to reestablish class boundaries and the tensions embedded within "help" and within "precarity management." Disciplining within these organizations reproduces middle-class norms that further differentiate and reproduce migrant difference and precarity. Acting from within norms becomes a form of privilege that allows middle-class volunteers and staff of assistance organizations to differently "other" groups who are outside of these norms. This act of differentiation not only creates the precarious subject but, in reinforcing normative boundaries, generates the privileged subject as well. This relationship between the privileged and the precarious blurs the lines between inclusion and exclusion, creating a far more nuanced relational politics of differential inclusion.

Normative Structuring of Precarity in Singapore

In a time when cities around the world are experiencing austerity cuts in welfare and various forms of public assistance, the Singaporean state continues to invest in public support. But as Derrida writes, "there is residual violence of the hospitable gesture, which always takes place in a scene of power" (in Leung and Stone 2009, 193). In this chapter, I have illustrated how domination is exercised through multidimensional processes of incorporation into existing structures of legibility. I have illustrated how the aggregate politics of race, class, citizenship, and migration together shape the contours of precarity in Singapore. The politics of these contours are located at the intersections of citizenship and race at the policy level as well as reproduced through the interactions between staff and volunteers of assistance organizations. Taken together, these practices and discourses produce the precarious subject in the zone of assistance.

I have explored in this chapter how the problem of poverty is the problem of precarity, contoured by sociopolitical relations of citizenship, race, and class. How citizens and citizenship are defined and experienced is particularly urgent to address because this shapes the definition and experience of precarity. The structuring of assistance is also divided by race, as seen by the overarching ideology of multiculturalism in which self-help groups are situated. Increasingly, populations in global cities are composed of significant numbers of noncitizens. Migrants at the lower echelons of the hierarchy often find themselves in employment and residence with migrants of similar status. Their adverse incorporation into the labor market and affective encounters with middle-class volunteers through assistance organizations differentiate them as the "poor other." These sociopolitical relationships situate precarity as a site of struggle.

As discussed here, migrants' lack of access to social support further compounds their marginality in the city. Such is the consequence of parameters of social support that are inflected not only by citizenship and migrancy but by race and class as well. Relational poverty, expressed through precarity, is multiply determined. It is constituted through the work of transforming, ordering, and governing identities, norms, and boundaries. It is modes of inclusion and integration that produce new sociospatial patterns of differentiation and "outsideness." This chapter has demonstrated the imperative of rethinking how we understand the implications of exclusion in the precarious present.

NOTES

1. "Absolute poverty" refers to what Jonathan Rigg calls "Poverty 1.0: the residual poor," who are challenged with the lack of food, health, facilities, education, clean water, and other "basic needs." The measurements of what is and who are the residual poor are usually in absolute and monetary terms based on $1.25 or $2 poverty lines (Rigg 2016, 9).

2. "Others" is a group comprising the other ethnic minorities in Singapore—Eurasians, Jews, Armenians, British, etc.

3. For a detailed explication of the principles that underlie these measures, see Teo (2014).

REFERENCES

Cacho, Lisa Marie. 2012. *Social Death: Racialized Rightlessness and the Criminalization of the Unprotected*. New York: New York University Press.

Chan, Robin. 2014. "Income + Wealth Inequality = More Trouble for Society." *Straits Times*, February 11. http://www.straitstimes.com/singapore/income-wealth-inequality -more-trouble-for-society (accessed June 23, 2017).

Chew, Ernest C. T., and Edwin Lee. 1991. *A History of Singapore*. Singapore: Oxford University Press.

Chua, Beng Huat. 1995. *Communitarian Ideology and Democracy in Singapore*. London: Routledge.

Chuan, Toh Yong. 2014. "Self Help Groups Get More Government Funding Help." *Straits Times*, August 31. http://www.straitstimes.com/singapore/self-help-groups-get-more -government-funding-help (accessed June 23, 2017).

Coe, Neil M., and Philip F. Kelly. 2002. "Languages of Labour: Representational Strategies in Singapore's Labour Control Regime." *Political Geography* 21, no. 3: 341–71. doi:10.1016/s0962-6298(01)00049-x.

Espiritu, Yen Le. 2003. *Home Bound: Filipino American Lives across Cultures, Communities, and Countries*. Berkeley: University of California Press.

Fraser, N. 1994. "After the Family Wage: Gender Equity and the Welfare State." *Political Theory* 22, no. 4: 591–618. doi:10.1177/0090591794022004003.

Goh, Robbie B. H. 2005. *Contours of Culture: Space and Social Difference in Singapore*. Hong Kong: Hong Kong University Press.

Gwartney, James, Robert Lawson, and Joshua Hall. 2014. "Economic Freedom of the World: 2014 Annual Report." N.p.: Frasier Institute. https://www.fraserinstitute.org/sites/ default/files/economic-freedom-of-the-world-2014-rev.pdf (accessed June 23, 2017).

Hoong, Chua Mui. 2015. "Integration Not Just about Fitting In." *Straits Times*, January 18. http://www.straitstimes.com/opinion/integration-not-just-about-fitting-in (accessed June 23, 2017).

Inland Revenue Authority of Singapore. 2017. "Wage Credit Scheme (WCS)." https:// www.iras.gov.sg/IRASHome/Schemes/Businesses/Wage-Credit-Scheme—WCS (October 2, 2015).

Lai, Ah Eng. 1995. *Meanings of Multiethnicity: A Case-Study of Ethnicity and Ethnic Relations in Singapore*. Kuala Lumpur: Oxford University Press.

Lawson, Victoria, and Sarah Elwood. 2014. "Encountering Poverty: Space, Class, and Poverty Politics." *Antipode* 46, no. 1: 209–28. doi:10.1111/anti.12030.

Leung, Gilbert, and Matthew Stone. 2009. "Otherwise Than Hospitality: A Disputation on the Relation of Ethics to Law and Politics." *Law and Critique* 20, no. 2: 193–206. doi:10.1007/s10978-009-9046-1.

Loong, Lee Hsien. 2014. "Prime Minister Lee Hsien Loong's National Day Rally 2014 Speech (English)." Prime Minister's Office of Singapore, August 17. http://www.pmo

.gov.sg/newsroom/prime-minister-lee-hsien-loongs-national-day-rally-2014-speech
-english (accessed October 1, 2015).

Mezzadra, Sandro. 2011. "The Gaze of Autonomy: Capitalism, Migration, and Social
Struggles." In *The Contested Politics of Mobility: Borderzones and Irregularity*, edited
by Vicki Squire, 121–43. London: Routledge.

Mezzadra, Sandro, and Brett Neilson. 2012. "Between Inclusion and Exclusion: On the
Topology of Global Space and Borders." *Theory, Culture & Society* 29, nos. 4–5: 58–75.
doi:10.1177/0263276412443569.

Ministry of Manpower. 2009. "Course Offerings under Skills Programme for Upgrading and Resilience (SPUR) Increased by Five-Fold." January 6. http://www.mom.gov
.sg/newsroom/press-releases/2009/course-offerings-under-skills-programme-for
-upgrading-and-resilience-spur-increased-by-fivefold (accessed August 10, 2017).

———. N.d. "Work Permit for Foreign Worker." http://www.mom.gov.sg/foreign-manpower/
passes-visas/work-permit-fw/before-you-apply/Pages/overview.aspx (accessed November 1, 2013).

Ministry of Social and Family Development. 2016. "Child Care/Infant Care Subsidy."
December 20. https://www.msf.gov.sg/assistance/Pages/Child-Care-Infant-Care
-Subsidy.aspx (accessed August 10, 2017).

———. 2017. "ComCare Long Term Assistance." February 1. https://www.msf.gov.sg/
Comcare/Pages/Public-Assistance.aspx (accessed August 10, 2017).

National Integration Council. 2010. "Community Integration Fund." https://www
.nationalintegrationcouncil.org.sg/CommunityIntegrationFund (accessed September 30, 2015).

Olds, Kris, and Henry Yeung. 2004. "Pathways to Global City Formation: A View from
the Developmental City-State of Singapore." *Review of International Political Economy*
11, no. 3: 489–521. doi:10.1080/0969229042000252873.

Ong, Aihwa. 2000. "Graduated Sovereignty in South-East Asia." *Theory, Culture & Society* 17, no. 4: 55–75.

———. 2006. *Neoliberalism as Exception: Mutations in Citizenship and Sovereignty.*
Durham, N.C.: Duke University Press.

Perry, Martin, Lily Kong, and Brenda Yeoh. 1997. *Singapore: A Developmental City State.*
Chichester: Wiley.

Population.sg Team. 2016. "Who Is in Our Population." August 25. https://population.sg/
articles/who-is-in-our-population (accessed August 10, 2017).

Rigg, Jonathan. 2016. *Challenging Southeast Asian Development: The Shadows of Success.*
Abington: Routledge.

Saad, Imelda. 2015. "Progressive Wage Model for Landscape Industry Launched."
Channel News Asia, April 24. http://www.channelnewsasia.com/news/business/
progressive-wage-model-for-landscape-industry-launched-8266052 (accessed June
23, 2017).

Schram, Sanford. 2000. *After Welfare: The Culture of Postindustrial Social Policy.* New
York: New York University Press.

Sennett, Richard. 2003. *Respect in a World of Inequality.* New York: Norton.

Somers, Margaret R. 2008. *Genealogies of Citizenship: Markets, Statelessness, and the Right
to Have Rights.* Cambridge: Cambridge University Press.

Teo, Youyenn. 2014. "Interrogating the Limits of Welfare Reforms in Singapore." *Development and Change* 46, no. 1: 95–120. doi:10.1111/dech.12143.

Wan, Guanghua, and Iva Sebastian. 2011. "Poverty in Asia and the Pacific: An Update." Manila: Asia Development Bank. doi:10.2139/ssrn.1919973.

World Bank. 2017. "Where We Work: Singapore: Overview." http://www.worldbank.org/en/country/singapore/overview (accessed June 23, 2017).

Yayasan Mendaki. 2016. "About Mendaki." http://www.mendaki.org.sg/about-mendaki/general (accessed October 3, 2015).

Ye, Junjia. 2013. "Migrant Masculinities: Bangladeshi Men in Singapore's Labour Force." *Gender, Place & Culture* 21, no. 8: 1012–28. doi:10.1080/0966369x.2013.817966.

———. 2014. "Labour Recruitment and Its Class and Gender Intersections: A Comparative Analysis of Workers in Singapore's Segmented Labour Force." *Geoforum* 51: 183–90. doi:10.1016/j.geoforum.2013.10.011.

———. 2016. *Class Inequality in the Global City: Migrants, Workers and Cosmopolitanism in Singapore.* Basingstoke: Palgrave Macmillan.

Yeoh, Brenda S. A. 2006. "Bifurcated Labour: The Unequal Incorporation of Transmigrants in Singapore." *Tijdschrift voor Economische en Sociale Geografie* 97, no. 1: 26–37. doi:10.1111/j.1467-9663.2006.00493.x.

CHAPTER 3

Illegality, Poverty, and Higher Education

A Relational Perspective on Undocumented Students and Educational Access

GENEVIEVE NEGRÓN-GONZALES

I meet Mariela at the downtown public library.[1] It is a sticky spring day in Fresno, California, the air heavy with heat but only a tease for the triple-digit temperatures to come in the weeks ahead. The library is hot and crowded. Mariela chose the location, and as we sit down, she apologizes for the fact that it is not an ideal location for an interview. She tells me, slightly embarrassed, that even though she Googled me extensively and determined that I was genuine after we spoke to confirm the interview, her mom insisted on the public library as a meeting place instead of a smaller café, "porque una nunca puede tener demasiado cuidado."[2] I had spent years interviewing, working with, and learning from undocumented student activists, students who proudly live by the phrase that has come to be the mantra of the undocumented student movement — *undocumented, unafraid, and unapologetic*[3] — students who faced police lines, chained themselves to the desks of U.S. senators, staged sit-ins in the middle of busy intersections. This new research, an outgrowth of that previous work in many ways, captured a different slice of the picture of what it is like to be undocumented and young in the United States.

Here in Fresno, the heart of California's Central Valley, the fear is palpable. The conversation with Mariela about her experiences as a student focuses not simply on school or schoolwork. She shares what it is like to work in the fields. She admits she is frequently up at night because she worries about her family's finances. Our conversation about her education is a story about familial separation through migration, low-wage work and low-wage life, racism, and the expectations she must repeatedly confront about what at times feels like an inevitable future working in the fields alongside her parents. We are talking about this year's cherry harvest, and how the historic California drought is changing the economic landscape of the Central Valley when she laughs, saying, "Sorry. We are supposed to be talking about school." I assure Mariela the aside is fine, and after collecting her thoughts for a moment, she says, "I don't know if it is like this everywhere, but here in the Valley everything is interconnected. If there's no water, there's no *cosecha* [harvest]. If there's no *cosecha*, there's no work. If there's no work, there's no money. If there's no money, there's no school. If there's no school, there's no future. You can't take these things apart from each other, they are all connected."

The question this chapter asks is a simple one: What happens when we examine the educational lives and educational trajectories of undocumented young people through the lens of poverty? There is a bourgeoning body of literature on undocumented students and educational access that spans several disciplinary fields; yet despite this interdisciplinarity, we have grown accustomed to thinking about the educational access of undocumented students as an "education issue" or an "immigration issue." Despite the reality that life in the United States for most new immigrants is marked by poverty, we rarely use poverty as a lens through which to understand the plight of these young people. We consider poverty to be the backdrop, the context, the landscape upon which the educational aspirations of this generation of undocumented young people are mapped. What happens, though, when we think of poverty not simply as context, but as a force that centrally configures who these students are, how they navigate the terrain of education, and how they think about their futures?

This chapter presents data from a study that examines the lives of a distinct group of undocumented students—undocumented community college students who live in the agricultural Central Valley of California. Their lives are explicitly defined by their proximity to poverty, liminality, and economic precarity. I posit that the conceptual and analytical frame of relational poverty helps make sense of the educational lives and educational trajectories of undocumented community college students in the Central Valley because their lives are profoundly shaped by poverty. The article discusses two concrete ways in which poverty shapes the lives of these students—(1) many undocumented community college students occupy a dual identity as both undocumented students and also low-wage "illegal" workers and (2) even those who make it to college are constrained by financial precarity and tethered to the difficulties of intergenerational familial poverty. I use a relational poverty framework to connect political economy, higher education, and immigration issues, highlighting the ways in which migrant "illegality" is (re)produced through the racialized spaces of higher education and showing how institutional forces shape opportunity and access.

This chapter develops a relational poverty analysis of the unique case study of immigrant students and in doing so contributes to the broader project of analyzing the multiple ways in which poverty is not an inevitably occurring phenomenon but rather is produced through institutional entanglements and structural processes. Situating the issue of educational access within a relational poverty analytic allows us to move away from the misguided notion that increased access to higher levels of education is the solution to the problem of persistent poverty. Rather, the story that emerges from these data illuminates the ways in which educational opportunities are configured through and constrained by ra-cially stratified labor markets, intergenerational poverty, and structural inequal-ity. This complicates the overly simplified conception of (higher) education as a path out of poverty and insists on an institutional analysis that demonstrates the ways in which impoverishment is produced through multiple, interlocking structural processes and how these processes are inextricably connected to de-bates around "illegality," belonging, and exclusion.

The California Context: The Valley of Contradictions

The Central Valley stretches approximately 450 miles through the middle of the state of California, home to nearly seven million people. It is one of the world's most productive agricultural regions, producing 8 percent of the nation's agri-cultural output by value (roughly $17 billion annually).[4] A critical part of this productivity is ready access to a plentiful, elastic reserve army of low-wage labor. The economic geography of the Valley and its proximity to the U.S.-Mexico border combine to create a particular economic arrangement that relies on the low-wage labor of mostly Mexican migrants to do the critical farm labor that keeps the Valley's economy afloat while simultaneously criminalizing and stig-matizing their presence (Chacón, Davis, and Cardona 2016).

It is estimated that the Central Valley is home to a hundred thousand undoc-umented immigrants (Hill and Johnson 2011). Of the estimated twelve million undocumented people in the United States, one million are children under the age of eighteen (Passel and Cohn 2011). Undocumented young people, especially those who migrate at a young age, are educated in U.S. schools, spend their formative years of identity development within the U.S. nation-state, and expe-rience many of the same rites of passage as their citizen counterparts. Like their parents, they repeatedly confront the constraints of their "tolerated illegality" (Oboler 2006, 15). The lack of a social security number limits their rights and opportunities, and they live under constant threat of deportation and family separation.

The Central Valley is a land marked by contradictions. It is a land of agri-cultural abundance, but many of its poorest residents who spend their days picking the crops that create this abundance are malnourished; a land marked by incredible wealth among ranchers and the landowners, and also home to some of the most extreme poverty in the nation; a land marked by migration and op-portunity and also characterized by the intergenerational (and, at times, trans-national) transfer of poverty. Children growing up in the Valley are educated in underresourced schools, and many will ultimately do the same backbreaking work their parents do. The Valley is critical to the California economy and to the global market, and production in the Valley is dependent on the wage of this low-wage workforce. The agricultural economy of the Central Valley and the structural inequities in the schooling system are often regarded as contextual, coexisting elements. However, an examination of the educational trajectories of these young people illuminates the ways in which impoverishment is produced through multiple, interlocking structural processes and the ways in which racialized illegality is embedded in those processes.

The young people in this study are the children of the workers who pick the strawberries we place on our kitchen tables; some are fieldworkers themselves. Many migrated to the United States as economic refugees fleeing the poverty of their homelands, often the result of U.S. intervention and foreign policy, only to find themselves navigating a different context of poverty in which they are marked "illegal." For many, education is seen as the way out of this conundrum. Undocumented children who grow up in the Valley navigate their family's poverty alongside their own educational lives. They are educated in schools that are underfunded, poorly resourced, and in many ways unable to meet their needs. Still, many strive toward college—they see higher education as the way out of the powerful clutch of poverty for themselves and their families. Many attend community colleges because the cost of even the least expensive four-year state university is out of reach. They navigate school with full-time employment, often working in the fields alongside their parents. These students fall squarely outside of the dominant, "nearly-American" image of DREAMers that the United States has begun to acknowledge.[5] The lucky ones, whose lives are not bound by the cycles of growth in the fields, do other kinds of low-wage, backbreaking work—they tar roofs in triple-digit heat, work long hours at construction sites, and do double shifts as janitorial workers or in restaurant kitchens. The lives of the undocumented young people in this region are profoundly shaped by the ways in which the agricultural economy and an inequitable schooling system are interconnected, structuring access and opportunity.

This chapter presents evidence from an ongoing qualitative, interview-based research project on the experiences of "illegality" among undocumented community college students in California's Central Valley. This chapter analyzes interviews conducted between 2013 and 2015 with thirty undocumented community college students, spanning eight different community colleges in eight Central Valley towns and cities. All interview participants are undocumented, are Latin@, and at the time of interviewing lived in the Central Valley, were between the ages eighteen and twenty-six, and either were currently enrolled in community college or had been enrolled in the previous term with plans to re-enroll.[6] Participants were recruited largely through outreach to relevant offices at area community colleges; some were recruited through personal contacts and snowball sampling.

I intentionally focus on students who are marginalized because of both their geographical and educational locations—living in the "invisible" Central Valley and enrolled in the California community college system. The California Master Plan created a three-tiered higher educational system in California—the community college system, the California State University (CSU) system, and the prestigious University of California (UC) system. As such, the institution of the community college is situated as a critically important site of access to higher education for marginalized students in the state. Though the Supreme Court's 1982 ruling in *Plyler v. Doe* secured the right to K–12 education for undocumented students, its limitations have become increasingly apparent. Undocumented youth graduate from high school and are faced with the daunting reality that they can neither legally work in the United States nor access federal financial aid to continue their education. The structural limitations of educational access for undocumented students gave rise to a nascent grassroots movement in the early 2000s. Initially this movement focused on educational access: activists fought several successful battles at the local, state, and national levels to repeal policies banning the enrollment of undocumented students in institutions of higher education and to allow them some access to in-state tuition and financial aid. The Student Adjustment Act, the precursor to the DREAM Act, was introduced in the U.S. House of Representatives in 2001 as legislation that offered a path to citizenship for undocumented students. Later that year, Texas passed HB 1403 (see Rincón 2008) and California passed AB 540 (see Seif 2004), which categorized undocumented students as in-state residents for tuition purposes at state colleges and universities. The DREAM Act, federal legislation that would provide a path to citizenship for undocumented young people after two years of college or military service, has failed to pass Congress despite numerous attempts since 2001. Although it has yet to become law, the DREAM Act has been successful in helping to cultivate a generation of undocumented youth activists by serving as a rallying point for their struggle.

In recent years this movement, sparked by the question of educational access for undocumented children, has matured in both size and scope, securing some impressive victories. California has been an epicenter of this struggle and these advances. Accompanying AB 540, the in-state tuition law that was passed in 2001, the California Assembly passed AB 130 and 131, enabling undocumented students to access some forms of financial aid. President Obama passed Deferred Action for Childhood Arrivals in 2012, which allowed undocumented young people who met a stringent set of criteria access to a work permit and temporary protection from deportation. The California legislature recently passed a driver's license bill. It also affirmed the right of an undocumented student who passed the bar exam to practice law in the state and is currently debating a professional license bill. However, my research demonstrates that not all students are experiencing increased access. In other work, I take up the question about the disconnect between the promise of inclusion embodied in these recent legislative shifts and the reality that citizenship status continues to constrain the educational experiences of undocumented students in California (Negrón-Gonzales 2017). My focus in this chapter is not simply this disconnect but rather an examination of the ways in which even within this context of greater access, poverty continues to profoundly constrain the lives of these students.

Relational Poverty as an Analytical and Conceptual Framework

I draw on the work of Sarah Elwood, Victoria Lawson, and the Relational Poverty Network in stating that the concept of "relational poverty" is one that "i) shifts from thinking about 'the poor and poor others' to relationships of power and privilege, ii) works across boundaries to foster a transnational, comparative and interdisciplinary approach to poverty research, and iii) involves multidirectional theory building that incorporates marginalized voices to build innovative concepts for poverty research" (Relational Poverty Network 2017). This intervention in mainstream poverty discourse to think about poverty in these ways also resonates with other work I have done on this topic (Roy et al. 2016) and makes an important intervention in what can, at times, be overly operationalized approaches to eradicating poverty. In particular, this relational poverty framework challenges ideas of poverty as a naturally occurring phenomenon with the assertion that poverty is actively produced through interrelating political, social, and economic processes (Elwood, Lawson, and Sheppard 2016). This conceptual framework makes an explicit attempt to disrupt North-centric (Roy 2010) approaches to poverty theory in which expertise from the Global North is situated as the solution to poverty in the Global South and also insists that we cannot separate an analysis of poverty from an analysis of the production of wealth (Wood 2003). Moreover, the production of poverty is intertwined in the processes that David Harvey (2003) calls accumulation by dispossession, a modern-day expression of the primitive accumulation that lies at the heart of the capitalist project. Within this conceptualization, an intersectional lens is critical; an analysis of poverty that does not wrestle in a nuanced way with how this process is enmeshed and constituted through race and gender, for example, is incomplete. Similarly, rather than treating social categories (e.g., "poor people," "the middle class") as fixed or distinct, a relational poverty perspective understands these categories as "emergent and co-produced" (Elwood, Lawson, and Sheppard 2016), which allows for not only a more nuanced understanding of these social actors but also a conception of poverty as a force as opposed to background context (Somers 1998; Mosse 2010).

I draw on this conceptual framework to extend my own analysis of undocumented students and the higher education system. Methodologically, I draw inspiration from others in this field who employ ethnographic methods as a way to push back on the quantitative obsessions with "measuring" poverty (Addison,

Hulme, and Kanbur 2009; du Toit 2009). Relational poverty is helpful both because it situates poverty as something that also happens "at home," not just "over there" in the Global South, and because it takes as central the idea of race and poverty as intertwined, not through a causal relationship but as a dialectic, co-constitutive dynamic. It is this sort of analytical conceptualization that allows us to think about the ways that illegality, low-wage work, and persistent poverty come together to shape the educational lives of undocumented young people.

Dual Identities: "Undocumented" Students Are Also "Illegal" Low-Wage Workers

Over the past several years, the conversation about immigration policy in the United States has rested on a distinction between what is largely understood as two groups—undocumented students and "illegal" low-wage workers. These two groups have been treated as distinct categories that constitute the broader aggregate of who undocumented people are in the United States. Following a long history of drawing distinctions between the "deserving" and "undeserving" poor (Beito 1993), this demarcation is both overtly and covertly deployed to assign a blatant differential associative culpability. Despite profound barriers faced by both undocumented students and undocumented workers, more progressive edges of the populace are beginning to coalesce around the idea that there should be some legal remedy for students who were "brought here through no fault of their own" (Perez 2009). Undocumented workers have not been included in this changing tide, continually regarded as a drain on the economy. Though not my focus here, in other work (Negrón-Gonzales, Abrego, and Coll 2016) I and my coauthors talk about the politics of "deservingness" and the deployment of the politics of respectability that are entrenched within this debate. For purposes of this conversation, however, I'd like to point out another reason that this distinction between the (innocent) undocumented student and the (culpable) "illegal" low-wage worker is dangerous—it is a fictitious divide.

There is no better way to see the overlap that exists between the categories of "undocumented students" and "undocumented workers" than by examining the lives and experiences of undocumented students who live in poverty. Work, to these students, is neither a secondary thought nor an auxiliary activity; for many, their identities as workers are more salient than their identities as students. Jose, a second-year community college student, shares, "I mean, school is what I do when I have enough time. But work is my priority. That's what I do. I wash dishes. I work in a kitchen. And then when I can, the best that I can, I go to school. But that's like a couple nights a week. What do I do with my time? I work. I wash dishes." His casual tone is not a reflection of each of these responsibilities; in fact, Jose is excelling in school and has plans to study neurobiology at UC Davis. His characterization of school as something that is done "when I can" is a reflection of the pragmatics of his situation; he is chipping away at classes one or two at a time while he works sixty hours a week in a restaurant. The majority of interview participants felt that the term "illegal worker" used in the media and popular discourse related to them, while also acknowledging that though they are students, they do not feel a connection to the label "DREAMer." "I mean, I guess technically, yeah, I guess technically I am a DREAMer. But when I hear that I think about someone who, like, goes to UCLA and they are a student activist. That's not my life." Though many undocumented students at four-year universities also work in order to pay for school-related costs, this work is often treated in the literature as an auxiliary activity—something they do on the side of school, which is assumed to be their primary commitment. Among these undocumented community college students, however, work is not auxiliary; it directly relates to their survival and the survival of their families. Zulma shares, "I am responsible for my parents. Cause my dad doesn't make a lot of money so I'm responsible for paying, like, the water bill, the PG&E bill. I was responsible for paying the mortgage last year because my parents were having a hard time. . . . They have paid taxes the whole time they worked because they worked with other people's social security numbers. But that money is gone. They don't have anything to fall back on like citizens do, now that they are old and cannot really work." A demarcation between "undocumented student" and "undocumented worker" does not match the lived experience of these students. Also embedded in these narratives are the multiple and overlapping roles these young people play in their families. They are not only both undocumented low-wage workers and undocumented students but also family members—sisters/brothers, daughters/sons, aunts/uncles, and grandchildren. In these familial roles, they also fulfill critical positions in their family units. These familial connections illustrate the ways in which the vulnerability undocumented migrants in a hostile political context face extends far beyond the realm of education.

The kind of work that these students do is consequential; they are disproportionately located in the lowest paid, least secure, most exploitative sectors of the labor market where protections are scarce and stability is nonexistent. These are not college students who also nanny or babysit or have a campus work-study job at the library. With the exception of one interviewee employed in an after-school tutoring program, all work in the low-wage service or manual labor sector. None are more than one degree of separation away from field work—either they have worked in the fields or their parents do. Gabriela shrugs when I make this observation: "I mean, it's the Valley. Everybody works in the field. Or they come from a family where people worked in the fields. Well, you know, of the Mexican families I'm talking about. It's everybody." Other students work in construction, roofing, hauling, and landscaping, work that is not only physically taxing but also difficult because it is mired with insecurity, abuses, and the difficulties that come along with the jobs that occupy the lowest rung on the economic ladder. These difficulties are magnified further by the risks that accompany life in a conservative, anti-immigrant context. Araceli shares, "I'm always afraid. It doesn't matter that I have DACA. If they really wanted to deport me, I don't think this paper is gonna save anything. Anyways, my mom doesn't have DACA. What happens if she gets picked up?" The duality that these students navigate between undocumented student and undocumented worker is not simply one in which they toggle back and forth between two parts of their lives. Rather, their experiences illuminate that this daily navigation entails particular risks and tensions they continually navigate as a part of this duality.

This tension directly impacts student achievement. Juliana's experience illustrates this dynamic. "It's hard. And sometimes it makes it hard to stay motivated. I have to leave my house at five AM to catch the bus to get to school. I go straight to work from there, and then catch the last bus to come back home. I get back at ten thirty. And then I still have to do my work and do it again the next day. But what are you gonna do? It's the only choice I have." Jaime and his brother are both community college students, and the navigation of this duality and the tensions it creates are something they figure out together.

> We drop out of school when my dad doesn't have work. We work full-time so that we can support the family. At one point, I had to drop out for an entire year. I did roofing. My brother dropped out during his first year here at [their community college] and he did landscaping. He tried to go back, but then he ended up having to drop out again. I went back after that year, but then had to drop out again to do roofing. And right now, we are working it out real good. We are working part-time, and going to school at the same time. Things are working good for now, but you know, you never know how long that's going to last.

The navigation of this dual identity as both undocumented student and "illegal" low-wage worker not only pushes against the problematic politics of respectability that we see emerge in the national discourse around immigration reform but also demonstrates a more nuanced way in which the lives of undocumented young people are shaped by the context of poverty in which they are enmeshed. Not only are these students also workers, but the negotiation of this dual identity fundamentally shapes their experiences in navigating higher education. They are not simply workers and also students; rather they are low-wage workers marked by their undocumented status in a context that repeatedly produces their "illegality" (De Genova 2004). They do the work this state and nation depend on, and the barriers they face in their pursuit of higher education crystallize the fact that the state prefers their bodies laboring in the fields rather than studying in the classroom. This (dis)connection—one that is firmly entrenched in the context of the state's dependence on low-wage work and the migrant bodies who do that work—is one that is forged and remade over and over again through the production of poverty. The world of low-wage work lives side by side with their educational pursuits, dialectically related and coconfiguring one another in ways that make them difficult to disentangle.

Financial Constraints and Precarity, Even for Those Who "Make It"

Though college matriculation is often regarded as the benchmark of success for low-income students, for undocumented community college students who are navigating familial poverty alongside their educational experiences, this threshold rarely brings certainty. My data demonstrate that the precarity that undocumented workers face due to their exploited position in the labor market both is mirrored in and also fundamentally shapes their educational experiences. This means that though California has recently adopted policies aimed at easing the path to higher education for undocumented students, poverty acts as a counterbalance to these policy advances. Understanding these students' educational experiences as fundamentally shaped by precarity, like their experiences in a labor force segmented by race and citizenship, is critical.

The persistent poverty that marks this low-wage life in the Valley means that families are quite literally struggling to meet their basic needs for survival; food, shelter, and clothing are not a given. An additional layer of poverty in the Valley that compounds this vulnerability is the temporal and insecure nature of agricultural work; crops are fickle, work is unreliable, and there are increasingly serious impacts of climate change and the drought. It is not an overstatement to say that these families sit perched on the edge of survival. In many ways, little has changed since Leo Chavez's seminal book *Shadowed Lives*, which documents the lives of undocumented migrant laborers living in illegal shantytown encampments plagued by persistent poverty, preventable diseases, and hunger (Chavez 1997). Thus, we have long known about the ways in which precarity marks the lives of these low-wage migrant laborers, teetering on the edge of survival. What I have found, however, is that educational access is also profoundly marked by this economic precarity.

Students who enroll in college are regarded as the ones who made it, those who are on the path to success. Years of research and experience demonstrate that not all students fare equally once they pass through the doors of the admissions office; race, class, and gender work together in complex ways to create differential kinds of experiences for students, even those at the same institution. It is of particular importance to this chapter to acknowledge the years of research that demonstrate how finances shape the lives of college students and how in that calculation poor students often lose out. We can see the ways in which nontuition, school-related costs often unanticipated by students can create financial strain particularly for students who do not have an economic cushion (Zerquera et al., forthcoming), how the impacts of financial stress weigh on educational achievement (Joo, Durband, and Grable 2008), and also how the value of a degree is altered for low-income students because the debt and financial strains they must deal with impact the kinds of jobs they choose, the sort of work they do, and the ways they build their lives post-graduation (Andrew 2010). The experience of undocumented community college students in the Central Valley illuminates the ways in which poverty creates a kind of precarity that shapes the educational experiences while they are in college. While all poor students face financial challenges, undocumented students shoulder the double burden of illegality and poverty that creates a kind of precarity that profoundly shapes their educational experiences.

How does poverty continue to shape the lives of undocumented community college students once they have overcome the myriad challenges in high school and have enrolled in college? All poor students struggle financially to make ends meet in college, particularly within the context of the trend toward decreased public funding for higher education (Mortenson 2012), and navigate the broader neoliberalization of higher education, which means less support, fewer services, and higher debts for students (Giroux 2014). However, undocumented students experience a unique manifestation of these broader processes. The educational trajectories of many students in the study are marked by rotating periods of enrollment and nonenrollment; enrollment is seldom linear or consecutive. They enroll when they have money and can afford to not work and don't enroll during semesters in which either they do not have enough money saved or the nature of their work mandates that they prioritize it. Viviana shares, "It can be hard sometimes because you never know if you'll have money to go to school again next semester. If there's not enough money, you just can't go." Viviana's experience demonstrates how a precarious work situation also creates a precarious and uneven educational experience. This sort of precarious enrollment situation also impacts students' academic achievement. Alejandra explains,

> Since we are an agricultural family, there is always that quick money for those three months when cherries are in season. So we work, and we save. And it's hard work, but you have to do it and you have to save it because everything for school is so expensive. . . . There was one semester where I wasn't going to work but money was tight so I had to, and then I started working in the fields, and I flunked my classes. Because it was just too much. And I am just cleaning up my academic record now from that, and I can't even apply for the California DREAM Act because it's GPA-based so I don't have that chance until I clean up my GPA, which is still messed up from when I had to work in the fields. So for now, I have to pay for everything. I have to pay out of pocket.

Alejandra's precarious work situation negatively impacted her grades, resulting in exacerbated financial difficulties by making her ineligible for state-based aid that she otherwise would have been able to access. Another student, Patricia, graduated at the top of her high school class and as a result was invited to participate in the honors program at the community college. Acceptance to the honors program comes along with support and resources such as getting your own advisor as opposed to having to get on the sometimes weeks-long waitlist to see a counselor. When Patricia's mother had to stop working in order to care for her little brother with a chronic illness, she decided that it would be best for her to drop out of school for a semester so that she could attend to her new role as the sole breadwinner. She explained that she thought it was a responsible move, prioritizing the financial security of her family while also making sure her grades did not suffer, convinced trying to do both would produce poor results. What Patricia did not realize is that this careful calculation ended up jeopardizing her role in the honors program, because participation in the program is contingent on semesters of consecutive enrollment. Gone were her counselor and other academic supports she had been awarded the previous semester. "I just felt so frustrated because it's like, the time when I really needed that support, that's when they took it away." For Patricia, then, academic achievement was at odds with the financial necessities that she was navigating as a low-wage worker, the sole breadwinner of her family. It was a no-win situation, created and intensified because of poverty, and Patricia's education was the unfortunate casualty.

Another way financial insecurity uniquely shapes the educational experiences of undocumented students is through deportation. Under the Obama administration, deportations increased sharply (Lopez, Gonzalez-Barrera, and Motel 2011), and Trump's vows to reinvigorate border enforcement and deportation promise to intensify this even more. Every student in the study knew someone close to them who had been deported in the past six years—several of them lost a parent to deportation, many lost siblings, and all knew people from their extended family or community who had been deported. Deportation, then, not only presents economic hardship but also acts as a structural process of impoverishment for these students; deportation actively produces poverty. Aside from the profound emotional, social, and psychological costs, there are often financial costs associated with deportation; this was a frequent theme that came up in student interviews. Even for students who were eligible to apply, the protection from deportation awarded by DACA caused financial strain. "I didn't apply for DACA at first, even though I was eligible, because I didn't have the money. I sort of felt like, okay, great that it passed, but I think that, like, most undocumented kids don't have an extra $465 laying around, you know?" Several students identified legal fees associated with fighting deportation cases of immediate family members as a source of strain on very limited family budgets. The most consistent theme related to this was how deportation means lost wages. When a family member is deported, the loss of a wage-earning provider means that the very delicate financial balance that has been established as necessary to keep the family afloat is thrown off-kilter. "Once my dad was deported, it was like, no question. I was gonna have to pick up more work. Because without his pay, it's like, there's just no way. There's no way that we could make that work. That's the first time I ended up dropping out of school." Thus, when a family is dealing with the aftermath of what is undoubtedly a traumatizing event, it must come to terms with not only the family separation and emotional impacts but also the financial dimensions. College-aged students in the family are often faced with the difficult necessity to withdraw for the semester or leave school permanently to increase wages coming to the family as a way of compensating for the lost earnings. Moreover, a unitary focus on educational access for students who are interfacing with the deportation regime (De Genova 2010) renders invisible the other institutional interactions that shape their intimate connection with poverty.

The undocumented youth who make it out are seen as the success stories, yet the experiences of these young people demonstrate the ways that unique financial challenges associated with a precarious legal status profoundly shape this experience and compound these difficulties. Their stories serve as a testament to the ways illegality and poverty continue to shape the lives of undocumented community college students, positioning them in a precarious situation in which studying and surviving are at times at odds with one another.

Toward a Different Future

Despite the financial, emotional, and academic challenges, Mariela is still pursuing her associate's degree at her local community college. The end does not seem particularly close, both because she continues to confront various barriers and because she has to chip away at the degree's requirements bit by bit while also attending to her familial responsibilities. Her educational life is profoundly shaped by not only her legal status but also the economic reality this status engenders. She keeps on, working toward a target that continuously feels just out of her grasp, both in pursuit of her own aspirations and because she is trying to make good on the promise she made to her parents—that they did not leave behind their homeland for nothing, that the daily pain of their migrant experience is not in vain, that Mariela will get an education and make a better life than would have otherwise been possible. She has her doubts, but for the sake of her parents, she pushes on.

Mariela and the other students in this study are clear examples of how educational opportunity is constrained by poverty, "illegality," liminality, and economic precarity. This intimate experience with poverty is configured through their illegality, an idea that the conceptual and analytical frame of relational poverty helps decipher. Through the discussion above of the ways in which poverty shapes the lives of undocumented community college students in the agricultural Central Valley, we are able to understand the ways in which understanding poverty through a relational lens—as co-constituted through other modalities of oppression and privilege—allows us a more nuanced understanding of not just how poverty looks, but also how it shapes lives, experiences, and outcomes.

These findings offer several charges to those of us concerned with the alleviation of poverty and who are particularly concerned with the ways poverty intersects with migration status to shape educational access. First, we must situate educational access, not simply as a question of policy, but within the domain of poverty. Though we have known for a long time that poverty shapes education, we must think in new ways about the ever-changing educational landscape around us and situate poverty not simply as a background or a context but as a character in that story. This means that our solutions to questions of educational access must wrestle honestly with questions of poverty and inequality. Second, we must reconceptualize the connection between illegality and poverty more broadly; the stories and institutional navigations of these students demonstrate the importance of understanding their co-constitutive relationship. There is an important point of connection to be explored between the ways that, as Nicholas De Genova asserts, migrant "illegality" is "produced" (2004) and the conceptual framework of relational poverty that insists on the coproduction of (rather than simply the existence of) poverty. The stories of these young people suggest that these are twin processes and must be conceptualized as such. Not only does poverty intersect and coproduce illegality and precarity, but undocumented status leads to forms of work and forms of access to education that reproduce a precarious quasi incorporation into the economy, society, and politics of the Central Valley. Last, these findings push us to think about the ways we situate education and educational reform efforts within the broader world of social problems of poverty and inequality. It is through an intersectional, relational understanding that we will be able to imagine—and ultimately bring about—a context in which access to education is a fundamental human right.

NOTES

I'd like to thank the undocumented students who shared their stories and their lives with me. I'd also like to thank the participants of the Relational Poverty Network Writing Retreat for their feedback on an earlier draft of this chapter, in particular Sarah Elwood, Victoria Lawson, Jeff Masgovsky, Jia Ye, and an anonymous reviewer. I would also like to thank my research assistant, Olivia Muñoz, doctoral student at the University of San Francisco, for her help in conducting these interviews.

1. All names are pseudonyms.

2. Translation: "Because one can never be too careful."

3. This phrase is attributed to the Immigrant Youth Justice League, whose members coined the phrase "undocumented and unafraid" during their National Coming Out of the Shadows Day in 2010 in Chicago. In 2011 the league amended the phrase to "undocumented, unafraid, and unapologetic."

4. This section draws from my previous article "Constrained Inclusion: Access and Persistence among Undocumented Community College Students in California's Central Valley" (Negrón-Gonzales, 2017).

5. The term DREAMer connotes someone who is eligible for the DREAM Act, a failed piece of federal legislation that would have provided a path to citizenship for undocumented young people after completion of two years of college or two years of military service. In recent years, many undocumented youth in the movement have distanced themselves from the word DREAMer, once a widely used identifier synonymous with "undocumented student," because they feel it reifies the idea that some members of the undocumented community are more "worthy" than others of a path to citizenship.

6. These parameters account for patterns of nonconsecutive enrollment term to term because of financial challenges.

REFERENCES

Addison, Tony, David Hulme, and Ravi Kanbur, eds. 2009. *Poverty Dynamics: Interdisciplinary Perspectives*. Oxford: Oxford University Press.

Andrew, Mark. 2010. "The Changing Route to Owner Occupation: The Impact of Student Debt." *Housing Studies* 25, no. 1: 39–62. doi:10.1080/02673030903361656.

Beito, David T. 1993. "Mutual Aid, State Welfare, and Organized Charity: Fraternal Societies and the 'Deserving' and 'Undeserving' Poor, 1900–1930." *Journal of Policy History* 5, no. 4: 419–34. doi:10.1017/s0898030600007533.

Chacón, Justin Akers, Mike Davis, and Julian Cardona. 2016. *No One Is Illegal: Fighting Racism and State Violence on the U.S.-Mexico Border*. Chicago: Haymarket Books.

Chavez, Leo. 1997. *Shadowed Lives: Undocumented Immigrants in American Society*. Belmont, Calif.: Wadsworth.

De Genova, Nicholas. 2004. "The Legal Production of Mexican/Migrant 'Illegality.'" *Latino Studies* 2, no. 2: 160–85. doi:10.1057/palgrave.lst.8600085.

———. 2010. "The Deportation Regime: Sovereignty, Space, and the Freedom of Movement." In *The Deportation Regime: Sovereignty, Space, and the Freedom of Movement*, edited by Nicholas De Genova and Natalie Peutz, 33–67. Durham, N.C.: Duke University Press.

du Toit, Andries. 2009. "Poverty Measurement Blues: Beyond 'Q-squared' Approaches to Understanding Chronic Poverty in South Africa." In *Poverty Dynamics: Interdisciplinary Perspectives*, edited by Tony Addison, David Hulme, and Ravi Kanbur, 225–46. Oxford: Oxford University Press.

Elwood, Sarah, Victoria Lawson, and Eric Sheppard. 2016. "Geographical Relational Poverty Studies." *Progress in Human Geography*. Advance online publication. doi:10.1177/0309132516659706.

Giroux, Henry. 2014. *Neoliberalism's War on Higher Education*. Chicago: Haymarket Books.

Harvey, David. 2003. *The New Imperialism*. Oxford: Oxford University Press.

Hill, Laura, and Hans Johnson. 2011. *Unauthorized Immigrants in California: Estimates for Counties*. San Francisco: Public Policy Institute of California.

Joo, So-Hyun, Dorothy Bagwell Durband, and John Grable. 2008. "The Academic Impact of Financial Stress on College Students." *Journal of College Student Retention: Research, Theory & Practice* 10, no. 3: 287–305. doi:10.2190/cs.10.3.c.

Lopez, Mark Hugo, Ana Gonzalez-Barrera, and Seth Motel. 2011. "As Deportations Rise to Record Levels, Most Latinos Oppose Obama's Policy." Washington, D.C.: Pew Hispanic Center. http://www.pewhispanic.org/2011/12/28/as-deportations-rise-torecord-levels-most-latinos-oppose-obamas-policy.

Mortenson, Thomas. 2012. "State Funding: A Race to the Bottom." *Presidency* 15, no 1: 26–29.

Mosse, David. 2010. "A Relational Approach to Durable Poverty, Inequality and Power." *Journal of Development Studies* 46, no. 7: 1156–78. doi:10.1080/00220388.2010.487095.

Negrón-Gonzales, Genevieve. 2017. "Constrained Inclusion: Access and Persistence among Undocumented Community College Students in California's Central Valley." *Journal of Hispanic Higher Education* 16, no. 2: 105–22.

Negrón-Gonzales, Genevieve, Leisy Abrego, and Kathleen Coll. 2016. "Introduction: Immigrant Latina/o Youth and Illegality: Challenging the Politics of Deservingness." *Association of Mexican American Educators Journal* 9, no 3: 7–10.

Oboler, Suzanne. 2006. "Redefining Citizenship as a Lived Experience." In *Latinos and Citizenship: The Dilemma of Belonging*, edited by Suzanne Oboler, 3–30. New York: Palgrave Macmillan.

Passel, Jeffrey, and D'Vera Cohn. 2011. "Unauthorized Immigrant Population: National and State Trends, 2010." Washington, D.C.: Pew Hispanic Center.

Pérez, William. 2009. *We Are Americans: Undocumented Students Pursuing the American Dream*. Sterling, Va.: Stylus.

Relational Poverty Network (RPN). 2017. "Relational Poverty Network: Connecting People and Ideas to Challenge Poverty and Inequality." http://depts.washington.edu/relpov/ (accessed June 8, 2017).

Rincón, Alejandra. 2008. *Undocumented Immigrants and Higher Education: Si Se Puede!* El Paso: LFB.

Roy, Ananya. 2010. *Poverty Capital: Microfinance and the Making of Development*. New York: Routledge.

Roy, Ananya, Genevieve Negrón-Gonzales, Kweku Opoku-Agyemang, and Clare Talwalker. 2016. *Encountering Poverty: Thinking and Acting in an Unequal World*. Oakland: University of California Press.

Seif, Hinda. 2004. "'Wise Up!' Undocumented Latino Youth, Mexican-American Legislators, and the Struggle for Higher Education Access." *Latino Studies* 2, no. 2: 210–30. doi:10.1057/palgrave.lst.8600080.

Somers, Margaret R. 1998. "'We're No Angels': Realism, Rational Choice, and Relationality in Social Science." *American Journal of Sociology* 104, no. 3: 722–84. doi:10.1086/210085.

Wood, Geof. 2003. "Staying Secure, Staying Poor: The 'Faustian Bargain.'" *World Development* 31, no. 3: 455–71. doi:10.1016/s0305-750x(02)00213-9.

Zerquera, Desiree, Vasti Torres, Tomika Ferguson, and Brian McGowan. Forthcoming. "The Burden of Debt: Exploring Student Experiences with Debt and Educational Expenses." *College Student Affairs Journal*.

CHAPTER 4

Staying Alive

AIDS Activism as U.S. Relational Poverty Politics

JEFF MASKOVSKY

On March 3, 2011, members of the Philadelphia chapter of the militant AIDS activist group ACT UP staged a protest to demand city funding for homeless people living with HIV and AIDS. ACT UP is the AIDS Coalition to Unleash Power, a nonviolent, radical democratic, direct action group that launched a powerful, politically militant response to the AIDS crisis in the United States and across the world. Its media-savvy demonstrations and dramatic acts of civil disobedience have been remarkably effective in combating homophobia and the stigma against AIDS, challenging governmental inaction in the face of a growing epidemic, contesting the exclusive power of medical expertise, demanding more effective treatments and better research, inventing more participatory models of research, social service provision, treatment, and prevention, and promoting the people-first language of people living with HIV empowerment, not victimhood. Among these and many other accomplishments, seventy ACT UP chapters have formed since the group was founded in New York City, in 1987, including ACT UP/Philadelphia, in 1988.

Shouting "Homes Not Graves for People with AIDS" from the balcony of City Council Chambers in City Hall, the activists disrupted Philadelphia Mayor Michael Nutter's 2012 budget address. In 2010, one of the protestors, Carla Fields, was both a member of ACT UP and a homeless person living with HIV who was eligible for AIDS housing. But she was forced to rely on the city shelters system because no housing was available. In a press release ACT UP issued before the demonstration, she said, "I have had 75 percent of my body eaten up by bedbugs in the shelter. The mayor apologized to me personally for having to suffer and get sick in the shelter system, but I don't want his apology. I want him to end the AIDS housing waiting list!"

The mayor's budget speech was a fitting moment to dramatize the plight of homeless people living with HIV. The Nutter administration (2008–16), as those in most major metropolitan areas in the United States, embraced fiscal austerity in the aftermath of the 2008 financial meltdown. In his 2012 budget address, he called for new wage and business tax cuts and pension reforms for city workers, and he proposed new funding in two reliable budget categories: downtown redevelopment and crime prevention/policing. This was part of an effort to make a "leaner, smaller, smarter government" as he put it, embracing a typical big city fiscal austerity agenda. In 2012, Philadelphia had a 23 percent poverty rate, the fifth highest HIV-infection rate among major metropolitan areas in the United States, a growing homelessness crisis, and a long-running shortage of investment capital (Nutter 2011).[1]

If ACT UP members were unsurprised by the mayor's budget priorities, they were also undeterred in their efforts to make AIDS housing a major public issue. Indeed, the budget speech protest was part of a long campaign in favor of AIDS housing. In 2010, with more than two hundred eligible people on a two-year-long waiting list, ACT UP began a series of actions to draw attention to the fact that Philadelphia's housing programs were not meeting the needs of homeless people living with HIV. The group engaged in the kinds of political tactics for which it has become famous as an inventive and effective political force (Crimp and Rolston 1990; Patton 1990; Shepard and Hayduk 2002; Maskovsky 2013). It issued attention-grabbing press releases, granted press interviews with homeless people with HIV, met with public officials, and engaged in direct action protests. In December 2010, for example, the group went Christmas caroling at City Hall and at Mayor Nutter's house, where they sang a version of "The Twelve Days of Christmas" that included the verses:

> On the twelfth day of Christmas,
> The mayor gave to me
> Lines for food and showers
> Expensive city clinics
> No beds to sleep on
> Rules for being sober
> Cold nights on the street
> TB in the shelters
> Less library hours
> Years on waiting lists
> ID requirements
> Foreclosed homes
> Shelters taking meds
> And no money for AIDS housing.

This creative, highly visible campaign exemplifies an important form of urban activism that has emerged in major U.S. cities, and elsewhere, during the period of what Jamie Peck calls "austerity urbanism" (Peck 2012). In an environment characterized by lean municipal government, new reductions in social service delivery, reduced fiscal capacity, and austerity politics (Peck 2012), urban activists are using rights- and justice-based frameworks to elaborate political demands for the preservation of life. And they are succeeding not only in gaining important concessions from stingy metropolitan governments but also in creating new political alliances and mobilizing new urban constituents, including some of the most vulnerable and marginalized of inner-city residents. For example, low-income African Americans like Carla Fields played key roles in ACT UP/Philadelphia's AIDS housing campaign.

I call this chapter "Staying Alive" to emphasize the fight for life itself that animates AIDS activism during the period of austerity urbanism. Fighting for life has been a central concern in AIDS activism since its inception (see, e.g., Shilts 1987; Chambré 2006). Yet it has taken on new meaning and has inspired new political practices as homeless and poor African Americans become mobilized as AIDS activists. In this chapter, I explore two interconnected aspects of this new fight for life as they are exemplified in the case of ACT UP/Philadelphia. The first is the internal dynamics that encouraged meaningful political participation by poor and homeless African Americans in a group founded mostly by middle-class gay white men and their allies. I chart the concrete changes that the group made to its radical democratic practice in order to manage race and class divisions that threatened to undermine its internal solidarity and to silence or marginalize its less affluent African American members. The second is the extent to which low-income African Americans enhanced the political vitality of ACT UP/Philadelphia, as the group mobilized to push the city of Philadelphia to expand its AIDS housing programs in a period of austerity urbanism. My broader argument is that although ACT UP/Philadelphia was unable to overcome entrenched race- and class-based inequalities, it managed them in ways that helped to sustain the AIDS activist movement during a challenging political period. This, in turn, created an important space of political participation for low-income African Americans, for whom movement participation restored essential civil rights, a sense of social value, and, for many, life itself.

The case of ACT UP/Philadelphia also shows an instance in which some of the most vulnerable and marginalized segments of the U.S. urban poor—those frequently referred to in U.S. mainstream poverty literature as "the underclass"—have mobilized effectively against the conditions of their impoverishment. What makes this case unique and important is how they did it. Rather than mobilizing solely against poverty, this group joined others to use their biological status as persons afflicted with disease to place demands on the city for rights, recognition, and resources.

By treating radical AIDS activism and the fight for life that it entails as a site of antipoverty mobilization, I seek to make AIDS activism thinkable as a form of relational poverty politics (see Elwood and Lawson's introduction to this volume). In mainstream poverty studies, scholars have a long history of using their formidable presence in academia to debate the cultural versus economic determinants of poverty in the United States.[2] On the one hand, those who focus on culture tend to blame the poor and their "culture of poverty" for their own impoverishment. On the other, those who focus on economics tend to focus narrowly on how best to attach the urban poor to low-wage labor markets. Both mainstream perspectives use a mono-causal explanation that reduces the complex political, economic, and governmental forces that produce poverty into a simple story of cultural pathology or economic "dislocation." Importantly, by ignoring the role of politics in the making of urban poverty, these approaches are mostly indifferent to the involvement of the urban poor in the fight for urban and economic citizenship (Goode and Maskovsky 2001; Fairbanks 2012). In contrast, my approach directs attention to the strategies that inner-city residents use not only to survive in conditions of impoverishment but to change them and to stake a claim to the urban present and future (see also Piven and Cloward 1977; Goode and Maskovsky 2001). I focus therefore on relationalities that are typically unthinkable in mainstream accounts of the making of poverty: on the urban poor's civic and political relationships with their more affluent counterparts—other activists, officials, policy experts, social service and healthcare providers, and academics—and broader political and governmental dynamics that shape the making of political subjects. Said differently, this study of relational poverty politics is not about finding a group of "dislocated" poor people and putting their "behaviors" under a microscope. Rather, it is about investigating their participation in broader urban political formations, theorizing the politics they enact in those circumstances, and ultimately making the political lives of the urban poor thinkable in a new way.

Poverty, Biological Citizenship, and the Politics of Inclusion

Central to my exploration of the political lives of the urban poor is consideration of the ways that they are interpolated as biological citizens. Many scholars have directed attention to citizenship projects that are organized around the commonality of a shared biological risk or classification, such as HIV infection, Parkinson's disease, ADHD, cancer, or depression, in contrast to political communities organized around race, gender, class, sexuality, ethnicity, or other social markers of difference and inequality that are typically associated with identity politics and conventional struggles for national citizenship (Rose 2007; Petryna 2003). One important aspect of the pursuit of biological citizenship is a shift away from the ideas of those afflicted by disease as mere supplicants to medical authority. Rather, increasingly, they are actively engaged, as Nikolas Rose puts it, "in the constant work of self-evaluation and the modulation of conduct, diet, lifestyle, and drug regime, in response to the changing requirements of the susceptible body" (Rose 2007, 154). By contesting the power of medical expertise, by viewing their diagnosis as an opportunity for empowerment and as a pathway for self-fulfillment, and by demanding more participatory models of research, social service provision, treatment, and prevention, AIDS activists are some of the earliest and most innovative biological citizens. They helped to usher in a new way of thinking about threats to health as manageable—not fatal, inexorable, or hopeless.

The idea of biological citizenship directs our attention to the political and governmental possibilities of grassroots mobilizations against disease, including the rise of biosocial communities organized around a shared health risk. Yet a full account of AIDS activists as biological citizens requires attention as well to social and political differences and inequalities, not just conceived as residual sites of identity and/or political struggle. Indeed, the making of poverty and social and political inequalities shapes—and is shaped by—emergent biosocial communities such as the AIDS community. In other words, issues such as poverty, homelessness, and racial injustice do not disappear with the advent and extension of struggles for life itself. They became freighted to those struggles and play out through them. With respect to AIDS politics, a key question is how racial and class politics shape—and are shaped by—the politics of homophobia and AIDS panic that have been present in U.S. cities since the beginning of the epidemic, and how they in turn have shaped activists' responses to AIDS. Austerity politics and governance further complicate this situation. In the context of austerity urbanism, urban elites in the United States have tended not to impose austerity by targeting particular subject populations for expulsion from social citizenship. They do not engage in the age-old practice of parsing out who is deserving of governmental support and who is not. Instead, in cities like Philadelphia, elites frequently recognize the demands of biological citizens agitating for rights, recognition, and resources based on shared biological risk. However, elites also refuse to allow those recognized as biological citizens to exercise the robust forms of social citizenship in which wealth redistribution, social welfare, or healthcare provisioning are implicated. An essential part of AIDS activism during this conjunctural moment is thus contesting an austerity politics that allows for *social inclusion but without social citizenship.*[3] This chapter explores these dynamics.

This chapter draws on fifteen years of historical and ethnographic research in Philadelphia on urban activism. I trace the relational poverty politics that arise in ACT UP, explore different positionalities within the group, describe how they change over time, and illustrate the ways that cross-class and cross-race alliances were produced. I then focus attention on the campaign for AIDS housing, which exemplifies the kinds of anti-austerity urban activism that were enabled and sustained by these alliances. I conclude with a critical discussion of mainstream poverty talk and scholarship in U.S. cities in the period from 2000 to 2015.

The Difference That Race and Class Make to AIDS Activism

The conventional wisdom among activists, pundits, and students of social movements is that radical AIDS activism crested during the period of direct action protests of the late 1980s and early 1990s.[4] A protracted period of movement decline followed, brought on by the lessening of stigma associated with AIDS, activist deaths and political burnout, the arrival of effective antiviral therapies in the mid-1990s, the attendant redefinition of AIDS from a "death sentence" to a "manageable disease," the advent of post-gay AIDS politics, the professionalization and bureaucratization of the AIDS community, state repression, and public and political disparagement of street protest tactics, among other factors (Altman 1994; Stockdill 2003; Gould 2009). So intensely felt is this sense of decline that some quarters have made a concerted effort to preserve and archive movement history (e.g., the ACT UP Oral History Project). Furthermore, newer generations of queer activists—those coming of age politically in the mid-1990s and beyond—frequently express nostalgia for ACT UP itself rather than interest in or identification with its ongoing campaigns (e.g., Hilderbrand 2006).

As is usually the case with conventional wisdom, this story of AIDS activism's rise and fall contains just enough truth to be misleading. Although involvement in radical AIDS activist groups such as ACT UP certainly decreased after the mid-1990s, as is evidenced by the declining size and number of active ACT UP chapters across the United States, participation by low-income African Americans increased dramatically during this period of purported decline. Focusing too narrowly on movement decline thus risks relegating low-income African Americans to the margins of AIDS activist history. It treats them as having arrived late to the cause, and minimizes their political impact. Scholars have acknowledged the contributions of people of color and low-income people in AIDS activism's earlier phases (e.g., Chambré 2006; Stockdill 2003). It is also important to view the later phases of AIDS activism not merely as moments of demobilization, but instead as periods during which the AIDS mobilization effort achieved its zenith in terms of diversity across gender, race, and class lines. This diversity was not an inevitable consequence of demographic shifts that placed low-income people of color, especially women and gay men of color, at the center of the AIDS epidemic. The increase in participation by low-income people of color in ACT UP/Philadelphia occurred for three interconnected reasons: subtle changes in ACT UP's informal leadership, an active and successful effort to diversify the group, and internal cultural changes that enabled broader participation in the deliberation process across race and class lines.

Informal leadership changes created subtle openings for different kinds of people afflicted with or affected by AIDS to become involved in ACT UP. The first wave of AIDS activists were those who established the first grassroots organizations serving people living with HIV and AIDS. The second wave were radicals who formed organizations such as ACT UP. In Philadelphia, most second-wave activists were gay white men and their allies influenced by gay liberation, the New Left, antiwar, and civil rights, as they were in many cities across the United States.[5] After the second wave was depleted by burn out, professionalization, or death, anarchist Gen Xers took over many of the informal leadership roles in a group that was organized around anti-hierarchical principles of radical democracy.[6] This third wave was attracted to the militancy of the movement. They also viewed it as a hospitable political space to express anarchist ideas about the corruptive and oppressive nature of the family, capitalism, and the state. Somewhat unique to Philadelphia, the third wave's ranks came mostly from the city's nationally recognized anarchist community. This wave was somewhat queerer than the first, in two senses: it embraced nonnormative sexuality writ large (and not exclusively that which was same-sex-identified), and it was not invested formally in lesbian and gay identity politics. Accordingly, it had a somewhat different take as to the intersection of sexual and AIDS politics. Whereas many of the activists in the second wave viewed homophobia and anti-gay bigotry as primary causes of the AIDS crisis, activists in the third wave saw sexuality as but one axis of inequality that shaped it. They perceived it as operating alongside other axes of inequality, such as gender, race, and class. In other words, although they did not ignore sexuality, they also did not prioritize it. The third wave thus embraced what is now widely called a "post-gay" politics of identity (Ghaziani 2011). Importantly, the third wave was no less white, nor less privileged along class lines, than the first or second.

The third-wave activists were under intense pressure to diversify the group. The push for diversity was inspired by many factors: an ideological commitment to racial and economic justice, the desire to have the group's demographics reflect those of the local epidemic, pressure from prominent local AIDS community leaders who criticized ACT UP for being unreflective—and hence out of step politically—with the vast majority of HIV-positive Philadelphians, and a slow and steady decline in political participation by gay white men, beginning in the mid-1990s. The third wave recruited new members at local AIDS service organizations, HIV clinics, recovery houses, homeless shelters, drug and alcohol programs, and mental health treatment programs. For example, one of the most important sources of new recruits was a community-based HIV treatment education program called Project TEACH (Treatment Education Activists Combating HIV). Project TEACH was designed to disseminate life-saving treatment information to HIV-positive people from low-income communities and communities of color. Over the course of each of the program's eight-week training periods, Project TEACH staff notified their students about ACT UP campaigns and other activist efforts. However, staff members were careful not to engage in explicit recruitment activities while the program was officially in session. In fact, they were deliberately cautious about *not* recruiting Project

TEACH participants to join ACT UP directly, and encouraging them instead to observe ACT UP demonstrations and other activities before making a decision to join. Yet, for their part, many Project TEACH participants were inspired by the people-first language of people-living-with-HIV empowerment and by the prospect of learning how to harness political power to gain control over the domain of medical research and treatment. For example, John Bell was a new recruit who told me that he was inspired by early AIDS activists' efforts to re-form the anti-HIV drug approval process. He simply could not believe, he told me, that a small group of people could force a government that he viewed as indifferent, inept, and prejudiced to change the way that it dealt with people who were suffering with a life-threatening illness. He joined ACT UP immediately after graduating from Project TEACH.

Nevertheless, ACT UP's diversification across race and class lines created new challenges inside the group. For example, new recruits were often put off by ACT UP's nonhierarchical culture and its consensus decision-making processes. This was not because they were averse to radical democratic political practices. On the contrary, it was because these practices were clearly not democratic enough. In fact, from many a new recruit's perspective, consensus decision making helped to produce and secure an informal leadership hierarchy based on race and class. John Bell also remembered feeling very alienated at his first meeting, not only because a group of insiders were talking about things he did not understand. He noted as well the way that this lack of understanding was racialized. He explained, "I'd be in this room with all these white, gay people. The gay thing was not an is-sue. The race thing was. And I couldn't understand. I couldn't understand." This helps to exemplify the dilemmas that ensue when race- and class-blind democratic practices guide the internal decision making of radical activist groups. That new participants often experienced race and class not just as social differences but also as sites of inequality is a problem that threatened to undermine the group's recruitment efforts. Of equal importance, that ACT UP's gay orientation did not bother Bell and many other low-income African Americans who were new re-cruits complicates dominant narratives about homophobia in the African Amer-ican community. Certainly homophobia exists in African American communities and many other communities. However, the fact that many African Americans are not homophobic—and that, in this case, many impoverished and homeless urban African Americans felt comfortable joining a pro-gay political group with a large and highly visible LGBTQ presence—is almost never mentioned in popular and political discussions about homophobia in the black community.

To overcome race and class dynamics that threatened to undermine the group's recruitment efforts, ACT UP/Philadelphia reinvented "consensus decision mak-ing" in ways that favored long-term participation by less affluent people of color. For example, it sometimes enacted "check-ins" before major decisions were made. This entailed going around the room, one person at a time, so that each person had his or her chance to comment on the discussion and to express approval or disapproval about a proposed plan of action. Check-ins are an explicit borrowing from the recovery movement (e.g., Alcoholics Anonymous), with which many new recruits were familiar. By using them, new members were no longer obligated, as with Robert's Rules of Order, to raise their hands to assert themselves, a practice that many found to be very intimidating. Robert's Rules of Order is the widely recognized rulebook for running meetings fairly and inclusively that most ACT UP chapters adopted at their inception. This did not change new recruits' perspectives that white middle-class members had disproportionate influence over the decision-making process. However, it created a new sense of responsibility among members of the group across race and class divides because the "check-ins" imposed on all members an obligation to lay out their concerns when it was their turn to speak or to accept the group's decisions fully as their own.

ACT UP/Philadelphia also provided financial and social support to new members. For example, the group started to distribute public transportation tokens at weekly meetings. This was controversial, even among new recruits themselves. Whereas some saw the transit tokens as a way of defraying the financial cost of going to and from meetings, others saw their distribution as tantamount to a bribe that encouraged attendance by individuals who otherwise would not be interested in the group's activities. Fascinatingly, the group engaged in a more than decade-long conversation about the politics and ethics of giving out transportation tokens, and decided several times to suspend their distribution, though never permanently. The controversy is itself instructive: it points to the careful balance that the group attempted to achieve between offering forms of social and financial support that might enhance participation by the less affluent on the one hand and maintaining an overall sense of pure, selfless, unremunerated political participation on the other.

Finally, and perhaps most important, is the agency of low-income African Americans themselves in managing racial hierarchies and class differences. José de Marco spent more than two decades as a member of ACT UP. Like John Bell, he joined the group after graduating from Project TEACH. And like Bell, he also remembers being too intimidated at first to participate at ACT UP meetings. But, as he told me, he was inspired by his gay uncle who had been active in the civil rights movement. And he decided to remain in ACT UP despite the unequal power relations within the group. He explains,

> Project TEACH actually opened my eyes to a lot of the issues and problems that face people with HIV and AIDS, especially people of color. Okay, now that my eyes have been opened to it, here's a group of people who are actually working on it. And, like, winning shit. They just don't talk about it; they just don't write letters. They accomplish the things. Eventually as time passes, you become stronger in your activism, in your skills. . . . I'm a good organizer now. I wasn't. I think I'm a

great organizer, around AIDS issues, of course. And I'm able to plan a campaign now. I don't think I would have been . . . no one else would have been able to teach me that, except ACT UP. You know? I've learned a lot of valuable skills. I stayed, you know. I saw the shit that was going on. I was living with AIDS. And ACT UP did shit, accomplished it. That's why I stayed. That's exactly why I stayed. And they made me, in the end, they made me feel a really big part of things.

Despite the race and class divisions within the ACT UP chapter, people like José also felt a sense of inclusion, and many learned to use the rules of deliberation to make the group more inclusive. As de Marco explained to me during an interview in 2005,

JOSÉ: I blocked consensus many times.
JEFF M: Really?
JOSÉ: Mmhmm. You know, and it was the sort of thing that when I blocked consensus because . . . we're making decisions that may impact large groups of people of color. You don't have a whole lot of people of color in this room to talk about it. So, a couple of times I blocked consensus. They got really, really angry with me.

Such actions by de Marco and others pushed the group to diversify further.

Under the rubric of people-living-with-AIDS empowerment, ACT UP/Philadelphia eventually become a political assemblage of white anarchist organizers and a rank and file that was predominantly poor and black. Then, over time, its leadership diversified, as many low-income African Americans assumed informal leadership positions. Educated middle-class people of color played an important role in ACT UP Philadelphia since its inception, though they were a minority in the first decade after the group formed. Occasionally, low-income whites also joined ACT UP, especially in the first decade as those who suffered financially because of their illness. But it was not until the mid-2000s when low-income African Americans—some gay, some straight—became the majority. And people of color, nearly all of whom were low-income Philadelphians, sustained the group as the third wave of activists who recruited them left ACT UP (many to form or work for new AIDS advocacy organizations elsewhere), and as an even younger generation of mostly white college-educated activists found their way into the group. Despite the pronounced race and class divisions within it, this configuration was surprisingly resilient: the Philadelphia group has held together longer during its political life span than most ACT UP chapters.

Fighting "Almost Deadness": Life Politics in the Age of Austerity

The post–2008 economic meltdown move toward austerity created new constraints on public health and welfare spending in Philadelphia. It is in this context that the city of Philadelphia's health authorities calculated the value of life for homeless people with HIV and for other "vulnerable" and "at-risk" populations for whom they crafted interventions. It might be tempting to assume that, in the context of austerity, municipal authorities gave no value at all to the lives of these populations, to assume that they treated homeless people with HIV as a disposable population shorn of civil and political rights, and that now survives on the margins of the city in a state of "bare life" (Agamben 1998). But the situation is more complicated, thanks in large measure to the efforts of AIDS activists who have fought for the creation and funding of AIDS and other health and welfare services, and who found new ways to elaborate political demands for the preservation of life in this hostile context.

One of AIDS activists' loudest complaints was that Philadelphia's health authorities used a threshold of "almost deadness" to calculate who is deserving of AIDS housing. As with most major U.S. metropolitan areas, public health officials in Philadelphia used biological markers to determine who was most urgently in need of access to AIDS housing units. The sicker the homeless person with HIV, the easier it was for him or her to gain access to housing. In fact, only those who were "advanced" enough in their disease progression to have an official AIDS diagnosis (evidenced by a low CD4 count or AIDS-defining illness), not just those who were HIV positive, were eligible for AIDS housing. The logic here follows established ethical guidelines for organ donation and other protocols for healthcare rationing. Activists insisted, however, that housing prevented HIV positive people from becoming sicker. Here the experience of ACT UP member Cliff Williams is instructive. His wife was on the list for AIDS housing because she had an AIDS diagnosis and cancer. When she died, he lost his place on the list because he did not yet have an AIDS diagnosis, just HIV. It was only after he got dangerously close to death that he again became eligible for AIDS housing. From Cliff's point of view, this was a catch-22, a choice between homelessness with HIV or housing with AIDS.

AIDS activists used various forms of political action to oblige the city to re-value life so that a broader, more diverse group beyond the "almost dead" could receive AIDS housing. One strategy they used was to push for new models for housing the homeless. As with most major U.S. cities, Philadelphia based its homeless policy on the Continuum of Care model, which makes psychiatric stability, substance abuse treatment, and sobriety prerequisites for permanent housing. City officials viewed the city's shelter system as the proper entry point in the Continuum of Care for the most vulnerable homeless populations. The logic here is that homeless people with acute psychiatric or substance abuse problems are too unstable for permanent homes. In its protests and in meetings with city officials, ACT UP members argued that this model has dangerous public health implications for homeless people with HIV and for the homeless in general. The organization produced a report, "Dying for Homes," that uses statistics and testimonials from homeless people such as Cliff to show that homelessness itself increases an individual's inability to safely manage illnesses, leaving those living with HIV at an increased risk for becoming sicker (ACT UP 2010). In contrast to the Continuum of Care model, activists promoted instead a Housing First model that offers immediate access to independent housing without requiring psychiatric treatment or sobriety. Adopting this model, they said, would prevent the spread of AIDS and enhance the health of those who are already infected. Their motto for this campaign was "Housing Equals Prevention, Treatment and Justice."

Housing First originated as a model for housing the chronically homeless on the West Coast of the United States in the late 1980s. It quickly spread across the country and internationally, and has been embraced by a variety of grassroots groups, national homeless rights advocacy groups, and municipal, state, and federal governmental agencies. According to ACT UP/Philadelphia member Max Ray, members of the group first learned about the Housing First model from AIDS and homeless rights activists outside of Philadelphia, who in turn brought the idea to the general membership. Members met with outside advocacy organizations, including the National AIDS Housing Coalition, which advocated a Housing First harm-reduction strategy for active drug users. ACT UP/Philadelphia also received support from CHAMP (Community HIV/AIDS Mobilization Project), a national advocacy group that provided funding and technical support for local campaigns. ACT UP/Philadelphia also partnered with students from the University of Pennsylvania, who helped the group to draft "Dying for Homes." ACT UP/Philadelphia has a long history of working with outside groups such as these, and in participating in transnational health and social justice activist networks. There is no doubt that ACT UP's more educated white middle-class members played an important role in importing the Housing First model into Philadelphia, and in facilitating its interactions with outside groups who offered assistance and helped in report writing. But this does not mean that low-income African Americans and other people of color in the group were uninvolved. For example, Cliff Williams almost single-handedly spearheaded the AIDS housing campaign in 2010. During an ACT UP planning meeting in 2011, Williams said to the group: "Okay, I called City Council people and set up a meeting. Now we need to get HIV-positive people and we need Penn students and med students who can come in with statistics, so I set those meetings up and called Penn students." As this case makes clear, low-income African Americans are not dupes of their more affluent white counterparts. To the contrary, they cultivate their own readings of privilege and unequal power relations in the course of their political participation, and this, in turn, informs the way that they act politically.

Moreover, this campaign was effective. In response to activist pressure, the city set aside twenty Housing First slots for HIV-positive people. ACT UP also called on the city to end the housing wait list, to keep better track of the homelessness crisis, and to streamline the bureaucracy that the homeless must navigate in order to get access to housing and healthcare. ACT UP also joined with other housing and health advocacy groups to fight successfully for more funding for affordable housing at the state level. Although Philadelphia itself never agreed to expand access to AIDS housing with a significant amount of city funding, by 2011 it abandoned all moral pretense that homeless people with HIV were not deserving of housing. This in itself marks an important activist victory.

Yet this acknowledgment also created new political challenges in the age of austerity urbanism. Activists I interviewed told me that Mayor Nutter and other city officials responded positively to the ACT UP AIDS housing campaign. Eventually the Nutter administration went so far as to embrace the basic tenets of the Housing First model, seeing it as a reasonable and cost-effective way of providing AIDS housing services. But the mayor also lectured AIDS activists that he "lives in a political world" in which powerful political constituencies have more influence than AIDS activists in the struggle over allocating shrinking pieces of the city government pie. ACT UP member Carla Fields had this to say after attending the November 2010 meeting with the mayor: "[His] response to the direct appeal from homeless people with HIV/AIDS was astounding. We come to the mayor and explain how he's clearly wasting money and leaving people to die on the streets and he's not willing to even say he'd try to find the money. It's crazy!"

Another important aspect of ACT UP's AIDS Housing Campaign was the call to demand that the city's nonprofit hospital systems and scientific and medical research facilities shoulder a fairer share of the city's tax burden, which they saw as a source of potential revenue to fund housing for homeless people with HIV. In the course of their activism, ACT UP members came to recognize that one significant dynamic limiting the city's business tax base is the disproportionate presence of tax-exempt nonprofit and educational institutions in Philadelphia's economy. Indeed, the University of Pennsylvania, with its large hospital system and academic research facility, is the largest employer in the city. Building on work done by ACT UP New York and by other social justice activists in Philadelphia and elsewhere, ACT UP/Philadelphia members began to see that Philadelphia's postindustrial economy was dependent on the needs and imperatives of knowledge and research hubs that supported health industries, biotechnology, and pharmaceuticals. They also saw that the city's attempt to exploit its academic health centers and teaching hospitals as sources of economic development intensified rather than ameliorated economic inequality and the healthcare crisis for low-income residents. By trying to compel the mayor to require large nonprofits to make payments to the city in exchange for the public resources that they use—in policy circles, this redistributive model is called payments in lieu of taxes or PILOTS—AIDS activists were not only seeking a means to secure more funding for AIDS housing. At the symbolic level, they were also challenging the widely held belief—cultivated studiously by those who lead them—that big nonprofits, universities, charities, and philanthropists, all play an inherently virtuous role in U.S. cities (Hyatt 2013). In ACT UP's report, "Dying for Homes," the group explained, "[The mayor] could also choose to make sure that the largest of non-profits, such as the several large universities in Philadelphia, contribute to the city for the resources they use. Payments in lieu of taxes (PILOTS) have been used effectively in other cities to make sure large, financially secure non-profits are a boon, rather than a burden, to cities." As such, the call for PILOTS contested top-down visions for economic development and called into question the privileging of the nonprofit sector as an unqualified social good. Calling out this structural inequity, radical AIDS activists challenge the austerity discourse of scarce resources, revealing these decisions as resolutely political.

The Political Lives of the Urban Poor

Broadly speaking, the assault against the urban poor intensified in the United States from the 2000s to the 2010s. The right's unrelenting attack on welfare dependency and inner-city depravity deepened in the context of austerity urbanism, and conservatives of all stripes continued to deploy the specter of a violent and pathological underclass, trapped in a culture of poverty, with notable popular and political effects. This was exemplified most dramatically by Donald Trump's characterization of the black and Latinx inner city as a "disaster," an assertion he made frequently while he was a presidential candidate and that he repeated also before and during the early months of his presidency (Maskovsky 2017). During the same period, liberal pundits, politicians, and mainstream poverty scholars defended technocratic postwelfare urban poverty governance schemes, often emphasizing the collective goodwill and cooperative capacities of inner-city communities. Their track record of refuting the right's assertions about the pathological underclass is rather mixed, however. And if liberal scholars and pundits discussed the political motivations of impoverished inner-city people, they tended to highlight the cooperative survival strategies and ingenious forms of social capital formation that are created and employed by many poor urban residents and to depict them as inspired narrowly and exclusively by the material "condition" of deprivation (e.g., Saegert, Thompson, and Warren 2005). For conservatives and liberals alike, the full political lives of the inner-city poor remained unthinkable.

In this chapter I have treated homeless people with HIV as full political subjects who, like their more affluent counterparts, act on a complex political stage, forging alliances where they can, and cultivating political subjectivities—such as the person living with HIV—that are not reducible exclusively to "local concerns" or "reactive politics." Instead, and also like their more affluent counterparts, they connect their personal and political experiences to extant and emergent movements, and in so doing, they reshape the movements in which they become involved. In this case, ACT UP/Philadelphia took on a far more overt antipoverty and racial justice stance as more low-income African Americans became involved in the group.

ACT UP/Philadelphia became one of the most successful radical democratic—or, in today's parlance, horizontalist—political groups operating in the urban United States with a cross-race, cross-class membership. Held together for more than two decades by a concerted effort on the part of its members to manage racial and class differences, even if they could never overcome them (Maskovsky 2013), the group provided an important avenue of political participation for the inner-city poor, particularly African Americans whose participation in the group transformed it into a poor people's organization.

The example of ACT UP/Philadelphia also shows that the most vulnerable segments of the racialized, inner-city poor were able to become biological citizens. Members of the group were able to use their identities as those afflicted by disease to make claims for healthcare, supportive services, and life itself in a context where austerity politics cut off other avenues for the pursuit of health and social welfare. The group's efforts also challenged the idea of homeless inner-city AIDS sufferers as urban exiles, as those in the city but not of it, abandoned to "bare life." Radical AIDS politics worked in many ways to enable new claims for rights, recognition, and resources, and it is but one example of the kinds of new and exciting demands for justice emerging of late out of unthinkable places.

NOTES

I thank ACT UP/Philadelphia members, past and present, for their helpful insights. Julie Davids, Max Ray, José de Marco, John Bell, Jane Shull, Waheedah Shabazz-El, and Paul Davis were especially helpful. This chapter benefited from comments by Sidney Donnell, Preeti Sampat, Genevieve Negrón-Gonzales, and Frances Fox Piven. I owe a huge debt of gratitude to Vicky Lawson and Sarah Elwood for their insightful and detailed comments on multiple drafts, and for pushing me to think more clearly about relational poverty. All mistakes or remaining points of confusions are of my own doing. And thanks to all participants in the November 2015 Relational Poverty Network Writing Retreat, where the idea for this chapter came into focus. Research was supported by the Ph.D. program in Anthropology at the Graduate Center, and by the Department of Urban Studies, Queens College, CUNY, and by grants from the Wenner Gren Foundation for Anthropological Research and the National Science Foundation.

1. The poverty rate in Philadelphia in 2013 was 26.3 percent (Pew Charitable Trusts 2015), and it has the highest rate of deep poverty among major American cities (Lubrano 2013).

2. A critical account of mainstream poverty research can be found in Goode and Maskovsky (2001) and Morgen and Maskovsky (2003).

3. I follow the relational approach elaborated by Elwood, Lawson, and Sheppard (2016) by seeking to develop a new kind of poverty knowledge born from a long-standing alliance with AIDS activists and antipoverty activists in Philadelphia. I was an active member of the Philadelphia chapter of ACT UP from 1990 to 1998 and of other U.S.-based AIDS activist groups from 1994 until 2009, including We The People with AIDS, a coalition of HIV-positive people in Philadelphia, and CHAMP, the Community HIV/AIDS Mobilization Project, a national-level activist training organization that bridged the HIV/AIDS movement with human rights and struggles for racial, economic, and social justice. As the demographics of AIDS shifted in the 1990s, and more poor people and people of color became involved in AIDS activist efforts, one of the central issues I engaged with in both my academic and political work was the differences that race and class make to AIDS activism and to urban activism more broadly.

4. This section of the chapter draws heavily from Maskovsky (2013).

5. As in ACT UP chapters in other cities, ACT UP/Philadelphia had a people of color caucus. It was formed by prominent AIDS activists Kiyoshi Kuromiya (1943–2000), and John Paul Hammond (1950–2010), among others. People of color were a relatively small minority in ACT UP until the mid-1990s, when their numbers began to increase. This was in part because most African American and Latin@ activists in Philadelphia became involved in other organizations, especially We The People with AIDS/HIV, the city's PWA coalition. For a detailed history of We The People, see Maskovsky (2000).

6. ACT UP operated as a leaderless collective, with similar horizontalist decision-making practices to those popularized by Occupy Wall Street and #BLM decades later.

REFERENCES

ACT UP. 2010. "Dying for Homes." http://static1.squarespace.com/static/53ca95b3e4b09ce5 b336eaa3/t/5696c0d705f8e2ea0ae4a6be/1452720343963/ACT_UP_Housing_Report.pdf (accessed April 18, 2016).

Agamben, Giorgio. 1998. *Homo Sacer: Sovereign Power and Bare Life*. Stanford, Calif.: Stanford University Press.

Altman, Dennis. 1994. *Power and Community: Organizational and Cultural Responses to AIDS*. London: Routledge.

Chambré, Susan Maizel. 2006. *Fighting for Our Lives: New York's AIDS Community and the Politics of Disease*. New Brunswick, N.J.: Rutgers University Press.

Crimp, Douglas, and Adam Rolston. 1990. *AIDS Demo Graphics*. Seattle: Bay Press.

Elwood, Sarah, Victoria Lawson, and Eric Sheppard. 2016. "Geographical Relational Poverty Studies." *Progress in Human Geography*. Advance online publication. doi:10.1177/0309132516659706.

Fairbanks, Robert P. 2012. "On Theory and Method: Critical Ethnographic Approaches to Urban Regulatory Restructuring." *Urban Geography* 33, no. 4: 545–65. doi:10.2747/0272-3638.33.4.545.

Ghaziani, Amin. 2011. "Post-gay Collective Identity Construction." *Social Problems* 58, no. 1: 99–125. doi:10.1525/sp.2011.58.1.99.

Goode, Judith, and Jeff Maskovsky. 2001. *The New Poverty Studies: The Ethnography of Power, Politics and Impoverished People in the United States.* New York: New York University Press.

Gould, Deborah Bejosa. 2009. *Moving Politics: Emotion and* ACT UP's *Fight against AIDS.* Chicago: University of Chicago Press.

Hilderbrand, Lucas. 2006. "Retroactivism." *GLQ: A Journal of Lesbian and Gay Studies* 12, no. 2: 303–17. doi:10.1215/10642684-12-2-303.

Hyatt, Susan Brin. 2013. "Philanthropia: Putting Policy-Making in the Hands of the 1%." Paper presented at the annual meeting of the American Anthropological Association, Chicago.

Lubrano, Alfred. 2013. "Of Big Cities, Phila. Worst for People in Deep Poverty." *Philadelphia Inquirer*, March 20. http://articles.philly.com/2013-03-20/news/37846947_1 _poverty-rate-deep-poverty-deep-poverty (accessed April 19, 2016).

Maskovsky, Jeff. 2000. "'Managing' the Poor: Neoliberalism, Medicaid HMOs and the Triumph of Consumerism among the Poor." *Medical Anthropology* 19, no. 2 (2000): 121–46. doi:10.1080/01459740.2000.9966173.

———. 2003. "Global Justice in the Post-industrial City: Beyond the Local/Global Divide." In *Reclaiming Cities*, edited by Jane Schneider and Ida Susser, 149–72. Oxford: Berg.

———. 2013. "Diversifying AIDS Activism: Lessons from ACT UP Philadelphia." In *Global HIV/AIDS Politics, Policies and Activism: Persistent Challenges and Emerging Issues*, edited by Raymond A. Smith, 401–22. Santa Barbara, Calif.: Praeger.

———. 2017. "Toward the Anthropology of White Nationalist Post-racialism: Comments Inspired by Hall, Goldstein, and Ingram's 'The Hands of Donald Trump.'" *HAU: Journal of Ethnographic Theory* 7, no. 1: 433–40.

Morgen, Sandra, and Jeff Maskovsky. 2003. "The Anthropology of Welfare 'Reform': New Perspectives on U.S. Urban Poverty in the Post-welfare Era." *Annual Review of Anthropology* 32, no. 1: 315–38. doi:10.1146/annurev.anthro.32.061002.093431.

Nutter, Michael. 2011. "2011 Budget Address Mayor Michael A. Nutter, Thursday, March 3, 2011." https://cityofphiladelphia.wordpress.com/2011/03/03/2011-budget-address -mayor-michael-a-nutter-thursday-march-3-2011/ (accessed April 20, 2016).

Patton, Cindy. 1990. *Inventing AIDS.* New York: Routledge.

Peck, Jamie. 2012. "Austerity Urbanism." *City* 16, no. 6: 626–55. doi:10.1080/13604813.2 012.734071.

Petryna, Adriana. 2003. *Life Exposed: Biological Citizens after Chernobyl.* Princeton, N.J.: Princeton University Press.

Pew Charitable Trusts. 2015. "Philadelphia 2015: The State of the City." http://www .pewtrusts.org/~/media/assets/2015/05/2015-state-of-the-city-report_web.pdf (accessed April 15, 2016).

Piven, Frances Fox, and Richard A. Cloward. 1977. *Poor People's Movements: Why They Succeed, How They Fail.* New York: Vintage.

Rose, Nikolas. 2007. *The Politics of Life Itself: Biomedicine, Power, and Subjectivity in the Twenty-First Century.* Princeton, N.J.: Princeton University Press.

Saegert, Susan, J. Phillip Thompson, and Mark R. Warren. 2005. *Social Capital and Poor Communities.* New York: Russell Sage Foundation.

Shepard, Benjamin, and Ronald Hayduk. 2002. *From ACT UP to the WTO: Urban Protest and Community Building in the Era of Globalization.* London: Verso.

Shilts, Randy. 1987. *And the Band Played On: Politics, People and the AIDS Epidemic.* New York: St. Martin's Press.

Stockdill, Brett C. 2003. *Activism against AIDS: At the Intersection of Sexuality, Race, Gender, and Class.* Boulder, Colo.: Lynne Rienner.

CHAPTER 5

India's Land Impasse

Infrastructure, Rent, and Resistance

PREETI SAMPAT

Land and other natural "resources" are again at the center of capitalist accumulation strategies globally. In so-called emerging economies, land and resource grabs for *growth infrastructures* are legitimized in the name of economic growth.[1] In India, the state invokes eminent domain for growth infrastructures, forcibly transferring land and resources to global and domestic capital. With appreciations in the value of land and built space in infrastructure project areas, state and private actors mop up rent from these transfers. Market-induced incentives for rentier gains complement forcible land and resource transfers within a growing *rentier economy* premised on access to especially large landholdings. The rentier economy incorporates actors differentially within its anticipated futures,[2] as state- *and* market-driven dispossessions combine to impoverish (or threaten) access to land, resources, livelihoods, and environments for many. Understanding the rentier economy around growth infrastructures consolidates a thinkable poverty politics that anticipates futures of rent. Dispossession and precarity are unthinkable from within this imaginary.[3]

Dispossession is tenaciously contested by peasant and citizen groups,[4] underlining how critical land and resources are to a large number of people who attach a range of sociocultural, environmental, and political-economic meanings to them. New and ongoing infrastructure policies and projects threaten to alienate large numbers of people from land and resources. As these are resisted, revised, and reversed, recurrent conditions of impasse unfold: the rentier economy is stymied by dispossession and resistance unimaginable from within its thinkable poverty politics of growth.[5] I term this dialectic of thinkable growth infrastructures and unthinkable dispossession and resistance as India's *land impasse*. India's land impasse is not only an impasse for capital or allied state actors however. Resistance to dispossession, while opening up alliances across the differential privileges of caste, class, and gender relations (see below), meets impasse within these historically differentiated power relations. Resistance to dispossession confronts capital over the institution of growth infrastructures in *contemporary* conditions of impasse. Yet inegalitarian relationships around land and resources confront these forces of resistance in a *historical* impasse over egalitarian development from below. In other words, the differential incorporation of allied actors in resistance to dispossession is a historical impasse that must be overcome for radically unthinkable and egalitarian counter-poverty politics to emerge in the present. The counter-poverty politics of alliance in India's land impasse thus references a *double dialectic of impasse*.

What are the differential incorporations and political imaginaries of infrastructure, rent, and resistance in India's land impasse?[6] How might we conceptualize the imaginaries and openings in impasse as counter-poverty politics of development from below? To explore these questions, I draw on research around the institution of the Dholera Smart City along the Delhi Mumbai Industrial Corridor in Gujarat state, and on the Regional Plan and special economic zones in Goa state in India. Dholera is a site of ongoing resistance, while the Regional Plan and special economic zones in Goa are instances of "successful" resistance that have resulted in policy cancellation.[7] I begin with a conceptual framework for what I term India's growth infrastructures and rentier economy. Through empirical cases of landgrabs and resistance against dispossession in Gujarat and Goa, I then discuss the dialectics of India's land impasse. I conclude with observations on the theoretical and political stakes of impasse, and the possibilities and challenges it opens for counter-poverty politics of development from below.

Growth Infrastructures and the Rentier Economy

The materiality of infrastructure allows for the possibility of exchange and circulation of goods, people, finance, power, waste, and ideas, among other things; it also signifies aesthetic and affective desire and possibility (cf. Larkin 2013). The possibilities of exchange, circulation, and aesthetic and affective desire in turn are animated by paradigms of development. In postliberalization policy discourse in India, there is a growing (if contested) conflation of development with capitalist growth, resulting in a predominant emphasis on capitalist growth infrastructures.

Growth infrastructures facilitate the circuits of capital by improving connectivity for deeper market reach, which is critical for the movement of capital and the absorption and expansion of excess surplus value.[8] Growth infrastructures are squarely posited as progrowth poverty politics. They include urbanization and real estate projects that activate land markets and often entail the enclosure of large swathes of land and resources, whether state or privately owned, or commons. They can be contrasted with decentralized infrastructures oriented to local needs, say local rainwater harvesting and micro-hydro- or solar-power-generating structures geared to household consumption.

India's growth infrastructures are distinct from preliberalization development infrastructures that also promoted capitalist development, but were under the formal control and regulation of state bodies and hence considered public infrastructures.[9] Postliberalization growth infrastructures involve greater control and direct benefit for capitalists, particularly over the past decade (cf. Nilsen 2010; Goldman 2011; Sampat 2017). Their legal frameworks emphasize the developmental role of capital, in partnership with or (at least formally) independent of state actors. While pre- and postliberalization infrastructures have both contributed to dispossession and experienced resistance, the intensification of postliberalization growth infrastructures with direct stakes for capital in recent years is generating recurrent conditions of impasse. There is additional friction in the institution of growth infrastructures, however, that emerges from the contemporary dynamics of accumulation and prevents productive linkages within the Indian economy.

The controversial special economic zones (SEZs) are exemplary growth infrastructures, ostensibly instituted to generate productive investments and employment in manufacturing, and to create "world-class" or, more recently, "smart" cities. Under India's 2005 SEZ law, they enjoy several tax concessions. However, initial investor enthusiasm for SEZs (by largely domestic capital) has faded due to a combination of factors. These include the global recession from 2008, and widespread resistance to land acquisition for especially large and midsized SEZs of over one thousand and four hundred hectares, respectively. According to the Comptroller and Accountant General of India, 52 percent of the land approved for allotment to SEZs remains idle and SEZs have not had any significant impact on India's economic growth, trade, infrastructure, investment, or employment (Government of India 2014). Most operational SEZs comprise information technology and related services that cannot incorporate peasants given their skill requirements. SEZs have often been slammed as real-estate-related landgrabs, as many controversial SEZs have sought land in the urban peripheries of large metropolitan centers (see Sampat 2017). To understand the failure of SEZs and their implication in the rentier economy, I analyze some relevant trends in the Indian economy below.

Manufacturing stagnated at 15 percent of India's gross domestic product for over two decades, despite incentives. On the other hand, in 2009–10, construction emerged as the second largest employer of workers in India with 11 percent of the workforce, after agriculture with 36 percent (Soundararajan 2013). In 2011–12 the shares of real estate and construction together accounted for 19 percent of the Indian economy, growing from 14.7 percent in 2000–2001 (Government of India 2013; Table 1).

The growth in construction and real estate has complementary effects in activating land markets. In his analysis of India's land markets, Chakravorty (2013) argues that land prices in India have risen phenomenally in recent years and growing real estate prices reflect the rise in the price of land, as construc-

TABLE 1. Share and Growth of the Real Estate and Construction Sectors

	2000–2001	2005–6	2006–7	2007–8	2008–9	2009–10	2010–11	2011–12	2012–13
Real estate, ownership of dwellings and business services	8.7 (7.5)	9.1 (10.6)	9.3 (9.5)	9.6 (8.4)	10.3 (10.4)	10.4 (8.3)	10.4 (6.0)	10.8 (10.3)	
Construction	6.0 (6.1)	7.9 (12.8)	8.2 (10.3)	8.5 (10.8)	8.5 (5.3)	8.2 (6.7)	8.2 (10.2)	8.2 (5.6)	8.2 (5.9)

SOURCE: Adapted from Central Statistics Office, Government of India (2013).
Shares are in current prices, growth in constant prices. Figures in parentheses indicate growth rate.

tion costs have risen stably along the consumer price index. He points out that the price of urban land increased fivefold in 2001–11,[10] and agricultural land prices in some rural areas have increased by a factor of five to ten over the past decade. Agricultural land prices are higher in the urban periphery than in interior districts (arguably because of potential real estate markets). He adds that the rising price of land is related to the expansion of the monetary supply in the economy in the postliberalization period in the following ways: expansion of credit markets, income growth for some sectors that in turn invest in land and property as status markers, rise in illegal money supplies (so-called black money), foreign investment from nonresident Indians, and scarcity of land with respect to location and intense fragmentation. The appreciation of land, in other words, is based on income inequality and precariously elite and illicit circuits of money that fuel rentier investments around growth infrastructures, without regard to redistributive economic linkages.

Rent accrues as appreciation of land when infrastructure projects are announced, and as appreciation of real estate as projects develop. But rentier activity incorporates landowners differentially. Large landowners able and willing to profit from rentiering and smaller landowners making distress sales for personal needs "give up" land without resistance for immediate returns. A large majority of peasants, however, are unable to profit from rentier gains as their landholdings are too small or nonexistent. Given their skill specialization in agrarian work, as land use is changed from agriculture, a crucial source of their livelihood is threatened or rendered precarious.

Investors and builders may or may not have direct stakes in productive linkages emerging from these infrastructures that can create additional jobs and that do not require specialized skills. Given this larger backdrop, it is unclear how or why more recent policy thrusts toward additional growth infrastructures, such as industrial corridors and smart cities, are expected to attract investments that create productive linkages within the domestic economy. In project areas such as Dholera, returns from rent are actively factored in policy and promoted as mitigating agrarian and other livelihood loss for landowners (see DSIRDA 2013;

Sampat 2016a). Without productive linkages with manufacturing, in effect, it is the rentier economy of anticipated gains from land and real estate appreciation that is fueling growth infrastructures and the consequential dispossession of existing relations with land and resources. Policy emphases on growth infrastructures thus complement the rent-driven logics of land commodification, accelerating downward pressures on agrarian and other relations around land and resources. I analyze below the dialectics of the land impasse in Gujarat and Goa to illustrate my argument.

Resistance and Impasse

For Lefebvre (1956/2016), the capitalist production of space is revealed through a focus on the constitutive trinity of capitalist society—land-labor-capital relations (see also Elden and Morton 2016; Marx 1894/1992). As Coronil (1997, 7–8) points out:

> Remembering nature—recognizing theoretically its historical significance—allows us to recast dominant histories of Western historical development and to question the notion that modernity is the offspring of a self-propelled West. A resignified nature allows us to include in our historical accounts not just a more diversified set of historical actors but a more complex historical dynamic. It enables us to replace what Lefebvre refers to as the "ossified" dialectic of capital and labor by a dialectic of capital, labor and land.

Placing land in the co-constitutive trinity of capital, labor, and land plays the double function of revealing the capitalist geography of uneven development, and the constitutive role of non-Western regions in the historical development of capital. It enables a more robust conceptualization of the dialectics of capitalist accumulation, and the historically foreclosed or potentially unfolding possibilities of resistance and impasse.

The historical foreclosure of redistributive land reforms after independence from colonial rule forms the underlying refrain for India's land impasse. The genesis of this foreclosure arguably lies in the 1793 permanent settlement of Bengal and its deeply unequal entitlements to landed property that facilitated revenue for the capitalist-colonial project.[11] These historical inequalities of access and private property entitlements were carried over postindependence in contemporary land relations due to the failure of land reforms, and constitute the historical impasse over egalitarian land relations.

Contemporary alliances against dispossession include differential incorporations that operate through caste, class, community, gender, and other axes of inequality. The political imaginaries of allied actors articulate possibility for egalitarian land relations. Yet the historical impasse over egalitarian land relations constitutes the underlying force field upon which the radical possibility of these imaginaries must be negotiated—at the limits of differentially incorporated alliance.

Struggles over land and resources are significantly shaped by historically and culturally particular local contexts, but their frequent recurrence in recent years across diverse regions in India is noteworthy. Several mobilizations resisting landgrabs across the country have secured success, although at tremendous cost over the years. Agitations against the infamous Indonesian Salem SEZ in Nandigram and the Tata automobile plant in Singur in West Bengal, the Mangalore SEZ in Karnataka, the Mumbai SEZ in Maharashtra, and the South Korean Pohang Steel Corporation SEZ in Odisha are some of the better known cases. Close to Dholera and also along the Delhi Mumbai Industrial Corridor, thirty-six of forty-four villages were exempted from the Mandal-Becharaji Special Investment Region in early 2014 on account of local resistance. In all of these areas, those resisting have refused to negotiate the terms of inclusion in a project (terms, for example, like "better compensation" and "rehabilitation"; see White et al. 2012). In rejecting the project altogether, they have created a "non-negotiating counterpolitics" (cf. Smith 2011) of impasse.[12]

The culmination of these struggles at the national level occurred during the ruling National Democratic Alliance government's 2015 attempt to amend the 2013 land acquisition law. The Right to Fair Compensation and Transparency in Land Acquisition Rehabilitation and Resettlement Act 2013 is itself a culmination of years of anti-dispossession agitations that came to a head with controversial landgrabs for SEZs in the late 2000s. The 2013 law replaced the colonial Land Acquisition Act 1894, bringing, for the first time, rehabilitation and resettlement of the affected project within the acquisition framework. The law included progressive measures such as mandatory social impact assessments of projects. It also controversially increased the scope of forcible acquisition for infrastructure, industrialization, and urbanization projects by the public *and* the private sectors. However, acquisition for private projects requires prior informed consent of 70 to 80 percent of affected parties, depending on whether or not the project is in partnership with the state (see Sampat 2013).

The 2015 amendments to the 2013 land acquisition law sought to exempt industrial corridor projects and other public and private projects (including entertainment, health, housing, and education projects) from social impact assessments, and private projects from mandatory consent provisions. The amendments were defeated by nationwide agitations that brought together peasants, big farmers, social activists, environmentalists, journalists, lawyers, academics, other concerned citizens, political parties, and trade unions on common platforms. This success brought landgrabs for capital to impasse nationally. However, rentier profits from growth infrastructures keep the stakes high for continuing attempts at landgrabs, as the cases below illustrate.

THE DELHI MUMBAI INDUSTRIAL CORRIDOR AND DHOLERA SMART CITY

The Delhi Mumbai Industrial Corridor (DMIC) was initiated in 2006 with an agreement between the governments of India and Japan.[13] During Prime Minister Shinzo Abe's visit to India in August 2007, the Indian consultancy firm Infrastructure Leasing & Financial Services prepared and presented the concept of the corridor that was subsequently approved. The DMIC maps a complex policy terrain along the 922-mile stretch between Delhi and Mumbai.[14] Approximately 180 million people, or 14 percent of the Indian population, will officially be affected by the corridor's development in six states—Uttar Pradesh, Delhi, Haryana, Rajasthan, Gujarat, and Maharashtra. The corridor envisages nine mega industrial zones (about 155 square miles each), one high-speed freight line, three ports, six airports, a six-lane intersection-free expressway connecting the country's political and financial capitals, and a four-thousand-megawatt power plant. Funds for the project are arranged from the Indian government, Japanese loans, investments, depository receipts issued through Indian businesses, and other foreign capital. Individual projects are to involve a host of private actors under public–private partnership arrangements. The role for capital is clearly laid out in the DMIC's complex legal infrastructure spanning national, state, and local governments and includes global as well as domestic capital.

The 572-square-mile Dholera Smart City covers twenty-two villages with a population of 39,300, and is among the first greenfield urbanization projects along the corridor. As 211 square miles of the Dholera area falls under the ecologically sensitive coastal regulation zone, around 361 square miles are available for the city's development, with some land reclaimed from the sea. Dholera's proposed land use includes residential, industrial, tourism, commercial, information technology, recreational sports, and entertainment zones.

The project is located in the Bhal region bordering the Gulf of Khambhat. Rain-fed wheat (the regionally coveted *bhaliya ghaun* variety), cotton, cumin, *jowar* (sorghum), and milch cattle with flourishing milk cooperatives complement local livelihood strategies with other occupations, including diamond polishing. The twenty-two villages fall within the Narmada river canal command area and irrigation canals have been awaited for over a decade. The villages were "decommanded" (removed from the canal command area) in 2014 in the wake of the Dholera project, but residents fought for reinstatement, and the area was subsequently "recommanded" in 2015 amid agitations, following which they were again decommanded later in the same year.[15]

The Gujarat government is using the mechanism of land pooling under Gujarat's town planning law to consolidate land. The use of the land acquisition law is deliberately eschewed in Dholera, presumably to avoid the controversies associated with forcible acquisition in recent years (especially around SEZs). Land pooling under the town planning law in fact allows the state authorities to escape the land acquisition law's elaborate measures for social impact assessment, consent of landowners, and compensation packages.

Land pooling is premised on the principle that the implementing authority brings together a *voluntary* group of land owners for land-use planning. The Dholera Special Investment Region Authority and other state and national-level DMIC officials claim that land pooling for Dholera is based on 100 percent public consultation and claim to have no knowledge of resistance on the ground. This is despite the fact that the authority has not managed to pool any land since 2010 amid ongoing litigation against the project by affected residents. My research shows that there is widespread dissent on the ground (see Sampat 2016a). Those resisting the project have made several petitions to the state authorities demanding exemption for their villages. Local residents have formed the Bhal Bachao Samiti (Protect Bhal Committee), with subcommittees in each affected village. Agitations have been continuing: a hundred people were detained and twenty-two arrested in February 2014 when protesting land acquisition (see "Govt Gives in to Farmers" 2013; JAAG 2014). Residents have also filed a writ petition in the High Court of Gujarat challenging the project. In December 2015, the High Court ordered a stay on all project implementation activity until the matter is duly heard (*Gujarat Khedut Samaj v. Gujarat State* 2015).

As the impasse in Dholera unfolds, uncertainty around Dholera's implementation is further accentuated by a general lack of investor interest in the project (Sampat 2016a). If and when land is consolidated by the project authorities, it can be presumed that developing and returning 50 percent of the land to the original owners will take a few years. What previous owners and others dependent on the land are expected to do in the intervening years for livelihood and food security is unclear, and this anxiety adds fuel to the unrest and resistance in the region. Whether or not the anticipated investment in the project will eventually come to fruition and ensure better livelihoods and living conditions for the local residents is a moot question. Residents across caste, class, gender, and community differences in the area articulate the need for greater support for agriculture, irrigation facilities, and egalitarian livelihood arrangements around land such as commons for pastures that will lead to local employment generation and development.

Pradyumna Singh Chudasama, a large landholding Darbar (so-called ruler caste) with fifty-four acres of land (and an additional thirty-five acres in his wife's name), is a retired officer from the state education department from Bavaliyari village and a key organizer in the anti-Dholera movement. Chudasama has collated details of the project through several applications under the right to information law and maintains the documents and records of all project details, petitions, appeals, communications, and relevant press cuttings for the Bhal Bachao Samiti. Chudasama is also a party in the writ petition challenging the project in the Gujarat High Court. While taking me through his meticulously maintained files, Chudasama argues that agricultural work offers gainful employment to all people irrespective of their abilities and capacities. The elderly as well as people with special physical and mental abilities can find gainful work in agriculture, but a factory will not hire everyone and will require specific skill sets (interview, May 20, 2015, translated from Gujarati).

Similarly, Lalita ben Bana Jadav of Sarasla village in Ambli panchayat is a Koli Patel (so-called lower caste) and has a small plot of about three acres as her husband's share that his family ironically received through redistributive land reforms.[16] She was an agricultural laborer but injured her back in 2013. While performing her chores in her kitchen garden, she explains to me that the villagers don't want a city and the women of the area will fight as the entire village is against giving their land to the project. If the project comes, she argues, people will die—what jobs will the uneducated get? She says that it is a lie that the villagers will prosper with land values appreciating, as the developed land allotted to them is closer to the sea and prone to flooding. With the majority of residents in the area being nonliterate, she is skeptical regarding local transitions to tourism and other service-oriented businesses. She adds that the farmers of the area need the Narmada canal water to enhance agricultural productivity (interview, May 22, 2012, translated from Gujarati).

Jadav and Chudasama, one peasant, the other a big farmer, ally together across their caste, class, and gender inequalities to oppose the Dholera project. They articulate local development needs and claim that agrarian development is more egalitarian. Their alliance represents the differential incorporation of social forces allied in resistance to dispossession, and in the political imaginaries of local infrastructures. This alliance simultaneously opens possibilities for articulations of egalitarian development from below, and indexes the historical challenge of inegalitarian relations with land and resources. If the Narmada canal reaches their villages, the agrarian infrastructure will benefit them unequally, given their unequal landholdings. Chudasama's historical and social privilege is at odds with that of the majority of the region's population, who, like Jadav, have previously benefited from redistributive land reforms. Beyond the pale of this alliance are the landless agrarian and largely *dalit* peasants.[17] If they manage to save their land from the project, the radical possibility of the alliance may well encounter its limits in confronting the historical challenge of egalitarian development for all, across caste, class, and gender inequalities. This co-constitutive tension of radical possibility and the historical challenge referenced by the land impasse finds resonance in Goa.

THE REGIONAL PLAN AND SEZS IN GOA

With Goa's relatively high human development indicators, migration to the state in combination with tourism has put it squarely on India's real estate map, exerting a pull on green areas (agricultural, *khazan*, forest, and slope areas), with their frequent (often illegal) conversion into settlement areas to enable construction.[18] The phenomenon of second homes or holiday homes for rich metropolitans from cities like Mumbai and Delhi visiting Goa for vacations, with their properties locked for most of the year, is seen to drive property prices beyond the reach of local residents. Violations of regulations for coastal zones, building heights, untreated sewage releases into the sea, and extraction of groundwater, causing the salinization of aquifers, are frequent. Sand dunes are denuded or razed for unhindered sea views; *khazan* lands are neglected; and land is increasingly converted for residential complexes, beachfront hotels, beach shacks, restaurants, other entertainment activities, and residential complexes (see Alvares and Gadgil 2002; Kazi and Siqueira 2006). Land conversions for real estate and conflicts over them in Goa must be seen as the backdrop for ongoing accumulation processes of land and resource appropriation.

Goa's first Regional Plan (RP) 2001 was approved in 1986, and set the growth-oriented land use and development policy of the state. It promoted "high-end" tourism, giving many concessions to capitalist hoteliers with relaxed construction norms in coastal and conservation areas, while restricting commercial expansion by peasant households providing petty tourism services (Trichur 2013). This differential incorporation in the economic development strategy of Goa subsequently paved the way for the growth of real estate investments in the state.

The process for a second RP 2011 was initiated in 1997, but finalized in 2006. When a resident of the popular tourist village Baga in North Goa district, Jamshed Madon, noticed construction on a local hill behind his house in late 2006 and made inquiries, he discovered that the entire hill was demarcated as settlement area in the final RP 2011 released earlier that year, whereas it was in reality a green area (forests, orchards, and farms). As he studied the plan with others, they discovered that a large extent of green area was being shown as settlement in the RP 2011. They raised the issue of conversions in their village and shared their findings widely. As word spread, an initial informal meeting of a heterogeneous group of professionals, nonprofits, and interested persons from across the state was convened in December 2006 in the capital city Panajim to discuss the discrepancies of the RP 2011.

During this meeting, an overall analysis of settlement land figures showed that 7,255 hectares of additional land had been converted into settlement between the 2005 draft and the 2006 final RP 2011. Alarmed at the scale of conversions and their implications for housing, land, resources, infrastructure, and the environment, the group galvanized into action quickly and spontaneously. Goa Bachao Abhiyan (GBA; Save Goa Campaign) was formed, campaign conveners were collectively chosen, and participants divided responsibilities among themselves. Comparative studies across various villages were undertaken to verify the scale of conversions and statewide public meetings were organized on the issue.

The advocacy efforts of the GBA members bore fruit, and the campaign gathered strength, with more participants from villages across the state undertaking analysis of the RP 2011. Research by campaign members revealed that large-scale conversions had begun in 1988, when the Town and Country Planning Board removed a critical clause in the Town and Country Planning Act 1974 that did not allow changes in the RP 2001 (from 1986) for five years to enable plan stability. Once this clause was removed, changes to the plan and land conversions were noted through gazette notifications through weekly and bimonthly notifications right until 2005. The RP 2011 then formalized the conversions that had taken place through the 1990s, while enabling more. The stakes of the RP 2011 were thus very high as it represented a lot of money already sunk into converted lands over nearly two decades. But this also revealed that laws were being changed and safeguards removed for facilitating further conversions and investments. It was not just real estate developers who were driving these conversions, but interests from within the state overseeing the growth of the Goan real estate market. The campaign demanded the cancellation of RP 2011, and on Republic Day in January 2007, several *gram sabhas* (village assemblies) took resolutions to scrap the RP 2011. The state government, then led by the Congress Party, was under considerable public pressure with state elections later that year, and eventually buckled under popular pressure.

The government announced the cancellation of the RP 2011 in February 2007, and initiated a participatory process with village-level plans made by local residents. What became the RP 2021 process, however, involving a Task Force with representatives of the GBA and others appointed by the government, was also controversial. The final RP 2021 disregarded the village development drafts made by village committees; the bottom-up planning process faced stiff political opposition. For a combination of reasons including the fierce anti-SEZ agitation in 2007, the opposition Bhartiya Janata Party subsequently came to power in Goa in April 2012, with the review of the RP process as an important part of its election manifesto. The RP process has been in abeyance since, although there are frequent political references to it; by default, the RP 2001 operates (see Sampat 2015b, 2016a).

The anti-RP agitation shed light on the extent of corruption in the implementation of laws and lawmaking processes that allowed land conversions with impunity, justified in the name of economic growth. The agitation also engendered hope and aspiration for locally determined development planning that was environmentally appropriate. In enabling residents in villages across the state to become map and policy literate, it empowered them. The Goan push for decentralization of developmental decision-making power from below, however, was not supported by state actors and led to an impasse after initial success.

The RP 2011 agitation also laid the groundwork for the anti-SEZ agitations in 2007–9, spearheaded by the SEZ Virodhi Manch (Anti-SEZ Front), as SEZs threatened the appropriation of *comunidade* commons for elite housing complexes or polluting pharmaceutical industries.[19] The anti-SEZ campaign resulted in the cancellation of the state's SEZ policy and fifteen approved SEZs by the state government.[20] As five private developers took the matter to court, the High Court of Bombay at Goa upheld the state government's decision in 2010. The matter is currently before the Supreme Court of India, although there are occasional reports of the state government holding talks for an amicable solution outside the court ("Compromise Deal" 2016).

The anti-RP agitation emphasized decentralized planning, and the anti-SEZ agitation demanded locally appropriate development. The spontaneous coalescence of both campaigns was partly the result of the critical legacy of previous environmental struggles in the state (see Sampat 2015a), and partly the result of the deep frustration among people with endemic state corruption. A living history of environmental activism and concerns combined with the following: mobilizations of a "Goan identity" and indigenous assertions over land and resources, popular frustration over corruption, a sympathetic media, the small size of the state, and resulting electoral contingencies. Livelihood concerns flowing from environmental and infrastructure stresses played a significant role, and relationships around land and resources were significant refrains in the campaigns. Both agitations brought together alliances across caste, class, gender, religious, and community differences to articulate egalitarian and democratic relations around land and resources (Sampat 2015a).

Ritu Prasad, an architect active in the RP agitation, points out that the RP for the state should be about policies that determine the physical land use based on socioeconomic needs of local residents that include agriculture, employment, education, and environment. She argues that the RP should follow a top-down process: "Real estate investors are determining land-use policy and land conversions in a top-down process through state agencies, but villagers should be determining the infrastructures required locally and determining policy in a decentralized manner" (interview, June 1, 2012).

Chinu Gawde of Kerim village in North Goa for instance, a nonliterate peasant from the scheduled tribe community and veteran in the SEZ agitation, argues that if factories are put up on the village commons, they will need technical expertise and such jobs are of no use to local peasants.[21] Using the land for cultivation will give work to the peasants. Other facilities like a hospital or an old-age home will be of use locally. She adds that if too many people come to their land (for industry and residential purposes), it will become polluted and their environment will be destroyed. She asks, "If their small plots of land get destroyed, where will they go?" (interview, July 5, 2012, translated from Konkani).

The differential incorporations of the alliances against the RP 2011 and SEZs underline the double dialectics of India's land impasse. With the RP process in abeyance, and SEZ lands in litigation, the possibility of instituting egalitarian relations around land and resources at the heart of both struggles is also under suspension. If locally determined village-level development plans can indeed be incorporated in a fresh RP process, the extent to which these serve egalitarian arrangements around land and resources will test the radical possibility of the local and statewide alliances of social forces forged by the anti-RP 2011 campaign. Similarly, if comunidade lands are returned to the villages impacted by SEZs, how they are put to use to address local development needs will reveal the challenges for counter-poverty politics of alliance in Goa. The political imaginaries of local development plans and infrastructures such as public hospitals and old-age homes contrast starkly with real estate and capitalist tourism infrastructures that alienate and dispossess local residents.

Incorporations and Imaginaries of Development from Below

The theoretical and political stakes of India's land impasse hinge on the possibilities and challenges that alliance politics from below pose for countering thinkable poverty politics in the rentier economy. How adequate are alliances against dispossession, forged across axes of inequality such as those witnessed in Dholera and in Goa, to such counter-poverty politics?

The local imaginaries of development infrastructures in the Dholera region include the Narmada canal network and other agrarian support. While strengthening the economic conditions of landowning peasants and big farmers (and arguably generating employment for landless peasants), these infrastructures will likely reinforce existing social inequalities, even as they protect people from outright dispossession and impoverishment. The differential incorporations of alliance can serve to support locally dominant political imaginaries and suppress or disregard radical possibilities of egalitarian development from below.

In addition, a deeper irony in the Narmada water politics militates against the representation of the canal network as an infrastructure for development from below. The preliberalization Sardar Sarovar Project that enables the canal network in the Dholera region has been constructed despite years of intense local opposition (which catalyzed into the well-known Narmada Bachao Andolan, or Save Narmada Campaign). This project has dispossessed thousands of indigenous and other communities in the Narmada river valley. Many of the dispossessed have received poor compensation, and many continue to struggle for resettlement, rehabilitation, and other legal entitlements at the time of writing (see Baruah 2014; see also Nilsen 2010). If the Dholera Smart City is canceled and the canal network is extended to the region, this will be at the cost of those dispossessed by the dam.

In Goa, land is often collectively owned as comunidades and leased by cultivators. Many of the controversial settlement zones of the RP and the entire land for SEZs in the state were acquired by the state government using eminent domain.

The differential incorporations of alliance notwithstanding, campaigns against the RP 2011 and SEZs have articulated the need for egalitarian infrastructures on these lands, such as hospitals, old-age homes, agricultural-processing units, and educational institutions that will not harm the environment or exploit local resources (see also Sampat 2015a). However, the radical possibility of alliance politics in Goa may also go no further unless the differential incorporations of the alliances are confronted head-on toward radical egalitarian agendas.

The historical lesson emerging from the experience of postindependence redistributive land reforms points to the absence of strong grassroots movements demanding egalitarian land- and resource-use rights that could compel the state to ensure egalitarian relations around land and resources. As a result, the reforms lost political expediency in the face of resistance from big landlords, historically reinforcing unequal relations around land and resources. A counter-poverty politics of alliance meets its limits as it encounters inegalitarian relations around land and resources, ones that even development infrastructures articulated from below may not resolve.

While the contemporary dynamics of India's land impasse may be resolved in favor of allied social forces resisting dispossession, a fundamentally egalitarian reconfiguration of relations around land and resources may not emerge until the historical impasse is resolved. Growth infrastructures combine with the rentier economy in India to differentially incorporate, impoverish, and exclude. While alliances across axes of inequality may resist dispossession successfully, a politics of development from below will push at the limits of the radical possibility of alliance politics.

NOTES

Earlier versions of these materials and arguments have appeared in Sampat (2015a, 2015b, 2016a, 2016b).

1. Growth infrastructures are often built where water is abundant, and extractive projects are related to such infrastructures through their materiality—sand, stone, and ore feed growth infrastructures in a backward linkage of dispossession and exploitation of labor, land, and resources. For a conceptual discussion on landgrabs, see White et al. (2012). Subsequent refinement has led some to describe landgrabs as only those executed through extra-economic force (see Borras and Franco 2013; Levien 2012; see also Hall 2013 for an overview). My preference is to go along with Adnan (2013), who contextualizes landgrabs within broader forces facilitating dispossession through "capitalism-facilitating accumulation."

2. In his work examining the Andhra Pradesh SEZ, Cross refers to special economic zones as "uniquely charged objects of conviction and anxiety" (2014, 4) that are "made into particular places for capital by planners and politicians, corporate managers and executives, farmers, workers and activists as they pursue different futures" (5) built on an "economy of anticipation" (6). My aim in invoking the anticipated nature of investments here is more modest, and points only to the tenuousness of the futures invoked in infrastructure and urbanization projects by various state and private actors.

3. See the introduction for the dialectic relation between thinkable and unthinkable poverty politics.

4. My use of the term "peasant groups" refers to medium to marginal landowning farmers with less than ten and two acres of land, respectively, landless agrarian workers, pastoralists, fisherfolk, forest dwellers, and other petty commodity producers. Peasants are also further stratified along caste, ethnicity, religion, and gender lines. Where necessary to distinguish, I use the term "big farmers" to refer to the rich peasantry.

The term "citizen groups" here refers to coalitions of individuals, often concerned professionals and representatives of nongovernmental organizations (NGOs) that coalesce around contentious issues. They are not NGOs in themselves, as they often do not take institutional funds or salaries or run projects, but groups of concerned people working voluntarily for campaigns and raising resources through individual donations.

5. Resistance to dispossession equally marks the many extractive projects facing opposition in India; here I focus on growth infrastructures to index their co-constitution with the rentier economy.

6. Thanks are due to the participants of the Relational Poverty Network retreat organized in November 2015 for articulating poverty politics as constituted by and constitutive of differential incorporations and political imaginaries.

7. The success of resistance should be qualified as similar projects and policies continue to threaten residents with alienation from land and resources, hence recurrent conditions of impasse.

8. Connectivity facilitates the "annihilation of space by time," and enables faster movements of goods, services, information, and money flows. As Harvey (1982) points out, infrastructure investments also mitigate crises of accumulation.

9. India's economic liberalization formally began in 1991, although processes toward liberalization had already begun by the mid-1980s (see Corbridge and Harriss 2007).

10. He points out that current urban land prices range from $833 per acre to $33 million per acre (at the then dollar-rupee rate of sixty rupees to one dollar).

11. State-level redistributive land reform laws were enacted soon after India's independence to break the concentration of land with large landlords and to strengthen the rights of landless (read title-less) tillers and tenants. They imposed ceilings on large landholdings and sought to redistribute the excess land thus nationalized but met limited success as they encountered resistance from the landed elite, with direct electoral implications for political parties (see Sampat 2013, 2016b).

12. Smith (2011) argues that the growing impoverishment of people confronted with capitalist growth is creating an absolute surplus population that can no longer engage in a "politics of negotiation" to the terms of a project, but instead creates a "non-negotiable counterpolitics" of resistance.

13. Under India's federal system, land laws are determined by the state governments, which can use national laws or create their own specific laws. While the Delhi Mumbai Industrial Corridor is a national-level corridor development project, land consolidation for Dholera Smart City is negotiated under Gujarat's laws. Goa's Regional Plan policy is similarly a state-level policy, and land consolidation for SEZs depends on state-level land acquisition frameworks.

14. For a map of the complete project scope and area, see Government of India (2016).

15. Ironically, the Narmada canal itself extends from the Sardar Sarovar Project, a large dam on the river that has dispossessed thousands, with many still struggling for resettlement at the time of writing (see discussion below).

16. Koli Patels is the majority community in the area (61.8 percent of the population); community members own a majority of marginal to medium (less than two and ten acres, respectively) land holdings that many received historically through redistributive land reforms.

17. Dalit is a political identity that translates as "broken" or oppressed people from historically oppressed communities—considered outside the fourfold hierarchy of the Hindu caste system and "untouchable" by Hindus.

18. *Khazans* are reclaimed from marshy mangroves by constructing dykes and sluice-gates.

19. Goa was a Portuguese colony until 1961. The Portuguese codified the traditional *gaonkari* system of collective land and resource ownership as comunidades in 1882. While some claim that the *gaonkari* system was originally caste egalitarian, the present-day comunidades have only so-called upper caste male members, although in some comunidades women, indigenous, and so-called lower caste cultivators have also leased land. Nevertheless, comunidade areas in villages have reduced considerably since 1961 with more privately owned fields, forests, and orchards and as a result of forcible land acquisition by the state government.

20. For discussions of Goa's experience with SEZs, see Sampat (2015a), Da Silva (2014), Bedi (2013).

21. Scheduled tribes are indigenous communities noted in the Indian Constitution and historically oppressed by dominant Hindu upper-caste and other communities. While scheduled tribe communities in Goa are not comunidade members and hence do not have direct comunidade holdings, land is leased out to them for cultivation, or they work as tenant farmers on a comunidade member's land.

REFERENCES

Adnan, Shapan. 2013. "Land Grabs and Primitive Accumulation in Deltaic Bangladesh: Interactions between Neoliberal Globalization, State Interventions, Power Relations and Peasant Resistance." *Journal of Peasant Studies* 40, no. 1: 87–128. doi:10.1080/03066150.2012.753058.

Alvares, Claude Alphonso, and Vidyadhar Gadgil. 2002. *Fish Curry and Rice: A Source Book on Goa, Its Ecology, and Life Style.* Mapusa: Goa Foundation.

Baruah, Rishika. 2014. "Sardar Sarovar Project Rehabilitation: Dam, Damned, Duped." *India Today,* June 13. http://indiatoday.intoday.in/story/sardar-sarovar-project rehabilitation -increase-in-height-of-narmada-dam/1/366748.html (accessed July 9, 2017).

Bedi, Heather P. 2013. "Special Economic Zones: National Land Challenges, Localized Protest." *Contemporary South Asia* 21, no. 1: 38–51. doi:10.1080/09584935.2012.757582.

Borras, Saturnino M., and Jennifer C. Franco. 2013. "Global Land Grabbing and Political Reactions 'From Below.'" *Third World Quarterly* 34, no. 9: 1723–47. doi:10.1080/0143 6597.2013.843845.

Chakravorty, Sanjoy. 2013. *The Price of Land: Acquisition, Conflict, Consequence.* New Delhi: Oxford University Press.

"Compromise Deal between SEZ Bosses and IDC." 2016. *Herald,* January 17.

Corbridge, Stuart, and John Harriss. 2007. *Reinventing India: Liberalization, Hindu Nationalism and Popular Democracy*. Cambridge: Polity.

Coronil, Fernando. 1997. *The Magical State: Nature, Money, and Modernity in Venezuela*. Chicago: University of Chicago Press.

Cross, Jamie. 2014. *Dream Zones: Anticipating Capitalism and Development in India*. London: Pluto Press.

Da Silva, Solano. 2014. "Goa: The Dynamics of Reversal." In *Power, Policy, and Protest the Politics of India's Special Economic Zones*, edited by Rob Jenkins, Lorraine Kennedy, and Partha Mukhopadhyay, 108–36. New Delhi: Oxford University Press.

DSIRDA. 2013. "Final Development Plan—DSIRDA: Report One." Gandhinagar: DSIRDA, 2013.

Elden, Stuart, and Adam David Morton. 2016. "Thinking Past Henri Lefebvre: Introducing 'The Theory of Ground Rent and Rural Sociology.'" *Antipode* 48, no. 1: 57–66. doi:10.1111/anti.12171.

Goldman, Michael. 2011. "Speculative Urbanism and the Making of the Next World City." *International Journal of Urban and Regional Research* 35, no. 3: 555–81. doi:10.1111/j.1468-2427.2010.01001.x.

Government of India. 2013. "Economic Survey 2012–13." http://indiabudget.nic.in (accessed November 18, 2013).

———. 2014. "Report of the Comptroller and Auditor General of India for the Year 2012–13: Performance of Special Economic Zones (SEZs)." New Delhi: Union Government Department of Revenue.

———. 2016. "Concept Paper: Delhi-Mumbai Industrial Corridor." New Delhi: Department of Industrial Policy and Promotion. http://dipp.nic.in/English/hindi/Schemes/DMIC/DMIC-Concept%20Paper%20(English).pdf (accessed July 31, 2016).

"Govt Gives in to Farmers, Withdraws 36 Villages from Mandal-Becharaji SIR." 2013. *Indian Express*, August 15.

Gujarat Khedut Samaj and Others v. Gujarat State and Others. 2015, December 10. Oral Order Pronounced in Writ Petitions 227 of 2014 and 57 of 2015.

Hall, Derek. 2013. "Primitive Accumulation, Accumulation by Dispossession and the Global Land Grab." *Third World Quarterly* 34, no. 9: 1582–1604. doi:10.1080/01436597.2013.843854.

Harvey, David. 1982. *The Limits to Capital*. New York: Verso.

———. 2001. *Spaces of Capital: Towards a Critical Geography*. New York: Routledge.

JAAG. 2014. "Once Again, the Voice of Dissent Is Sought to Be Suppressed in Gujarat. Leaders of DSIR Arrested from a Public Sammelan." News release, February 9.

Kazi, Saltanat, and Alito Siqueira. 2006. "Bridging Local and Global Concerns: A Study on Globalized Tourism and Its Implications on Land-Use and Land-Cover." In *Multiple Dimensions of Global Environmental Change*, edited by Sangeeta Sonak, 62–86. New Delhi: TERI.

Larkin, Brian. 2013. "The Politics and Poetics of Infrastructure." *Annual Review of Anthropology* 42, no. 1: 327–43. doi:10.1146/annurev-anthro-092412-155522.

Lefebvre, Henri. (1956) 2016. "The Theory of Ground Rent and Rural Sociology." *Antipode* 48, no. 1: 67–73. doi:10.1111/anti.12172.

Levien, Michael. 2012. "The Land Question: Special Economic Zones and the Political Economy of Dispossession in India." *Journal of Peasant Studies* 39, nos. 3–4: 933–69. doi:10.1080/03066150.2012.656268.

Marx, Karl. (1894) 1992. *Capital: A Critique of Political Economy*. Vol. 3. London: Penguin.

Nilsen, Alf Gunvald. 2010. *Dispossession and Resistance in India: The River and the Rage*. London: Routledge.

Sampat, Preeti. 2013. "Limits to Absolute Power: Eminent Domain and the Right to Land in India." *Economic and Political Weekly*. 48, no. 19: 40–52.

———. 2015a. "The 'Goan Impasse': Land Rights and Resistance to SEZs in Goa, India." *Journal of Peasant Studies* 42, nos. 3–4: 765–90. doi:10.1080/03066150.2015.1013098.

———. 2015b. "Right to Land and the Rule of Law: Infrastructure, Urbanization and Resistance in India." Ph.D. diss., City University of New York.

———. 2016a. "Dholera: The Emperor's New City." *Economic and Political Weekly* 51, no. 17: 59–67.

———. 2016b. "India's Land Impasse." Seminar, July 11. http://www.thehinducentre.com/multimedia/archive/02928/682_Preeti_Sampat__2928517a.pdf (accessed August 12, 2017).

———. 2017. "Infrastructures of Growth, Corridors of Power: The Making of the Special Economic Zones Act 2005." In *Political Economy of Contemporary India*, edited by R. Nagaraj and Sripad Motiram, 230–59. Cambridge: Cambridge University Press.

Smith, Gavin A. 2011. "Selective Hegemony and Beyond-Populations with 'No Productive Function': A Framework for Enquiry." *Identities* 18, no. 1: 2–38. doi:10.1080/1070289x.2011.593413.

Soundararajan, Vidhya. 2013. "Construction Workers: Amending the Law for More Safety." *Economic and Political Weekly* 48, no. 23: 21–25.

Trichur, Raghuraman. 2013. *Refiguring Goa: From Trading Post to Tourism Destination*. Goa: Goa1556.

White, Ben, Saturnino Borras, Ruth Hall, Ian Scoones, and Wendy Wolford. 2012. "The New Enclosures: Critical Perspectives on Corporate Land Deals." *Journal of Peasant Studies* 39, nos. 3–4: 619–47. doi:10.4324/9781315871806.

CHAPTER 6

Abject Economies, Illiberal Embodiment, and the Politics of Waste

DAVID BOARDER GILES

Bodies That Matter out of Place

This essay explores the possibilities for what I'll call illiberal embodiment—both of the personal body and the body politic—incipient within the discarded surpluses of liberal markets and publics: edible food discarded by supermarkets, homes shuttered by real estate speculators, people displaced by gentrification or abandoned by neoliberal welfare "reforms," and so on. My story begins with the ethnographic worlds of anarchist soup kitchens, "do-it-yourself" grassroots community centers, and other shared social spaces constituted by dumpster divers, squatters, and other scavengers in Seattle, San Francisco, New York, and Melbourne—sites that reconfigure people, places, and things devalorized by market and state. I ask what these surplus worlds tell us about the material and discursive constitution of class, capital, and state power. What political and economic exclusions produce such surpluses? How do they manufacture the scarcity and vulnerability betokened by the word "poverty"? And in contrast, what emergent, effusive forms of life do they enable that might yet be called "poverty politics"? With a certain optimism of the will, I sketch out new directions for research into the kinds of unexpected, heterogeneous coalitions these surplus worlds make possible.

Based on multisited ethnographic fieldwork, I discuss projects that reappropriate and revalorize these surpluses—particularly Food Not Bombs (FNB), a global movement of anarchist soup kitchens that recover wasted commercial food surpluses (by donation or "dumpstering"), prepare them, and redistribute them publicly, often in contravention of anti-homeless-feeding prohibitions. FNB is a complex assemblage with an open structure, no formal leadership or membership requirements, and consensus-based organization; it cultivates a heterogeneous and often ephemeral community. FNB often brings together sheltered and unsheltered people, for example, both at public food sharings and also in the kitchen, in relationships not possible within the sharp distinctions between volunteer-providers and clients typical of liberal soup kitchens or food banks. The community spaces, squats, and low-rent communal houses where FNB often cooks cultivate a permissive atmosphere and, importantly, tend to disavow any reliance on the carceral state. This permissive atmosphere, informal structure, and the plentitude of its resources therefore cultivate what geographers Victoria Lawson and Sarah Elwood have called "spaces of encounter" within which a range of people may collaborate, with some of the usual classed and racialized differences attenuated, if never entirely suspended (2014). Similarly, FNB and other anarchist projects are often spaces of encounter for new arrivals in a city—including a transnational spectrum of itinerant, train-hopping punks and squatters, university students, precariously employed migrants from the Global South, tech employees, and others for whom FNB represents a welcoming touchdown space. To the extent that they create more egalitarian spaces of translocal encounter, not premised on market or state recognition (and even hostile to these things), these social projects queer national, classed, and racial imaginaries.

Over six years of collaborating with FNB chapters in each aforementioned locale, from 2005 to 2011, I got to know a cross section of the diverse, transnational, alternative economies of activists, anarchists, punks, dumpster divers, squatters, scavengers, and others who constitute the movement. These collaborators, in turn, taught me a great deal about the politics of homelessness, food insecurity, and the cultural economies that valorize or abandon people and things in each city. Their high-stakes markets and publics incorporate and exclude bodies according to diverse kinds of enculturated affects and dispositions, from genteel germ-phobia to homelessness, all underwritten by class, race, nation, gender, sexuality, and ability—because, as Audre Lorde puts it, "institutionalized rejection of difference is an absolute necessity in a profit economy which needs outsiders as surplus people" (2007, 115). In these "world-class" cities, the outsiders are diverse, ranging from underemployed students to radical queers, undocumented migrants to homeless itinerants, all of whom come together through projects like FNB.

These are not outsiders a priori, however. Their exclusion is biopolitical. In other words, it is constituted by practices and dispositions that reproduce bodies themselves, and that organize them into political and economic systems. Indeed, as this volume illustrates, the word "poverty" itself refers not to an essential set of characteristics or conditions but to the social and spatial distribution of bodies, resources, and privileges within prevailing liberal regimes of economy and governance. I argue therefore that it is not just surplus people, places, or things that are excluded from liberal markets and publics, but rather *modes of embodiment* themselves. These exclusions are conditioned by the contemporary configuration of market, public, and state that anthropologist Elizabeth Povinelli calls "late liberalism" (2011). As such, in this essay I distinguish between those *liberal embodiments* that structure late liberalism, and those *illiberal embodiments* that evade or obstruct it.

Moreover, scaling up from the example of FNB, I sketch out some of the ways in which illiberal embodiment may become politically productive—and, indeed, reframe the very domain of the political. Late liberal markets and publics, for example, also exclude a wealth of commercial waste from public circulation—from less-than-perfect food spurned by urbane consumers to real estate abandoned to property speculation and gentrification. These ex-commodities, still useful but abandoned nonetheless, become, in Mary Douglas's famous phrase, "matter out of place" (1984). Projects like FNB, I argue, bring both excluded goods and bodies together in novel, out-of-place formations, ephemeral but politically meaningful, in ways that are not wholly legible according to the hegemonic terms of liberal markets and publics. In so doing, they expand the possibilities for a politics of "poverty," beyond the negative frame of exclusion from liberal markets and publics.

A Note on Method

The social worlds I describe are nonetheless often framed within the ambit of liberal politics by participants and critics alike, in ways that obscure their illiberal dimensions. To name these dimensions, we must sidestep the implicit liberal underpinnings of prevailing political epistemologies. Despite FNB's anarchism, for example, a popular slogan is that "Food Is a Right, Not a Privilege," invoking the liberal tradition of natural rights. Meanwhile, detractors on the left disparage dumpster diving and squatting as "drop-out culture" or "lifestyle activism" precisely for their disengagement from prevailing political and economic institutions. Both frames rely on liberal vernaculars that render illegible modes of living and organizing otherwise.

Indeed, late liberalism is organized by a discursive project of recognition that disciplines difference according to the norms of liberal markets and publics. Therein, difference is either erased—reduced to homo economicus or the individuated neoliberal subject—or neutralized, as in that neoliberal refraction of identity politics that evacuates embodied difference from identity. On the right, for example, these moves are expressed in valorizing shallow corporate representations of "diversity," and on the left in upholding essentialist conceptions of feminist or antiracist politics that ignore the dissent and differences among their constituents. Queer essayist Mosley calls the latter "peak liberalism" (2017), a form of rigidly partisan identity politics that envisions different positionalities strictly as competitors on a two-dimensional terrain of privilege, obscuring both the fluid intersections of struggle highlighted by feminists of color such as Audre Lorde and Kimberlé Crenshaw (cf. Lorde 2007; Crenshaw

1993), and the potential vectors of solidarity that might dissolve or reframe those privileges.

Perhaps in the same vein, even among progressives FNB's politics are sometimes interpreted as a kind of veiled privilege, its members dismissed as disaffected white youth for whom the inescapable recourse to the protections of whiteness undermines their intended (or pretended) radicalism. To be sure, the privileges are real. FNB and its affiliated movements are largely, though far from exclusively, white. The intersections of material, cultural, and social capital this affords them are a topic of vigorous conversation for many participants. Indeed, as I argue, many of those very privileges emerge from late liberal configurations of power—to which, as Foucault famously said, there is no "outside" (1978/1986). The narrow representation of these movements' political significance along a single vector of privileged identity, however, *itself bears a resemblance to that liberal project of recognition* described above. And in the process, it overlooks the everyday material collaborations of a heterogeneous, shifting assemblage of migrants and travelers from the Global South, their American-born children, indigenous activists, homeless activists, low-income single mothers, feminist riot grrls, queers, poor and itinerant punk rockers, APOC (Anarchist/Autonomous People of Color), non-neurotypicals and differently abled volunteers, and others whom I met through my time with FNB, and who have collectively shaped the movement even while none of them have constituted a majority. Indeed, the liberal project of recognition that has excluded them from political representation may also render the politics of their ephemeral collaborations illegible. In part, my project here is precisely to make them visible.

To capture these intersections of privilege and exclusion, and the unexpected coalitions, support structures, and avenues for political agency they facilitate, I take cues from queer theorists and feminist theorists of color who draw our attention to the untidy and intersectional *matter* (read: both "topic" and "materiality") of "enfleshment," that is, "the interface of the individual and society, as a site of embodied or 'enfleshed' subjectivity" (McLaren 1988, 58; cf. Butler 1993; Weheliye 2014). Below, following Gibson-Graham's call to "queer economy" (2006, xxxvi), I'll theorize the proliferation of economies and subjectivities with a queer or abject relationship to prevailing markets and publics, assembled from bodies and goods discarded by them. Within such projects of reclamation is the raw material for illiberal political formations and unwritten futures.

Disidentification and the Dirty Habits of Abject Economies

The ethnographic worlds in which I've moved are dirty. Not necessarily filthy, although on occasion they're that too. But more often the sensory worlds of dumpster divers, squatters, punks, FNB chapters, and other anarchist projects illustrate Mary Douglas's dictum that "dirt" is merely matter out of place. In *material* terms, they're harmless: in six years of ethnographic research, I met just two people who'd fallen ill after eating dumpstered goods or dining with FNB (a better ratio than that boasted by many commercial establishments). But in *semiotic* terms, the sights and smells of anarchist soup kitchens and their ilk are beyond the pale of public decency. Like the anarchist and punk subcultures in which they are embedded, they are crowded with signifiers of obsolescence, valuelessness, disorder, and waste. They share a rough, unfinished aesthetic, from salvaged pots and battered appliances to dumpster-dived produce and a patent rejection of bourgeois body ritual. Indeed, all the FNB kitchens where I have cooked have shared a certain *je ne scent quoi*—a common sensory palette that can often be identified by smell alone (slightly overripe produce, unwashed punk rockers, and so on).

These are deliberate symbolic rejections of the status quo, to be sure. More than that, however, they facilitate a dis-interpellation of goods, people, and embodied practices from the hierarchies of value that structure privilege and poverty. This dis-interpellation sustains an alternative configuration of economic and social relations that I call an "abject economy," a diverse constellation of outsiders and surpluses with respect to prevailing liberal markets and publics. As Dylan Clark argues in his ethnography of dumpster-diving punk rockers in Seattle, those markers of newness, tidiness, cleanliness, and safety that confer exchange value not only are constitutive of the commodity—and in their absence, of valuelessness and waste—but, at a larger scale, are some of the signifiers that constitute bourgeois identity and whiteness (2004). This is no less true in Melbourne, San Francisco, or New York. By his logic these are tertiary but constitutive components of what Lorde called the "mythical norm," that set of embodied signifiers (she lists "white, thin, male, young, heterosexual, Christian, and financially secure" but we can surely add more) within which, she says, "the trappings of power reside" (Lorde 2007, 116). "In this sense," as Clark puts it, *"the downward descent into a dumpster is literally an act of downward mobility"* (2004, 28, emphasis added).

This mobility is complicated, of course, by the privileges and struggles different participants bring to it. The cultural and social capital of whiteness or bourgeois heritage, for example, may mitigate these symbolic pollutions—whereas the homeless are read as polluted without so much as touching a bin. Moreover, notwithstanding that dumpster diving isn't illegal in the United States, and rarely prosecuted in Australia, potential contact with the police is riskier for the people of color, the economically precarious, the disabled, and the non-passing queers and trans folks I met through FNB and dumpster diving than for the white, middle-class, able-bodied, or straight dumpster divers and squatters. Across this constellation of embodied differences, however, the act remains symbolically transgressive, and never wholly risk-free. Indeed, the only dumpster diver I knew who reported police contact was a young, straight, working-class, cisgendered white man dumpstering with a few other white punks behind a Buffalo supermarket. He was detained and assaulted by the officer but not charged.

To describe these transgressive dis-interpellations, I'm borrowing the terms *counteridentification* and *disidentification* from queer theorist José Esteban Muñoz. In contrast to the direct interpellation of political subjects within hegemonic symbolic systems, for Muñoz, "counteridentification" reflects a performative turning-against that nonetheless "validates the dominant ideology by reinforcing its dominance through . . . controlled symmetry" (1999, 11). In a sense, counteridentificatory subjects remain interpelated in the prevailing social structure. For example, in contrast to the assimilationism of Booker T. Washington, who called for black inclusion within liberal social contracts, Muñoz describes the separatism of black nationalists like W. E. B. Du Bois as a counteridentification: it left intact the logic of exclusion it rebuked (Muñoz 1999, 18). For Muñoz, assimilation and separatism, identification and counteridentification, are of a piece. And certainly, for many dumpster divers, a righteous but fragile anticapitalism follows precisely this pattern—adhering almost religiously to symbolic languages that embrace the dirty or deviant values imposed on them by bourgeois society. For example, a litany of anarcho-punk band names popular with FNB collaborators illustrates the point—"Filth," "Nausea," "Capitalist Casualties," "Shoplifting," and so on.

It is all too easy to end our story here (and many do), either romanticizing or dismissing these symbolic rejections as mere gestures (heroic or hubristic, respectively). But transgressive practices like dumpster diving do more than breed reactionary anticapitalist identities. In contrast to such counteridentifications, Muñoz invokes disidentification to describe a signifying practice that sidesteps the dichotomy: "Disidentification is the third mode of dealing with dominant ideologies, one that neither opts to assimilate within such a structure nor strictly opposes it. . . . Instead of buckling under the pressures of dominant ideology (identification, assimilation) or attempting to break free of its inescapable sphere (counteridentification, utopianism), this 'working on and against' is a strategy that tries to transform a cultural logic from within" (Muñoz 1999, 11). Muñoz was describing the signifying practices of many queers of color, for whom no stable recourse to identity (resistant or hegemonic) is possible. Their queerness estranges them from mainstream people of color while their race marks them in queer, predominantly white spaces. Disidentification, then, describes the renegotiation of unstable or compromised identities, in ways that are not easily legible. In contrast to the political endgame of legibility that often demands recognition or redress (in the formula, for example, of "Black Lives Matter" or "We Are the 99 Percent"), disidentification facilitates a politics often liberatory from within but opaque from without—queer counterpublics that refuse inclusion in heteronormative publics; neighborhood watch coalitions that seek neither sanction nor support from the police; nonmarket community economies that spurn inclusion in capitalist markets; and so on.

Beyond the fragile counteridentifications described earlier, FNB and the punk scene in which it is embedded foster just such spaces of liberatory illegibility. Paralleling Muñoz's analysis, for example, Chicana punk rocker Alice Bag describes the liberatory potential of the early Los Angeles punk scene—a kind of "home" where she felt freer to find a powerful feminine voice than amid the misogyny and gendered violence she associated with her Chicano childhood. "It was an exciting and hopeful time," she writes, "when our ethical and aesthetic values were being demolished and rebuilt, where each one of us on the scene could challenge one another in an attempt to tear down the old icons and virtues" (Bag 2011, 297). In like fashion, people come to punk through diverse pathways of exclusion, counter-, and disidentification—be they personal trauma, gender nonconformity, non-neurotypical cognition (some punks reject terms like "bipolar," "borderline," etc.) or other stigmatized identities. As one friend and FNB co-conspirator said bluntly (himself disabled, mixed-race, indigenous, and a trauma survivor), describing the reasons of many participants for seeking out FNB, punk rock, or anarchist politics: "we're all broken." Not everyone would accept his superlative or negative description, but the embodied differences he describes are nonetheless important parts of the punk landscape, of anarchist politics, and FNB.

In this context, the "downward mobility" of punks, dumpster divers, and FNB volunteers amounts to a disidentificatory signifying practice. Beyond rejecting consumerism, it serves a creative function that echoes and transforms the marginalization many participants already experience. The FNB kitchen, too, functions as such a site of downward mobility and disidentification, a semiotically gregarious space, marked by a paucity of economic and cultural capital, for the encounter between people and things who, in ways small or large, permanent or passing, precipitate out from Lorde's mythical norm.

What is especially important about such disidentifications in FNB's case, however, is that they do more than perform an identity. As J. K. Gibson-Graham argues, social relationships are the very foundation of an economy, and therefore reframing them is the key to "taking back the economy" (2013). Likewise, FNB's resignifications are embodied, material practices. FNB participants scavenge. They cook. They eat. They do unpaid caring labor. They seek shelter (if only a couch for night). In each city I met a wide range of people for whom dumpster diving, squatting, and other kinds of scavenging made possible new lives and new communities. And in aggregate—across hundreds of FNB chapters in dozens of countries, and innumerable networks of dumpster divers, squatters, and so on—these practices constitute an economy in the strictest sense: a system for distributing goods and services.

Chief among these economic practices is the reclamation of surpluses: dumpstering for food and other goods, wearing secondhand clothes, squatting in abandoned buildings, or simply living cheaply in undervalued neighborhoods—all devalorized surpluses that are near the end of their social lives according to the logic of market exchange. By design, the post-Fordist consumer economy's cup runneth over with these excess goods (Packard 1960/2011; Liboiron 2013). They sooner or later find themselves forgotten at its margins—their exchange value often negated long before their use value has expired. Often they're obsolete before they're sold. Elsewhere, I have argued that capitalist value is premised on the abandonment of these valuable surpluses—which cannot be recirculated publicly without undermining the logic of scarcity that inheres in market exchange. Insofar as these abandoned goods retain a use value, and therefore an unrealized exchange value, they are a kind of "abject capital" (Giles 2014). In other words, the scarcity of capitalist exchange is at least partly a manufactured scarcity. Such abandoned commercial surpluses mark the discursive and material horizons of a market. Their disposal is massive and regular—in the United States, for example, 5.4 billion pounds of unspoiled food is disposed of annually by retailers before ever reaching a point of sale (Kantor et al. 1997). Their abandonment in the dumpster, their boarded up windows, and so on constitute a sort of cultural point of no return.

That certain enterprising scavengers instead revalorize these ex-commodities amounts to a "dirty," out-of-place sociality from the average consumer's perspective. Inspired by Mary Douglas, the psychoanalyst and philosopher Julia Kristeva used the term "abjection" to describe the visceral, embodied experience of such moments of out-of-placeness with respect to the formation of self, identity, or ego (1982). Abjection for her is that unsettling revulsion that occurs within us at "the place where meaning collapses," whether that collapse is prompted by a corpse or the skin on a glass of unhomogenized milk (2). The subdued horror, germ-phobia, and creeping suspicion often attached to discarded, surplus, or secondhand goods could well be described in such terms. In this sense, the market economy is bounded by an affect of disgust.

This beyond-the-pale economy, which disidentifies and reorganizes both excluded bodies and abject capital, is therefore an *abject* economy—abject because it is not legible according to the norms of market exchange, but also not separable from them. It is where the meaning of market exchange breaks down. In contradistinction to prevailing liberal economies, it relies on a principle of surplus, and relies upon the capitalist economy for its raw materials. In the same fashion, markets themselves rely on aftermarket economies to make their surpluses disappear—from grocery surpluses donated to food pantries to outdated electronics and clothes shipped to the Global South for recycling. The constellation of squatters, dumpster divers, FNB chapters, and other scavengers I've described, of course, is only one example of such an abject economy. We might look to other nonmarket configurations of capitalist surpluses for further examples—the squatters of Rio de Janeiro or the garbage pickers of

Mexico City, perhaps—but that is beyond the scope of this essay. What I argue below, drawing on my work with FNB, is that such abject economies may be politically fruitful and live in productive tension with late liberal structures of power. I now turn to those structures of power and the embodiments through which they are constituted and which, in turn, constitute relations of privilege, poverty, and oppression.

Late Liberalism and Liberal Embodiments

No market is "free." The liberal economies that discard such surpluses are deeply embedded in a spectrum of polities and political institutions. Indeed—free-market dogma notwithstanding—*all* economies are socially produced through everyday practices, institutions, and cultural values. The value of things reflects the values ascribed to *life* and, more to the point, the differing values of *different* lives. Feminist scholars and theorists of racial formation, for example, have long argued that the construction and exploitation of gendered and racial differences are fundamental to capitalist accumulation (e.g., Gibson-Graham 1996; Lipsitz 2006). In other words (and at the risk of stating the obvious), liberal capitalism is always political, and always embodied.

Here I flesh out (take or leave the pun) some of the ways in which this is so in the political present. I'll connect certain ontological dots between three scales of analysis: on-the-ground forms of habitus and hexis; collective formations of identity and enfleshment; and the broad biopolitical structures of "late liberalism." In naming the multiscalar assemblages so constituted, I suggest a tentative theoretical apparatus to trace the distribution of late liberal discipline across a spectrum of differences that crisscross the fleshy palimpsests that are our bodies, impoverishing or privileging them in different ways, but always already incorporating them into the biopolitical regimes of market and state. These assemblages are what I call *liberal embodiments*.

Povinelli (2011) uses the term "late liberalism" to describe a broad configuration of cultural, economic, and state power distinctive to recent decades. Late liberalism weaves together many threads—from the direct administration of racialized state violence to the selective deployment of compassion in the public sphere and the normative discursive power by which differences are disciplined and logics of economic calculation privileged. She situates this confluence within a long genealogy of liberal states and capitalism. Her framework captures congruencies between a range of contemporary liberal iterations, from the postcolonial condition of indigenous peoples to the heteronormative discipline of reproduction and caring labor.

For Povinelli, late liberalism is overdetermined by two definitive features: neoliberalism—a form of governmentality that measures the value of all social life according to the criteria of the market—and the paradoxical imperative to mark and manage the participation of a spectrum of social differences in a realm defined by the abstract individuation of its participants—the project of recognition described at the outset. Late liberalism is therefore that set of technologies and discourses by which difference is incorporated into the social contracts of market and state. It responds equally to challenges both from within and without, recuperating resistance from indigenous movements, postcolonial studies, poor people, people of color, feminists, and myriad Others. The doctrine of multiculturalism, in which difference and culture are celebrated, and made economically productive at the same time as they are politically annulled, is a classic project of late liberalism. Marriage equality is another.

Indeed, as I described earlier, even more radical, critical voices are partly absorbed within late liberal vernaculars—consider FNB's invocation of natural *rights*, or the conception of cultural *property* that underwrites criticisms of "cultural appropriation," or even the master term common across the left, social *justice*. There are, of course, sound illiberal arguments too for sharing food, not exploiting cultural heritage, and distributing power and opportunity equally—but those are the subject for a different essay. As these differences are absorbed, they are also circulated more and more in the fashion of what Nancy Fraser has called "subaltern counterpublics": discursive arenas that emerge through exclusion from larger public spheres, whose primary function is to act *in parallel* with and influence them (1990). In a sense, difference in Fraser's counterpublics becomes imagined as mere partisanship, and politics becomes a matter of identifying with some parties and against others, always with the goal of influencing the larger liberal whole. (This is perhaps also what Mosley meant by "peak liberalism.")

In this incorporation and management of difference, late liberalism is intimately concerned with bodies. It works simultaneously at the scale of shared ideologies that underwrite market and state, and shared habitus and hexis—concrete embodied practices and dispositions through which those ideologies are, in Judith Butler's terms, "materialized" (1993). Markets are founded, for example, on everyday waste-making practices that produce such abject capital as I describe above, and the larger prejudices and valorizations that surround the waste once made. Precisely such multiscalar assemblages constitute liberal embodiments. They marginalize bodies and modes of enfleshment to produce surfeit and scarcity, privilege and poverty. The terms "habitus" and "hexis" capture the mechanism of this enfleshment. They express an ontological framework that explicitly roots social structure in everyday embodiments and vice versa. Habitus, as Pierre Bourdieu describes it, is a kind of socialized second nature (1977). Everything happens as if by design in a given social structure, he says, because the sociocultural, economic, and political patterns within which individuals live are imprinted upon them as a set of seemingly commonsense predispositions, which tend to reproduce those same sociocultural, economic, and political patterns. Hexis simply refers to embodied habitus, from body language to culinary preferences.

Liberal embodiments, then, might include any of the myriad sorts of hexis by which liberal markets and publics are sustained over other forms of political and economic behavior. The visceral trust placed in over-the-counter medicines as opposed to home remedies, for example. Or the social anxieties and fears of contagion and deviance buried in the endocrine responses that prompt our individuated consumption of transport, security, and brand recognition.

But liberal embodiments encompass a broader range of affects, identities, and hexeis than the things that keep us working and shopping. As the theorist Eva Cherniavsky (2006) has suggested, subjects are *differentially incorporated* into the basic structure of capitalist social relations precisely according to their form of embodiment: "I am calling 'incorporation' or 'incorporated embodiment' a specific idea of the body as the proper (interior) place of the subject, and my claim is that incorporation emerges as the privileged form of embodiment for a modern social and economic order predicated on mobility: the geographic mobility of the labor force relative to centralized manufacturing zones, for example, or the abstract mobility of 'free' economic agents to enter into and terminate contractual relations" (xv). In this way, Cherniavsky's framework draws our attention to the importance of a spectrum of embodiments that transcend the simple formula of labor and class exploitation, and yet are constitutive of capitalist social relations. The bodies of undocumented manual laborers are no less incorporated into late liberal formations, for example, than the bodies of bourgeois shoppers with their distinct palates and preferences. In other words, where Marx and Engels predicted all class struggle could be subsumed within the antagonism between bourgeoisie and proletariat, for Cherniavsky, class *qua* class is merely one of many social relations of production and consumption. These relations entail both everyday forms of habitus and hexis, and larger relations among collectively incorporated identities. All of these relations constitute capital, and all of them are embodied. The same can be said of their integration into the larger projects of late liberal governmentality that enable these relations of production and consumption.

Thinking about liberal embodiment this way cuts against the grain of some of the more celebratory usages of "liberal," and the correspondingly pejorative, theoretically narrow use of "illiberal" to describe politics beyond a framework of law and rights. Some readers might see the illicit figure of the undocumented migrant, for example—economically incorporated but legally without sanction— as anathema to a nominally rights-driven liberal order. But Povinelli echoes a long line of critics, from Aimé Césaire to Giorgio Agamben, who highlight the *exceptionalism* at the heart of liberalism (Césaire 1972/2000; Agamben 1998). The liberal social contract is inescapably built upon "relations of exception"—

classes of life "included through [their] own exclusion" (Agamben 1998, 170). Even the very origin story of that most pioneering of experiments in liberalism, the U.S. Constitution, rests on that most explicit relation of exception, chattel slavery and the Three-Fifths Compromise.

The biopolitical force of liberalism, therefore, rests not on a sacred recognition of rights, but rather on the power to distribute entitlements and to organize lives and bodies according to them — to "make live" or "let die" in Foucault's formulation (1978/1986). And where bodies are differentially incorporated, it exercises the capacity to *make live differently*, capacitating myriad lives and embodiments in such ways as to enable the projects of market and state. In this fashion, we might imagine a spectrum of racialized, classed, gendered, sexualized, and differently abled embodiments, from the suspected terrorist or urban "superpredator"—both marked for indefinite detention—to the bourgeois white consumer, from the victorious beneficiaries of marriage equality to the objects of legislation prohibiting transgendered subjects from using their preferred bathrooms. These all amount to liberal embodiments insofar as they reflect a differential incorporation made legible within regimes of production, consumption, and governance. They produce legible, embodied modes of vulnerability and exploitation ("poverty" produced in stark, interlocking enactments of oppressions). In this way, the overlapping politics of race, class, citizenship, sexuality, gender, and ability have classically been shaped by liberal projects of embodiment. This is true whether we are describing their ontological basis in technologies of governmentality and biopolitical incorporation—from Jim Crow to the war on drugs, from the law of coverture to the erosion of *Roe v. Wade*—or in those liberatory and redemptive movements that have aimed to incorporate them differently—from the civil rights movement to marriage equality.

All of the above are examples of liberal embodiments, which persist as historically specific formations largely to the extent that they are policed, both figuratively and literally, by the disciplinary power of liberal institutions. Differential embodiments of race in the United States, for example, continue to be underwritten by the expansion of the carceral state and the militarization of the border. Differential embodiments of class are underwritten, in part, by the carrots of tax credits and the sticks of what advocates have called the criminalization of homelessness—those municipal ordinances that penalize the everyday practices of people without permanent shelter, like public sleeping, eating, and excreting. The latter example throws into sharp relief the entanglements between the axis of collective embodiments and the axis of hexis. It is not, after all, homelessness itself that is criminalized, nor poverty, black and brown skin, "mental illness," or queerness—although poor people, people of color, non-neurotypicals, queers, and LGBT communities are all overrepresented among the homeless—but rather a range of minor embodiments that are juridically and spatially excluded from the public sphere. In just such ways are minor embodiments key components of the larger liberal assemblages of embodiment. It is partly the exclusion of these minor embodiments—and their corresponding production as discursively legible and disciplined objects—that constitutes larger liberal embodiments themselves.

Illiberal Embodiment and Radical Social Projects

At this point, the reader could be forgiven for feeling a familiar post-Foucauldian paralysis. Is there not the smallest gesture that escapes liberal discipline? No resistance that is not recuperated—or, treasonously, already formed in the mirror image of market or state? But perhaps we need not seek a utopian "outside" to power when, as Povinelli contends, it has *interstices*. Late liberal discourses, she argues, live in an ongoing process of "aggregation" and "disavowal" (2011). And in those bodies and goods disavowed, there is the possibility for reassembling what Povinelli, ever prosaic, calls "the otherwise"—those forms of subjectivity that dis-integrate or circumnavigate late liberal norms. I outline below how such embodiments might be constellated in enduring assemblages that I call *illiberal embodiments*, what role abject economies might play, and what sort of relational poverty politics they might enable.

But first, a caveat: illiberal embodiments should not be confused with "resistance" or "agency," concepts that theorist Alexander Weheliye suggests "assume full, self-present, and coherent subjects working against someone or something" (2014, 2). Whether through "strenuous denial or exalted celebration," the two notions obscure other sorts of freedoms. "Why are formations of the oppressed," he asks bluntly, "deemed liberatory only if they resist hegemony and/or exhibit the full agency of the oppressed?" In contrast, he points toward the messy ontological grounds of everyday lives.

In my own fieldwork, illiberal embodiments emerged from just such everyday moments in which liberal assemblages of embodiment were temporarily suspended or disarmed. Moments as simple as the willingness to let a homeless stranger sleep on a spare couch or floor, as unpredictable as the collaboration of Seattle software workers, recovering junkies, and devout Muslim immigrants around the FNB kitchen, as fleeting as the joy of finding the perfect peach in the dumpster. While we mustn't romanticize these moments as resistance, they nonetheless add up to a distinctive social world, and they *matter*.

Above all, they matter on the terrain of the body. Illustrating this, Weheliye uses the term "habeas viscus" ("you shall have the flesh") to "signal how violent political domination activates a *fleshly surplus* that simultaneously sustains and disfigures said brutality" (2014, 1–2, emphasis added). While he writes from within black feminist studies, his framework equally helps us think about a broader range of disavowed surpluses. Sometimes framed negatively as "bare life" for this disavowal (e.g., Agamben 1998), both Weheliye and Povinelli instead emphasize their positive materiality. Weheliye writes, "the flesh, rather than displacing bare life or civil death, excavates the social (after)life of these categories: it represents racializing assemblages of subjection that can never annihilate the lines of flight, freedom dreams, practices of liberation, and possibilities of other worlds" (2014, 2). In this way, Weheliye gestures toward an illiberal politics of impoverishment, within which something other than the lack and exclusion usually denoted by the term "poverty" becomes imaginable.

The meaningful assemblages composed of such lines of flight, such other worlds, are what I would like to make visible with the term "illiberal embodiment"—from the queer, disidentificatory performances of Alice Bag to the mutual aid economies of FNB and other scavengers. These practices of freedom must be made meaningful in and through the body. Let us define an illiberal embodiment, therefore, as that larger assemblage composed of enfleshments, affects, practices, or hexeis that confound liberal recognition and differential incorporation and yet meaningfully organize participants' social worlds. It may evade liberal governmentalities altogether—ideally hiding in plain sight—or it may become visible but illegible to liberal vernaculars. (Here we might think, for example, of the complaint that Occupy Wall Street somehow "didn't do anything" despite mobilizing thousands.)

What role does our abject economy of dumpster divers, squatters, FNB chapters, and so on, play in constituting such assemblages? Of what significance are they if not "resistant"? From one perspective, their material practices are illiberal by definition, revalorizing surpluses abandoned by liberal publics. As I described above, however, they also serve a disidentificatory function, cultivating new forms of habitus and hexis that are not so much *exceptional* (excluded, legible) as *abject* (confounding, illegible) with respect to late liberal governmentality. Moreover, that abject hexis may facilitate coalitions and collaborations that cut across the hegemonic lines of embodiment and enfleshment inscribed within prevailing liberal economies. Povinelli (2011) describes such aggregations of people, things, and counterdiscourse simply as "radical worlds." Of course, these worlds do not exist in a romantic undiscovered country where people and things go on to lead social afterlives free of the logic of capital. Nor, however, do liberal economies or polities command all spaces and social worlds equally. The churn of late liberalism's aggregations and disavowals creates interstices for assembling the otherwise. As one former Seattle squatter, dumpster diver, and FNB participant put it: "I never felt that squatting was in itself anything radical, but the time that it gives you—I mean sure, it takes a lot of time to scavenge but beyond that—it gave us the time to not have to pay off a landlord, to engage in meaningful projects like Food Not Bombs or Books to Prisoners." The ready availability of surpluses, therefore, and the embodiments that avail themselves of this waste are the ontological substrate of Povinelli's radical worlds, along with the forms of nonmarket labor and identification capacitated by them.

Indeed, FNB is only the most prolific of radical political movements to be built on reclaimed commercial excesses. Its genealogy dates back to the free breakfast programs of the Black Panthers or the feed-ins of the San Francisco Diggers, which both served grocery surpluses. Moreover, FNB's access to such surpluses—independent of 501C3 nonprofit status, permits, grants, and other mechanisms of recognition—underwrites its refusal of outdoor feeding prohibitions that partially criminalize homelessness. Most meal programs rely on the same surpluses, but reappropriate them into precisely those circuits of neoliberal governmentality established by these prohibitions—which they scrupulously observe to maintain their legal status.

Povinelli describes such disidentificatory efforts simply as radical "social projects." "Social projects," she writes, "disaggregate aspects of the social worlds and aggregate individual projects into a more or less whole . . . they are not 'things' so much as aggregating practices" (2011, 7). They represent queer rearrangements of prevailing discursive norms, complex assemblages of matter and meaning, of practice, affect, and signification" (10). As just such a complex assemblage, FNB has indeed persisted, growing from a single chapter in 1981 to hundreds of chapters on six continents, enacting a grassroots internationalism that cuts across the vernaculars of nation, language, and ethnos. Through my time with Seattle FNB, for example, I and other participants met visiting FNB activists, anarchists, and punks from Argentina, Australia, Canada, Colombia, France, Germany, Mexico, New Zealand, and Russia, not to mention dozens of U.S. cities. Furthermore, this assemblage produced social networks (online and offline) that circulated information even more widely—so that, for example, when in New York I met a volunteer from the Moscow chapter (Russia, not Idaho), I already knew about their recent conflicts with white supremacists, which had resulted in the murder of one of her collaborators.

The privileges and oppressions of late liberalism do not, of course, simply disappear at the doorstep. As one black punk rocker put it, in James Spooner's brilliant documentary *Afropunk*, his fellow white punks, can often just "put on a suit" and blend back into mainstream society, a privilege not available to punks and anarchists of color (2003). Indeed, participants often bring with them to the FNB kitchen the habitus of their privileges in the wider world. L. A. Kauffman has argued, for example, that the very structure of formal consensus used by most FNB chapters reflects a bourgeois habitus alienating to communities of color (Kauffman 2015). It is also telling that FNB meetings are still sometimes dominated by heterosexual, cisgendered men—sometimes dubbed "manarchists" by queer and feminist participants. It is telling too, however, that in my experience these individuals very often present as non-neurotypicals, who are dismissed in more mainstream circles for their atypical demeanor and therefore find FNB a safer space to assert some form of control. Nonetheless, on numerous occasions women have used FNB's consensus process to censure aggressive manarchists, and even eject them from the chapter. My favorite example of feminist intervention, though, comes from the Seattle chapter during the early 2000s, who established an all-male feminist dishwashing contingent upon noticing that the typical gendered habituses of the wider society were playing out in the kitchen, and men had been letting the women do all the cleaning up after the meal! As I've suggested above, therefore, late liberal privileges do not command all spaces equally. Such spaces of encounter as these also often work to disrupt such privileges and queer subjects' interpellation within liberal embodiments.

So What? How Else to Constitute a Politics

This essay has wrestled with a question posed to FNB and movements like it in numerous guises. Those for whom FNB represents "lifestyle activism," or for whom Occupy Wall Street "didn't do anything," for whom these movements represent white privilege in radicalism's clothing, or whose theory of change relies on the petitions of subaltern counterpublics for recognition by larger liberal publics, all seem to ask a rhetorical "so what?" The implicitly absent reply flattens the labors of such movements to insignificance according to the terms of power and privilege that constitute late liberalism. This essay's response is twofold: it describes the operations of power under late liberalism; and it offers one account of how else to constitute a politics.

I have theorized late liberalism as that array of discourses and technologies through which difference is disciplined in the pursuit of the projects of market and state. To make visible the linkages between the scale of everyday practice, collective identity, and liberal biopolitical regimes, I identified a species of assemblage, which I call liberal embodiments. These embodiments serve to both administer difference and incorporate it within relations of production and consumption. As such, they also offer a framework for thinking beyond class, and beyond identitarian counterpublics for understanding the distribution of privilege, power, and impoverishment with respect to market and state.

Furthermore, I have theorized the possibilities for a novel, illiberal politics at the level of embodied practices and subjectivities—what Weheliye calls "different genres of the human." I have argued that a range of embodiments are excluded by liberal discourse and discipline, and that these represent the raw material for alternative lifeworlds and alternative politics. Echoing my earlier formulation, I describe those enduring constellations of everyday practice, shared vernaculars, and political horizons that constitute these worlds "illiberal embodiments." I insist on the political significance of these radical worlds in their illegibility to and endurance alongside liberal forms of life and difference. Anarchists sometimes put this prosaically: "another world is possible, and exists in the shadows of this one."

By grounding my argument in the materiality of body and flesh, I have argued that, to a large extent, that world may be built of abandoned material surpluses of people, of places, and of things, in precisely the fashion that the globally contiguous ethnographic worlds of FNB are constellated. In wasted or undervalued spaces, fueled by those wasted surpluses, excluded bodies and practices are freer to convene, and to constitute enduring worlds wherein they may imagine their relationships differently than under the prevailing liberal discourses. A more radical world in this sense not only is possible but endures in the detritus of the political present.

REFERENCES

Agamben, Giorgio. 1998. *Homo Sacer: Sovereign Power and Bare Life*. Stanford, Calif.: Stanford University Press.

Bag, Alice. 2011. *Violence Girl: East L.A. Rage to Hollywood Stage. A Chicana Punk Story*. Port Townsend, Wash.: Feral House.

Bourdieu, Pierre. 1977. *Outline of a Theory of Practice*. Translated by Richard Nice. Cambridge: Cambridge University Press.

Butler, Judith. 1993. *Bodies That Matter: On the Discursive Limits of Sex*. New York: Routledge.

Césaire, Aimé. (1972) 2000. *The Discourse on Colonialism*. Translated by Joan Pinkham. New York: Monthly Review Press.

Cherniavsky, Eva. 2006. *Incorporations: Race, Nation, and the Body Politics of Capital*. Minneapolis: University of Minnesota Press.

Clark, Dylan. 2004. "The Raw and the Rotten: Punk Cuisine." *Ethnology* 43, no. 1: 19–31. doi:10.2307/3773853.

Crenshaw, Kimberlé. 1993. "Mapping the Margins: Intersectionality, Identity Politics, and Violence against Women of Color." *Stanford Law Review* 43, no. 6: 1241–99. doi: 10.2307/1229039.

Douglas, Mary. 1984. *Purity and Danger: An Analysis of the Concepts of Pollution and Taboo*. London: Ark.

Foucault, Michel. (1978) 1986. *The History of Sexuality, Volume I: An Introduction*. Translated by Robert Hurley. New York: Random House.

Fraser, Nancy. 1990. "Rethinking the Public Sphere: A Contribution to the Critique of Actually Existing Democracy." *Social Text*, nos. 25/26: 56–80. doi:10.2307/466240.

Gibson-Graham, J. K. 1996. *The End of Capitalism (As We Knew It): A Feminist Critique of Political Economy*. Cambridge: Blackwell.

———. 2006. *A Postcapitalist Politics*. Minneapolis: University of Minnesota Press.

———. 2013. *Take Back the Economy: An Ethical Guide for Transforming Our Communities*. Minneapolis: University of Minnesota Press.

Giles, D. B. 2014. "The Anatomy of a Dumpster: Abject Capital and the Looking Glass of Value." *Social Text* 32, no. 1 118: 93–113. doi:10.1215/01642472-2391351.

Kantor, Linda Scott, Kathryn Lipton, Alden Manchester, and Victor Oliveira. 1997. "Estimating and Addressing America's Food Losses." *Food Review* 20, no. 1: 2–12.

Kauffman, L. A. 2015. "The Theology of Consensus." *Berkeley Journal of Sociology*, May 26. http://berkeleyjournal.org/2015/05/the-theology-of-consensus.

Kristeva, Julia. 1982. *Powers of Horror: An Essay on Abjection*. New York: Columbia University Press.

Lawson, Victoria, and Sarah Elwood. 2014. "Encountering Poverty: Space, Class, and Poverty Politics." *Antipode* 46, no. 1: 209–28. doi:10.1111/anti.12030.

Liboiron, Max. 2013. "Modern Waste as Strategy." *Lo Squaderno* 29: 9–12.

Lipsitz, George. 2006. *The Possessive Investment in Whiteness: How White People Profit from Identity Politics*. Philadelphia: Temple University Press.

Lorde, Audre. 2007. *Sister Outsider: Essays and Speeches*. 2nd ed. Berkeley, Calif.: Crossing Press.

McLaren, Peter. 1988. "Schooling the Postmodern Body: Critical Pedagogy and the Politics of Enfleshment." *Journal of Education* 170, no. 3: 53–83.

Mosley, Pat. 2017. "Un-identity: Climbing down the Other Side of Peak Liberalism." May 14. https://patmosley.blog/2017/05/14/un-identity-climbing-down-the-other-side-of-peak-liberalism/ (accessed May 18, 2017).

Muñoz, José Esteban. 1999. *Disidentifications: Queers of Color and the Performance of Politics*. Minneapolis: University of Minnesota Press.

Packard, Vance. (1960) 2011. *The Waste Makers*. Brooklyn: Ig.

Povinelli, Elizabeth A. 2011. *Economies of Abandonment: Social Belonging and Endurance in Late Liberalism*. Durham, N.C.: Duke University Press.

Spooner, James. 2003. *Afropunk: The Original "Rock and Roll N***er" Experience*. Independently released.

Weheliye, Alexander G. 2014. *Habeas Viscus: Racializing Assemblages, Biopolitics, and Black Feminist Theories of the Human*. Durham, N.C.: Duke University Press.

CHAPTER 7

Crushing Red Shirts and Restoring *Amart* Privilege

Relations between Violence, Inequality, and Poverty in Thailand

JIM GLASSMAN

Studies of poverty and inequality—and thus of poverty understood relationally—have often reposed on economism. Structural economic phenomena alleged to drive or undermine polarization are workhorses in mainstream explanations of poverty (e.g., Kuznets 1955; for critique, see Piketty 2014, 13–15), and they even play a somewhat similar role in certain forms of Marxist political economy (e.g., Cohen 1978; for critique, see Lebowitz 2005, 39–61, 247–71). I wish to critically challenge any such economism. My contention is that varied forms of violence are integral to—not external to or merely functional for—the kinds of (gendered and racialized) class relations that produce poverty and inequality within capitalist societies. Social polarization and poverty are products less of economic dynamics conceived abstractly than of concrete *class* relations, conceived as simultaneously economic, political, military, social, cultural, and ideological.

I supply a fuller theoretical argument for this last proposition elsewhere (Glassman, forthcoming). Here, I outline some key theoretical claims and utilize them in a brief analysis of a particular case of inequality and poverty, that of Thailand. My central argument is straightforward. Structural features of the Thai economy—e.g., imbalance between urban-industrial and agricultural productivity or poor educational performance—are regularly invoked to explain Thailand's high levels of socioeconomic inequality. Yet I contend that violent repression of social movements by Thai elites has played a crucial role in perpetuating and deepening such inequality, substantially augmenting and (re)producing structural forces. Repression has a long history within Thailand, but I focus especially on the latest incidents of state violence, the repression of the Red Shirt movement, a movement struggling against inequality, poverty, and authoritarianism.

The Red Shirt movement is a good example of what Lawson and Elwood call "unthinkable poverty politics," intended by the members of the movement to disrupt existing meanings of poverty and the social power relations that generate them. This movement is "unthinkable" in that royalist and military elites have repressed it not only by carrying out extraordinary physical violence against the movement but by denying the legitimacy of Red Shirt claims to relative poverty, legitimate grievances, and the political right to change existing social relations. As such, the violence I analyze here has in fact been deployed precisely with the aim of making the claims and the relational poverty politics of the Red Shirts unthinkable.

In the first section, I outline some theoretical propositions that underpin my analysis. In the second section, I sketch some of the historical material that illustrates the importance of violence to the maintenance of inequality and poverty in Thailand. In the third section, I extend this historical analysis to Thai social struggles since 2000, and especially the past ten years. In the concluding section, I reflect on strategic implications of this analysis.

Theorizing Inequality and Poverty: Class Struggle and Violence

Within mainstream economics, a long line of theories—ranging from older modernization accounts of income disparity U-curves to more recent attempts to explain income inequality by differential educational opportunities and job skills—has naturalized economic inequality, reducing it to an outcome of largely unavoidable economic dynamics (e.g., agrarian transition and urbanization, development of high-tech industries). While such accounts don't necessarily eschew forms of "state intervention" to redress inequality and poverty (e.g., Keynesian growth pole strategies during the Cold War, education- and technology-promotion strategies during the neoliberal globalization era), they tend to regard a substantial amount of inequality as inevitable and only partially susceptible to change through state practice.

A major form of "state intervention" that is routinely disregarded in neoclassical economics, and that is cordoned off into analytically separate areas of study such as "politics," is the use of police and military force to impose (or reduce) specific forms of inequality. Yet, far from being something that can be analytically partitioned into a separate category, violence is integral to the class structures and relations of any class-based society, not least those that are capitalist. As such, violence—whether deployed by "the state" or by private forces—should be considered a major factor in the development of capitalism, something that needs to be analyzed in explaining inequality and poverty. While mainstream analysts occasionally allow for the possibility that violence produces poverty, they tend to limit this consideration to cases such as "failed states" or highly "underdeveloped" societies—and then the violence is not characterized as integral to capitalism but is seen as an outcome of the failure to develop a successful capitalist economy. In contrast, I argue that violence is integral even to successful capitalist development, and the ways it is deployed are as important to consider in analyzing income inequality and poverty as are factors such as the forms of urbanization or the structure of industrial employment.

Unlike in neoclassical economics, violence has not been a marginal issue for Marxist theory. Marx famously recognized the importance of violence to the genesis of capitalism. For example, he ironically noted at the end of volume 1 of *Capital* that the "rosy dawn" of capitalist production was marked by "idyllic" (violent) forms of primitive accumulation that belied capitalists' claims to have gotten wealthy through working hard and saving (Marx 1867/1977, 915). He also recognized the more general significance of power relations within capitalist class processes, noting in the chapter on the working day that both capital and labor claim a right to the surplus, with such claims being susceptible to determination only by force (Marx 1867/1977, 344). As such, violence is broadly integral to capital for Marx in a way it has never been within neoclassical economics (see Harvey 2003).

At the same time, and particularly in *Capital* volume 1, Marx located the day-to-day functioning of capitalist accumulation (expanded reproduction) within a context where the already achieved process of dispossessing agrarian producers subjected them to the "dull compulsion" of the market for survival, thus obviating the need for regular military-style intervention in support of capital (Marx 1867/1977, 899). As Michael Perelman argues, moreover, Marx clearly did not want the pathologies of capitalism, as a form of social organization, to be laid at the doorstep of war or violence in general, rather than being attributed to fundamental relationships between wage labor and capital (cited in de Angelis 1999). Marx thus emphasized the degree to which capitalism could be differentiated from other modes of production in which the process of surplus appropriation was itself more marked by direct violence, feudalism being the major example. For leftist scholars following Marx, this has created a complex legacy, one in which violence within capitalist societies, while recognized, can potentially be pushed to the analytical margins when discussing capitalist production proper—in spite of the fact that Marx himself notes that economic relations such as wage labor and the use of machinery often developed earlier within the military than within "the interior of bourgeois society" (Marx 1939/1973, 109).

The notion that violence may be left analytically on the sidelines in discussions of capital is one that is to some extent congenial to reformist political projects in which the "norms" of liberal capitalist democracies are taken to be adequate to the objectives of working-class and leftist struggle. Differences of opinion over this matter famously rent the early twentieth-century European left, but in spite of the damage done to social democracy by World War I, reformist approaches that largely sideline capitalist policing and military repression, analytically, have remained central to much Marxist thought and practice—even, for example, in David Harvey's alert reading of contemporary primitive accumulation (Harvey 2003; see Glassman 2005 for discussion). This has been possible not only because of the residual attractiveness of social democratic approaches but because of the increasing implausibility of militarized leftist struggles like those of the communist parties in Russia and China. Thus, while Marxist theory has not neglected the general importance of force within social struggle, there has been a tendency in recent generations for Marxists to undertheorize military and policing activity.

While fully elaborating a Marxian approach that theorizes violence as deeply internal to the day-to-day class relations of capitalism would require much more space, here I outline the rudiments of such an argument. I suggest ways that what I call "policing"—including everything from localized forms of domestic policing to large-scale transnational military ventures—can be seen as integral to capitalist production and social reproduction, rather than merely being external, functional, and invoked as needed by class elites. My use of the term "policing" corresponds roughly to the phenomena Charles Tilly analyzes when discussing "specialists in violence" (2003, 34–41). If capital is construed as containing the violent moment of expropriation within itself on an ongoing basis—what Massimo de Angelis (1999) refers to as primitive accumulation being an ontological *condition* of capitalist production rather than a historical precondition—it becomes necessary to more fully theorize the role of specialists in violence within capitalist class processes, including those that generate inequality and poverty.

My perspective on policing regards expenditures on the means of violence, within a capitalist framework, as not only integral to capital because of ongoing primitive accumulation but as situationally rational, from the perspective of various capitalists. This is so because it secures and helps reproduce the social property relations within which capitalists operate. In this sense, like other forms of social reproduction, expenditure on the means of violence can be construed as indirectly productive—i.e., generative of profit—insofar as it is productive of forms of control that generate confidence among capitalists and encourage further investment. Policing and forms of militarized violence should thus be seen as basic features of capitalist social relations, not as external processes that are invoked only for primitive accumulation, when crisis hits, or when external "security" threats become evident.

To these broadly Gramscian considerations about the ongoing "war of position" in capitalist societies it needs to be added—as Paul Baran and Paul Sweezy long ago emphasized (1966)—that production of the means of violence itself is an integral part of the social division of labor and a major productive activity, directly generating profits for its investors. The policing of a given society, like the U.S. military's attempts to police the world, requires the production of police and military goods, the commodity production of which (including by private sector contractors) is in fact central to the entire dynamic of policing, as well as to the growth dynamics of the larger economy.

Furthermore, even those aspects of military policing that are not typically seen as directly producing profit have the salutary result for capital of training large numbers of young people (particularly men) into forms of work discipline, respect for hierarchical authority, and a sense of national belonging (Cowen 2008; cf. O'Connor 1973, 97–123). As such, labor in the military functions—like other forms of social reproductive labor—to reproduce the producers of surplus value. Thus, whether the discipline is that of the police academy or the military boot camp, policing in general can be seen as integral to the social reproduction of labor power—and to the kinds of social relations capitalists require for the generation of profit.

In sum, I argue that the *capital* (i.e., social relations) constituting those social reproductive processes that sustain militarized violence is essential and in no way external or peripheral to capitalist accumulation. Just as banking capital plays a central role in the production of material life and the reproduction of capitalist social relations, even though it is not in and of itself the most direct form of production, so too repressive activities such as policing are central to both production and social reproduction. Marx insisted that financial capital is an essential facet of capital, yet must be maintained in a proper relationship to fractions such as industrial and merchant capital in order for the totality of capitalist relations to function properly. So, too, the segments of capital that can be identified with policing are facets of capital as a totality and require a proper relationship to activities such as manufacturing and trade in order for capital as a totality to function properly.

I conclude this brief discussion of militarized violence within capital by giving the last word to a proponent of such violence. A California Special Training Institute training manual, approved for use in the 1970s by Louis Giuffrida (later head of the Federal Emergency Management Agency under the Reagan administration), put the matter in especially pointed fashion:

> The truth is that expansionist whites in a quest for power and wealth, largely in the name of the government, systematically annihilated thousands [*sic*] of Indians and claimed their heritage, the land, in the name of national progress . . . the winners incarcerated the losers and have kept them incarcerated for more than 100 years.
>
> . . . [Our] mission can be accomplished only if we understand that . . . legitimate violence is integral to our form of government for it is from this source that we can continue to purge our weakness. (Lawrence 2006, 16)

The argument for the centrality of violence to ongoing processes of capital accumulation can be further explicated theoretically (see Glassman, forthcoming). But here I examine the ways violence has been integral to ongoing reproduction of inequality and poverty in Thailand. I show the analytical traction that can be gained by regarding violence as central to capitalist class relations, rather than as something external and readily susceptible to being overturned within the process of capitalist class rule.

Sustaining Inequality through Violence: Thailand in the Twentieth Century

Thailand has a very long history of evolving inequality and poverty, as well as an intertwined history of military dictatorship and social violence. I do not summarize histories of military and political violence in Thailand (which are legion), but rather here I provide an account of why and how violence continues to be central to the production of inequality and poverty in Thailand since the turn of the twenty-first century—a phenomenon not typically predicted by either the modernization theoretic or neoliberal analyses that have largely dominated Thai economic studies. What I do in summarizing the geographical-historical literature is simply to pursue several claims about class formation and dynamics during the period from the end of the nineteenth century to the end of the twentieth. From these foundations, I build an account, in the ensuing section, of Thailand's violent and inegalitarian present.

Basic forms of sociospatial inequality prominent in Thailand today—e.g., income and wealth disparities between Bangkok and the Northeast of the country—have a very long history (Hewison 1989; Suehiro 1989; Baker and Pasuk 2004; Glassman 2004b). Thailand was formed, over the course of the nineteenth century and the early twentieth, from the imperial and subimperial maneuvers of both European powers and the Bangkok-based Chakri dynasty. Among the many aspects of these maneuvers that continue to resonate today, two can be highlighted. First, in a series of nineteenth-century wars with Laotian kingdoms such as Vientiane and Champassak, the Bangkok-based Kingdom of Siam took control of a substantial portion of the formerly "Lao" labor force, relocating many corvée-providing peasants to the Korat Plateau and setting in motion the long and racialized history of uneven development that marks Thailand to the present. When Red Shirt supporters from the Northeast today bridle at their treatment by Bangkokians, who derogatorily refer to them as both "Lao" and "water buffalo," they articulate a critical response to this long history of denigration and exploitation at the hands of Thai rulers and their cadres.

Second, in a series of specific political projects for which the case of the Lanna Kingdom (based in Chiang Mai) can be taken as an example, the Siamese elite collaborated with British imperial rulers to incorporate formerly independent tributary kingdoms into the modern Thai nation state. Lanna's incorporation took place over the late nineteenth century and the early twentieth, facilitated by the deployment of Sino-Thai tax farmers—who generated revenues for Bangkok from previously untaxed activities (Butcher, Dick, and Sullivan 1993)—and enforced by military repression of resistors, the British Gatling gun proving an especially effective weapon against machete-wielding peasants. The result of these kinds of processes was incorporation and political subordination of the North, Northeast, and South, with Bangkok's governance being modeled on colonial practices such as those in British India (Chaiyan 1994; Thongchai 1994).

When Red Shirt supporters in Chiang Mai today announce their desire to create an independent Lanna Republic, they articulate a critical response to this long history of political-territorial subordination. Indeed, British-Siamese collaboration set in motion a crucial feature of twentieth- and twenty-first-century Thai military history. Protected externally by powerful military allies—first Great Britain, then the United States—the Thai military has served elite (royalist and capitalist) interests and focused on internal regional and class politics, rather than on external security threats (Anderson 1978).

Within these broad contours of racialized uneven development and militarized class politics, Thailand's twentieth-century transformation was prominently marked by a sociospatially uneven process of class transformation, in which both the racialization of Thai capital and primitive accumulation were important. The racialization of Thai capital was (and continues to be) a function of the fact that the most powerful merchant groups have typically been Sino-Thais, many descendent from the Teochiu-speaking populations of Guangdong province that migrated in large numbers during the nineteenth and early twentieth centuries. These Sino-Thai capitalists became major economic players within the Thai economy by the middle of the twentieth century, eventually becoming closely tied to the military and dominating much of what existed in the small industrial sector, as well as agribusiness, and the commanding heights of trade and finance (Skinner 1957; Hewison 1989).

Sino-Thai merchant capital was in part descendant from nineteenth- and early twentieth-century tax-farming operations like those involved in the incorporation of the former tributary kingdoms. Unable to effectively rule distant subjects on their own, the Chakri rulers contracted with Chinese merchant groups that could exercise "muscle" and make tax collection effective. In this sense, the formation of a growing Sino-Thai merchant class was linked to processes of primitive accumulation that began to monetize the rural economy, forcing peasants out of agriculture and into varied forms of wage labor (Chatthip 1999).

Primitive accumulation intensified after World War II, especially under the impetus of U.S.-sponsored, Cold War–era counterinsurgency and development programs (Charoensin-o-larn 1988; Hirsch 1990; Glassman 2004b). While monetization of various activities was crucial, it was never the sole reason for peasants' difficulties in maintaining viable agrarian livelihoods. Specific state activities favoring capital, such as the rice tax imposed from 1955 to 1985, played an important role in redistributing the agrarian surplus to urban industrialists (Glassman 2004b, 62). And when peasants organized to counter landlord power, they were met with campaigns of repression: for example, the Farmers' Federation of Thailand (FFT), formed in the 1970s to fight for land rent control, was dismantled by a series of assassinations during 1974–75, backed by the more general violence of the Thai state in the village (Anan 1989; Bowie

1997; Haberkorn 2011). In sum, rural incomes did not lag behind urban incomes in Cold War Thailand simply because of a natural dynamic of uneven returns to urban and agrarian labor; state policies and violence played an important role in keeping agrarian incomes low, and redistributing the surplus to capitalists.

Once dispossessed farmers began flooding into Bangkok, their large numbers helped to depress urban-industrial wages. But Thai capital and the Thai state did not simply repose on the "reserve army of the unemployed" to keep wages low. Instead, violence was also deployed to fragment and repress labor organizations. As with the FFT, labor unions in Bangkok and elsewhere faced considerable state and private violence during the postwar period, especially in the 1960s and 1970s (Glassman 2004b, 79–92). Those workers who could ultimately survive this repression often ended up in small, fragmented, and co-opted unions. The well-documented weaknesses of these labor organizations contributed materially to the fact that even as Thailand's industrial economy boomed from the 1950s to the 1970s, workers' wages remained flat, falling well behind productivity and exacerbating the already large disparities between capital and labor (Glassman 2004b, 105–9).

Ultimately, the violence exercised by Thai capital and the Thai state never strictly targeted peasant or labor organizations per se but also any political movements that could potentially challenge the entrenched power of capitalist and aristocratic elites, or the *amart*, as today's Red Shirts call them. Thailand's long history of coups is not merely a history of class-fractional struggle or military-royalist intrigues—though it is that—but also reflects elite responses to the challenges thought to be posed by any political organizations or social movements that might represent peasant and worker interests directly within the Thai state (Bell 1978). This was the case with the 1947 coup, played a role in the 1957 and 1971 coups, and was crucial to the coups in 1976, 1991, 2006, and 2014. A member of the amart, speaking to a U.S. diplomat at a time (July 1968) when U.S. leaders were encouraging elections to legitimize the military government, pronounced on the issue in a fashion that expresses well the enduring attitudes of Thai elites toward political change. Alarmed that elections allowed openings for actors who might try to undermine existing social relations, the Thai official voiced concern that even the noncommunist opposition harbored "extreme economic egalitarians whose idea is to take from the rich and obstruct the kind of rapid economic development taking place in Bangkok and spread the money evenly over the entire population" (U.S. Department of State 1968).

The dimensions of violence indicated here—and their integration with processes of class formation that affect the distribution of wealth and income—continued to play a role as the Thai economy boomed in the 1980s and 1990s, contributing to the fact that this boom disproportionately favored the upper 10 to 20 percent of the income distribution (Glassman 2004b, 161–68). Indeed,

Thailand's development from the end of the Second World War until the end of the twentieth century was an almost unrelenting process of increasing disparity in both income and wealth, abetted and punctuated continuously by the forms of violence against agrarian producers, urban workers, and "extreme economic egalitarians" that allowed the amart to keep this development trajectory from being derailed.

Thai economist Pasuk Pongpaichit has recently summarized statistically this history of wealth and income concentration. Income inequality, as measured by the Gini coefficient, increased from an already high .413 in 1962 to an exorbitant .536 in 1992, largely stagnating across the rest of the 1990s and then declining slightly in the 2000s, as I discuss below (Pasuk 2016, 407). Concentration of wealth has been even more marked, and in fact continued to increase even as income disparity began to level off in the 1990s (Pasuk 2016, 409–10).

Apologists for Thailand's elite have typically countered that since the economy was growing rapidly during the 1950s to 1990s, income and wealth disparities haven't much mattered—the economy, they claim, has been a rising tide that lifts all boats. Moreover, there has long been an expectation that the "natural" inequalities associated with economic development would decline—in U-curve like fashion—once a certain "stage" of development (or educational attainment for the general population) was reached. In addition, for those who expect all good things to come together with capitalist development, the hope has been that increasing general prosperity will also bring more social peace—even an end to military coups and political violence. That none of this has happened in Thailand calls deeply into question the theoretical perspectives on which these assertions rest, whether modernization theoretic or neoliberal.

Even before the 2006 to 2016 period, however, many aspects of the conventional celebratory rhetoric had been called into question by the economic crisis of 1997. The most important consequences of this crisis were not for the Thai economy per se, but for the legitimacy of the elite that had proclaimed its own virtues in economic management. In the wake of the crisis, a new round of class struggle and a new aspirant to leadership emerged. Moreover, in the wake of the crisis, voices of discontent with Thailand's "miracle"—voices that had long been present but frequently ignored or repressed—could not so readily be ignored.

The Ongoing Legacies of Violence: Thailand in the Twenty-First Century

Markedly high and growing inequalities—exacerbated by the consequences of the 1997 economic crisis—gave rise to the political campaign of right-wing populist businessman Thaksin Shinawatra. Thaksin appealed to both leaders of ailing Thai businesses and the large population of farmers and workers who felt that development had not in fact been a rising tide lifting their boats. Thaksin's Thai Rak Thai (TRT) party, with no competition from the left (leftist parties being banned or subject to extreme obstacles) formed because of support by disgruntled business and political leaders, but prospered because it garnered massive support from rural and working-class voters. TRT easily won the 2001 elections, some of the first to be held in Thailand, and took office with a clear mandate to buttress the prospects of the poor, on which it partially acted. Thaksin's government moved quickly on campaign promises such as a debt moratorium for small farmers and national health insurance (the so-called thirty-baht healthcare system). What it was willing or able to do in the redistribution of wealth or income from capital to labor was at best limited, and it by no means transformed the violent practices of the Thai state (Glassman 2004a, 2007). What it actually did was nonetheless politically consequential.

Able, for the first time, to participate somewhat meaningfully in electing a government that made promises about policies, the majority of the Thai working-class population (urban and rural) participated enthusiastically in elections, handing TRT successively larger parliamentary majorities (Glassman 2010). By 2005, along with delivering on some of its campaign promises in ways that arguably contributed to slightly greater rural prosperity and declining inequality, TRT had developed a powerful stranglehold on government and was moving to reshuffle the bureaucracy in ways more conducive to fulfillment of its various projects. This placed it at odds with older elites, and eventually with discontented business leaders and professionals. Thaksin is a Sino-Thai business elite himself, and he originally had strong backing from key business allies. Yet by 2005 former business and royalist allies who felt he was favoring his own economic and political interests at their expense began to organize against him (Kasian 2008). Unable to overcome TRT's massive electoral support, these opponents—eventually dubbed Yellow Shirts (for their royally colored protest attire)—took to the streets to destabilize Thaksin's government, leaning on business and royalist backing, along with the campaigning of middle-class reformers who deemed Thaksin corrupt. While they were unable to directly bring down the TRT government, their constant protests and unwillingness to accept the results of the TRT-sponsored snap election of early 2006 legitimized the military coup that took place that September, abetted by the flight from Thaksin's camp of key capitalists such as the powerful Chearavanont and Lamsam families (Glassman 2004a; Connors and Hewison 2008; Thongchai 2008). Allied especially strongly with the older amart (McCargo 2006), major military leaders lined up with anti-Thaksin insurgents and pushed TRT out of office.

The military's intervention did not result in permanent military dictatorship immediately after 2006, in large part because military leaders hoped that by rewriting the constitution, disbanding TRT, and banning leading TRT members from politics, they could lure a critical mass of the popular voting bloc supporting Thaksin into switching its allegiance to the party preferred by the amart, the Democrat Party. Yet this did not turn out to be the case. The 2007 election returned to office a Thaksin-connected party, the People's Power Party (PPP), formed by former TRT members who had not been banned after the 2006 coup (Glassman 2010). This result was still objectionable to those who had supported and carried out the coup. Consequently, actors involved in the 2005–6 protests took to the streets again in 2008, first occupying Government House throughout the year to make governance by PPP more difficult, then occupying and shutting down the two major Bangkok airports during December to encourage a court decision disbanding PPP and mandating the formation of a new government. The Yellow Shirt protests were countered by groups of pro-Thaksin protestors who for the first time became identified as Red Shirts. The Red Shirt protests were contained by the police and the military—something not done in the case of the Yellow Shirt airport occupations, which had the implicit authorization of the military. Meanwhile, the courts went forward with the disbanding of PPP and the banning of leading PPP politicians, while the military helped broker a political agreement that enabled the Democrat Party to form a new government without general elections (Chambers and Napisa 2016, 433–44).

This "judicial coup," as it has been called, led to an intensification of Red Shirt struggles during 2009–10, culminating in the massive demonstration of April and May 2010, which called for the Democrats to step down and hold new general elections. Instead, Democrat Party leaders and the military responded with violent assaults, dispersing the protests and leading to the death of some ninety people and the injury and imprisonment of many more (Glassman 2011; Montesano, Chachavalpongpun, and Chongvilaivan 2012). Again, however, military leaders seemed to hope that their latest actions would undermine popular support for Thaksin-connected parties and thus allowed elections in 2011. Yet these were once again won by a Thaksin-connected party, the Pheua Thai (PT) Party, headed by Thaksin's sister Yingluck and comprising unbanned former TRT/PPP politicians. PT was able to govern uneasily from 2011 until 2014, by which point Yellow Shirt protests—now under the name of the People's Democratic Reform Committee (PDRC)—again destabilized the government. PDRC protestors began demanding Yingluck's resignation in late 2013, then disrupted the early 2014 elections, paving the way for the May 2014 coup. In the aftermath of this coup, the military has made clear that it has no immediate plans to step down from power. The business elites and professional cadres who backed the coup have likewise indicated that they do not wish to see any immediate retreat from authoritarian governance (Veerayooth and Hewison 2016; Baker 2016; Mérieau 2016; Prajak 2016; Veerayooth 2016).

While the ways the military has entrenched itself had something to do with its leaders wanting to be in a dominant position to control the royal succession (Marshall 2014), the class basis of the Yellow Shirt and military-royalist project is crucial. The staying power of the TRT/PPP/PT bloc has been a function of its popular support among workers, farmers, and provincial business and political leaders (Somchai 2006, 2016; Glassman 2011; Walker 2012). The military and the Yellow Shirts are openly committed to dismantling this bloc, with Yellow Shirt supporters frequently branding Red Shirts as uneducated "water buffalo" who are unworthy of the right to vote.

Red Shirts, nonetheless, remain unmoved even as they are being repressed. Even with the structural and self-imposed limits of the TRT reforms, the record of inequality over the period since Thaksin rose to power helps explain the class basis of support for the Red Shirt project. Along with class-relevant policies like the national health insurance program and the debt moratorium for farmers, the overall policies of the TRT and PT governments—including the latter's increase in the official minimum wage—have contributed to a small decline in income inequality. Pasuk credits Thaksin's programs for a slight reduction in the Gini coefficient—which is particularly sensitive to changes in the middle of the distribution—to .465 by 2013, the last full year that Yingluck was prime minister (Pasuk 2016, 408). Moreover, the national health insurance scheme has been credited with bringing about substantial improvements in health outcomes for lower income groups (see Gruber, Hendren, and Townsend 2014). Between these kinds of policies and the crucial matter that Thaksin-connected parties have courted the majority population as potential voters (and consumers), while the Yellow Shirts have denigrated and attempted to prevent this population from voting (Prajak 2016), most members of the Red Shirt movement have been willing to look past the many deficiencies of Thaksin-connected parties. Red Shirts have tended to see Thaksin's agenda as far preferable to the long-standing elitist political leadership of the Democrats and the pro-royalist bureaucracy, the latter of these having been maintained in power by decades of military dictatorship that systematically privileged royalist elites and major capitalists (Somchai 2006, 2016).

By the same token, Yellow Shirts and other supporters of the military coup regime have been cornered in this class-relevant struggle and unable to respond with anything other than ongoing military repression and authoritarianism, typically buttressed with moralistic and elitist discourse about corruption and the failings of "Western" electoral democracy (Thorn 2016). As the 2014 coup unfolded, for example, "civil society" groups such as university presidents and doctors opposed new elections and supported the removal of the Yingluck government (Veerayooth 2016). The PDRC and conservative NGOs also stepped up to oppose new elections and support the violent disruption of the electoral process PT had initiated (Prajak 2016).

The conflict here is clearly class-based and distributional—not only in the sense of being a conflict over distribution of income and wealth but more importantly distribution of the political power to undertake policies affecting the former. The groups that have fought to displace "Thaksinomics" include not only the various professionals appointed by the military to draft new constitutions and run new governance organizations but the business elites that have made out spectacularly both before and after the coup (Mérieau 2016; Veerayooth 2016). These include, especially, the top families that broke from Thaksin in 2006, including Chearavanont, the richest family in Thailand besides the royal family. Pasuk (2016) points out that even during the period when TRT/PPP/PT policies were contributing to a decline in income inequality within the middle of the income distribution, the top 1 percent of Thai income recipients saw their shares of the national income increase spectacularly, at the relative expense of everyone else in the income distribution, particularly the bottom 40 percent. More importantly, wealth is especially highly concentrated. Some of the first studies to assess this in recent years estimate a Gini coefficient for wealth distribution of .700 in 2013. They also show striking degrees of concentration in specific indicators of wealth such as land ownership (the top 10 percent of land owners own 61 percent of all titled land) and bank deposits (a mere 0.13 percent of all deposits account for just under 50 percent of the total value of deposits). Moreover, the wealthiest families have increased their shares of total wealth since the 1997 crisis: the four wealthiest (private-sector) families in the country held 45 percent of the wealth of the top fifty families in 2013—this not including the enormous holdings of Thailand's wealthiest "family," the monarchy (Pasuk 2016, 409–13; see Porphant 2008). By 2016, two years after the 2014 coup, the top fifty families were listed by *Forbes* as controlling $106 billion in assets, of which the top four families controlled $55 billion, or over 50 percent.[1] In this context, it is not surprising that top business elites have been backers of the coup, having clearly benefited from the protection the military provides, including for deals that financially benefit military leaders as well.[2] Nor is it surprising that among the main undertakings of the current coup regime have been attempts to undermine reforms such as the minimum wage and the national health insurance policy (Seo 2015).

Given the limits of the TRT/PPP/PT reform project, neither capitalism nor Thailand's wealthiest have really been threatened by the Red Shirts or "Thaksinomics." But neither they nor the Thai military—continuing to fatten on militarized forms of accumulation as they have for many decades—are willingly letting go of the forms of dominance that have secured their position in Thailand's class structure. The latest coup, like those before it, is not necessarily about securing the conditions for capitalist growth in general, but it is unquestionably about securing the conditions under which a historically specific class elite can maintain its power and privilege within the process of capitalist accumulation. It is also about repressing and attempting to make unthinkable the vast resistance to such privilege manifest in the now-dismembered Red Shirt movement.

Learning from Struggles against the *Amart*

It would be misleading to characterize the aspects of the Thai case that I sum-marize here as highly unique. The use of violence by dominant classes, especially to suppress militant social struggles, is unexceptional. Even in contexts of far greater affluence than Thailand, where strategies of hegemony might seem more readily available, the use of sometimes extraordinary violence to suppress those who wish to reorganize society is common. In the United States, for example, early twentieth-century labor and socialist movements were violently repressed by privately hired corporate gunmen and state-organized repression. Half a cen-tury later, the FBI's COINTELPRO campaign successfully carried out repres-sion of groups such as the American Indian Movement and the Black Panthers.

The strategic lessons that might be conjured from the Thai case thus have broad reach. The most basic lesson follows from the notion that violence is deeply integral to capitalist class relations. Insofar as this is the case, then not only is it inadequate for those struggling for greater economic equality to await a structural economic turnaround, it is also inadequate merely to argue for social struggle as a means to achieve that end. Social struggle is a necessity, but how those involved in social struggle can counter the violence that will come their way is a vexed matter.

For some communist parties of the past, the answer was autonomous mil-itary struggle—a project that had some success, but that had clearly outlived its historical prospects in most of the world by the period when Maoists seized power in China. Today, rural insurgents—e.g., the Zapatistas—find that how-ever tactically significant a military project is, it is neither sustainable nor ade-quate over time to achieve the aims of the insurgents.

Such a reality might lead to pessimism about the prospects for militant and radical struggle, but a military strategy is not the same thing as fielding an army. Among the implications of the Red Shirt struggle is the implication that social forces fighting for substantive change need to have a strategy that includes means of avoiding the ferocious military repression that will almost surely be unleashed when power is threatened, and that underpins day-to-day class processes. If that cannot mean fielding an autonomous military, it nonetheless might open onto strategies for challenging not just the legitimacy of military rule but the numerous processes that instill militarism within the gendered and racialized class structures of capitalist society. In short, social movements of the poor need to challenge policing and military violence—not as processes abstracted from capitalist rule but as integral elements of such rule. The specific ways this can be done are not part of my brief here, nor are they something that individual authors should propose. They are projects to be un-dertaken and developed by the social movements struggling to undermine the forces generating ongoing poverty and inequality through unthinkable poverty politics. This means that they are also worthy projects for relational poverty studies.

NOTES

1. See Karmali (2017)
2. See, for example, "Big Business, Wealth, Royal Connections and Fines" (2016) and "Protecting the Corrupt" (2014).

REFERENCES

Anan Ganjanapan. 1989. "Conflicts over the Deployment and Control of Labor in a Northern Thai Village." In *Agrarian Transformations: Local Processes and the State in Southeast Asia*, edited by Gillian Hart, Andrew Turton, and Benjamin White, 98–122. Berkeley: University of California Press.

Anderson, Benedict. 1978. "Studies of the Thai State: The State of Thai Studies." In *The Study of Thailand: Analyses of Knowledge, Approaches, and Prospects in Anthropology, Art History, Economics, History, and Political Science*, edited by Eliezer Ayal, 193–247. Athens: Ohio University Center for International Studies.

Baker, Christopher. 2016. "The 2014 Thai Coup and Some Roots of Authoritarianism." *Journal of Contemporary Asia* 46, no 3: 388–404.

Baker, Christopher, and Pasuk Phongpaichit. 2004. *A History of Thailand*. Cambridge: Cambridge University Press.

Baran, Paul A., and Paul M. Sweezy. 1966. *Monopoly Capital: An Essay on the American Economic and Social Order*. New York: Monthly Review Press.

Bell, Peter F. 1978. "'Cycles' of Class Struggle in Thailand." *Journal of Contemporary Asia* 8, no. 1: 51–79. doi:10.1080/00472337885390041.

"Big Business, Wealth, Royal Connections and Fines." 2016. *Political Prisoners in Thailand*, March 21. https://thaipoliticalprisoners.wordpress.com/2016/03/21/big-business-wealth-royal-connections-and-fines/ (accessed June 23, 2017).

Bowie, Katherine Ann. 1997. *Rituals of National Loyalty: An Anthropology of the State and the Village Scout Movement in Thailand*. New York: Columbia University Press.

Butcher, John, Howard Dick, and Michael Sullivan. 1993. *The Rise and Fall of Revenue Farming: Business Elites and the Emergence of the Modern State in Southeast Asia*. Basingstoke: Palgrave Macmillan.

Chaiyan Rajchagool. 1994. *The Rise and Fall of the Thai Absolute Monarchy: Foundations of the Modern Thai State from Feudalism to Peripheral Capitalism*. Bangkok: White Lotus.

Chambers, Paul, and Napisa Waitoolkiat. 2016. "The Resilience of Monarchised Military in Thailand." *Journal of Contemporary Asia* 46, no. 3: 425–44. doi:10.1080/00472336.2016 .1161060.

Charoensin-o-larn Chairat. 1988. *Understanding Postwar "Reformism" in Thailand: A Reinterpretation of Rural Development*. Bangkok: Editions Duang Kamol.

Chatthip Nartsupha. 1999. *The Thai Village Economy in the Past*. Chiang Mai: Silkworm Books.

Cohen, G. A. 1978. *Karl Marx's Theory of History: A Defense*. Princeton, N.J.: Princeton University Press.

Connors, Michael, and Kevin Hewison. 2008. "Introduction: Thailand and the 'good Coup.'" *Journal of Contemporary Asia* 38, no. 1: 1–10.

Cowen, Deborah. 2008. *Military Workfare: The Soldier and Social Citizenship in Canada.* Toronto: University of Toronto Press.

de Angelis, Massimo. 1999. "Marx's Theory of Primitive Accumulation: A Suggested Reinterpretation." Manuscript, University of East London. http://homepages.uel.ac .uk/M.DeAngelis/PRIMMACCA.htm (accessed March 11, 2016).

Glassman, Jim. 2004a. "Economic 'Nationalism' in a Post-nationalist Era." *Critical Asian Studies* 36, no. 1: 37–64. doi:10.1080/1467271042000184571.

———. 2004b. *Thailand at the Margins: Internationalization of the State and the Transformation of Labour.* Oxford: Oxford University Press.

———. 2005. "The New Imperialism? On Continuity and Change in U.S. Foreign Policy." *Environment and Planning A* 37, no. 9: 1527–44. doi:10.1068/a37157.

———. 2007. "Recovering from Crisis: The Case of Thailand's Spatial Fix." *Economic Geography* 83, no. 4: 349–70. doi:10.1111/j.1944-8287.2007.tb00378.x.

———. 2010. "'The Provinces Elect Governments, Bangkok Overthrows Them': Urbanity, Class and Post-democracy in Thailand." *Urban Studies* 47, no. 6: 1301–23. doi:10.1177/ 0042098010362808.

———. 2011. "Cracking Hegemony in Thailand: Gramsci, Bourdieu, and the Dialectics of Rebellion." *Journal of Contemporary Asia* 41, no. 1: 25–46.

———. Forthcoming. *Drums of War, Drums of Development: The Formation of a Pacific Ruling Class and Industrial Transformation in East and Southeast Asia, 1945–1980.* Leiden: Brill.

Gruber, Jonathan, Nathaniel Hendren, and Robert M. Townsend. 2014. "The Great Equalizer: Health Care Access and Infant Mortality in Thailand." *American Economic Journal: Applied Economics* 6, no. 1: 91–107. doi:10.1257/app.6.1.91.

Haberkorn, Tyrell. 2011. *Revolution Interrupted: Farmers, Students, Law, and Violence in Northern Thailand.* Madison: University of Wisconsin Press.

Harvey, David. 2003. *The New Imperialism.* Oxford: Oxford University Press.

Hewison, Kevin. 1989. *Bankers and Bureaucrats: Capital and the Role of the State in Thailand.* New Haven, Conn.: Yale University Southeast Asia Studies, Yale Center for International and Area Studies.

Hirsch, Philip. 1990. *Development Dilemmas in Rural Thailand.* Singapore: Oxford University Press.

Karmali, Naazneen. 2017. "Thailand's 50 Richest 2017: The Nation's Wealthiest Rise against the Odds." *Forbes,* May 30. http://www.forbes.com/thailand-billionaires.

Kasian Tejapira. 2008. "Toppling Thaksin." *New Left Review* 39: 5–37.

Kuznets, Simon. 1955. "Economic Growth and Income Inequality." *American Economic Review* 45, no. 1: 1–28.

Lawrence, Ken. 2006. *The New State Repression.* Portland: Tarantula. http://zinelibrary .info/files/staterepression.pdf (accessed September 30, 2014).

Lebowitz, Michael A. 2005. *Following Marx: Method, Critique, and Crisis.* Chicago: Haymarket Books.

Marshall, Andrew MacGregor. 2014. *A Kingdom in Crisis.* London: Zed Books.

Marx, Karl. (1939) 1973. *Grundrisse.* New York: Vintage.

———. (1867) 1977. *Capital*. Vol. 1. New York: Vintage.

McCargo, Duncan. 2006. "Thaksin and the Resurgence of Violence in the Thai South: Network Monarchy Strikes Back?" *Critical Asian Studies* 38, no. 1: 39–71. doi:10.1080/14672710600556429.

Mérieau, Eugénie. 2016. "Thailand's Deep State, Royal Power and the Constitutional Court (1997–2015)." *Journal of Contemporary Asia* 46, no. 3: 445–66. doi:10.1080/00472336.2016.1151917.

Montesano, Michael J., Pavin Chachavalpongpun, and Aekapol Chongvilaivan. 2012. *Bangkok May 2010: Perspectives on a Divided Thailand*. Chiang Mai: Silkworm Books.

O'Connor, James. 1973. *Fiscal Crisis of the State*. New York: St. Martin's Press.

Pasuk Phongpaichit. 2016. "Inequality, Wealth and Thailand's Politics." *Journal of Contemporary Asia* 46, no. 3: 405–24. doi:10.1080/00472336.2016.1153701.

Piketty, Thomas. 2014. *Capital in the Twenty-First Century*. Cambridge, Mass.: Harvard University Press.

Porphant Ouyyanont. 2008. "The Crown Property Bureau in Thailand and the Crisis of 1997." *Journal of Contemporary Asia* 38, no. 1: 166–89. doi:10.1080/00472330701652018.

Prajak Kongkirati. 2016. "Thailand's Failed 2014 Election: The Anti-election Movement, Violence and Democratic Breakdown." *Journal of Contemporary Asia* 46, no. 3: 467–85. doi:10.1080/00472336.2016.1166259.

"Protecting the Corrupt." 2014. *Political Prisoners in Thailand*, October 11. https://thaipoliticalprisoners.wordpress.com/2014/10/11/protecting-the-corrupt/ (accessed June 23, 2017).

Seo, Bo Kyeong. 2015. "Thai Public Health Care Suffering by Association." *East Asia Forum*, April 15. http://www.eastasiaforum.org/2015/04/15/thai-public-health-care-suffering-by-association/ (accessed June 23, 2017).

Skinner, G. William. 1957. *Chinese Society in Thailand: An Analytical History*. Ithaca, N.Y.: Cornell University Press.

Somchai Phatharathananunth. 2006. *Civil Society and Democratization: Social Movements in Northeast Thailand*. Copenhagen: NIAS Press.

———. 2016. "Rural Transformations and Democracy in Northeast Thailand." *Journal of Contemporary Asia* 46, no. 3: 504–19. doi:10.1080/00472336.2016.1166258.

Suehiro, Akira. 1989. *Capital Accumulation in Thailand 1855–1985*. Tokyo: Center for East Asian Cultural Studies.

Thongchai Winichakul. 1994. *Siam Mapped: A History of the Geo-body of a Nation*. Honolulu: University of Hawaii Press.

———. 2008. "Toppling Democracy." *Journal of Contemporary Asia* 38, no. 1: 11–37. doi:10.1080/00472330701651937.

Thorn Pitidol. 2016. "Redefining Democratic Discourse in Thailand's Civil Society." *Journal of Contemporary Asia* 46, no. 3: 520–37. doi:10.1080/00472336.2016.1164229.

Tilly, Charles. 2003. *The Politics of Collective Violence*. Cambridge: Cambridge University Press.

U.S. Department of State. 1968. "Memorandum of Conversation." July 18, document 396. In *Foreign Relations of the United States 1964–68, Volume XXVII, Mainland Southeast Asia; Regional Affairs*. http://history.state.gov/historicaldocuments/frus1964-68v27/d396.

Veerayooth Kanchoochat. 2016. "Reign-Seeking and the Rise of the Unelected in Thailand." *Journal of Contemporary Asia* 46, no. 3: 486–503. doi:10.1080/00472336.2016.1165857.

Veerayooth Kanchoochat and Kevin Hewison. 2016. "Introduction: Understanding Thailand's Politics." *Journal of Contemporary Asia* 46, no. 3: 371–87.

Walker, Andrew. 2012. *Thailand's Political Peasants: Power in the Modern Rural Economy.* Madison: University of Wisconsin Press.

CHAPTER 8

Thinking from June 2013 in the Brazilian Metropolis

New Urban Political Assemblages, Old State-Society Relations

FELIPE MAGALHÃES

Brazilian cities have witnessed in the past decade a new period of strong political mobilization in social movements and civil society organizations, composing a myriad of different kinds of politics and platforms. In June 2013, this underlying political assemblage erupted into one of the largest waves of political protests in the country's history. The events broke new ground in urban democracy, marked by a heterogeneity of forces brought together by different purposes but in many cases also in conflict with one another. This chapter explores the dynamics behind the "jornadas de junho," which open up opportunities for a renewed understanding of how poverty is produced relationally in the Brazilian metropolis. Thinking with and from June 2013 in urban Brazil reveals the ways in which neoliberalism meets persistent forms of patrimonialism and clientelism, and traces a genealogy of urban democracy against persistent injustice, in a historical setting of repeated restrictions on distribution, democracy, and welfare. It also provides openings for understanding a larger new wave of social movements that shaped the June 2013 protests in contrast with the last cycle of (antidictatorship) struggles that culminated in the government of the Workers' Party (Partido dos Trabalhadores — PT).

These movements comprise both old and new forms of poverty politics and alliances across differences in class, ethnicity, socioeconomic position, or political platform. Their struggles involve new configurations of power relations that reproduce barriers to a deepening of democracy, or, in some of the movements' own discourse, to the construction of "popular power" that they actively seek. This chapter builds a relational poverty analysis, specifically examining the ways in which these street protests express, in particular moments, a complex blending of differential incorporation and alliances.

The economic and political model of Brazil's PT, in power from 2003 until the present coup d'état,[1] has gone through a significant crisis in recent years. The post-2010 conjuncture has witnessed much lower GDP growth, partially as a late effect of the 2008 crisis and the 2014 commodity market bust, threatening the foundations of the cross-class alliance that sustained a distributive model of governance that managed to take millions out of poverty. This alliance had its base in economic growth driven by commodity exports, achieving income distribution through policy that fueled an intensive expansion of an internal market dominated by large oligopolies in many sectors. The dead end for this capital-labor pact that sustained the PT model resulted in the abandonment of elite support and a strong sudden growth of direct opposition from the right to this agenda, culminating in the current coup.

The landscape of urban social movements has also shifted. As demonstrated by Holston (2008), Abers (1998) and Fernandes (2007a, 2007b), Brazil's urban movements coalesce around long trajectories of persistent exclusion from housing and access to urban land in general, constituting strong alliances between the (homeless, favela, suburban) poor and middle-class activists, politicians, academics, and intellectuals.[2] In the previous cycle, which gained momentum in the mid-1970s and became known as the Urban Reform movement, such encounters also happened through the Catholic Church, labor unions, and political parties. The recent cycle witnesses more diverse points of contact, with examples in the black people's movement (Movimento Negro), or in collectives of feminist activist lawyers. Tracing these shifting alliances as they play out in urban spaces reveals the forms alliances take when a commons is constituted and what results from those struggles.

The first part of this chapter uses Brazilian classical theorists of the country's social formation to better theorize our sociopolitical history and contemporary processes. So-called northern theory is obviously not absent from such perspectives, but is taken as an input and *cannibalized* in constructions of other ways of seeing and understanding Brazil's sociopolitical trajectories and the resulting relationalities, reflected in our own situated theoretical terms. The second section explores the ambivalences of the 2004 to 2010 economic boom, which are related to the progrowth alliances described above. The boom and related alliances had important positive effects for a very large portion of Brazil's urban poor, while at the same time strengthening the contradictions behind the June 2013 events. In the end, I contrast the June 2013 events with a subsequent wave of protests, organized in 2015 by those who had lost the 2014 elections as a conservative reaction to the federal government and the social movements. The latter resulted in Dilma Rousseff's impeachment process in 2016 and, in stark contrast to June 2013, involved radically opposed forms of interaction between the middle classes and the urban poor.[3] This analysis reveals the geohistorical specificity of the politics activated in cross-class alliances.

Throughout, the notions of poverty and the poor I refer to correspond to those who live not only in conditions of material deprivation—an aspect that has largely improved in Brazilian cities in the twenty-first century—but in harsh everyday living conditions and larger vulnerability, distress, and heteronomy.

As Catholic bishop Dom Mauro Morelli argues, poverty, if understood as "living well with little," should not be seen as a problem. Rather, it is concentrated wealth and its "firstborn child" *misery*—real material deprivation coupled with unacceptable living conditions—that should be confronted.[4] This chapter rearticulates poverty in this same way, arguing that the struggles over poverty I address involve people living with little but not well—precisely because of the set of sociospatial relations that reproduce the relational attributes that define the substance of such poverty.

Theorizing Singularities: Brazil's Social Formation Revisited

Thinking from localized specificities in social formations has made a comeback in recent years in the spatialized disciplines. Contemporary debates in relational poverty and urban theory (Elwood, Lawson, and Sheppard 2016; Peck 2015) are largely influenced by poststructuralist elaborations concerning assemblages, networks, pluralized and multifaceted relations, associations, and localized processes that may or may not be interpreted in conjunction with their insertion in wider scales (corresponding also to larger economic/political dynamics). It is impossible to comprehend how poverty is relationally (re)produced through inner workings of urban neoliberalism in metropolitan Brazil without understanding how this mode of *governmentality* is blended with renewed versions of deep-rooted social relations constructed through patrimonialism and clientelism. These older oligarchic political forces correspond largely to those who are taking direct control of the federal government at this moment. Their representation in congress comprises politicians known as the BBB platform: *bala* (bullet), *bíblia* (Bible), and *boi* (cattle), including large *latifúndio* landowners in violent opposition to agrarian reform movements, environmentalists and the demarcation of Amerindian land, and keepers of slave labor perpetuating debt peonage in the country's backlands. Poverty, in these contexts, is reproduced not only through peripheral blends of modern capital in its Latin American versions (extensively analyzed in the developmentalist, or dependency theory sociological tradition) but also in the persistent renewal of older oligarchic sociospatial and power relations.

This chapter constructs theory as a counterpoint to imported ideologies and theoretical frames by building a situated analysis of Brazilian sociological singularities and their potential contribution to contemporary understandings of sociospatial and cross-class relationalities (as in Elwood, Lawson, and Sheppard 2016). This fine-grained interpretation of Brazil's social formation is situated in our own peripheral condition and stands as a theoretical response to the prevailing racialist and evolutionist conservative thinking that dominated Brazilian social thought from the late nineteenth century. Anthropologist Gilberto Freyre started this turn, focusing on the cultural and sociological specificities of Brazilian society. Many later social scientists and intellectuals undertook this task, including Raymundo Faoro and Sérgio Buarque de Holanda, and after the 1950s emergence of dependency theory and Latin American developmentalist economic thinking, Caio Prado Jr., Celso Furtado, and Florestan Fernandes, among others. Apart from the latter's interpretations of economic underdevelopment as resulting from a postcolonial condition and the continued patterns in international economic relations that reproduced it, these mid-twentieth-century social theorists concentrated on several interrelated sociological themes. Some examples include the persistence of a long history of patrimonialism and clientelism in the relations between elites and the state (Faoro 1957);[5] the specificities of modern class formation and our "bourgeois revolution," marked by the absence of the classic conflict between the bourgeoisie and the landed aristocracies (Fernandes 1975);[6] the consequences of Brazil's many historical and social differences to Spanish America and the history of personalized relations between rich and poor (Holanda 2012).

The full implications of this expanded theoretical dialogue require further analysis. I would point out, *en passant*, that engaging these genealogies reconstitutes theory to inform the many relational ways that contemporary state-society interactions reproduce poverty, and how social movements and protest events respond. These genealogies also point to the geohistorical specificities of political relations and historical trajectories behind the reproduction of poverty (and the resultant mobilization of the poor) in their diverse local forms. Advancing the epistemological contribution of this collection, I explore the making of poverty knowledge, in drawing connections between the Brazilian case, informed by Brazilian theorists, and a critical relational analysis of the insertion of external flows of power and capitalist accumulation from larger scales.

Cities and the 2004–2010 Cycle of Inclusive Growth

The new cycle of urban movements arises from a context of growth with distribution—an apparent paradox that speaks directly to the relational poverty politics deeply involved in these struggles. Brazilian cities are rich empirical grounds to analyze how relations (re)produce poverty in situated terms of localized singularities. The visible precariousness these cities engender, including lack of access to basic infrastructure, insufficient housing and collective services, and resultant vulnerabilities for the majority of their residents (including exposure to urban violence), points to sociospatial relations connected to the production of the city itself. This production of space is largely a result of conflicting interests and actions of different groups, involving a hegemony that tends to repress those who attempt to escape or directly oppose its forms of domination. Such hegemonic formations are always specific to place, resulting from local historical trajectories, but obviously connected to external relations and processes. In colonial contexts, this hegemony has frequently involved the historical conformation of elites who were aristocratic and oligarchic long before learning to be bourgeois. Parts of these groups are born through their direct cooperation with the colonial system, and go through subsequent periods of renewal in forms of exploitation of the colonized (which involve the poor as a productive input, along with the abundance of land and extractive resources), engendering a process of internal colonialism. This process fractures territories into a deep sociospatial fragmentation, isolating areas that command and control the extraction of surplus from the rest of society and space through the formation of large pools of cheap labor supply and through resource extraction. The resulting contemporary weaknesses of public space and the public sphere have a historical origin, and contemporary urban neoliberalism is inserted in long genealogies composed by prior patterns of elites producing space.

Since the 1930s, Brazilian sociology has analyzed how old oligarchies have declined with the turn toward industrialization and urbanization (Freyre and De Onís 1963). Later trajectories of industrial and urban development kept shifting this logic, with the state and institutions tending to gain a larger deal of complexity, operating somewhat through the rule of law and a higher degree of isonomy.[7] Though more solidly developed democratic institutions do open opportunities for emancipatory transformations through organized popular movements,[8] inheritances from these genealogies of oligarchic relations tend to persist behind modernized façades. Contemporary examples include the absence of democratic reform through regulatory apparatuses for many sectors, including the media; the violent reproduction of extreme levels of land tenure concentration (both rural and urban spaces); state creation of channels for reproducing specific capitals above a general level of remuneration through concessions; the lack of democratic control/public transparency in several domains of the state, including the police forces; and the distribution of local TV and radio concessions to politicians and powerful regional oligarchs. As Holston (2008) demonstrates, these genealogies of restricted access to land tenure connect back to a nineteenth century nexus of postindependence imperial power in partnership with regional oligarchs for policing a large and unintegrated territory, later moving on to a complex series of legal practices for normalizing illegality, fraud, and exclusion. The racist and patriarchal character of this profoundly exclusionary process is also clear in its entanglements with the late nineteenth-century transition to a postslavery republic in which significant fractions of public land would be privately incorporated, most frequently by those inserted in networks that reproduce power and privilege.

Struggles for democracy, in this context, are fights against the renewal of this nexus—not simply tackling invested capitalist interests in the state and in policy, but also resisting the reproduction of relations between elites and power structures through clientelism and patrimonialism. Social movements are aware of this logic. Their demands and projects are stopped by the following: violent elite opposition to agrarian reform and to indigenous and *quilombola* land demarcations, barriers to formulating housing policies in progressive and democratic terms, and opposition to democratic management and planning of public transit by those who control its operations, among others. June 2013 partially comes from these conflictual relations that reproduce poverty, and from the ways in which the city assembles these relational assemblages. Some movements frame their struggles as fights for rights against privileges, and against forms of privileges and poverty that are relationally established by the state in service of capitalist interests and through patrimonialist/clientelist channels.

In the mid-2000s, a shift in the social movements' landscape came about with the strengthening of a new lineage of civil society groups and organizations dedicated to housing and public transit, along with a wide variety of political platforms, such as women's rights, police violence, and prison reform. These movements started organizing and acting independently from the older wave of 1970s urban "right to the city" movements in which the *urban reform* organizations were included, and that culminated in progressive planning experiences in cities where the PT won elections during the 1990s (Abers 1998; Fernandes 2007a, 2007b). These newer groups comprise varied blends of student organizations; urban activists for public transit and social housing and against the eviction of favelas; feminist movements; the Movimento Negro; political parties to the left of PT (including some of its leftist sections); and the so-called youth movement, composed of often socioeconomically precarious and vulnerable students and other young people. As in the previous cycles of movements, the city is an important aspect and agent of their activism, crosscutting and producing many issues, processes, and assemblages that they stand for or against. Economic growth coupled with income distribution through policy appears in the post-2003 context, acting as a balsamic in some of its specific situations and dynamics—such as the important alleviation of poverty for the very bottom of the pyramid. However this growth also worked as fuel on the fire, partly because collective structures remained relatively unchanged, but also due to old relations of power being recycled by growth itself being channeled through them. Economic growth with distribution coupled with the reproduction of poor collective services during the 2000s created enormous private markets in the four sectors involved in public service provision: education, health, housing, and transport. All four markets have seen explosive growth along with the post-2004 rise of a new lower middle class in Brazil (formerly much poorer groups of people previously excluded from the internal consumer markets) due to the distributive policy shift.

This dynamic of income distribution was inserted in a larger pact that constituted a strong political base for the economic-political model of *lulismo* (Singer

2012), involving labor unions and important fractions of the large business oligopolies. The strategy aligned big business conglomerates and the poorer electorate behind the PT's victories in the polls: the idea being that income flowing to the bottom of the pyramid through policy would bounce back up through consumption. The insertion of the oligopolies in this political pact points to the need to understand political dynamics and their results through the persistence of deep-rooted patrimonialist forms of state-society-space relations. The initial spark for June 2013 came from protests against private companies operating public bus lines, with the relations between these contractors and the state being full of unknown conditions and hidden accounting practices to the point that activists refer to these agents as the "bus mafia".

It is important to stress that while high economic growth brought poverty alleviation for many metropolitan residents, it also translated into significant urban restructuring involving fast-paced land rent valorization. This created a construction boom and gentrification vectors evicting poorer populations, frequently coupled with large urban projects clearing favelas and other poorer areas from bus corridors. Many in the newer movements act and organize against such urban consequences of growth, although recognizing the importance of successful distributive policies and the resulting alleviation of poverty for many.

New Political Spaces and the Situated Antecedents of June 2013

By the beginning of the 2010s, urban activism in Brazil was already highly connected, and used digital networking resources as a central feature of its actions. These new political spaces have their antecedents in the 1990s when the Internet appeared as a point of encounter for activists in different fronts and regions. By the first World Social Forum in Porto Alegre in 2001, *cyberactivism*, as it was called then, was already an important political trend, operating mainly through independent online media initiatives, along with blogs, email lists, and newsgroups. The arrival of social media in 2004 furthered this circuit, as did widening access to devices and the Internet itself.

A parallel development that also gained momentum during the 2000s was the appearance of the new cycle of urban social movements organized around housing, transport, and a broader "right to the city" platform. It was in this context that post–Arab Spring multitudinous forms of political interaction between digital and urban spaces arose in Brazil. In October 2011, responding to Occupy Wall Street's call for global action, several *ocupas*—or *acampas*—appeared in the center of Brazilian cities, some lasting for several weeks before being evicted. In the São Paulo *acampa* experience, rising tensions with parts of the area's homeless population led to difficult interactions between the predominantly middle-class white activists and the poor, frequently black, inhabitants of the center's streets who felt their places invaded. These interactions between middle-class activists and the homeless did not result in the latter's direct engagements in the protests, in spite of the activists' strong attempts to do so. Nonetheless, other forms of alliances appeared between the many different groups of activists, artists, students, artisans, and intellectuals that gathered in those spaces. These resulted in the formation of networks of many sorts, and forms of interaction with a larger public than usual because of the social movements' use of media and communications. Such channels would be an important part of the story of how the events of June 2013 quickly gained ground.

The spark for the 2013 multitudes in the streets came partially from the specific effect of high economic growth in the 2004 to 2010 period: a massive increase in cars and motorcycles circulating in the major cities, coupled with a continued precariousness and increasing costs of public transport, and lack of transparency in public management of the transit system and its private operators. After large cuts in subsidies to public buses as part of 1980s and 1990s austerity measures that hit local governments, public transit declined in quality and number of users, a vicious cycle that continues. Contracts regulating the operation of bus networks by private concessionaries allow them to change the number of buses running in cases of declining passengers, but with no public accountability whatsoever for these adjustments. Slower buses and higher prices make more passengers switch to cars and motorbikes, feeding into the vicious cycle, further slowing buses. Without subsidies or revenues apart from the bus fares themselves, prices are readjusted each year, maintaining an unknown and unpublished level of remuneration to investors in the bus concessions. Adjustments usually occur in empty cities in early January, when many people in major urban centers are away for summer holidays. Meanwhile, federal government subsidies for cars reached unprecedented levels as a measure of pushing growth through private consumption after the 2008 crisis.

A few smaller social movements focusing on these public transport problems (and organized by students and other young urban activists of varied class and racial positions) started gaining ground in the early 2000s. They promoted large street demonstrations responding to bus fare increases in the cities of Salvador in 2003 and Florianópolis in 2004 and 2005.[9] The Movimento Passe Livre (Free Pass Movement—MPL) was founded in 2005 in the Fifth World Social Forum, held in Porto Alegre, in a meeting organized by smaller local movements composed mainly of student activist organizations demanding free bus fares for students. Some such organizations, such as Belo Horizonte's Tarifa Zero (started during the June 2013 events), demand more transparency and accountability between private bus operators working under public concessions, and have been explicitly and repeatedly denied by the city. In the case of Belo Horizonte, activists highlight that there is no public access to the concessionaries' spreadsheets—hence to the information outlining their actual profits. This indicates, for these groups, the existence of a form of protection to private interests from a specific sector infiltrated in the state for guaranteeing its own minimal conditions of capital accumulation above a certain average market level. This is the kind of intraelite (neo)patrimonialist and clientelist relation that renews its façades and forms of action, and blends with more institutionalized, impersonal neoliberal policy in this specific regulatory context.

In June 2013, due to requests by President Dilma Rousseff to postpone bus fare readjustments, as part of a series of hands-on government interventions to tackle inflation through restrictions on managed prices, the rise in prices came during a time of year when people were not away from the major cities for the holidays. This arbitrariness was the unusual spark that gave momentum to anti-tariff protests, with the São Paulo section of MPL claiming on placards each day they went to the streets, "If the fare does not decrease, the city will stop."

New Assemblages in Dispute: June 2013

The first June 2013 protests were restricted to the city of São Paulo, with the MPL taking a leading role. The corporate media turned radically against the protestors and openly favored repression.[10] Within a few days, with police violence against journalists covering the events reaching levels unprecedented since the end of the military government and with the population's growing approval of protestors, the media switched sides and began trying to use the opportunity to turn June 2013 against the PT and the federal government.[11] This coincided with a call for protests in the large cities across the country by local independent movements—mainly connected to the 2014 FIFA World Cup—and turned the first day of national-scale events into a heterogeneous multitude of different groups out on the streets together at the same times and in the same spaces.

Protestors were mainly young people, with a large group of secondary and college students, and a wide variation of income levels. Demands on placards were extremely heterogeneous, frequently individualized and without any organized collective platforms behind them. The largest crowd reached one million people in one night in Rio de Janeiro, whereas most protests in the other major cities involved a few hundred thousand protestors in each occasion. The organized groups that took part in the progressive/libertarian wings of June 2013 included the new wave of urban social movements, political parties to the left of the PT, and dozens of local activist groups. A huge mass of mainly white, higher middle-class unorganized individuals also quickly showed up to protest against generalized corruption, in response to the large media presence, causing instantaneous confusion among those who are more regular attenders of political protests. They tended to wear Brazilian national team jerseys, bring Brazilian flags, paint their faces green and yellow, sing the national anthem and chant nationalist slogans, and engage in direct, often violent confrontation with activists carrying the red flags of organized movements or political parties (including the PT in some cases). These conflicts appeared due to opposing attitudes concerning the presence of leftist political parties and organizations with their red flags in the marches, a generally antipolitical party stance from the yellow-shirt nationalist crowd, and radically opposing views on policy, the state, and capitalism itself. The poverty politics of the nationalist crowd have become clearer more recently, as they have created their own organizations to protest directly against the government, as detailed below. The largest events of June 2013 comprised this big multitude of radically different political elements, and reached record numbers only because of the presence of these non-leftist, anarchist, progressive, and organized middle-class crowds.

This combination of nationalist discourse with violent behavior toward leftist parties and the support of the traditionally conservative media for the protests triggered a fear of a rightwing coup d'état against the PT in the progressive sectors of June 2013, even though most of them were part of a leftist opposition. This created a strong ambivalent sentiment, in which most leftist activists avoided directly attacking the federal government, in a practice of seeing the *state as assemblage* (DeLanda 2006) of heterogeneous elements and scales of action. They defended the PT from its more reactionary critics, at the same time criticizing it for not pushing for deeper democratic and institutional reform. Although the government would later support harsh repression of these movements during the World Cup, President Dilma Rousseff's early responses to June 2013 were sensitive to these voices. She proposed a major reform of the country's political-electoral system and even a new constitutional assembly, passing the problem on to Congress, which reacted with silence and later, an even more conservative agenda. In 2014, the presidency also attempted to institutionalize a National Policy for Social Participation, opening spaces for citizen participation in policy making and translating to the federal level the participative budgets, policy councils, and other urban planning practices initiated by PT mayors in the 1990s. This proposal, which Congress would ban later in that year, caused strong reactions from many sectors, including the media, who treated the would-be federal-level participatory spaces as authoritarian *Bolivarian soviets*.[12]

The third phase of June 2013 started when the action of anarchist/black bloc groups became prominent in the protests, including *property damage* as a deliberate politicized action as a way of displaying the violence of capitalist physical assets in a context of extreme inequality. Black blocs in the events included a large number of poor peripheral young men, some using the opportunity to respond to their daily experience of police abuse, and at other times using masks in the protests simply to protect themselves from being chased by the police afterward. This was when the large crowds started abandoning the streets, and the media returned to their initial condemnation of activists. Meanwhile, in some places the protests generated open and horizontal *popular assemblies*, as spaces of political discussion, which grew to large forums where the wide and diverse current ecology of social movements would gather and discuss. A fourth and final stage lingered on until the 2014 World Cup, and witnessed the ubiquitous presence of heavily armed police forces and a retreat of many organized movements from the streets.

The 2011 *ocupas* witnessed the formation of new networks between activists and the general public that were decisive in spreading the flames from the initial sparks of June 2013. These events created an enormous amount of such interactions, and provided decisive force for the new wave of social movements that started them. Another remarkable fact of June 2013 is that a significant amount of protesters belonged to the poorer population of big cities. This is a rare occurrence, given the brutal repression of police forces that they live with every day, that leads them to feel that they do not belong in the cities' important and central public spaces, not to mention in protest actions. MPL is inserted in a lineage of movements that have traditionally had a large participation of student activists and middle-class leftists, with black and/or poor members entering in supporting roles and/or as those who benefit from the vanguards' plans, a character that has shifted considerably over the years. Today, not only do poor people engage in direct action, as in the large series of squats that have taken over many Brazilian cities in the past decade, but they are increasingly protagonists of the movements. June 2013 provided a good portrait of this change, with a visible presence of a larger number of poor, nonwhite suburban activists in the events. Hence, contemporary encounters between feminist groups, the Movimento Negro, and these transversal platforms (such as housing or transport) tend to switch the more traditional class politics terrain—more frequently related to that division of labor between middle-class intellectualized organizers and their beneficiaries—to a politics in which the protagonists are frequently black, female, *and* inhabitants of the poorer favelas or distant, metropolitan peripheries.

An important difference between Brazil's 2013 and the 2011 Occupy movements in North America is that concrete changes in the regulatory framework aiming at *radical reform* were a clear part of June 2013's agenda, if we look at the organized groups and movements that composed it. This radical reform can be characterized as a set of demands that connect to a deepening of the democratic process and a radical critique of the representative model, but also to ways of confronting patrimonialism and clientelism. Theorizing from the Brazilian context suggests that such demands for the construction of a true public sphere in the context of metropolitan Brazil—deeply affected by years of neoliberal regulation in the macro scale—have different political meanings related to their geohistorical singularities. It is fair to affirm that the second part of Karl Polanyi's double movement (Polanyi 1944)—of capitalist development followed by distribution and the strengthening of social policy, along with forms of compensating for the effects of the free market's social construction—never fully took place in most Latin American countries. In Brazil, the construction of a democratic *res publica*, when not tackled by the persistence of neopatrimonialist relations between elites (whether bourgeois or oligarchic) and the state, appeared in connection to the "order and progress" ethos of nationalist developmentalism. In its hegemonic versions from 1930 to 1984,[13] this nationalist conservative modernization project performed distribution only through its populist labor legislations, not inclusion. Distribution took corporatist forms, with all labor unions directly connected to the presidency, and with the direct repression of communist and anarcho-syndicalist forces, through a legal framework for organized labor during Getúlio Vargas's Estado Novo dictatorial period that was directly inspired by Mussolini's Carta del Lavoro.

In Belo Horizonte, the Assembleia Popular Horizontal (APH) was one of the popular assemblies cited above. After it began during June 2013 as an attempt to organize the demonstrations, it worked as a big forum of activists, articulating working groups divided by broad themes (from human rights and police violence to public transit, environmental policy, and urban reform), and arranging meetings with both the mayor of Belo Horizonte and the governor of the state of Minas Gerais. The group requested guarantees from the governor, to whom the militarized police responds, that the protests of the following days would not be violently repressed. They presented concrete demands for public policy reform and questioned elected leaders directly on the legitimacy of the basic legal-bureaucratic framework of the Brazilian state and the crisis of representation, all with live Internet transmission by *mediactivist* channels. This attempt at direct democracy involved alliance politics of many sorts among the groups situated in the progressive zones of June 2013, generating encounters and the formation of new alliances, but also many conflicts between the heterogeneous groups and individual activists in this new assemblage that was born in the middle of the June 2013 events.

Relational Reactions

It is useful to look at June 2013 as a large urban political assemblage (in DeLanda's 2006 terms) of many heterogeneous politicized elements in interaction, alliance, and conflict. It was a resulting assemblage of the encounter and interaction between other previously constituted elements: the politicized metropolis with a renewed energy in autonomous social movements and other forms of bottom-up political attempts at social change, with the Internet working as a platform for these agents. Assemblages (*agencements*), being active agents and catalyzers, give birth to new potentialities through the intensified interactions between their parts, and also change them, in a process of *becoming* through the affects with the *other*.

A political assemblage like the June 2013 protests is a profusion of subjective singularities in encounter, engendering new political subjects and subjectivities. Such new potentialities compose alliances of many sorts: poor with middle-class activists, labor organizations with *cycleactivists*, LGBT and feminist/black movements with housing and right to the city organizations, student activists with environmentalists, anarchists with *mediactivists*, and so on—not without conflicts, but most frequently in agonistic terms of constructive debate. The alliance with political parties always stops in difficult conversations, in which the issues of horizontality and the aversion of representative politics heat up debates with more traditional organizational structures, a few of them like the Partido Socialismo e Liberdade attempting to change their inner rigidities in these directions, but with little success so far. This stands in a clear contrast to the previous cycle of movements that tended to support the PT and participate actively in their campaigns and local administrations to the point of co-optation.

Another friction arises between movements that have become stronger in recent years—such as LGBT, black, feminist, environmental, indigenous, housing—and more traditional, labor-based organizations. In one specific June 2013 march in Belo Horizonte conducted by labor-based groups, the mutual discomfort became quickly clear to all, not only in terms of radical democratic horizontality versus vertical organizational structures, but also in terms of political content, such as intentions around economic/industrial growth and development, to which indigenous and environmental groups have been standing in opposition. Hence alliances with the traditional organized left tend to occur in terrains where labor unions do not predominate and where more plural platforms can better penetrate. These frictions created an anti-June 2013 attitude in important parts of PT's support base, who accuse the new movements of naïvely contributing to a restrengthening of the conservative agenda.

Several new vectors resulted from the alliances and encounters formed in June 2013, such as new movements, many of which are acting at small-scale grassroots levels, but also new forms of organization and struggle. One example of the latter is the 2015 student occupation of 196 public secondary schools in the state of São Paulo, against a reorganization plan that involved shutting down 92 schools. By the end of the year, the governor had backed down from the plan, but not before sending the police to repress students, who managed to resist and sustain their occupation and self-management experience. These struggles have given rise to a new kind of activist: operators of alliances, who are able to form networks, who situate themselves in several different connected webs and help tie them together. With an increasing heterogeneity in the types of struggles and platforms, this subject gains importance as a translator between groups. Notably, these actors are often lower income young adults with direct contact with the poor, the favela, or distant urban peripheries, and are also very frequently nonwhite and female. Many come from collectives of *popular lawyers* that have grown in number in recent years and that act in support of the poor—whether involved in activism or not—in situations of vulnerability in court cases such as eviction threats.

The uncertainty derived from the radically open character of June 2013 was an input for strong organized reactions from the other side of the political spectrum, including many in the conservative sections of June 2013. That group, also an assemblage/alliance formed during those events, separated itself from the larger assemblage and created its own, pure anti-PT movement. Unsurprisingly, this happened with strong support from media conglomerates that later openly promoted their marches. After the PT's victory in the 2014 presidential elections, their platform was fueled by an attempt to connect the president to a series of corruption scandals involving the national oil company, Petrobrás. These large crowds, composed mostly of older, white, higher income groups, hit the streets in major demonstrations in 2015 and 2016 demanding the president's impeachment due to her supposed involvement in corruption. Significant numbers of them framed the Latin American turn to the left as a "communist threat," and the crowds included small sections of extreme right-wing, openly racist, and anti-LGBT groups demanding military intervention against the government.[14]

The highly contrasting and diametrically opposed events of June 2013 and 2015–16 have interesting historical parallels with the pre-1964 military coup moment. Large masses of labor unions and social movements gathered in the streets in support of João Goulart's structural reform plans, followed by a series of demonstrations by the nationalist conservative sections of the white, richer sections of the middle class. The Marcha da Família com Deus pela Liberdade (March of the Family with God for Freedom) created a strong basis of political support for the coup, exactly in the strategic political ground inhabited by the middle classes. In both moments (the 1960s and the 2000s), we find two opposing political dynamics predicated on very different patterns of relations between the middle classes and the poor and advancing different poverty politics. On the one hand, we find progressive times and spaces involving active efforts by middle-class activists, academics, intellectuals, politicians, community organizers, social assistants, and others to connect directly with the poor who are in need and willing to organize in collective action—through tactics that are diversified over time and between movements with respect to their theoretical and ideological backgrounds. On the other hand, we find reactionary events that produce another sort of interaction between the middle classes and the poor in which discourses of meritocracy and blaming the victim openly come together in the defense of more effective forms of *discipline and punishment*.[15]

These interactions between the poor and the middle classes form a privileged "middle of the chessboard" political terrain that works as a fundamental battleground for both sides of the political spectrum. The different formats of action and political dynamics involved in these encounters generate significant results for the poor, for better or for worse. The city, by intensifying these encounters and affects in a variety of positive and negative ways, acts as a laboratory for diverse sorts of poverty politics. The current historical moment represents a new turning point in their long genealogies and resulting sociospatial processes with important effects in the entanglements of society and space, engendering multiscalar results with profound political consequences. This account demonstrates the political effects of partial incorporation of poorer sectors into political processes, the rise of alliances across difference that are neither stable nor necessarily leftist, as well as the importance of reading relational poverty politics through history and place.

NOTES

I would like to thank all the participants of the RPN writing retreat in the San Juan Islands in November 2015, with whom I have learned a great deal, for comments on earlier versions of this chapter. Special thanks to Vicky Lawson and Sarah Elwood for so generously making it all happen, and to Jia Ye, Jeff Maskovsky, and Antonádia Borges for giving me the privilege of their careful readings of my piece followed by sessions of very good advice. The remaining problems are my own responsibility.

1. As I finish this chapter, Dilma Rousseff has just started a 180-day suspension from office for her investigation due to impeachment procedures undertaken by an opposing congress completely dominated by the current interim president's party. It is safe to see this process as a new form of coup d'état. Instead of the direct employment of armed forces as in 1964, it has been clearly orchestrated by the large unregulated media oligopolies, in tandem with an openly politicized instrumentalization of the nation's judiciary branches. The story offers a rich example of the design of more aggressive terrains in implementing policy shifts, instituting a state of exception aimed at redefining a neoliberal regulatory fix in extreme crisis conditions. Anderson (2016) offers a rich empirical account of this unfolding event, although missing key geopolitical aspects related to the recent political/institutional strengthening of the BRICS.

2. The middle classes to which I refer are a diverse group that has grown in size and heterogeneity since the turn of the century. Apart from simple socioeconomic categories, the line separating the middle classes from the poor is their degree of vulnerability and exposure to situations of material deprivation, as well as sociospatial relations that engender precarious living conditions of everyday violence, where the poor lack urban infrastructure and collective services.

3. See Note 1.

4. See "Devemos combater a riqueza" (2013).

5. See also Sorj (2000).

6. On Florestan Fernandes's contribution to sociological interpretations of Brazilian patrimonialism, see Portela (2012).

7. It is commonly argued that patrimonialism is a consequence of lacking *isonomy*— understood as the basic legal democratic principle of "equality before the law"—in legal-institutional apparatuses.

8. As in Holston's (2008) approach to urban social movements in São Paulo in their relation to the (rule of) law.

9. Among many others not widely diffused in the news, where pressure from organized anti-bus tariff groups led to reversal of price increases in some cases, before the major June 2013 protests. This happened earlier that year in the cities of Porto Alegre, Natal, and Goiânia, without spreading the movement to other places.

10. Mostly large media conglomerates, controlled by a few families and evangelical churches, that still function without antitrust laws or an economic regulatory framework, even thirty years after the end of the authoritarian regime. A significant number of politicians control local subsidiaries of the larger television channels. This configuration speaks to the persistence of patrimonialism, connected to a lack of isonomic rule of law, which works through a well-detailed regulatory legal framework in many countries.

11. To whom these media groups tend to stand in opposition, usually in favor of the center-right Partido da Social-Democracia Brasileira (PSDB). For details on the media's first approach to the protestors as "vandals" and their later effort to use June in favor of their own political agenda, see Judensnaider et al. (2013).

12. See, for example, the May 29, 2014, editorial of *O Estado de São Paulo*, which interpreted the proposal as an attempt at regime change through presidential decree. For a general analysis on the transferring of participation practices in local institutionalized spaces to the national level, see Pogrebinschi (2013).

13. This notwithstanding a small period with President João Goulart, who was unseated by military coup in 1964.

14. Researchers at Universidade de São Paulo and Universidade Federal de Minas Gerais conducted surveys during the April 12, 2015, events in São Paulo and Belo Horizonte, respectively, capturing the socioeconomic profile and the general perceptions of the protestors. Results can be seen at www.lage.ib.usp.br/manif and at Grupo Opinião Pública's website, http://opiniaopublica.ufmg.br/site/pesquisas/perfil-ideologico-e-atitudes-politicas-dos-manifestantes-de-12-de-abril-belo-horizonte.

15. The surveys cited in the previous note reveal a perception of these groups that the direct cash transfer policy of *Bolsa Família* makes the poor "lazy and unwilling to work for wages".

REFERENCES

Abers, Rebecca. 1998. "From Clientelism to Cooperation: Local Government, Participatory Policy, and Civic Organizing in Porto Alegre, Brazil." *Politics & Society* 26, no. 4: 511–37. doi:10.1177/0032329298026004004.

Anderson, Perry. 2016. "Crisis in Brazil." *London Review of Books* 38, no. 8: 15–22.

DeLanda, Manuel. 2006. *A New Philosophy of Society: Assemblage Theory and Social Complexity*. London: Bloomsbury.

"Devemos combater a riqueza com sua filha primogênita, a miséria." 2013. *Cáritas Brasileira*, December 23. http://caritas.org.br/devemos-combater-a-riqueza-com-sua-filha-primogenita-a-miseria/22987 (accessed June 23, 2017).

Elwood, Sarah, Victoria Lawson, and Eric Sheppard. 2016. "Geographical Relational Poverty Studies." *Progress in Human Geography*. Advance online publication. doi:10.1177/0309132516659706.

Faoro, Raymundo. 1957. *Os Donos do Poder: Formação do patronato político brasileiro.* São Paulo: Globo.

Fernandes, Edesio. 2007a. "Constructing the 'Right to the City' in Brazil." *Social & Legal Studies* 16, no. 2: 201–19. doi:10.1177/0964663907076529.

————. 2007b. "Implementing the Urban Reform Agenda in Brazil." *Environment and Urbanization* 19, no. 1: 177–89.

Fernandes, Florestan. 1975. *A Revolução Burguesa no Brasil: Ensaio de interpretação sociológica.* Rio de Janeiro: Zahar.

Freyre, Gilberto, and Harriet De Onís. 1963. *The Mansions and the Shanties: The Making of Modern Brazil.* Berkeley: University of California Press.

Holanda, Sérgio Buarque de. 2012. *Roots of Brazil.* Notre Dame, Ind.: University of Notre Dame Press.

Holston, James. 2008. *Insurgent Citizenship: Disjunctions of Democracy and Modernity in Brazil.* Princeton, N.J.: Princeton University Press.

Judensnaider, Elena, Luciana Lima, Marcelo Pomar, and Pablo Ortellado. 2013. *Vinte Centavos: A luta contra o aumento.* São Paulo: Veneta.

Peck, Jamie. 2015. "Cities beyond Compare?" *Regional Studies* 49, no. 1: 160–82.

Pogrebinschi, Thamy. 2013. "The Squared Circle of Participatory Democracy: Scaling-up Deliberation to the National Level." *Critical Policy Studies* 7, no. 3: 219–41. doi:10.2139/ssrn.2104699.

Polanyi, Karl. 1944. *The Great Transformation.* New York: Farrar & Rinehart.

Portela, Aristeu, Jr. 2012. "Florestan Fernandes e o conceito de patrimonialismo na compreensão do Brasil." *PLURAL, Revista do Programa de Pós-Graduação em Sociologia da USP, São Paulo* 19, no. 2: 9–27.

Singer, André. 2012. *Os Sentidos do Lulismo: Reforma gradual e pacto conservador.* São Paulo: Companhia das Letras.

Sorj, Bernardo. 2000. "The Seven Faces of Brazilian Society." *Cahiers du GELA-IS*, no. 3. http://www.bernardosorj.com/pdf/sevenfacesofbraziliansociety.pdf.

CHAPTER 9

"Check Your Privilege"

The Micropolitics of Cross-Status Alliances in the DREAM Movement

THOMAS SWERTS

In June 2012, President Obama announced Deferred Action for Childhood Arrivals (DACA), an executive action that allowed eligible undocumented youth to receive a temporary work permit and exemption from deportation. Although DACA fell short of demands by the DREAM movement, it was a substantial symbolic gesture of the Obama administration toward sustained efforts by undocumented youth activists to make their voice heard. In Chicago, the announcement set the stage for a meeting between Representative Luis Gutierrez (D) and the Immigrant Youth Justice League (IYJL). A press conference was organized at the office of the Illinois Coalition for Immigrant and Refugee Rights (ICIRR), an umbrella organization that had formed a strategic alliance with IYJL. The director of ICIRR, community representatives, and the congressman gave speeches for the camera crews. In his speech, Gutierrez celebrated the work done by youth organizers and applauded the coalition that made this "victory" possible:

> What it demonstrates is if you're forceful, if you're tenacious, if you're forthright, if you're fighting for justice, you can win, and we won last Friday. *I want to thank the tenacity, the courage, the ingenuity of all of the DREAMers across this nation who came together and said to their friends and their allies: "Join us, we will lead," congratulations to you, this is a victory that is marked by your tenacity, I want to thank you, it is great when you are working with such a coalition of people.*[1]

From a social movement perspective, this coalition was indeed crucial to achieve this outcome. For sure, the strategic alliance between IYJL and ICIRR was instrumental in facilitating contacts with the congressman, ensuring media coverage, and linking undocumented youth to the broader immigrant rights movement. These macro–alliance politics have been extensively studied by social movement scholars (see, among others, Van Dyke and McCammon 2010; Beamish and Luebbers 2009; Snow et al. 1986). In this chapter, I shift attention to the often neglected micropolitics of allyship that take place within the DREAM movement. The term "micropolitics" refers here to the perpetual intersubjective exchanges between activists in unequal positions of privilege that affect how social movement organizations operate.

Returning to the scene of the press conference, a slot had been reserved for undocumented youth to speak. When IYJL member Yolanda took the stage, five fellow members wearing their "Undocumented, Unafraid" T-shirts and holding up sheets with pictures and stories of soon-to-be deported immigrants backed her up.[2] She gave the following testimony:

> My name is Yolanda and I'm undocumented. I came to this country when I was four years old and I am currently attending the University of Illinois at Chicago. As an undocumented student, I was pleased to hear that President Obama has finally decided to take a stand with DREAM Act–eligible youth. After two years of undocumented youth coming out of the shadows, participating in civil disobediences, and occupying President Obama's campaign offices nationwide over the last two weeks, he is unable to ignore us any longer. . . . As immigrant rights advocates respond to this announcement, we urge you to take into account the voices of undocumented youth who have been taking risks to call attention to this issue. . . . *We invite Congressman Luis Gutierrez, Senator Dick Durbin, advocates and allies, and other undocumented youth to work together to hold the administration accountable to its words and prepare for the work left ahead.*

At first sight, this scene seems to be an example of the increasing openness and boldness of undocumented youth activists in publicly claiming their right to rights. Indeed, undocumented youth have been able to gain agency by strategically relying on storytelling and emotion as political tools (Swerts 2015). But what is equally important in analyzing such speech acts is to investigate *those who do not speak* in this setting. The shout-out to "allies" and the discursive distinction between "allies," "advocates," and "undocumented youth" was not a coincidence. The latter group raised their "voices" and "took the lead" while the former groups played a supportive role. Two of the T-shirt wearers were citizen members whom I had come to know through my fieldwork. The fact that they were allowed to wear these shirts as a badge of honor already reflected their ally status. Due to her Arab background, ally Rhadia did not really stand out in the scene. As a college student, she became involved in the movement through her commitment to her undocumented friend. Ally Scott was the only white person on stage. As an anthropology student at an elite university, he was inspired to become an ally by seeing the effects of deportation policies firsthand while interning at a Guatemalan NGO.

Unlike the macropolitics of coalition building, the stories of allies like Rhadia and Scott are easily overlooked. The complex social processes through which the subject position of the ally comes into being within the DREAM movement can teach us about the potentials and limits of alliance politics. In an era wherein lack of legal status causes immigrants to be excluded from citizenship rights and privileges, subjected to state violence and stigmatized by illegalizing discourses, mobilizing to voice the grievances of the undocumented is a daunting task. I argue that precarious subjects like undocumented youth rely on forging cross-status alliances with citizen activists to sustain their political organizations. The term "cross-status" refers to the gap between activists with and without citizenship status. In effect, citizenship as a historically and politically constructed form of privilege constitutes the main boundary that separates allies from non-allies in IYJL. In line with objectives of this volume, I adopt a broader use of relational poverty as the generalized condition of economic, cultural, social, and political precariousness that results from being excluded from citizenship as privilege.

In what follows, I draw on two and a half years of ethnographic fieldwork in Chicago, in-depth interviews with IYJL members, and content analysis of speeches, organizational publications, and blog posts to study how power differentials become negotiated between citizen allies and DREAMers. First, I outline a relational perspective on the micropolitics of cross-status alliances. Second, I sketch a historical overview of the representational struggles within the DREAM movement. Third, I compare and contrast documented and undocumented perspectives on what being an ally means. Throughout, I argue that building cross-status alliances implies *boundary bridging*, or the process whereby power differentials are negotiated through the mechanisms of equalization and differentiation. Both mechanisms contribute to the social construction of the ally by making citizen supporters structural equals who remain symbolically unequal. It is precisely this mixed status of being "unequal equals" that turns potentially overpowering and privileged citizens into productive allies for DREAMers. These findings underscore the importance of adopting a relational approach to the study of political subject formation among precarious actors.

Setting the Stage: Allies in the DREAM Movement

With millions of people on the move and migrants' basic human rights often suspended or violated in the name of refugee containment, denial of citizenship is a crucial process of impoverishment. The boundaries of citizenship delineate the terms for inclusion and exclusion to the polity. They are a crucial instrument of exclusionary governance for Western governments under pressure to preserve existing levels of welfare and wealth in the wake of state deficits, foreign debt, and economic crises. In effect, having citizenship status has become a privilege tied to what Shachar (2009) depicts as a worldwide "birthright lottery." The overriding importance of undocumented status as a gateway to poverty is well captured by the recent work of Gonzales (2011, 2016). Gonzales borrows the term "master status" from Everett Hughes to grasp illegality's stigmatizing quality, which tends to subsume the ability of other traits or acquired statuses to avoid poverty (Gonzales 2016, 15). Indeed, in many places, citizenship status is a basic requirement to secure access to healthcare, jobs, housing, and higher education; being undocumented renders the de facto cultural, social, economic, and political integration of immigrants null and void.

For the estimated 2.1 million undocumented youth who arrived to the United States with their parents and grew up attending American schools, making American friends and consuming American pop culture, the transition into illegality mostly takes place during adulthood (Gonzales 2011). Since the Supreme Court ruled the exclusion of undocumented youth from primary and secondary education to be in violation of the Equal Protection Clause of the Fourteenth Amendment, schools provide a "safe space" for undocumented youth during childhood. When youth reach the age when their friends are taking driving classes, contemplating college, or traveling abroad, they are confronted with the daunting reality of their "illegality." Pointing to the fact that these populations find themselves in a quasi-permanent position *in between* legal categories rather than being completely excluded from "legality," this illegality is a form of what Menjívar (2006) has called "legal liminality." Undocumented youth, who make up roughly one-fifth of the total population of undocumented immigrants in the United States, embody this liminality to an even greater extent than their adult first-generation counterparts.

This experiential gap in the lived reality of what it means to be young and undocumented led to representational struggles within the immigrant rights movement. Nicholls (2013) argued that when the DREAMers burst into the political scene in the 2000s, their politicization changed the modus operandi of the immigrant rights movement at large. Whereas immigrant leaders first relied on portraying undocumented youth as victims of the broken immigration system, these youth started coming out in public as "undocumented, unafraid, and unapologetic." The feeling that others were speaking *for* them urged undocumented youth activists to strive for autonomy and develop their own style of being political (Nicholls 2013; Swerts 2014). This feeling is well captured by Cynthia, who told me during an interview that "undocumented people are finally taking the lead and they're deciding what's right for them and their communities rather than having these executive directors of really well-known national organizations decide on . . . legislation that will not affect them at all." This quote demonstrates a strong sense that overpowering citizens—with or without immigrant background—had been telling them for too long how to behave politically.

This brief background of internal movement conflicts between undocumented youth activists and allies sets the stage for what is at stake when we talk about the micropolitics of allyship. In situations where noncitizen actors must fight for their right to speak for themselves against more privileged citizen "allies," cross-status coalitions are fragile and precarious (also see Enriquez 2014, 165–70). Put differently, the emancipation from citizen voices that constantly risk overpowering them is a crucial part of the political subject formation process whereby undocumented youth gain a voice of their own. Yet, as in any movement, forming strategic alliances with more privileged actors can also create political and symbolic openings for precarious subjects. Furthermore, engaging in mutual exchange with diverse partners potentially generates learning opportunities that can strengthen political organizations. Hence, the puzzle that DREAMers faced was how to bridge the gap between the lived experiences of illegality and citizenship in a way that optimally negotiates power differentials.

A Relational Approach to Cross-Status Alliances

My analysis of the micropolitics of allyship in the DREAM movement relies on a relational approach to studying the processes whereby alliances between documented and undocumented activists are forged. More traditional social movements studies on alliance politics tend to focus on forging coalitions among diverging political actors (Van Dyke and McCammon 2010), alliance building across social movements (Beamish and Luebbers 2009), and constructing overarching movement "frames" to bridge differences (Snow et al. 1986). The unit of analysis here is almost always the social movement organization, portrayed as a strategic undertaking aimed at maximizing the bundling of resources to attain predefined political goals. This focus on the interorganizational and intermovement levels obscures the significant micropolitics of allyship within organizations among a movement's diverse membership. In this regard, Enriquez's pioneering study on cross-status coalitions (2014), which argued that a shared social justice ideology accounts for the formation of cross-status coalitions, represents a significant step in the right direction. Although this analysis shies away from interpreting coalition formation as a strategic endeavor, reducing citizen members to bearers of "electoral power" (Enriquez 2014, 164) does not do the complexities of allyship justice. Furthermore, the emphasis on *preexisting* social justice ideologies as a binding factor downplays the explanatory power of cultural schemas that originate in the interaction between citizens and noncitizens.

The relational theorizations of poverty that inform this volume (see Lawson and Elwood 2014; Elwood, Lawson, and Nowak 2015) are better equipped to provide a fine-grained analysis of the micropolitics of alliance building. Such a perspective starts from the claim that poverty as a social phenomenon is mutually constituted by the meaning-making and place-making practices of the privileged. The production of middle-class ideologies and privileges, for example, coproduces poverty by rendering the poor "other" visible (Elwood, Lawson, and Nowak 2015, 127). In a similar way, the production of citizenship ideologies enables distinctions between migrants "deserving" of legalization, as exemplified by the hardworking valedictorian DREAMer, and "undeserving" unemployed, unassimilated, or criminal "illegal aliens" (see Chauvin and Garcés-Mascareñas 2014). The very fact that we are talking about *co*production already hints at the possibilities for the contestation of moral and class binaries of deservingness. In contrast to the inevitability of class reproduction that is implied in Bourdieusian concepts of habitus and doxa (Bourdieu 1984), a relational perspective locates the potential for a progressive poverty politics in the realm of intersubjective relations.

Lawson and Elwood (2014) explore how ideological understandings that delineate the deserving from the undeserving poor are enacted and contested in "spaces of encounter." These spaces of encounter are reminiscent of what Pratt (1991, 34) calls contact zones, or "social spaces where cultures, meet, clash and grapple with each other, often in contexts of highly asymmetrical relations of power." The DREAM movement and, more particularly, IYJL is an organization that constitutes a contact zone. In the "safe space" of IYJL, citizen and noncitizen activists actively try to come up with ways to supersede and negotiate the asymmetrical power relations that underpin citizenship in the United States. At the same time, these encounters trigger conversations about the positionality of activists with diverging legal statuses. What happens then when citizens are turned into allies is illustrative of Pratt's notion of translation as a process that involves "the purposeful creation of nonequivalence" (2002). In effect, the meaning of membership in the DREAM movement becomes differentiated for allies as they are assigned a place in the margins rather than at the center.

Purposefully establishing a negotiated form of nonequivalence between citizen and noncitizen activists in the DREAM movement requires a great deal of boundary work. Boundaries have regained in importance over recent years as an analytical tool to scrutinize phenomena like class, ethnicity and migration (Bourdieu 1984; Lamont and Molnár 2002). Lamont and Molnár (2002, 168) conceptually differentiate between symbolic boundaries, referring to "conceptual distinctions made by social actors to categorize objects, people, practices, and even time and space," and social boundaries, referring to "objectified forms of social differences manifested in unequal access to and unequal distribution of resources (material and nonmaterial) and social opportunities." In the "contact zone" of IYJL, symbolic boundaries between allies and DREAMers are dominated by the stigmatizing and criminalizing effect of legal status as a categorical marker that paves the way for pervasive unequal access to college grants, driving, or traveling abroad. The DREAM movement seeks to shift how social boundaries are drawn for the undocumented community by reworking the symbolic boundaries that determine how undocumented youth are categorized.

Since migration scholars theorize boundary change at the level of society at large, they implicitly take dominant modes of membership as their reference point while neglecting the possibilities for contestation in everyday spaces of encounter (see Alba 2005; Zolberg and Woon 1999; Wimmer 2013). Lamont and Bail's (2007) work on the everyday antiracism is far more revealing since it outlines how stigmatized groups make variable use of equalization strategies aimed at bridging boundaries and, thereby, establishing equality with members of the dominant majority. While this argument is compelling, the way that boundary bridging is operationalized assumes power differentials can be mediated only by creating chains of equivalence. However, echoing Pratt's notion of translation, one can also imagine boundary-bridging strategies that create nonequivalence based on differentiation as a mechanism. Below, I use the case of IYJL to demonstrate how both equalization and differentiation inform the micropolitics of cross-status alliances.

Becoming Unequal Equals

As an ethnographer, my initial plan was to ask if I could participate in IYJL's activities and internal meetings, disclosing my research goals and seeking to be formally admitted to conduct observations.[3] When I presented myself at an open meeting, I did not get the anticipated response. References to my training in sociology and my interest in undocumented activism seemed to be anything but reassuring. Instead, I was asked why I cared so much about the issue and what kinds of experiences I had. I improvised on the fly and told them the story of how my encounter with the sans-papiers during a charity concert in Brussels had opened my eyes to the exclusion of undocumented immigrants. I would learn to fall back on these foreign experiences that I brought with me as a European immigrant. Since storytelling was a central community-building technique at IYJL, I was often urged to share my personal experience. I distinctly remember being touched by the emotional stories of hardship, deprivation, and despair of undocumented youth as they went around the circle during "shout it outs." When it was my turn to speak, I felt nervous because I thought I had nothing to offer. "But you migrated to the U.S. too, right?" someone suggested, leading me to recount my experiences moving from Belgium and getting settled in Chicago. Through these exchanges in the "safe space" of IYJL, I was confronted with my own positionality on the folding lines of race, class, and citizenship. The "asks" they made of me as a citizen member, which ranged from driving people around to using resources on campus, being part of the security team during rallies, and building the stage for "coming out" speeches, were part of the process of becoming an ally. Through trial and error, I survived what Emily called the "informal interviewing process" for IYJL allies:

> There's an informal interview process. So I think like the norms of IYJL that are written on the board aren't necessarily the real norms of IYJL. . . . You can't be

with IYJL and not be angry immensely about the way the system is structured. . . . There's a humility that you have to have because otherwise you won't stick in the group because you have to accept that sense of humility to fit in. And I think that's why a lot of the allies come and go, they're not used to that. You have to have your own pain I think, your own personal pain. You can't come from a position of a lawyer, like you can't come there to watch or experience in full, like you have to be there to work and do stuff. I think that those are some of the big norms.

Emily's statement contains the four major elements of allyship in the organization. First, allies need to demonstrate their emotional investment in the movement, rather than providing a calculated reasoning of why they joined. This corroborates Jasper's (1997) findings on the importance of emotion as a mobilization factor. But emotion also serves to create equalization, since the public demonstration of your personal pain as a citizen can be used to connect with the hardships of undocumented youth. Second, allies have to "accept a sense of humility" to fit in. Humility entails allies "stepping down" or "stepping back" at the appropriate times. Third, allies cannot speak from a position of privilege, since such a position would prevent them from "experiencing membership at IYJL in full." Finally, allies "have to be there to work and do stuff"—be engaged and make sacrifices for the movement.

Emotional investment, humility, reflexivity, and sacrifice are norms that DREAMers installed for citizens to comply with in exchange for movement membership. Like Emily stated, the "real norms" of IYJL were not necessarily those "written on the board" but the ones implicitly demanded of allies in interaction. Yet, during my time as an ally at IYJL, allies and undocumented youth alike pushed to formalize some of these norms to clarify expectations. From the very beginning, the "points of unity" made it clear that undocumented youth take the lead in the organization: "We believe in the right of those most affected to lead our own movements for liberation, and thus believe in an organization where undocumented youth are at the leadership, working with the support of allies." In a reversal of roles, citizens are assigned a supportive role, while the "most affected" are the only legitimate movement leaders. Below are other operational "IYJL norms" that were agreed upon for all members (internal IYJL correspondence):

What is said here, stays here; what is learned here, leaves here
No one knows everything, together we know a lot
Leave space for humor and play
"I" statements: recognize we speak from our own experiences
Be curious
Express discomfort
Boundaries: everything is an invitation; draw your own boundaries and respect
   those of others

In addition, one norm applied to citizens only: "Check your privilege." Since more and more would-be allies presented themselves at IYJL over time, an "Ally Sheet" was drafted with tailored norms adapted from the AB 540 Ally Training Guide. This sheet contained recommendations under the headings of awareness, knowledge, skills, and action. Awareness involved challenging yourself and others to think critically about how undocumented immigrants are portrayed in the media. Knowledge referred to the need for allies to familiarize themselves with policies, laws, and other practices that impact undocumented immigrants. Finally, allies had to use their privileges to seek out groups to get involved with, opportunities to speak in support of the cause and to learn to let undocumented people take the lead.

Analyzing these informal and formal norms reveals that allies never achieve full equal status but remain "unequal equals." The public enactment of emotion and sacrifice creates chains of equivalence between noncitizens and citizens that reinforce social ties within the organization. Conversely, the embodied enactment of humility and the reflexive unlearning of privilege create chains of non-equivalence that center the undocumented and their lived experiences as the legitimate subjects and subjectivities of the DREAM movement. Next, I outline how differentiation and equalization are deployed as mechanisms to negotiate power differentials at IYJL.

Learning to Be an Ally = Unlearning Privilege

The role of the ally is hardly fixed, but defined intersubjectively in practice. I draw here on my interviews with IYJL members to show how the meaning of allyship is perceived from an undocumented and a documented perspective. Contrasting people's narrative reflections on respectively dealing with and being an ally reveals that allyship is rendered meaningful in spaces of encounter. Despite attempts to institutionalize the role of the ally in the DREAM movement, allyship is brought to life only in the fuzzy messy space of cross-status interactions. Jobito's statements below pay testament to this complexity and instability of the allies' role. In positioning themselves toward allies, undocumented youth face the double task of wanting to keep their allies close enough to bear the fruits of their support yet not too close to risk being overpowered:

> I think . . . with allies, [we are] just *trying to figure out what their role is in this organization.* We're trying to learn what the allies' role is [laughs], it's not like they're allies. Like it's weird, like it's a weird space. I definitely feel comfortable with all of the allies in IYJL and speaking to them about anything I would be comfortable speaking to anyone who's undocumented, but I think *learning experiences* of what it means to be an ally, and *learning to stand back* kind of thing, is a learning expe-

rience like, with allies. Right? Because we know that we're here, we know we want undocumented youth to speak for themselves, but we definitely realize that allies are vital to what this organization is doing.

Learning to stand back is another way of saying that citizen allies in the DREAM movement need to unlearn their citizenship privileges. For Spivak (1988), unlearning privilege is an epistemological prerequisite for ethical encounter with precarious subjects. For citizens to become allies they must self-subject to the norms defined by the undocumented and be ready to represent the movement's cause on their terms. The transformation in the subjectivity of the ally implies a responsibility to the other that stems from being called by and being answerable to the other rather than from the duty of the "fitter self" (Spivak 2004, 535–37).

A blog post by undocumented member Araa specifically calls fellow citizens in the movement to be more answerable and vocal about their responsibilities as allies. In a subtle way, she describes unlearning privilege as a reflexive subjectivity that spurs allies into action. What it does not represent, however, is feeling sorry or guilty about the unequal distribution of citizenship privilege, since this cripples the possibility of allyship altogether.

> I wish you were more unapologetic. Yes, you, the citizen. When I say *check your privilege*, I don't mean apologize for it, I don't mean feel guilty for it, and I sure as hell don't mean don't take full advantage of it. All I'm saying is be more considerate of folks who don't have that privilege, recognize the system that marginalizes both of us in different ways and sets us up against each other by giving you a piece of dignity and denying it to me. Own up to it and do something about it. It's not an accusation, it's a challenge.

The creation of (non)equivalence is achieved here by focusing outward on "the system" that pits citizens and noncitizens against each other and by demonstrating the relevance of the DREAMers' rallying cry, "undocumented, unapologetic, unafraid," to citizens.

Allies tend to reply to calls for answerability through similar discursive means, sharing behavioral guidelines based on their experience that can be replicated by other allies. For example, Ricardo's blog post gives a hypothetical answer to a question that many citizens struggle with while forming their subjectivities as allies:

> "Why are you in this?" Many have asked me this. What they mean is: if you are a citizen, why the hell are you fighting for the rights of undocumented people? Here is my answer: *I fight because I can't stand my privilege* knowing that my boyfriend, my friend, my cousin and 12 million more people can't take the things I do for granted. . . . It means that I have to make time. That I will attend rallies and organizational meetings. That I will call my representatives when necessary. That I will send faxes to DHS when the need arises (hopefully never). That I will spread

the word about the struggle. That I will listen to my friends when they come to me and will not share what they reveal to me in confidence. It means *sacrifices*, but still, I cannot compare mine to those of my undocumented friends. It is their struggle after all.

Ricardo's narrative exemplifies the ally who distances himself from things he takes for granted as a citizen and who actively brings "sacrifices" in terms of time and effort for the movement. Equalization takes place by discursively aligning himself with his "undocumented friends" and the hardships that they go through and emotionally expressing discomfort about his own privileges. Some allies, like Ian, went further by choosing to no longer travel abroad to honor the "check your privilege" pledge. While he had traveled to Central America before he joined IYJL, he no longer felt comfortable doing so as an ally in the face of his undocumented friends' inability to do so:

> It causes a lot of discomfort, when, people [undocumented youth] know that can travel across borders do it. . . . When I realized the anguish that that causes in people that I know, *I decided that I won't.* . . . A few days ago I was actually hanging out with some friends, a few of whom are Guatemalan. And they were talking about how some of them are going to move to Guatemala and, "Oh you should come visit." And I said, "Well actually, I'm not sure if I could do that, because all of the people that I know can't. And I would be really uncomfortable doing that."

Both Ricardo and Ian explicitly point to and name the experiential gap between citizens and noncitizens in order to legitimize their actions. For many allies, this gap in lived experience leads to doubts and concerns about when it is appropriate to speak up. Emily expressed this by identifying the main challenge as "knowing when to help": "I feel like I have a sense about when to be vocal, but I think about not knowing when to help and when it's appropriate to help and I think I know that there's some times where I honestly can't be there for them because I don't know how it feels to be undocumented no matter what." Ian also struggled with this question, informed by his knowledge of the representational conflicts in the movement:

> I was trying to figure out what if anything I could add . . . what's relevant. Um, because some things that I learned, even specific to immigration organizing, I realized was not really relevant. Like, you do two separate things for citizens and noncitizens. And the whole point of IYJL was to reject that kind of fucked up way of having a movement. . . . It has to do with the power of oppressed people and the power of not oppressed people. Where previously the movement had been segregated as the decisions were being made by people who had papers, or were even passing as having papers, like my friend, she was undocumented but was operating as someone with papers. And then we were, and we would make decisions on what would be safe and doable for them. And we were always assumed to be people with papers.

Even when we were people like myself who were citizens that the decision-making agent was assumed to be undocumented and operating from that experience.

What Ian alludes to is that the DREAMers' past experience of being overpowered by citizens led them to draw a symbolic line in the sand about what is undocumented-only territory and what is not.

My interview with IYJL member Reyes further clarifies the learning processes involved in making ally subjects. Reyes describes the initial position of allies in the movement as inspired by Spivak's concept of the duty of the "fitter self," since citizens speaking in the name of the poor defended their leadership as a way to protect the poor from the risk of repression:

> Early on we had a lot of allies and, and it's also because the immigration movement was still in the position where um, I'm willing to take that risk for you, because I am an ally, I am a citizen, I don't want you to put your name out there and face deportation. So I'm gonna go out there, I'm gonna speak for you, and this. . . . We had a lot of them telling us you shouldn't come out, you shouldn't speak out, you shouldn't get arrested, and in a way that was very upsetting because we wanted to create this safe space where we could have our own voice and not have someone telling us, you shouldn't do this. So there was a lot of *growing pains* with this whole allied concept. So I think over time, as the movement progresses, *what an ally is has become more well defined.* . . . So I think a lot of allies have begun to realize is not to really step aside, but to like sponsor the whole thing, and to realize that they *do have a role, they do have a part in the story that is valuable, but at the same time realizing that they cannot speak for an undocumented view.*

The positive content of this supportive role is well illustrated by undocumented member Ulises's remarks on the role of the ally, which stress not only that allies must unlearn their privilege but that *checking* their privilege can set in motion a process whereby privileges are turned into potential strengths from a movement perspective:

> I think *allies also have their own strengths*, their members, and their own special abilities. Special abilities, you know not like superheroes, *special skills, special privileges that they can use to help to organize or help IYJL* in some way. And I think when it comes to like discussions I think they bring in some new perspective or help contribute in some way. . . . *I think they're like the gateway to the other world, if that makes sense.* They play that supportive role, like undocumented folks, but they bring in that new perspective that is not being undocumented. And I think that's important, and this movement, that we're not just like undocumented folks, we wouldn't get very far."

Ulises highlights that allies bring in a new perspective, and that some political openings become apparent from the vantage point of the citizen. Citizen allies at

IYJL also imported ways of organizing, access to resources deriving from their professional networks and experiences from different movements that proved to be useful.

Differentiation as a boundary-bridging mechanism operates through naming and valuing diverging traits, roles, and skills of undocumented youth and allies. The organizational ritual at the start of every IYJL meeting exemplifies these naming practices. Typically, one of the founding members would start by introducing herself or himself as "Hi, my name is X and I am undocumented." Citizens would in turn use the expression "Hi, my name is X and I am an ally." Even when everybody in the room knew each other, IYJL members swore by this formula as if it were an initiation rite that had to be completed before anything could take place. It did not take me long to embrace the ally label, as it offered me a ready-made identity within the movement. But since I was involved with IYJL as a researcher first and foremost, I questioned whether my use of the label was justified. A session I attended with other citizen members at an IYJL retreat helped to reassure my ally status. While undocumented youth gathered in the room next door, our task was to think about some questions: Why did you join? Why did you stay? What is your role? What can we do better? Noah expressed the view that allies should have "no asks," "check their privilege," and be self-reflexive. Scott admitted that people asked him "Who are you?" when he joined and that having to disclose intentions had been intimidating. Several allies highlighted that it was at times unclear for them how they could "step up." To my surprise, Emily then said that the way that I had volunteered to preside over a session on college applications for undocumented youth had inspired her to take more initiative as an ally herself. In this way, she commended how I had shared my experience in and knowhow of the educational field as an ally. Naming and valuing practices thus serve to acknowledge citizen members as allies and define the differentiated role that allies can take up.

The ethical imperative to "step up" as an ally sometimes results in powerful moments of equalization. As outlined before, storytelling and sharing of emotions were key vehicles for bridging differences. Among the citizen members that I knew at IYJL, Noah was one of the fiercest and most outspoken. In a blog post addressing allyship, he argued that "not speaking out" equals "hurting" the undocumented:

> When you see injustice, it is your responsibility to speak out against it. And if you don't—if you sit in your car, if you stay silent you are helping the forces of hate, you are helping the forces of injustice. . . . What I want to say more than anything else is that, *as an ally, you need to speak out.* If you don't, not only do you hurt the person being unjustly treated, but you hurt yourself as well. You wound yourself. And that when you act, when you go to meetings, when you speak out, you can heal yourself, and by healing yourself you help heal the world.

Noah's statements illustrate several equalization strategies. The running thread through his argument is that citizens and noncitizens are emotionally connected subjects and that speech acts (or the lack thereof) have very real effects on the other. Storytelling as a practice helps create chains of equivalence between allies and DREAMers. No organizational practice clarifies allyship as the process of becoming "unequal equals" better than the "coming out" speeches. In preparation for the 2011 Coming Out rally, it was decided that Rhadia would come out as an ally. The very fact that she received this "privilege" illustrates the evolution that allyship had gone through since the organization's inception. On March 10, 2011, this is what she exclaimed on a makeshift stage in downtown Chicago:

> My name is Rhadia and I am an ally. Growing up I had always felt that the immigration issue was taboo. After the 9/11 attacks, I remember hearing the whispered tones of the elders in the Arab Muslim community discussing undocumented immigrants leaving the country in fear of discrimination and uncertainty. A few years later I was sitting in a computer lab when in an effort to make light of a situation that I found both awkward and confusing, I cracked a joke about my mom trying to find a citizen wife for my brother. My lab partner, Cynthia, started laughing and confided that she was actually in the same boat. In our search to find help for Cynthia's college situation we found ourselves sitting at an immigration event just a mere month later. That day Cynthia came out and spoke about her life as an undocumented student to a room full of people. As her speech was coming to a close we made eye contact. When the reality that her secret was now out in the open hit us, we burst into tears. It was at that specific moment that I remember thinking "if Cynthia can do this, the least Rhadia can do is go to a few meetings from now on." It wasn't my brother or watching friends and families disappear from my community that sprung me into action. It took seeing my friend cry and hearing other undocumented youth come out that made me make that choice. The least I could do is get past any of my personal insecurities and fears. Mama, Baba, I am going to stay out late because I'm going to act, go to meetings, organize, and speak out. And no, you are wrong. This issue does affect my life. Friends, classmates, and professors use the word "undocumented." I can and WILL walk out of this conversation. Your judgments no longer hurt. Staying silent and allowing the forces of hate to continue, that hurts. I am ready. My name is Rhadia. I am an ally, I am unafraid, and I am unapologetic.

The story is built around her Arab immigrant background, the personal connection she developed with her undocumented friend Cynthia, and the impact this encounter had on her subjectivity. The speech demonstrates equalization with the undocumented through empathy, emotion, and friendship and differentiation through distinguishing allies from the undocumented. As such it represents a telling example of the possibility for and potentiality of cross-status alliance politics.

Building Alliances for (and against) Citizenship

Citizenship (or lack thereof) is a strong norm and marker of political belonging and recognition. Undocumented immigrants represent extremely excluded populations. In this light, there is a greater need than ever to develop analytical tools to grasp the prospects of alliance politics. Drawing on the DREAM movement, I show how cross-status alliances can be constructed between citizens and noncitizens. I borrowed insights from cultural sociology and geography to conceive of allyship as a relational boundary-bridging process that involves strategies of equalization and differentiation. On the one hand, equalization requires allies to "unlearn" their citizen privilege, self-submit to IYJL's community norms, and publicly demonstrate their emotional and personal commitment to the cause. On the other hand, power differentials are negotiated through differentiation strategies whereby citizen allies are asked to "step down" during strategic decision making and, conversely, "step up" to play a supportive role by facilitating access to resources and networks. I showed that these strategies, while deployed to uphold cross-status alliances, are inherently in tension with one another as undocumented activists remain wary to avoid being overpowered. The subject position of a citizen ally is therefore never fixed, but rather constantly in flux as it is intersubjectively defined and redefined through community practice.

This case study also entails several insights for other types of alliance politics. First, the durability of intramovement alliances between citizen and noncitizen actors depends on the putting into place of certain dos and don'ts. These community norms serve to give feedback on allies' current behavior as well as guidance for future actions. Second, there are learning processes involved in creating alliances that presuppose flexibility and reflexivity from allies and the capacity of organizations to adapt themselves to changing circumstances. Third, alliances offer opportunities for precarious actors to do a *role reversal* whereby they take the lead and allies get a supportive role. Hence, if precarious actors can determine the rules of the game, it can help to increase their agency and ability to negotiate existing power differentials. Fourth, despite attempts at equalization, a gap remains between the lived experience of those most affected and those who are not directly affected by social injustice. Acknowledging this experiential gap is a prerequisite for allies to embrace an appropriate role within progressive movements for social justice. Finally, precarious actors can strategically rely on the privileges and strengths of their allies to further their cause. While the risk of being overpowered tends to loom over the shoulder, it is a risk worth taking in view of the benefits and enrichment allyship can entail for precarious subjects.

NOTES

1. All italics in parts of oral or written statements in this chapter have been added by the author.

2. All real names were replaced by pseudonyms as per the IRB's request.

3. This section touches upon the ways wherein my positionality as a Caucasian European male on a student visa affected my ethnographic fieldwork. For a more elaborate discussion on the methodological and ethical challenges concerning this fieldwork, see Swerts (2014, 44–88).

REFERENCES

Alba, Richard. 2005. "Bright vs. Blurred Boundaries: Second-Generation Assimilation and Exclusion in France, Germany, and the United States." *Ethnic and Racial Studies* 28, no. 1: 20–49. doi:10.1080/0141987042000280003.

Beamish, Thomas D., and Amy J. Luebbers. 2009. "Alliance Building across Social Movements: Bridging Difference in a Peace and Justice Coalition." *Social Problems* 56, no. 4: 647–76. doi:10.1525/sp.2009.56.4.647.

Bourdieu, Pierre. 1984. *Distinction: A Social Critique of the Judgment of Taste.* Cambridge, Mass.: Harvard University Press.

Chauvin, Sébastien, and Blanca Garcés-Mascareñas. 2014. "Becoming Less Illegal: Deservingness Frames and Undocumented Migrant Incorporation." *Sociology Compass* 8, no. 4: 422–32. doi:10.1111/soc4.12145.

Elwood, Sarah, Victoria Lawson, and Samuel Nowak. 2015. "Middle-Class Poverty Politics: Making Place, Making People." *Annals of the Association of American Geographers* 105, no. 1: 123–43. doi:10.1080/00045608.2014.968945.

Enriquez, Laura. 2014. "'Undocumented and Citizen Students Unite': Building a Cross-Status Coalition through Shared Ideology." *Social Problems* 61, no. 2: 155–74. doi:10.1525/sp.2014.12032.

Gonzales, Roberto G. 2011. "Learning to Be Illegal: Undocumented Youth and Shifting Legal Contexts in the Transition to Adulthood." *American Sociological Review* 76, no. 4: 602–19. doi:10.1177/0003122411411901.

———. 2016. *Lives in Limbo: Undocumented and Coming of Age in America.* Oakland: University of California Press.

Jasper, James M. 1997. *The Art of Moral Protest: Culture, Biography, and Creativity in Social Movements.* Chicago: University of Chicago Press.

Lamont, Michèle, and Christopher Bail. 2007. "Bridging Boundaries: The Equalization Strategies of Stigmatized Ethno-racial Groups Compared." Working Paper No. 154, Centre for European Studies, Harvard University.

Lamont, Michèle, and Virág Molnár. 2002. "The Study of Boundaries in the Social Sciences." *Annual Review of Sociology* 28, no. 1: 167–95. doi:10.1146/annurev.soc.28 .110601.141107.

Lawson, Victoria, and Sarah Elwood. 2014. "Encountering Poverty: Space, Class, and Poverty Politics." *Antipode* 46, no. 1: 209–28. doi:10.1111/anti.12030.

Menjívar, Cecilia. 2006. "Liminal Legality: Salvadoran and Guatemalan Immigrants Lives in the United States." *American Journal of Sociology* 111, no. 4: 999–1037. doi: 10.1086/499509.

Nicholls, Walter J. 2013. *The DREAMers: How the Undocumented Youth Movement Transformed the Immigrant Rights Debate.* Stanford, Calif.: Stanford University Press.

Pratt, Mary Louise. 1991. "Arts of the Contact Zone." *Profession* 91: 33–40.

———. 2002. "Arts of the Contact Zone." In *Professing in the Contact Zone*, edited by Janice Wolff, 1–20. Urbana, Ill.: National Council of Teachers of English.

Shachar, Ayelet. 2009. *The Birthright Lottery: Citizenship and Global Inequality*. Cambridge, Mass.: Harvard University Press.

Snow, David A., E. Burke Rochford, Steven K. Worden, and Robert D. Benford. 1986. "Frame Alignment Processes, Micromobilization, and Movement Participation." *American Sociological Review* 51, no. 4: 464–81. doi:10.2307/2095581.

Spivak, Gayatri. 1988. "Can the Subaltern Speak?" In *Marxism and the Interpretation of Culture*, edited by Cary Nelson and Lawrence Grossberg, 217–33. Champaign: University of Illinois Press.

———. 2004. "Righting Wrongs." *South Atlantic Quarterly* 103, no. 2/3: 523–81.

Swerts, Thomas. 2014. "Non-citizen Citizenship: A Comparative Ethnography of Undocumented Activism in Chicago and Brussels." Ph.D. diss., University of Chicago.

———. 2015. "Gaining a Voice: Storytelling and Undocumented Youth Activism in Chicago." *Mobilization: An International Quarterly* 20, no. 3: 345–60. doi:10.17813/1086-671x-20-3-345.

Van Dyke, Nella, and Holly J. McCammon. 2010. *Strategic Alliances: Coalition Building and Social Movements*. Minneapolis: University of Minnesota Press.

Wimmer, Andreas. 2013. *Ethnic Boundary Making: Institutions, Power, Networks*. New York: Oxford University Press.

Zolberg, Aristide, and Long Litt Woon. 1999. "Why Islam Is Like Spanish: Cultural Incorporation in Europe and the United States." *Politics & Society* 27, no. 1: 5–38. doi:10.1177/0032329299027001002.

CHAPTER 10

Ethnographic Alliance

Hope and Knowledge Building through a South African Story

ANTONÁDIA BORGES

To Thembeni Khubeka (In Memoriam)

In South Africa, "poverty" is a term largely used in English as self-descriptive or as a category for academic analysis. Those who use it to describe themselves do so in an attempt to make the complexity of their lives more intelligible to an interlocutor who generally does not speak their mother tongue, such as landless people summarizing their lives to a passing visitor. In this case it is possible to say that the term's lack of precision is minimalized by the generosity of its user: more important than conceptual exactitude is establishing a dialogue that can lead to transformation. Unfortunately, the same goodwill is not used as broadly among those who speak exclusively English and understand the word "poverty" as a floating signifier to be assigned meaning according to their own interests: sometimes for accusation, other times for commiseration.

Debates about relational poverty such as those found in this volume are urgently needed for analyzing contemporary capitalist experiences in South Africa and many other places, where the category is often used indiscriminately without proper consideration of the underlying economic metrics that are accepted as universal. The constant dispossession that the African continent experiences corresponds to the descriptive and political usurpation that the term "poverty" implies when used by powerful actors. The relationship between capitalist usurpation and the perversion of analytical and descriptive simplifications used to describe the poor occurs alongside several other daily denials. In contrast, relationally appropriating the term involves dedicating oneself to negating the negation imposed by colonialism, both yesterday and today. Negating the negation is the political tonic of intellectual efforts such as those by Frantz Fanon, Archie Mafeje, and many others. This relational appropriation involves a refutation of poverty as an ontology attributed by the oppressor. The simultaneous (1) rejection to conform and (2) investment in creative meaning-making acts constitute what we shall call combative ontology (Mafeje 2001).

The people found in this article dedicate their lives to hopeful practices focused on creating forms of belonging that go against hegemonic models that segregate and annihilate their living potential. We believe that an ethnographic alliance is an exercise as political and theoretical as it is aesthetic and ethical, forming collaborative subjects devoted to authentic interlocution. The people I do research with are nonacademic ethnographers. They are what Mafeje (2001) called *authentic interlocutors*, due to their ability "to decode local 'vernaculars': the encoded local ontology and modes of comprehension" (cf. Adesina 2008, 146; Borges et al. 2015; Nyoka 2012). Following Mafeje's definition, the main objective is to challenge the idea that (1) wealth is one-and-only and universal, but merely unequally distributed, and (2) that equality can be reached by sharing this circumscribed stock of valuables. In short, this chapter's aim is to relate unacknowledged forms of understanding and sensing to neglected ways of living.

I focus on matters related to the house and to the home in order to demonstrate how scarcity is not equal to a shard of a whole but a whole in itself that comprises knowledge and freedom. A shelter, as we will see in the following pages, enfolds subtle paths to understanding notions of space, time, and transformations of being in the world in opposition to ideals of completeness (Nyamnjoh 2015). I especially use the idea of scarcity to demonstrate that people defined by what Mafeje calls their *combative ontology* are not deceived by investments meant to definitively solve their problems, much less their "poverty." They disagree with the overarching developmentalist premise that poverty is merely a matter of not having or *lackness*, and that taming it and accumulating wealth are a universal human drive. Rather, they understand that living means *relating to incompleteness*. The false promise of ending needs, of fighting poverty without mentioning inequality or racism is one more criminal assault made by the state and capitalist apparatuses against their knowledge.

I also want to make evident that storytelling, like any ethnographic account, entails more than a pure description of the world "as it is." On the contrary, it provides concrete means—which, like poetry, are powerful and ethereal at the same time—for building knowledge and hope against a double dispossession: (1) subtracting knowledge and (2) reducing people from what they are to amorphous and anonymous entities, the poor.

Ethnography is not something anthropologists do to a pregiven world; rather ethnography is people acting upon the world and themselves simultaneously, rather than merely living in it. As I develop in this chapter, ethnography is a sort of combative epistemology, a kind of knowledge that makes its own sense out of the struggle to be alive, and therefore is able to continuously produce additional challenging knowledge. It is in this sense that the knowledge and hope produced by those I do research with challenge patronizing projects intended to fight inequality through unreachable redistributive plans. Instead of coping with such chimerical policies, it is widely acknowledged by the nonacademic ethnographers I dialogue with in this chapter that scarcity is not fought in order to reach completeness. Scarcity is fought because fighting is what makes a life meaningful.

In the realm of the so-called poverty studies, such a perspective challenges a supposedly descriptive approach devoted to rendering the world "visible," or in other words, depicting the world as it is, how wealth and opportunities are unevenly distributed and how those with the smallest share live. Instead of accepting an established world order (a capitalist one) and its detraction, ethnographic knowledge on poverty should entail a less epistemologically subjugated politic. It should privilege narratives that challenge hegemonic ways and places where wealth is located and acknowledged. In this sense, storytelling necessarily confronts master narratives in which poverty is only equated to the lack of something that is abundant elsewhere.

I insist that what an academic (me) and her hosts in the field (all ethnographers like myself) produce in terms of knowledge cannot be restricted to what is lacking in their world. Neither is the reason for such a conclusion a defense of alienation, for example, they cannot know and therefore miss what they do not have. This kind of condenscending perspective does not acknowledge other ways of being in the world (or ethnographies or stories) that are not devoted to taming developmentalist mentality. The reason behind my assumption is better defined as hope: a hope that this overpowering and silencing master narrative may one day be defeated.

A day is coming when, instead of being seen as the have-nots, people called poor for their lack of wealth will be seen as knowledge producers, whose main invention will have been challenging those trying to silence their voices with the false promise of equal distribution of wealth. Instead of believing that everyone should live in the same predatory and opulent way, the people I do research with strive with all their might to remain autonomous in their desires. In their daily life, they show how precarity is something developmentalists do not wish to share with them. Not because the wealthy do not want to go down, to submerge, but because they lack something vital: alliances with others who are also engaged on a daily basis in vanquishing death and its perpetrators, who refuse to die, and refuse to be quiet.

Redistribution as a Panacea

South Africa can hardly be pictured as a poor country if we take into account features such as its mineral reserves or its leading role in local and even global geopolitics (Ribeiro et al. 2015). Nevertheless, academic literature from all fields places the country among the most unequal in the world. Inequality in this particular case is very often related to long-lasting racism and income concentration (Gradín 2013; Leibbrandt, Finn, and Woolard 2012). Recent successful economic trajectories of black individuals are rare, and not significant enough to jeopardize this pattern of economic growth and accumulation. Some authors considered the impromptu prosperity of the pejoratively labeled "black diamonds" as evidence that not much has been challenged in the post-apartheid nation in order to subvert perverse logics of consumption and segregation (Neocosmos 2008; Posel 2010). Others go even further, highlighting how nowadays state regulations pave the way to a neoliberal definition of citizenship, associated with consumption and constantly threatened by increasing debt (James 2012). Amid a common though diverse theoretical tradition where there is almost no hope in the transformative role of recent policies of wealth redistribution in South Africa, some authors acknowledge, nevertheless, that it is urgent "to credit and respect the vernacular aspirations to social relationality that are so puzzling to an emancipatory liberalism" (Ferguson 2015).

Redistribution is one of many land reform approaches that has been adopted in South Africa to address present land concentration and social inequality, which is deeply connected to former racist dispensation and various policies of territorial plundering. Land redistribution roughly consists of a program used by the democratic government to offer grants to families that can prove they fit into the farm dweller or labor tenant category, meaning black people who live and work in rural areas legally belonging to mainly white farm owners. Different legal acts have assured farm workers of their right to stay in the housing area they occupied when working for a farm owner, even if their labor is no longer hired (e.g., the Land Reform [Labour Tenants] Act [3 of 1996] and the Extension of Security of Tenure Act [62 of 1997]). For landlords, any new regulation that acknowledges dwellers' rights to land imposes rules that force them to obey labor laws, which apparently make their businesses less profitable and their land "unsalable" due to its litigious component. Families applying for redistribution differ from restitution claimants since they do not have title deeds or other archival evidence to prove previous private property ownership. Instead, they must be able to substantiate a livelihood that is deeply linked to the land in question through labor relations with the (white) owner of the farm where they have been residing (Ntsebeza and Hall 2007).

The singular situation I here deal with has emerged from years of research alongside a black South African family that has been fighting for land as compensation for decades of governmental planned uprooting of its living members and ancestors. Through their housing experiences, it becomes clear that the desired house is intended to shelter a better future that has been denied to the family. But it is also meant to reconfigure a usurping historical narrative of belonging that has restrained—through dispossession, displacement, removals—them from creating a space of existing in which living and dead or "ancestral shades" can dwell together.[1] In their struggle, they have done many experiments in order to build a new world or realm, where space/time causal chains of their confinement could be broken. Where, in short, they could demonstrate that their life goes beyond striving between material scarcity and opulence. In this striving, they do not expect this new world of coexistence and mutuality to be exempted from conflicts. Wherever diversity coexists, adversities are a sign of life itself. Completion is an undesired accomplishment, insofar it alludes to death, the extreme opposite of being alive. Herein we find a challenging definition, where poverty means lacking the resources to fight against death and, therefore, "an ontological object, . . . a theoretical concept and an object of intervention" (Lawson 2012, 2). Thus, wherever death is deliberately produced, such as in cases of obliteration, disappearance, being forgotten, or immobility, there will be poverty.

Chewing Poverty

Certainly not, but probably yes, the birth of a child is an occasion where one is suddenly put face-to-face with uncertainty and unpredictability in a highly punching way.

Langelihle was born in 2011. Her mother, Danisile, is a young Zulu-speaking woman in her mid-twenties who although born in the township of Thokoza (Gauteng province) has spent most of her adult life between the township of Madadeni and her family home in the surrounding rural village of Ingogo (Kwazulu-Natal province).

I have known Danisile since 2007.

The first time I talked to her, she was a teenager, nevertheless strongly in charge of her house duties. At that time, she and her family lived in what they call their home: a homestead of four mud houses located within land owned by a white farmer (Hall 1984). Danisile and her relatives used to refer to the place I mention here as -khaya (home/house), despite the fact that officially the land where it was located belonged to another person.

As with many other farm dwellers, Danisile's family presence inside the farm was not welcome at all. Their daily life was pervaded by various menaces meant to evict them from the farm owner's land. Playfully, people in Ingogo and in the surrounding areas I have been with call the systematic method used by farmers to expel undesired people from their land "constructive eviction." Because the farmer could accuse them of trespassing and legally sue them (as I have seen happen), as a child and later as a teenager, not allowed to take a short cut, Danisile experienced exhausting walks from her house to school in the village and other common challenges farm-dwelling children face in South Africa—long walks, lack of school books and stationary, dehydration, cold, hunger, a single school uniform, and no water at home to wash it properly.

One day in 2010, when greeting Danisile a year after my last visit, I noticed her body had changed. She had put on some weight and her breasts were more pronounced than before. Her father told me she had just had a miscarriage.

I didn't push him or her with any further question; his only concern was his daughter's health and well-being since due to high blood pressure she had lost the baby. Nothing yet could hide a deep sense of sadness from Danisile's eyes in face of the death.

When she got pregnant the second time, she was determined to slow down. Although quite happy with her pregnancy, Danisile could not avoid being worried about her child's future. Luckily her oldest brother (who was recovering from a disease that had also set him in a battle against death) had moved from Thokoza to live in and help his family in the new house they had just moved into.

The ancestors' occupation of that landscape from time immemorial entitled them to pursue state compensation for their family dispossession, especially for the usurpation of their land by an intruder. As a result, after years of waiting (Oldfield and Greyling 2015), they were granted a farm in compensation for their losses. Although their dream to get back their home, the land where the patriarchal homestead is, has not been fulfilled, they were satisfied the farm they received in the redistribution process lies less than ten kilometers from the farm where his forebears are buried. Nineteen family members have settled the claim as a trust, which means they decided they prefer a piece of land they can use as a group rather than splitting small pecuniary compensations individually, which they said would not reunite them: not just the living, but also the dead scattered in different resting sites. The eldest man of the sibling group (Danisile's father) was chosen to move to the newly acquired farm along with his nuclear family in order to keep the land as one piece. It was also his duty to ritually inform their ancestors of their achievement (the farm, the new house) and to ensure they would be made to feel at home and welcome to visit any time. His ancestors and his wife were the first to be informed about the farmland, named after his late father.

While visiting them in June 2011, the toddler, as any of us, was alive but fighting against the cold weather. In the new house in which they were now living, unlike other children in many mud houses in Ingogo, Langelihle was not being warmed around a fire or a paraffin heater inside a shack on the verge of catching fire.

Late in that winter night, while Langelihle sleeps, we are ready to go to bed. Sibongile, daughter of Thembeni, Danisile's oldest sister, offers us some "poverty." We, adult women, decline it. Children enjoy and call this snack "poverty" because it is cheaper than brand-name ones. The chewing of "poverty" is noisy. Sibongile chews it playfully, making fun of all the ambiguities that pervade the occasion. She is in her grandfather's new house for a short visit. Like us, she had experienced an amazing, opulent feast that very same day. Chewing poverty is therefore a performative excess. Nevertheless, she says, when in Johannesburg, where she strives to get through the unending academic pitfalls reserved for black students from rural backgrounds like hers, sometimes there is not even a loaf of bread or eggs to eat in the evening. There she chews poverty to chase away the ghosts of hunger that threaten her.

Poverty—the snack—gives us an opportunity to sensorially, though no less conceptually, experience what it means to be a human being in a world that classifies people as if they were snacks. It is a powerful meaning to see how human beings might be addressed, thought of, and valued as snacks: people are given different values despite being supposedly made of the same substance (like the rise of apartheid after the Universal Declaration of Human Rights was proclaimed) and granted unfair chances to circumvent death (as their family have experienced since they were granted land while their neighbors and other relatives were still landless). We all laugh about the situation.

Despite the freezing weather, all of us were happily well protected in that room. The new house had brick walls and carpet on the floor. A heater was turned on. Electricity, though expensive, was provided by the public energy company ESKOM (which belongs to the South African government) after an endless negotiation to reestablish its delivery to the farmhouse.

The brick house was of course much more a shelter than others they had lived in before: the mud hut or the township house mockery known as a matchbox. However, their surprise and disappointment was immense upon their arrival months earlier when they saw a depleted place. Although wealthy upper- or middle-class people (or brand-name snacks, if we follow the analogy) scarcely ponder that to keep an immense house warm electricity is a necessity, when they arrived there was no power, no wiring, and no operating cold room, which is essential to the butchering process. The issue was not about being able to pay for the bill, but rather the lack of supply from the very same government that had granted them the land. The former owner who had sold the farm to the government swore he handed over the farm "as it was" to the redistribution program. He accused some black families from a vicinity of stealing cables and machineries from the storehouse, seeding disagreement and hate among neighbors whose relations were already under threat due to the unequal reach of compensation policies post-apartheid (Bähre 2007). Government officials were not able to answer why the farm was given to Danisile's family in ruins, notwithstanding the exorbitant amount paid in the negotiation (Chitonge and Ntsebeza 2012).

The interior of the house was also empty. There was no furniture left, no appliance to turn on. The electric pump was no more. There was neither electricity nor running water. In short, no hot bath, no warm food. Cleaning the huge brick house was a Sisyphean task. The stream where the women had to go fetch water was up in the mountains. The water supply was never enough.

It was an error to think they would move to a house where they would no longer worry about carrying water from the stream or collecting wood to cook. They could not believe that behind those red brick walls was hidden the old hardship they have been through their entire life—this time proportionally magnified.

Anyone with taming eyes and a developmentalist mentality who visited them after they moved into the farm would easily blame them for not being "diligent," for "spoiling" the house, for "not caring" about the once spotless garden and fruit trees that surrounded the farmhouse, for "not cleaning" the swimming pool, for "not watching" the flock, for a missing sheep, a sick sheep, a dead sheep. . . . One by one, all the flock they had compulsorily acquired as a "starting pack" was dead a couple of months after their settlement. Danisile's father cursed them: Useless beasts! Despite her and her older brother's efforts to herd the flock, they wandered. Maybe what made them obedient were the electric wires. . . . But, with no electricity, it was hard to ask them to be respectful. Sheep, though supposedly docile, were not goats, an anarchic but resilient animal. Everyone knows it. People from the government know it as well. However, since the farm was a sheep farm, the "starting pack" they got "with" the farm was intended for them to start a business. No matter if the family had no interest in sheep. No matter if there was no electricity on the farm. When they were given the farm, a mandatory "pack" of sheep was handed to them.

After the sheep pack, a second step was taken in the five-year governmental development project for the farm: hydroponic vegetable tunnels. The shining plastic tents that cost a fortune also hid an endless chain of tasks to produce tomatoes, spinach, zucchini, and so forth, which a few retired women from the village would buy on their pension days with coins that would do little to help cope with the increasingly astronomical electricity bill for watering those crops. Again, there was no state-coordinated plan to make their production as relevant as their white neighbors' subsidized maize plantation. Either oblivion or a deliberate plot was behind the production of their farm as a failure. Years later, in 2013, as if following a script, they asked ESKOM to cut their electricity supply in order to negotiate an exorbitant debt they had accumulated after years of overspending to produce veggies that were too expensive for old gogos (as grandmothers are called) from the village to afford.

State Power

Among the many other families who were similarly involved in social movements that fight for land, and also registered and waiting for reparations because their ancestors had been forcefully removed from their lands, this family was honored with a plot of land. It was not the land where their ancestors are buried, but a farm not far from there. Although from a developmentalist point of view (democracy, human rights, humanitarian governance), the fact that they now have a house means they are no longer poor; but it is a mistake to take a solid roof for a home. For them as for other families in the same struggle, a house where the living and the dead can dwell together is by definition an unfilled object: it evolves from continuous engagement in its building as a realm of conviviality rather than a physical place.

The asymmetrical relationship between the family and the power of the state becomes tangible in the continuous and violent relationship with ESKOM. The point here is not simply about how state agencies—the department of land reform, rural development, and public electricity—lack communication because of bureaucratic discordancy. We want to go deeper and question the moral judgments made in South Africa about the beneficiaries of programs that compensate for historical debt, and why so little attention is given to the state as the orchestrator of failure, despair, and often death. Our question is this: is the state a mediator or a buffer, or does it play the hatchet man role?

We know their experience is not an isolated case in South Africa. A market-oriented land reform that benefits mainly those who sell their farms to the government works as a Trojan horse, especially for those families who decide to move into the farms rather than individually sharing the grant (Hall 2004). Family trusts that get their land back—because of their wealth and urban location—and decide to lease it to professional administrators do not face the same constraints. The stigma of "failure" falls on the shoulders of the weakest groups, those who need to live in and from the land they fight for.

On one hand there are land reform detractors who are worried about the low productivity of the properties occupied by black people, who are inexperienced in farm work. These critics fail to recognize the many years some people spent separated from the land, which in ancient times had belonged to their ancestors. On the other hand, there are the governing state powers. It is impossible to ignore the sluggishness and restricted reach of the compensations granted under the pledged land reform program. In the "successful" cases, such as the one being discussed here, huge sums guaranteed good deals for the white landowner and for the large companies that supplied the farm inputs or livestock. Transferring state capital to the market is considered a more appropriate and less flawed strategy in the governmental land transferal processes that address historical debts and misdeeds from the past, especially because the beneficiaries are inexperienced in dealing with large amounts of money, which could lead to the misuse of resources. The state asserts that it must manage the retaking of the lands in a protective manner so as to ensure success. However, as we have seen, this state management is not parsimonious, efficient, or transparent. Regardless, beneficiaries are expected to demonstrate their gratefulness at seeing public funds being spent in their name, albeit in a way that completely ignores their objections. They are not allowed to question state procedures, although their lives continue under threat. In summary, the few successful cases are owed to large state investments in projects that in no way alter the status quo or the development and income distribution model in the country. On the contrary, they ensure that the beneficiaries are to blame when things "go wrong."

In the end, what we have is a continuous production of death—which extends from people, to plantations, to animals. The state's mandate to intervene, to minimize the effects of inequality, opens the door to its installation within people's houses; in other words, their existence and their dependency upon the state are inexorable, in a vicious circle. State intervention to reduce outrageous living conditions are carried on based on a chimerical project of achieving completeness, fulfillment, and social harmony despite the intrinsically unbalanced nature of power relations or, in other words, despite the absolute disparate distribution of chances of living or dying among members of the same society. State intervention makes the state itself meaningful insofar as it reclaims the power to control, to reach completeness (Nyamnjoh 2015). Its legitimacy to intervene toward betterment leads also to the individual blaming of the failing ones.

No Longer Trespassing

Sibongile's mother had joined forces with other women in her family to finalize her parents' wedding. Although they had five children and were married by law, Thembeni's parents had not yet sealed their union according to full tradition.

Being far from their home villages (in a township near Johannesburg, Thokoza, where many families since the 1960s have been living and working—usually after being forcibly moved there after their eviction or as temporary migrant workers) gave them the opportunity to meet each other. However, at the same time, such a location, entangling "the rural in the urban," was also the source of many troubles they faced throughout their lives as "a combination of forced removals . . . Bantu education . . . and of the tightening grip of influx control" (Mamdani 1996, 231). Amazulu, Basotho, and many others were living in urban peripheries to work in the factories and mines or as domestic servants. Her father had been a soccer star whose brilliant career was overruled by the need to work in different factories (Rosa 2011). Her mother used to work as a domestic servant for white families living in the whites-only neighborhoods.

Townships were intended to temporarily house workers. The seasonality of labor providers was ensured by different regulations ranging from short-term labor contracts to the prohibition of civil marriages and governmental regulations of traditional customs regarding weddings. In other words, marital unions outside the "reserves" were strongly repressed. Thembeni's mother and father had children in a marriage that challenged official regulations, a decision that had translated into daily threats to their lives under apartheid.

When the racist, nationalist regime collapsed in the mid-1990s, a succession of battles was enacted in the township where they lived: first the taxi business war and later the so-called East Rand War. According to their memories, an escalating wave of violence among taxi owners disputing marketing and against neighbors who were Zulu took place around their house. At this time her father was no longer working in the local factories. He owned a taxi business, and his main task became driving people from his hometown in Kwazulu-Natal to the township of Gauteng.

One certain day, during the war, his cars were destroyed. Houses were plundered and set ablaze, people were shot dead, and others were raped and violated. ANC militias paved the township streets with blood and flames. The East Rand War is commonsensically understood as a conflict between Zulus (Inkhata's supporters) and Xhosas (ANC supporters): "In South Africa in 1994, narratives of atrocities, told from one side to another, travelled almost instantaneously. In these conflicts, the IFP was often understood simply as 'Zulu' (even though many Zulus were members of the ANC), and from the opposite point of view, it was usually possible to label any ANC group as 'Xhosa'" (Donham 2011, 91). Being a Zulu, her father was supposed to support the Inkhata Freedom Party. He was sure that his family was in danger due to his ambiguous political loyalty—a Zulu supporting the ANC—which could at any time be added to his unconventional marriage to a Sotho woman. On the verge of seeing his family torn apart or even killed, Thembeni's parents went in search of a shelter in his home province (KZN— KwaZulu-Natal), where his family homestead is, inside a white farmer's land. The situation was so desperate that after the assassination of some close acquaintances and neighbors (the boyfriend of Thembeni was shot dead, leaving her and their firstborn daughter Sibongile behind), they decided that it was safer to send each child to live in a different place (in Gauteng and KZN) with other relatives until the turmoil ceased.

After fleeing from Johannesburg, her parents rented a house in another industrial decaying township close to his home village in KZN, Madadeni (Hart 2002). The father worked as a taxi driver locally, while the mother continued cleaning the houses of the whites to make ends meet and raise their small children. Things had calmed down by that moment and they were really committed to move back to Thokoza, where they had their own house. One day, in 1999, because of his increasing commitments to a land struggle social movement, he was not able to join his wife on a trip to Johannesburg.

The father had a very bad feeling that something was not right that day her mother went to Thokoza. His intuition was justified when his fellow taxi drivers came to him with the tragic news that his wife had been killed in a car accident (Lee 2011).

Thembeni's mother and father had not been able to complete the series of ceremonies to seal their marriage in a short period of time, so they celebrated the various stages at different stages in their lives, sometimes with yearlong intervals (Ngubane 1987). But before the rituals had been concluded, her mother had passed away. The entire family experienced years of unrest, partly because their mother had departed so abruptly, and partly because their living conditions were becoming increasingly more precarious. After her departure, they went through an endless period of suffering. Her father's engagement in a land struggle kept him away from any real possibility of earning enough money to raise their children. Finally he decided to move from the Madadeni township rented house to the countryside, where he could rely on his relatives to feed his younger children, but where, at the same time, in retaliation for his political activities in the Social Movement, the farm owner hurled death threats at him and his old father.

There is a line of flight between tradition and modernity, a dimension outside a Cartesian plan, outside of the linear time and space of temporal narratives and modern history. This other dimension requires constant effort/engagement in convivial negotiation that is not understood as harmonious. Moving back to the farm to be closer to relatives who could take care of the children while the father was out leading the landless movement brought relief and despair. Being close to kinfolk did not necessarily mean that his children would be safer. In addition to the farm owner and hunger, there were suspicious and uneasy relatives who saw themselves as stuck in the countryside while a kin member was mobile, doing politics, and being seen—never mind that such recognition implied being arrested and taken to court for political activism. Challenging and cheating death was not a matter of strategy but the result of analytical attention given to the plasticity of reality. For people whose existence relies on what we can call a combative ontology, surviving is a matter of analyzing not a chain of causes but a constellation maze of changing effects.

Colonial legislation created precise codes for regulating weddings in order to limit the flow and reproduction of people and the taxes imposed on their homes and production (Guy 2014; Ross 2015). It could have never predicted that people would marry *in absentia* after they no longer "existed" as contributors (taxpayers), or in other words, that people would exist in a dimension that is illegible to the state and that could not be regulated or governed.

Sibongile, the same one who chewed poverty, had ritually played the role of her deceased grandmother for the final step of her wedding. One day she was ritually behaving like a *makoti* (bride) is supposed to do, the other day traveling to the city to study information technology at the University of Johannesburg, where sometimes she has no food. She is the first woman in her family who went to the university. I admire Sibongile. Years before, when I met her, she was a schoolchild who loved to play soccer and almost cried when her grandpa gave her a pair of sport shoes. At that time I would never have bet that in a couple of years she would be on the verge of being admitted to the university (Ndlovu-Gatsheni 2015). How had a poor girl from Madadeni made her way to Johannesburg to study? I have no doubt that her present happiness and hope are linked to the fact that her grandfather and his siblings got a farm back in redistribution.

Although from a market, profit-oriented perspective the farm activities might be seen as a failure or even a catastrophe (Wolford 2007), literature often misses the effects they have on producing hope in the future—not future as a temporal real, but future as a location where the means to address unpredictability are available. Sibongile's life—a young woman from a matchbox/RDP house in Madadeni who studies in Johannesburg, who comes to her family's home in Ingogo on her holidays to perform her grandmother, who chews poverty before sleeping in a warm, square, carpeted bedroom in a farmhouse—is a puzzle to all who want to engage with those who do cope with uncertainty in contemporary South Africa.

Caught in a transitioning world, Sibongile chews poverty while dreaming about being a professional, driving an Audi, partying in Ibiza. She shares her dreams with me: "I wish my family to be proud of me: my grandpa, my mother." I try to say to her they are already proud. She smiles. She knows they love her, but she wants to be admired. Thembeni also knows it, and because of her concern about her daughter's future, she has been committed to finish her father and mother's wedding. As an avatar of her deceased grandmother, Sibongile was somehow also "frozen" in the middle of a ritual process they, as a family, have the obligation to properly seal. Sibongile's future was probably at stake if her mother had not made her parents' wedding happen.

Thembeni sealed her parents' wedding after overcoming numerous obstacles in her own life, even without having consummated any union with Sibongile's father. The historical facts state that the marriage was not possible because he had been killed while both were still teenagers, soon after she gave birth to her daughter. He had been murdered in the aforementioned wars, when the family lived in Thokoza township. Maybe someday someone will think about marrying them, thus joining the living and the dead on both sides of the family. Whoever does it, however, will face significant challenges, maybe even greater than those faced by Thembeni in sealing the union between her living father and dead mother.

Sibongile's present and her desired future allow us to prospectively think about her baby niece sleeping next to us (Chevalier 2010). Following White's (2010) argument, it is plausible to state that Langelihle wellness was reached through a ceremonial tour de force in which her cousin's performance was fundamental. We can also assume that a year before, when Danisile had a miscarriage, neither her mundane nor her transcendental world was being addressed and experienced in what is locally considered a proper way to pave a cheerful future. She and her family were fighting for their land; her deceased mother was not pleased since her wedding had never been concluded. How could her children, like Danisile, be cheerful? In a hopeless world, how could a new baby be raised in peace?

The case explored here would be uninteresting but for two aspects (Azevedo 2013). First is the fact that the ceremony took place in the new house, on the farm the family received in a redistribution case after more than ten years of waiting. The wait had not been passive, in that Thembeni's father had been involved in a social movement that fought for land. However, neither was it decisive, in that many militants in the movement were not as lucky. The second aspect is that Thembeni's mother had died several years earlier. Although there is abundant literature about rituals by proxy, I would stress here how this family's way of life constantly challenges the illusion portrayed by cynical political actions intended to solve problems once and for all. Although one could say that the farmhouse was sine qua non to completing the ritual, that conclusion would be a mistake. Thembeni's father and Danisile are certain the same thing would have happened in other circumstances. What is important to understand is that although the rituals had been concluded, their problems had not.

Three years after finalizing her parents' wedding, Thembeni also passed away. One night, when I was in Brazil, I received a message from Danisile on Facebook. It was four forty the morning of June 6, 2014. Danisile wrote: "Thembeni is very very sick. I'm scared."

I asked her if there was anyone close by who could take her to a hospital. I offered to help in any way I could, despite the distance between us. My reaction was that of someone who could dodge death. However, a few hours later, at five after eight, Danisile sent another message: "Dudu passed away." Several months passed and she wrote me again, saying her father was very ill. At one point she asked herself, "Is this God living or dead?" Another time she said, "I feel like crying . . . can't bear to see my father like [this] . . . wish God will stop taking my loved ones away from me."

Fortunately her father recovered and did not die. This time, for now, life had triumphed. If there is any lesson to learn, maybe it could be summarized in the following manner. A continuous fight with the incommensurable and with unpredictabilities from enmeshed realms—erroneously and neatly separated in two, the temporal (like the state or threatening diseases) and atemporal (like invisible spells of envy or recalcitrant demands from ancestral spirits)—shows us that a relational approach to poverty should inscribe and take into account a vast array of experiences that challenge current and more common concepts of poverty. Unpredictability is part of being alive. Escaping it does not mean pursuing an unreachable and illusory state of plenty. What people need to live are the conditions for addressing their problems. To do so in the context of our research means being mobile (Tutuola 1952; Nyamnjoh 2015), having the freedom of movement to cross realms that are apparently uncrossable—whether the mundane (such as the borders of private property) or the atemporal (such as the borders that separate the living and the dead).

Despite our engagement, we cannot escape the trap: for us in general, the problem of exclusion is summarized as being outside politics, which keeps us from questioning the pertinence of representative politics as defined in supposedly democratic contexts where the vernacular is obliterated by the presumed efficiency of the colonial-liberal administration language. The political activities of the father of the Kubheka family within the social movement are completely entangled with both his daughters' and his ancestors' illegible political activities that unfold outside the supposedly only acknowledged realm where rights must be conquered and poverty must be fought. The effects of all these intangible, illegible, invisible politics are undeniably powerful in their ability to react to the silencing approaches that reduce the meaning of their lives to what is known (lack of wealth) instead of acknowledging what inspires them: an unbreakable engagement in producing knowledge and hope that goes beyond the modern and colonial hegemonic stranglehold on their thoughts and actions.

In examining the experiences of the women who belong to the Kubheka family, I sought to demonstrate that their sense of insufficiency and loss was not determined by modern apparatuses or institutions (state and market). Neither were the (partial) solutions that had been forged to deal with the fragility of existence limited to what these instances provided.

The attention Thembeni gave to the past and the effort she made to marry her parents seemed to tell me about politics in other terms. By pushing for their union, she challenged the segregation and the violence that had separated them during apartheid. Yet the most important aspect of the politics she defines or is engaged in is the awareness that there is no definitive intervention that can end all problems. Problems are infinite because they are related to the issues of life and death.

The unpredictability of existence places the continuity of hope at risk. And the state often makes it impossible to have the means to forge ways out of oppression—which leads to the death of any combative ontology.

Ethnography as a Combative Epistemology

Ethnography remains a term permeated by mystery and well-known secrets. I do not mean definitions of ethnography as a method or tool. I mean the broad gamut of approaches that have one thing in common: defending ethnography as a theory (Peirano 2014). I especially disagree with the adaptations made by those such as Gibson-Graham (2014) regarding Geertz's concept of thick description. I disagree because I do not believe the facts are small, or that the issues are large. Like Obarrio (2015, 276), I believe in how easily "the violence of abstraction . . . effaces each singular subjectivity and life-world." I prefer to fight against the illusive idea of a theory that embraces everything. At the same time, like the cited authors, I appreciate notions of "performative ontology" that ethnography uses to describe "ethical acts." The same happens with the notion of Archie Mafeje's "combative ontology." In his writings against anthropology and its colonial legacy, Mafeje refuses a fundamental concept: culture (Mafeje 2001). According to him, culture is a panacea that allows social scientists to juggle two irreconcilable issues: particularism and universalism. Poverty as a concept faces similar challenges: it is at once considered a particular experience and a universal phenomenon, and both are trapped in a single capitalist narrative. In refusing the conceptual wild card of culture, Mafeje realizes that what makes people different from one another are their incommensurable ethnographies (or modes of understanding and therefore being in the world), and not an inventoriable set of things that ideally circumscribe a specific society.

Likewise, I argue an ethnographic theoretical stance is built upon the intellectual experiments we have been engaged in, along with those with whom we do research (Borges 2009). The "story" of the women from the Kubheka family introduced in this chapter does not even come close to summarizing their story and the possibilities of narrating it (Borges 2013). It is more about a possible engagement or, better said, an analytical engagement that was made possible by my interlocution with them and their ethnographies over a period of years, and by the academic literature that incessantly produces other ethnographies. More than theoretical, an ethnography is necessarily a meeting point, a collision, with other ethnographies. Narratives begin with what is in hand (analytical facts and artifacts produced by our interlocutors inside and outside academia), and their limitations are established by what is not in hand (what has happened in the past that we don't know about, or the "twists" of other ethnographical theories that we could have dialogued with but didn't . . . yet).

This chapter builds an open but extremely solid narrative that depends on alliances with those who entrusted us with their stories who can continue intervening in the narrative, and with those who are faced with the narrative and observe the possibility of transforming and condensing it. All the people who have hosted me during my fieldwork articulate epistemological investments and different struggles to remain alive—as living people or as ancestral shades. As we have seen, combative epistemology transforms our understanding of what would otherwise be dismissed. Poverty politics is not a politics of poverty, but a politics of hope and alliance. The people I am ethnographically allied to believe that the way to be and become truly alive is by rising against the silencing cloud that overshadows their forms of existence. For them, chewing poverty is doing politics against living on crumbs.

NOTES

Vicky Lawson and Sarah Elwood have given fundamental support and vivid inspiration to this chapter. I also acknowledge the colleagues who took part in the writing retreat, whose contributions have been decisive in this final cut. Earlier versions of the chapter benefited from debates with Divine Fuh, Heike Becker, Jill Haring, Richa Nagar, and Sophie Oldfield, to whom I am thankful as well.

1. The term "shades" refers to deceased kin members with whom the living can continue to talk daily if the conditions for appropriate rituals are ensured.

REFERENCES

Adesina, Jo. 2008. "Archie Mafeje and the Pursuit of Endogeny: Against Alterity and Extroversion." *Africa Development* 33, no. 4: 133–52. doi:10.4314/ad.v33i4.57349.

Azevedo, Aina. 2013. "Mulheres de Zuluness. Casa e casamento entre a família Khubeka falante de isiZulu na África do Sul." Tese de doutorado, Universidade de Brasília.

Bähre, Erik. 2007. "Reluctant Solidarity: Death, Urban Poverty and Neighbourly Assistance in South Africa." *Ethnography* 8, no. 1: 33–59. doi:10.1177/1466138107076136.

Borges, Antonádia. 2009. "Explorando a Noção de Etnografia Popular: Comparações e transformações a partir dos casos das cidades-satélites brasileiras e das townships sul-africanas." *Cuadernos de Antropología Social* 29: 23–42.

———. 2013. "Mulheres e Suas Casas: Reflexões etnográficas a partir do Brasil e da África do Sul." *Cadernos Pagu (UNICAMP. Impresso)* 40: 197–227.

Borges, Antonádia, et al. 2015. "Pós-Antropologia: As críticas de Archie Mafeje ao conceito de alteridade e sua proposta de uma ontologia combative." *Sociedade e Estado* 30: 347–69.

Chevalier, Sophie. 2010. "Les Black Diamonds Existent-ils? Médias, consommation et classe moyenne noire en Afrique du Sud." *Sociologies Pratiques* 20, no. 1: 75–86. doi:10.3917/sopr.020.0075.

Chitonge, Herman, and Lungisile Ntsebeza. 2012. "Land Reform and Rural Livelihood in South Africa: Does Access to Land Matter"? *Review of Agrarian Studies* 2, no. 1: 87–111.

Donham, Donald. 2011. *Violence in a Time of Liberation: Murder and Ethnicity at a South African Gold Mine, 1994*. Durham, N.C.: Duke University Press.

Ferguson, James. 2015. *Give a Man a Fish: Reflections on the New Politics of Distribution*. Durham, N.C.: Duke University Press.

Gibson-Graham, J. K. 2014. "Rethinking the Economy with Thick Description and Weak Theory." *Current Anthropology* 55, no. S9: S147–53. doi:10.1086/676646.

Gradín, Carlos. 2013. "Race, Poverty and Deprivation in South Africa." *Journal of African Economies* 22, no. 2: 187–238. doi:10.1093/jae/ejs019.

Guy, Jeff. 2014. "Colonial Transformations and the Home." In *Ekhaya: The Politics of Home in KwaZulu-Natal*, edited by Megan Healy Clancy and Jason Hickel, 23–47. Durban: UKZN Press.

Hall, Martin. 1984. "The Myth of the Zulu Homestead: Archaeology and Ethnography." *Africa* 54, no. 1: 65–79. doi:10.2307/1160144.

Hall, Ruth. 2004. "A Political Economy of Land Reform in South Africa." *Review of African Political Economy* 31, no. 100: 213–27. doi:10.1080/0305624042000262257.

Hart, Gillian Patricia. 2002. *Disabling Globalization: Places of Power in Post-apartheid South Africa*. Berkeley: University of California Press.

James, Deborah. 2012. "Money-Go-Round: Personal Economies of Wealth, Aspiration and Indebtedness." *Africa* 82, no. 1: 20–40. doi:10.1017/s0001972011000714.

Lawson, Victoria. 2012. "Decentring Poverty Studies: Middle Class Alliances and the Social Construction of Poverty." *Singapore Journal of Tropical Geography* 33, no. 1: 1–19. doi:10.1111/j.1467-9493.2012.00443.x.

Lee, Rebekah. 2011. "Death 'On the Move': Funerals, Entrepreneurs and the Rural-Urban Nexus in South Africa." *Africa* 81, no. 2: 226–47. doi:10.1017/s0001972011000040.

Leibbrandt, Murray, Arden Finn, and Ingrid Woolard. 2012. "Describing and Decomposing Post-apartheid Income Inequality in South Africa." *Development Southern Africa* 29, no. 1: 19–34. doi:10.1080/0376835x.2012.645639.

Mafeje, Archie. 2001. *Anthropology in Post-independence Africa: End of an Era and the Problem of Self-Redefinition*. Nairobi: Heinrich Böll Foundation.

Mamdani, Mahmood. 1996. *Citizen and Subject: Contemporary Africa and the Legacy of Late Colonialism*. Princeton, N.J.: Princeton University Press.

Ndlovu-Gatsheni, Sabelo. 2015. "Decoloniality in Africa: A Continuing Search for a New World Order." *Australasian Review of African Studies* 36, no. 2: 22–50.

Neocosmos, Michael. 2008. "The Politics of Fear and the Fear of Politics: Reflections on Xenophobic Violence in South Africa." *Journal of Asian and African Studies* 43, no. 6: 586–94. doi:10.1177/0021909608096655.

Ngubane, Harriet. 1987. "The Consequences for Women Payments in a Society with Patrilienal Descent." In *Transformation of African Marriage*, edited by David J. Parkin and David Nyamwaya, 173–82. Manchester: Manchester University Press.

Ntsebeza, Lungisile, and Ruth Hall. 2007. *The Land Question in South Africa: The Challenge of Transformation and Redistribution*. Cape Town: HSRC Press.

Nyamnjoh, Francis B. 2015. "Incompleteness: Frontier Africa and the Currency of Conviviality." *Journal of Asian and African Studies* 52, no. 3: 253–70. doi:10.1177/0021909615580867.

Nyoka, Bongani. 2012. "Mafeje and "Authentic Interlocutors": An Appraisal of His Epistemology." *African Sociological Review* 16, no. 1: 4–18.

Obarrio, Juan. 2015. "A Matter of Time." *Hau: Journal of Ethnographic Theory* 5, no. 3: 273–84.

Oldfield, Sophie, and Saskia Greyling. 2015. "Waiting for the State: A Politics of Housing in South Africa." *Environment and Planning A* 47, no. 5: 1100–1112. doi:10.1177/0308518x15592309.

Peirano, Mariza. 2014. "Etnografia Não é Método." *Horizontes Antropológicos, Porto Alegre* 20, no. 42: 377–91.

Posel, Deborah. 2010. "Races to Consume: Revisiting South Africa's History of Race, Consumption and the Struggle for Freedom." *Ethnic and Racial Studies* 33, no. 2: 157–75. doi:10.1080/01419870903428505.

Ribeiro, Gustavo Lins, Tom Dwyer, Antonádia Borges, and Eduardo Viola. 2015. *Social, Political and Cultural Challenges of the BRICS*. Bamenda, Cameroon: Langaa Research and Publishing Common Initiative Group.

Rosa, Marcelo. 2011. "Mas eu fui uma estrela do futebol! As incoerências sociológicas e as controvérsias sociais de um militante sem-terra sul-africano." *Mana* 17, no. 2 (2011): 365–94.

Ross, Fiona C. 2015. "Raw Life and Respectability: Poverty and Everyday Life in a Postapartheid Community." *Current Anthropology* 56, no. S11: S97–107. doi:10.1086/682078.

Tutuola, Amos. 1952. *The Palm-Wine Drinkard and His Dead Palm-Wine Tapster in the Dead's Town*. London: Faber & Faber.

White, Hylton. 2010. "Outside the Dwelling of Culture: Estrangement and Difference in Postcolonial Zululand." *Anthropological Quarterly* 83, no. 3: 497–518. doi:10.1353/anq.2010.0000.

Wolford, Wendy. 2007. "Land Reform in the Time of Neoliberalism: A Many-Splendored Thing." *Antipode* 39, no. 3: 550–70. doi:10.1002/9781444306750.ch7.

CHAPTER 11

Theater, Hunger, Politics

Beginning a Conversation

DIA DA COSTA AND RICHA NAGAR

In this conversation we offer hunger as a critical conceptual link in articulating the relationship between theater and politics. We begin with a foundational question: when the meanings of the "political" are as diverse and shifting as the sites of engagement from and through which political theater is mobilized, then *what makes political theater political?* As coauthors whose associations with theater in India are grounded in different histories, locations, relationships, and methodologies, we are guided by a shared investment in political theater as an embodied, collective critique that grapples relationally with transgressions, pedagogies, and solidarities. Such critique enables fresh theorizations and interventions while also troubling the preexisting terrain on which discursive and performative practices pertaining to poverty politics and alliances are created, circulated, absorbed, and remade.

The conceptual lever of "hunger" reimagines views of hunger as the archetypal sign of poverty alleviated by income to buy food. By contrast, the diverse worlds of theater and politics we address in this chapter highlight hunger as a multidimensional bodily experience that is simultaneously material, ideological, creative, and affective. Rather than establish a simplistic equivalence or hierarchy among different types of hungers, we advance a relational conception of poverty where hunger is an intangible ontological phenomenon that is entangled in, and constitutive of, material relations and material-psychological-spiritual-political effects. In the first two sections Dia Da Costa explains that activist performers' formulation of hunger for theater speaks of politics in terms of willful resistance and unanticipated revolt, of a dance between critical challenge and ambivalent subjection. In the subsequent notes from an ongoing journey, Richa Nagar elaborates on political theater as a site for co-ownership of stories and theories through their collective coevolving (re)interpretation, and the challenges of sustaining a hunger called theater. Through different, overlapping, and complementary modes of engagement and writing, we consider how theatrical practices reimagine the politics of caste, community, and poverty by articulating the hunger for political potential, creativity, and unanticipated relationships across divisive hierarchies and gulfs. In embracing fluid and open-ended practices of narration, we search for coauthored articulations that refuse to fix the entangled meanings of hunger, politics, and theater while also pushing for fresh reimagining(s) of alliance politics.

A Hunger Called Theater

I have often heard activist performers speak of their hunger for theater. Before he became a full-time rural activist performer, landless agricultural worker Pradeep Sardar balanced the need for money with the need for doing theater. He said, "Yes I can earn more but, in life, I am not pursuing money alone. I like this [theater] work. I have other hungers than money. . . . I want to . . . create more people who will think of people." Another activist performer, Ankur Garange, a resident of an informal settlement in Ahmedabad city, spoke of acute experiences of hunger and then his initial awe of theater: "a new hunger was born whose name was theatre" (Budhan Theatre 2011). Kalpana Gagdekar, from the same settlement, spoke of her compulsion to continue doing theater when her father-in-law was in jail and her household struggled to make ends meet. Through it all, "we just kept doing theatre" (Budhan Theatre 2011, 13).[1]

Indeed, the felt reality of what Pradeep, Ankur, and Kalpana meant largely escaped me due to my unwillingness to do theater. Initially, I interpreted the hunger for theater as a passionate but metaphorical expression, that is, a *representation* of a desire for art as politics, not art or politics itself. I knew theater was more than a safety-valve source of hope in the face of hopelessness; nonetheless, I worried about treating this hunger as a real hunger, on par with hunger for the *real* food that feeds bellies and reproduces life, labor, and capital. Yet, diversifying my conceptual tools to understand the hunger for theater as discursive subjection, ideological manipulation, or representation still shortchanged the vitality and gravity of what people meant. Over time, I began to hear "hunger for theater" as articulating a drive, an understanding, and an attachment. I became attuned to what Nagar and Geiger call "situated solidarities," thereby taking seriously people's hunger for creative practice as theoretical and political formulation, rather than as raw material to be theorized by experts through "appropriate" frameworks and channels of knowledge production (Sangtin Writers and Nagar 2006; Nagar 2014).

The hunger for theater signals repertoires of embodied knowledge that are singular, enduring, and powerful for requiring presence as means of transmission (Taylor 2003). Rather than being interpreted against theoretical debates that secure their own categories of knowledge, this hunger must be taken seriously as knowledge, art, and politics, in its own right. This is not just hopeful vitality, but a yearning for creativity coming from the very depths of despair, arising out of living and laboring under heteropatriarchal, colonial capitalism. To hear only romantic hope or tragic despair in this phrase can be a mark of emotional inertia or inertness to certain sources of embodied knowledge. Our conception of relational poverty knowledge thus takes a page out of Spivak's championing of aesthetic education as potentially producing "an uncoercive rearrangement of desires" when the metropolitan subject learns to learn from the subaltern. Accordingly, taking hunger for theater seriously involves "suspend[ing] oneself in the text [lifeworld] of the other," refusing to think of oneself as the better, indispensable, educated, enabled person who can right wrongs and theorize artistic and political practice, and instead training ourselves to "learn from the singular and unverifiable" (Spivak 2004, 532). In short, we view hunger for theater as an ontological, viscerally material phenomenon, ensconced in material relations and with material effects, and simultaneously felt as intangible, "singular and unverifiable."

This hunger is not a deferred need that kicks in once real hunger is assuaged, as in the standard model of recreation after social reproduction. Livelihoods that earn a dollar a day do feed hunger, to use the minimalistic terms of the World Bank. However, art and political action do not necessarily follow from satiated stomachs. Ultimately, the transition narrative "if fed, then art" and the safety-valve, compensatory narrative of "when hopeless, then art" are entirely inadequate. Although scholars from Gramsci to Lorde have long critiqued the base-superstructure perspective that grants these narratives progressive legitimacy, the minimalist ways in which "hunger" is conventionally taken up endure, thereby upholding the violence of development projects that are blind to the soul and creativity of life, when they aim to satiate hunger through earnings of a dollar a day. Such minimalism feeds on bourgeois assumptions about "knowing" the primary needs of the poor and reverberates within governmental surveys on poverty and within fields such as development studies, where despite copious debates and capacious frameworks, a lingering minimizing of what counts as *real* hunger remains. Against this emotional barrier and ideological heel digging, we take seriously subaltern politico-aesthetic yearnings as sites of reimagining caste and poverty politics.

Hunger for theater is not equivalent to hunger for food or money as a materiality apprehended within the calculus of exchange value and the social reproduction of labor power. Yet, the materiality of this creative hunger is commensurable with hunger for food because both hungers are experienced bodily, in immeasurable, albeit in different kinds of intangible ways. Not equivalence, but commensurability and coexistence deconstruct the distinction between hungers momentarily upheld here. In fact, the distinction undermines the significance of the coexisting materiality of creative survival as a mode of being, instead of a secondary accessory of existence. Hunger for theater feeds a hunger for serendipitous creativity through which people most acutely subject to the disciplinary and divisive violence of social reproduction "create more people who will think of people." It signals desire for renewed living with "dormant structures" of ethics and responsibility within subaltern lifeworlds that tend to get epistemically exiled by colonial capitalism (Spivak 2004, 558).

In consuming and nourishing the mind-body-soul, the hunger for theater *becomes* an affect emanating from a body's capacity to be moved by and to move (Massumi 2002) creative constructions of art and politics.[2] Here, the body (not easily separable from mind or soul) is a vehicle of material *and* immaterial experience, the latter variously felt as divine, virtual, or potential experience. Art and politics are of course themselves identifiable by the capacity to move people and social relations, respectively, in the midst of all that corrupts and congeals the ultimately unstable categories of art and politics. A hunger called theater points to a hunger for all that makes life serendipitous in the face of one's apparent total captivity to unifying logics and structures of power. It bears witness to the ambivalent, unsettling, and uncertain (often unverifiable) potential that makes life a moving, unforeseeable becoming, still worthy of being called life, rather than a still life that is prefigured as ever captive to current configurations of power and current imaginings of how transformation might come.

However, capitalism is also a social, relational, moving, colonizing formation—a "one that is a many"—because it too has a hunger for the kind of serendipity that emerges from other normative systems of value and a voracious appetite for creative potential that can constitute new frontiers of value (Gidwani 2008). Nonetheless, the history of capital/labor does not subsume the history of creativity itself. Attending to theater as a hunger is driven by the conviction that the labor of creative practice is worthy of being explored in terms of the pleasures, desires, and affects that make life dynamic and move bodies into creative becoming *as much as* for how it potentially spells reproduction. If Gramsci emphasized the ongoing intellectual (de)construction of hegemony and counter-hegemony, our inflection on embodied creativity and affect suggests critique and ambivalence. We see a *dance* of capture, collusion, critique, and creative flights that demands that we seriously rethink poverty politics by recognizing that performances and pleasures are simultaneously "scenes of subjection" and occasions for momentary flights from captivity (Hartman 1997). As a process of embodied, soulfully felt knowledge production, theater is inseparable from poetic, ethical, historical, political, and theoretical knowledge production. As such, the hunger for theater signifies a *resistance* where "politics" is defined by the transgression of social norms: Pradeep transgresses the normalized desire to prioritize money as the only survival story about the poor. Queering reproductive temporality and its normative geographies (Halberstam 2005), he lives with an ontological hunger for a new social future where a willful "waste" of potential labor time spent on doing theater fosters empathy and care among people, while refusing the "if fed, then art" or "when hopeless, then art" formulations of leftist politics and critical development epistemologies.

Simultaneously, Pradeep's hunger for theater also expresses what Georgis contrasts as the *revolt* of queer affects where "politics" is defined by a nonintentional feeling that wells up, "an unpredictable affect that refuses to live by social logic" (Georgis 2013, 21). Here, the hunger for theater is a serendipitous political that emerges in those affects that "arrive as a surprise or an interruption to the symbolic" and have the potential of "present[ing] an emotional occasion for learning" (Georgis 2013, 16). Pradeep's hunger for theater not only satiates a consciously willed politics of resistance where teaching and learning involve transgressing and imagining emancipation from the violent "community of money" that locks his survival to the social reproduction of capitalism itself. It also allows for learning from enduring the sufferings inherent to the violence of money, which insist on leaving him little room for other hungers than money. Pradeep's story *expresses ambivalence* in relations of subjection and power: how *to* suffer and live with the violence of money (i.e., revolt expressed by doing theater) and not just how to overcome suffering (i.e., overcome the violence of money through resistance). An aesthetic education with no guarantees studied in practice reveals that the rearrangement of desires is tentative, not definitive — an unending dance between creative enduring and overcoming of suffering.

Potential Politics

When framed in terms of relational poverty politics, a hunger called theater foregrounds political potential by underscoring the unanticipated elements of creativity in relation to the hegemonic capture of creativity. Take, for example, Budhan Theatre, a community-based performance troupe among the Chhara of Ahmedabad, Gujarat. This troupe resists the stigma of criminal tribe status accorded them in colonial India and still manifest in their second-class citizenship and livelihoods of liquor production and thievery. Colloquially referred to by police and caste superiors as "born criminals," Chhara face severe discrimination in the job market, and often get arrested for crimes they did not commit.

The performers of Budhan Theatre willfully articulate Chhara marginality and transgress statist and casteist accounts of Chhara criminality. In thus *resisting* dominant terms of Chhara citizenship, excluded citizens enable their interpellation by postcolonial citizenship. In addition, Alok Gagdekar captures how political theater generates politics as *revolt* and not just resistance: "Before 1998 [when I joined Budhan Theatre] it was not necessary for me to think about society because at that time I had much to think about. Father's illness, debt, the circus of earning daily meals — I was caught up in all these things. But when I juxtaposed Budhan Sabar's circumstances with a fresh look at my own, I found the knots in me untied" (Budhan Theatre 2011, 9–10). Alok is captive to the violence of money, debt, illness, and earning daily meals. Although he sees the hunger for food in cynical terms (it is a "circus"), being captive to the circus of social reproduction means that Alok is not prompted "to think about society." Hunger for food consumed Alok until theater about Budhan Sabar (a person from another tribe) taught him about notorious police brutality, custodial death, and a rights-based struggle for criminal tribe communities. Alok describes a becoming through theater, an unannounced, creative politics of revolt emerging through performance. By recognizing individual suffering in social terms, his willful resistance onstage conditions the production of a revolt experienced through theater, that is, a serendipitous, unanticipated sensual epiphany and political line of flight that affectively refuses being locked into the circus of earning money enough for daily food. This affective refusal of total captivity to social reproduction is effectively manifest in Alok's recurring hunger for theater. Theater generates an emotional occasion for learning, including novel desires and ways of seeing himself, Chhara history, and politics.

Alok's epiphanies do not protect creative potential from turning into cultural capital and governmentality. He went on to become the first Chhara graduate of India's prestigious National School of Drama. Indeed, Budhan Theatre's politics of resistance willfully mobilizes belonging via normative vectors of citizenship and cultural capital. But this embrace of mainstream inclusion also manifests revolts that move people to exceed lives ruled by vicious circles and intractable conditions of normative citizenship and social reproduction, by reminding them of coexisting and effaced hungers.

Consider a final example of what makes political theater political, beyond individual experiences. Gujarat is well-known as the laboratory of violent contemporary Hindu fundamentalism. Here, Muslims are subject to extreme discrimination and often presumed guilty of terrorism. In 2002, Chharas participated in riots mobilized by right-wing Hindu cadres, municipal leaders, and politicians, killing Muslims and destroying Muslim property. On this occasion, Chhara were not just dupes of Hindu leaders, but active participants in riots mobilized on the basis of ordinary patronage networks to which Chhara had already been subject. Police informants, policemen, "social workers," musclemen, and politicians regularly seek bribes from Chhara, destroy liquor stills, and ultimately restore and protect illegal liquor production securing Chhara social reproduction. These are also the very people who mobilized votes and foot soldiers for riots on behalf of the Hindu right. The intersections of a violent and patronizing Hindu fundamentalist and neoliberal state are apparent in these divisive, violent, and deadly majoritarian patronage politics. Riot and patronage politics keeps the surplus population alive while killing minorities within it, thereby reconciling the contradictions of contemporary neoliberal capitalism that make "welfare for all" an impossibility (Berenschot 2011). Job discrimination against them ensures that Chhara cannot easily access noncriminal livelihoods, while police brutality and protection lock Chhara into criminal livelihoods, which played out in Chhara violence against Muslims in 2002. Chharas are thus held captive to modes of survival that reproduce their stigma and the violence against Muslims unless they can nurture alternative livelihoods.

In this context, creative economy jobs appear to be alternative livelihoods in respectable, clean, socially just jobs, even though some of these opportunities are tied up in violent aesthetic visions and divisive political histories informed by Hindu fundamentalist reinventions of heritage and bourgeois articulations of clean, green, "world-class" cities (Da Costa 2015, 2016). While Budhan Theatre explicitly mobilizes a politics of resistance against criminalized livelihoods by nurturing networks, livelihoods, and aspirations for such creative economy jobs, theater praxis also occasions moments of unanticipated revolt and creative modes of belonging and becoming that can provide a line of flight outside the viciously intersecting violence of masculinist Hindu fundamentalism and neoliberalism in contemporary Ahmedabad.

For instance, Budhan Theatre's adaptation of Jean Genet's play, *Another Accident*, embarked on a significant reconstruction of community criminality by satirizing police brutality against Muslims, instead of focusing on police brutality against Chharas. In the political context of Ahmedabad, where expressing solidarity with Muslims has been largely rendered impossible, and considering Chhara involvement in anti-Muslim violence, Budhan Theatre's numerous public performances of this play are a revolt against divisive violence as the primary mode of relationality defining poverty and caste politics within Hindu nationalist terms of belonging and citizenship. In one of their first performances, they invited twenty Muslim POTA families to watch the play. "POTA families" is an administrative, and now colloquial, designation for (disproportionately Muslim) families accused under the Prevention of Terrorism Act of 2002. POTA was instituted after the Indian Parliament was attacked that year, but repealed in 2004 after the discovery of its misuse by state governments to persecute political opponents.

So commonplace is the terrorization that the accused refer to themselves as POTA families, and next of kin avoid interacting with POTA families to evade accruing stigma and criminality by proxy. Budhan Theatre is exemplary in countering such normalization publicly. "POTA family" members watching the Budhan play cried and exchanged stories with Chharas about their respective patrons of criminality and stigma. Budhan Theatre's revolt craves and constructs a space for Chhara and Muslim becoming together, which is especially significant considering Chhara involvement in killing Muslims. Again, this kind of line of flight speaks of the "political" in political theater as both resistance and revolt, resistance against the prevailing terms of Hindu majoritarian patronage politics that makes Chharas (suspected) rioters and killers. But there is also a revolt at work here, a queer hunger to construct solidarity with Muslims against the social logic in Gujarat that makes hatred of Muslims the condition of survival, belonging, and community building. Where space for solidarity with Muslims has been structurally extinguished, Muslim and Chhara bodies hunger for and manifest an unanticipated revolt that articulates the possibilities for a different relationality emerging from shared tears and stories of criminalization.

The shared tears and tales may not accomplish something as definitive as lasting solidarity against divisive violence, but the despair emerging from mutual fear and obstinate divisions is momentarily overcome. The hunger for theater speaks of the need to creatively realize on- and offstage the virtual possibility of giving ordinary human regard to mutually suspected Muslim and Chhara killers, despite such regard being socially inadmissible within the logic of belonging to neoliberal, Hindu patronage politics. Rather than suffering the isolation of stigmas borne in worlds apart, these performance encounters nurture alternative feelings and imaginaries for the criminalized and suspected in ways that do not begin and end with criminality as caste history and compelled by poverty, or the criminal as abject or duped. Figures as despised as the suspected Muslim and the Chhara facing an intractable ordinary reality may well hunger for this kind of unanticipated epiphany and creative revolt that conjures new modes of belonging that refuse the reproduction of their stigma as an inevitable condition of social reproduction.

In producing unanticipated insights, the encounters initiated through performance enable unforeseen alliances by asking actors and audiences to dwell on the ambivalent humanity and subjection of reviled people. These theatrical encounters manifest the ways in which the Chhara actor onstage is not just a "born criminal," killer of Muslims, and liquor producer and "congenital" thief. Importantly, this involves a capacious political potential that is not solely about emancipation from criminal livelihoods and denial of killing. Rather, its ambivalence dwells on the Chhara who *may well have* killed, but nonetheless deserve regard because they are also actors, satirists, sharp critics of police brutality and state criminality, people with strong sentiments about Muslim suffering at their hands and the hands of others, and above all, people with aspirations to be perceived as good and creative. These kinds of uncoercively rearranged desires and unanticipated political potential emerge from intense theatrical encounters, which keeps some Chhara hungry for ongoing immersion in performance.

Notes from an Ongoing Journey

One hunger burns the stomach, the other burns the heart. Stomach's hunger can be extinguished by eating from another's plate, but the hunger for theater can only be satisfied by one's own creativity. . . . In political theater, this creativity must be collectively owned.[3]

The hungers for food and theater are neither equivalent, nor sequential. Rather, a hunger for theater—as Dia Da Costa evocatively argues above—resists captivity to existing configurations of power as well as to current imaginings of how transformation will come; it yearns "for all that makes life serendipitous" and that bears witness to the "ambivalent, unsettling, . . . potential" that makes life an "unforeseeable becoming . . . still worthy of being called a life." In this brief exploration, I reflect on the possibilities and challenges posed by this hunger for enriching our collective articulations of relational poverty politics. I draw upon one of my recent collaborations with Tarun Kumar, where we have tried to realize—in and through theater—new embodied understandings of the interbraided politics of caste, class, gender, location, and language.[4] Specifically, this exploration focuses on theater as a form of politics that craves freedom from the chains of existing imagination through creativity that must be articulated and sustained collectively.

PREMCHAND'S *KAFAN* AS *HANSA*

To me, *Kafan* . . . will always be . . . a story of two merciless brutes who merrily eat roasted potatoes while Budhiya is dying from labor pains. . . . This is what is imprinted on my mind. I came to your rehearsal fully prepared to hate Madhav and Ghisu. Instead, I'm . . . crying and empathizing with these two . . . [I'm] fall[ing] in love with two men I was supposed to hate. This can't be *Kafan*. . . . [Yet,] it is *Kafan!*[5]

In 2014–15, Tarun and I co-organized an intensive political theater workshop in Mumbai, which brought together twenty people to grapple with issues of caste, class, gender, and religion through a focus on Hindi/Urdu fiction. Nineteen of these participants have migrated to Mumbai from rural areas of Uttar Pradesh, Madhya Pradesh, Haryana, Bihar, Jharkhand, Chhattisgarh, Karnataka, and Gujarat. While half of them identify as upper caste/*sawarn*, the other half identify as dalit, dalit Muslim, "OBC" (other backward caste), or *adivasi*. Although the majority of them aspire to make a successful career in the film industry, five provide domestic help in the homes of film and television artists in the Yari Road area of Mumbai and had never seen a play before participating in the workshop.[6]

The workshop culminated in *Hansa, Karo Puratan Baat*, a play in Awadhi whose title is inspired by a song of the mystic poet Kabir.[7] Written and directed by Tarun, the play evolved from continuous readings and improvisations by the workshop participants of Premchand's last short story, "Kafan" ("The Shroud"), which he published in Urdu (1935) and Hindi (1936). The story revolves around two men—Ghisu and his son, Madhav—who sit by the fire outside their hut on a cold winter night eating roasted potatoes after combating acute hunger for two days. As they eat, reminisce, and philosophize about the good and the bad, Madhav's wife, Budhiya, screams with labor pains and dies by the end of the night. Father and son then try to gain sympathy from everyone in the village, collecting money for Budhiya's shroud, which they eventually spend on liquor and delicious food.

Often seen as a "classic" along with many other works of Premchand, *Kafan* was cited for several decades for its complex engagement with casteism, feudalism, religious hypocrisy, and women's oppression in rural northern India. In recent years, however, the story has been heavily critiqued in dalit thought, primarily on the grounds that as a *sawarn* writer, Premchand has been insensitive in his portrayal of Ghisu and Madhav as two inhuman *chamars*.[8] The critique has produced uncomfortable silences around Premchand's writing. The collectively created *Hansa* broke these silences by providing a fresh perspective to the story: placing Ghisu, Madhav, and Budhiya in their place and time in ways that served as prelude to and analysis of the story of Budhiya's death and Ghisu's and Madhav's response to it. Through a collective reinterpretation of the story in Awadhi—the first language of the majority of the workshop participants who have themselves moved from deeply impoverished rural areas of India to Mumbai in search for stable livelihoods—the play did at least two things. First, it retheorized the violence of Brahmanical capitalist patriarchy across time and place. Second, the actors tapped into their lived experiences and memories to create a richly textured drama with romance, humor, suffering, and irony, in ways that both moved the audience and refused their grasp. Through an unexpected and raw musicality and an unyielding linguistic mode, *Hansa* radically blended Premchand's critique of class and caste-based violence with Kabir's spiritual questioning of humanity's material investments, while complicating the definitions of "hero" and "antihero," exploitation and suffering, cruelty and benevolence, and life and death.

In December 2014, the group performed four shows of *Hansa* before packed audiences, followed by long discussions between actors and audiences.[9] Members of the audience rejoiced, sang, and cried with the actors and said that they were "mesmerized" and "disturbed" by what they found to be "an unforgettable play."

REIMAGINING DALIT/SAWARN POLITICS

I haven't read much about . . . "the dalit question," but I lived sawarn-dalit politics in my village . . . for more than two decades. . . . Premchand wrote *Kafan* in 1935 and here we are in 2014 in Mumbai. . . . As an [often] unemployed actor from Hardoi [rural Uttar Pradesh], I feel that most of us in this room are no different than Ghisu or Madhav. We are the chamars of today's Bollywood and they are the chamars of rural UP.[10]

Ghisu turns Budhiya's death into an *utsav* [festival], not because he is heartless but because he has a penetrating critique of the world in which he and Madhav are treated like crap . . . I keep returning to this seven-page long story . . . sometimes in the middle of the night . . . even after memorizing its text by heart. . . . Ghisu's wisdom is like that of a saint. That doesn't mean he is not witty and smart and cunning. His . . . wisdom includes all of this. That's what I have been trying to internalize so that I can transmit all of this through my body. . . . I can't think of myself as Bhagwan Das anymore. I have become Ghisu. Grappling with *Kafan* has changed how I approach life.[11]

Playing Budhiya, and singing the songs of *Hansa* make me come alive. I have never felt so alive and happy. . . . [Alok] makes me free and light. Unburdened. . . . My daughters and grand-daughters . . . can't recognize me anymore . . . I wrap up all my work quickly because I can't wait to get to the rehearsals. . . . I used to work in seven homes; now I just work in six because I need more time for myself in order to feel like Budhiya.[12]

When the workshop began, I hadn't ever imagined that Mumtazji, a mother and grand-mother who goes from one house to another to cook meals, would become my Budhiya. . . . I had expected a beautiful Budhiya of my own age to appear from somewhere. But . . . today when Mumtazji enters the stage in her green sari and bright red bindi on her forehead, she looks no less than any Budhiya that I might have imagined for myself. Her commitment and devotion to this work astound me. I am forced to think: "Yaar, even after running around between seven houses and completing a hundred chores in each place, Mumtazji's face always glows with an energizing smile when she enters the [rehearsal space]. Can I ever come close to this dedication?"

In the beginning I used to see Mumtazji, Meenaji, Sajjan, and Anil differently— "Arey yaar, how will these people do real acting? How will they get along with us [real actors]?"[13] My head was burdened with previously learned ideas about theater, dialogue, etcetera. But I slowly learned that each one of them is a far more alive and truthful actor than the rest of us [trained actors]. Perhaps because they have not learned acting in a school, they have learned acting from life.

. . . In the scene of Budhiya's death, Mumtazji wears my mother's green sari. Because of that sari, I am able to live Madhav's pain at the . . . cruel death of his young wife. Sometimes it is hard for me to control myself because I see my mother in that sari. But that connection with my mother's body does not interfere with the connection I feel with Budhiya's body.[14]

The question of whether someone who is not born dalit can represent or do justice to dalitness in the Indian context has acquired enormous salience, especially in dalit thought emerging after the 2001 World Conference against Racism in Durban. Debates on this question have led critics to distinguish between *atmakatha,* or story of the self as a chiefly sawarn or privileged mode of self-narration, and narratives of *swaanubhuti,* or experiences of the self that establish "Dalit personhood as a figure of suffering" and that regard "the protagonist as the representative of the Dalit community and Dalit identity" in order to goad the moral imagination of the reader and to demand ameliorative action (Sajid 2016, 114). Although such deployment of swaanubhuti has triggered important conversations about representation, consumption, and manipulation of dalit lives and struggles (Rege 2006), the tendency to delimit dalit literature and representations of dalit selfhood vis-à-vis caste politics has negated this literature's potential to reinvent itself in ways that can allow for border crossings. Sajid (2016) draws on the work of the novelist Mohandas Naimishraya to provide powerful examples of dalit writing that insist on looking beyond experiences of a single caste in order to create a literature that deploys empathy or connectedness of feeling (*samaanubhuti*) to create a politically and aesthetically rich poetics of alliance (*samanvaya*) and equality (*samata*), and to reflect critically upon Indian society. The making of *Kafan* as *Hansa* embodied these poetics of alliance by cocreating intimacies, analyses, and community across the borders of histories, geographies, hopes, dreams, and desires often defined around the suffocating politics of caste, religion, gender, location, and language.

The preceding quotations locate several actors of *Hansa* in relation to their own personal and political journeys while providing glimpses of the ways in which the collective process of making *Hansa* opened up a space to reengage the concepts of swaanubhuti, samaanubhuti, and samanvaya. For example, Gaurav arrived at samaanubhuti through a self-reflexive comparison between the treatment suffered by Ghisu and Madhav and the ways that Hindi-speaking migrant actors from rural areas are treated in Bollywood. By comparison, Mumtaz came to regard herself—and be regarded by other participants—as "much more than a poor dalit Muslim who cooks and cleans"; she became an "artist" not only who could grapple deeply with the pain of Budhiya because of her own experience (samaanubhuti) but whose involvement inspired other actors to feel and enact *Kafan* differently. Mumtaz's presence made *Kafan/Hansa* as much a story about Budhiya as it is about Ghisu and Madhav in the dominant imagination (see Vineet's quote). Alok and Bhagwan Das worked extremely hard for months to love, respect, and *own* Madhav, Ghisu, and Budhiya as parts of themselves, and the process was marked by deep psychological and emotional transitions for them, one during which they found themselves unable to undertake any other acting assignments. Theater became a politically and aesthetically aware praxis to collectively articulate ethics *and* dreams in deeply embodied, affective, and relational ways, allowing for theoretical, spiritual, and lived reimaginings that may otherwise seem impossible.

EXTINGUISHING AND SUSTAINING HUNGERS

Whereas the hunger that burns one's stomach must be extinguished, the creative hunger for political theater requires sustenance. The ongoing possibility of creativity and critique through political theater is centrally entangled with the challenge posed by this codependent distinction between the two hungers. This challenging codependence also makes it necessary to recognize political theater as a process comprising at least three forms of co-constitutive production that enable alliance through a creative refusal of inherited interpretations and a continuous *embodied* reworking of analytical frameworks: first, the creation (e.g., a play) through which political messages are articulated; second, the building and sustaining of a collectivity that must converse and coexist productively with the individualized hungers for creativity (and hungers of the creative egos) in the collective; and third, the building of political theater that must wrestle with the making of audiences that can sustain that theater without reducing it into a series of commodities. This last aspect connects political theater's survival to the risks and sociopolitical contradictions of funding, professionalization, and NGOization.

The making of *Hansa* in Mumbai involved an intense exploration of the systemic and psychic dimensions of exploitation, desire, greed, attachment, and indifference. The collective emotional and creative labor of the workshop participants—which included difficult dialogues rooted in each actor's encounters with multiple hungers—complicated in aesthetically rich ways the dominant reading of *Kafan* as a story of hunger (for food), untouchability, and inhumanity in the context of prevailing structures of caste, class, and gender. It entangled Ghisu's, Madhav's, and Budhiya's hunger for food with their hunger for emotional and sexual intimacy; for aesthetic, sensuous, spiritual, and intellectual comforts; and for their desire to feel "charitable." Moreover, it reinterpreted Budhiya's death as liberation from the exploitative materiality of class, religion, and the body itself.

The intense process of making *Hansa*, and the manner in which it moved its audience in each show, produced a hunger—among both actors and spectators—for continuing theater that allowed domestic workers in the Yari road area to continue to read, reflect, and perform with professional actors. However, while all of those actors who earned their living as domestic help (Mumtaz, Meena, Sajjan, Anil, Yasmin) were willing to let go of some of their paid work in order to continue to build a political and creative platform through theater, several young men who aspired for success in Bollywood (Alok, Bhagwan Das, Gaurav, Neeraj) felt that their continued participation in such theater would injure their future prospects. As much as this theater continues to pull them, they fear that its all-consuming nature—in terms of time, energy, and emotional and political labor—seriously threatens their chances of earning recognition and sustained livelihood in the long run. While the transgressive energy from the collective creation of *Hansa* sparked new relationships, interpretations, and analytical frameworks, it has been challenging to translate those transgressions into continuous creative labor for social transformation because of these very real fears. Yet, the group members also express hunger for finding ways to realize again the creative and political energy *and* community that they built through *Hansa*.

For example, Sajjan, a sixteen-year-old adivasi from Bihar, came to Mumbai in May 2014 when his two brothers who are already employed as domestic help in Mumbai found him a job that involves taking care of three dogs in the home of a Bollywood actor. Sajjan's employers, Narendra and Uma,[15] encouraged him to fully participate in the theater workshop between June and December, in part because they felt that he could "not utter even a sound from his throat" and the theater workshop would help him become "smarter" and better adjusted to his new social atmosphere. Two of Uma and Narendra's nephews—who had recently arrived in Mumbai from Haryana and UP (Uttar Pradesh)—also participated in the workshop. Although Narendra and Uma were out of town during the shows, they heard rave reviews from their family about Sajjan's incredible performance—especially as someone who never learned "proper Hindi"—and they were immensely proud of "his new personality and confidence."

Five months later, however, Uma and Narendra complained to Tarun and me that the theater workshop had spoiled Sajjan for life: Sajjan had opened a Facebook account where he logged in with their Internet password to entertain himself with pornographic material. Furthermore, when they scolded him for his ill manners, he talked back while looking them straight in the eye, something he had never done when he first arrived. It is no longer possible for Uma and Narendra to love Sajjan like a "family member" because rather than being grateful for what he is getting, he assumes that he deserves "equality and space" all the time. Sajjan is stepping out of what is deemed by them to be his *auqat*, or proper place, and both Sajjan and his employers attribute its credit or blame to the theater workshop. At the same time, the inability of the workshop participants to continue as a collective means that Sajjan no longer has access to the political, creative, and aesthetic space of theater to process his new struggles, experiences, and understandings—a painful reminder of the limits of all resistance and revolt, including those enabled by theater.

The process of awakening a hunger for theater occurred in each of the sites that we have worked in, allowing participants to articulate and internalize new political interpretations of their pasts and presents, in profoundly relational terms, through a penetrating embodied immersion in stories, texts, and languages whose previously inherited meanings they had often taken for granted. This hunger has also allowed for creation of innovative "texts" that were possible to imagine only collectively with the specific (hi)stories, memories, passions, and commitments that each participant brought to the making of the process. In so doing, each exploration in political theater has triggered spaces for new alliances that inspire fresh engagements with life and its possibilities and limitations. Since neither of these theatrical exercises was burdened by a need to seek resources that could sustain the activity and provide livelihoods to the actors, the plays did not become commodities to be sold for profit.

At the same time, Sajjan's example points to the structural limits of such work to sustain the creative and political hunger that it generates. Unless backed by an ongoing movement as a key resource for its sustenance, theatrical productions do not readily translate into projects that can continue in the absence of a registered organization or support from individual donors. While building registered organizations creates new risks of NGOization and threatens to make political theater a process of manufacturing commodities, it also takes us back to the key contradiction in the dance of hungers: How to continue living—and performing—the hunger for transformative politics relationally through theater? How to learn in alliance with those whose locations in the theater of the "margins" allow them to push dominant imaginations associated with poverty politics in the most radical ways while also ensuring that the burden of reproducing their own bodies does not threaten to take away their transformative creativity?

Continuing Conversations

This collaborative intervention into discussions of relational poverty knowledge theorizes the political hunger and creativity of theater workers who build personhoods and alliances to courageously resist structural impediments, and to refuse statist categorizations and frameworks that hierarchize, segregate, and kill. Differentiated and embodied hungers work in conjunction to move the production and reception of theater by actors and audiences, and varied hungers dance with, defer to, or obscure each other's becoming. Within the encounters of hungers, we delve into what makes political theater political, or otherwise forestalls its political potential. Alok's hunger for theater and Budhan Theatre's relationship with Muslims offers no bracing portrayal of Chhara transforming hegemonic caste and poverty politics. Rather these hungers express the deep ambivalence of willful resistance and unanticipated revolt that combine into a politics better characterized as a dance between survival, reproducing normative belonging, and creating novel modes of relationality. As authors with "diasporic distance" writing on contemporary India and its deepening heteropatriarchal, capitalist, casteist and Hindu nationalist violence, we ourselves collaborate with and hunger for a politics that enables border crossings and alliances emerging from empathy and epiphany. The standard politics of resistance and emancipation often privilege standpoint-based experience of Chhara history and political identity or dalit swaanubhuti. Insofar as these political articulations do little to fortify against the divisive communal violence that has emerged *within* and *across* marginalized communities, a hunger called theater manifests the belief that another political theater is possible.

In this political theater, the politics of belonging are imagined through collaborative alliance-building where collective creativity works through empathy and unanticipated articulations of the participants' own histories and geographies (swaanubhuti) while also laboring for new analytical resonances and epiphanies through samaanubhuti (e.g., Mumtaz identifying as Budhiya *and* as an artist and coeducator in a collective process). Such collaboration invites us to rearticulate alliance by rethinking marginality and by refusing to lock politics into familiar divisions of caste, class, or location. Sajjan's experience shows that the politics of alliance needs collectivity and relational groundedness of theater to be sustained in order for a hunger for theater to go from awakening to nourishing body-mind-souls toward new social futures. In a politics that challenges the simultaneous violence of Hindutva, developmentalism, commodification, and NGOization, such a hunger for theater is hard to sustain. However, once this hunger is implanted, it keeps actors restless for the next opportunity for collective creation through theater. The hope of ongoing alliances through political theater lies in this continued embodied yearning—yearning that demands radical shifts in the ways that we produce knowledge with and about those who are named poor or precarious, and who are deemed erased or excluded in "our" vocabularies.

NOTES

Shukriya to members of Budhan Theatre and to the team that created *Hansa* with Parakh-Mumbai, for fulfilling partnerships that made this work possible. Thanks, also, to Nosheen Ali, Alex Da Costa, David Faust, Jim Glassman, Nida Sajid, and RPN members for their comments on earlier drafts of this chapter.

1. For a more detailed discussion of the hunger for theater felt by those in privileged sociopolitical locations, see Da Costa (2016).

2. Northern Pakistanis sometimes refer to poetry as *rooh ki giza*, "nourishment for the soul" (Ali 2012, 16).

3. Tarun Kumar, theater and film artist, in a Skype discussion with Richa during the writing of this chapter, Mumbai, July 21, 2015.

4. This collaboration has focused on organizing theater activities in four diverse locations where we have built long-term relationships with communities and struggles in the context of our lives: villages of Sitapur district, Uttar Pradesh (2006–present), Minneapolis (2008), Lucknow (2014), and Jogeshwari, Mumbai (2010–13).

5. Vineet Kumar, theater and film artist, Mumbai, December 21, 2014.

6. Only three participants—Mumtaz Sheikh, Meena Bariya, and Yasmin Patel—were women, and all three were domestic workers. This acquired significance in the relationships that developed during the workshop as well as the aesthetics pertaining to the adaptation of *Kafan* into *Hansa*.

7. Awadhi, literally the language of Awadh, is often marginalized by "standard" Hindi and Urdu speakers as a *dehati zubaan* (language of the village), which is often contrasted with *khadi boli* ("standard" Hindi that is taught in schools and associated with urban sophistication). Awadhi is predominantly spoken in the rural areas of central and eastern Uttar Pradesh.

8. Chamars regard themselves as dalit.

9. Bal Auditorium of Central Institute of Fisheries Education in Versova was selected for these performances because it was free of charge, and attracted a large audience who was interested in seeing *Kafan* in Awadhi.

10. Gaurav Gupta (workshop participant), journal entry and workshop discussion, August 8, 2014.

11. Bhagwan Das (workshop participant), journal entries and notes from discussions, December 19 and 21, 2014.

12. Mumtaz Sheikh (workshop participant), journal entries (dictated to coparticipants) and discussions, December 21, 24, and 25, 2014.

13. Sajjan is an alias.

14. Alok Panday (workshop participant), entries from journal 3, pages 5 and 6; and unnumbered entry from August 12, 2014.

15. Aliases.

REFERENCES

Ali, Nosheen. 2012. "Poetry, Power, Protest: Reimagining Muslim Nationhood in Northern Pakistan." *Comparative Studies of South Asia, Africa and the Middle East* 32, no. 1: 13–24. doi:10.1215/1089201x-1545336.

Berenschot, Ward. 2011. *Riot Politics: Hindu-Muslim Violence and the Indian State*. London: Hurst.

Budhan Theatre. 2011. *Stories, Mine and Yours*. Chharanagar, Ahmedabad.

Da Costa, Dia. 2015. "Sentimental Capitalism in Contemporary India: Art, Heritage, and Development in Ahmedabad, Gujarat." *Antipode* 47, no. 1: 74–97. doi:10.1111/anti .12103.

———. 2016. *Politicizing Creative Economy: Activism and a Hunger Called Theater*. Champaign: University of Illinois Press.

Georgis, Dina. 2013. *The Better Story: Queer Affects from the Middle East*. Albany: State University of New York Press.

Gidwani, Vinay K. 2008. *Capital, Interrupted: Agrarian Development and the Politics of Work in India*. Minneapolis: University of Minnesota Press.

Halberstam, Judith. 2005. *In a Queer Time and Place: Transgender Bodies, Subcultural Lives*. New York: New York University Press.

Hartman, Saidiya V. 1997. *Scenes of Subjection: Terror, Slavery, and Self-Making in Nineteenth-Century America*. New York: Oxford University Press.

Massumi, Brian. 2002. *Parables for the Virtual: Movement, Affect, Sensation*. Durham, N.C.: Duke University Press.

Nagar, Richa. 2014. *Muddying the Waters: Coauthoring Feminisms across Scholarship and Activism*. Champaign: University of Illinois Press.

Rege, Sharmila. 2006. *Writing Caste, Writing Gender: Reading Dalit Women's Testimonios*. New Delhi: Zubaan Books.

Sajid, Nida. 2016. "Resisting Together Separately: Representations of the Dalit-Muslim Question in Literature." In *Dalit Literatures in India*, edited by Joshil Abraham and Judith Misrahi-Barak, 108–27. New Delhi: Routledge.

Sangtin Writers and Richa Nagar. 2006. *Playing with Fire: Feminist Thought and Activism through Seven Lives*. Minneapolis: University of Minnesota Press.

Spivak, Gayatri Chakravorty. 2004. "Righting Wrongs." *South Atlantic Quarterly* 103, nos. 2/3: 523–81.

Taylor, Diana. 2003. *The Archive and the Repertoire*. Durham, N.C.: Duke University Press.

CONCLUSION

Politicizing Poverty

VICTORIA LAWSON AND SARAH ELWOOD

> This collection aims to overcome the current *regime of disappearance* by redirecting
> poverty studies toward a repoliticization of poverty and inequality.
>
> **—Goode and Maskovsky (2001, 17)**
>
> Repoliticizing inequality is an ongoing project, one that increasingly demands
> vigilance and creativity. . . . I offer one approach to the task of repoliticizing inequality:
> The resignification of poverty as a critical concept.
>
> **—Roy (2016, n.p.)**

The foundational agenda of *Relational Poverty Politics* is that of repoliticizing
poverty and bringing into consideration a range of rebellious, creative, and hopeful projects of unthinkable poverty politics. Over fifteen years ago, Judith Goode
and Jeff Maskovsky's *New Poverty Studies* showed how long-standing poverty
policies, discourses, and norms in the United States make poverty "disappear" by
positioning impoverishment as seemingly unrelated to racial capitalist economic
structures and relations, and therefore not a matter of collective societal attention
and action. Ananya Roy (2016) unpacks the political effects of an ascendant discourse of "inequality," arguing that it decenters a focus on specific multifaceted
processes of impoverishment (integral to racial capitalism) and keeps poverty
knowledge and actions contained within the normative (thinkable) terms of
white, Western liberal democracies. *Relational Poverty Politics* takes up the charge
laid down by these critical scholars: poverty must be creatively and insistently
repoliticized to recognize unthinkable politics that challenge Western, colonialist
knowledge and its practices of dispossession, violence, and accumulation that
reproduce impoverishment. This book explores contradictory and incommensurable (but coexisting) entanglements of thinkable and unthinkable poverty
politics to offer creative insights about other subjects, worlds, and futures.

This book extends much relational poverty analysis by foregrounding poverty politics. The contributors theorize a range of poverty politics being mobilized against enduring inequality and impoverishment. They explore who is

involved, what is thinkable, what kinds of (transformed) subjects and relations emerge, what and who remain unthinkable (within normative frames) but are anyway creating meaning and action. The collection makes visible both forms of politics that reproduce ongoing processes of impoverishment and their social arrangements, and forms of politics that mark the outsides of existing power hierarchies or that are unrecognizable under its normative and ideological terms. The volume engages in dialogic learning across diverse sites, subjects, and forms of action, revealing new forms of poverty politics through transnational relational analysis. In bringing these rich and varied cases into conversation here, we build a relationality of theory that expands what counts as poverty politics, learns from those excluded from knowledge making, and develops new insights for theory and action that arise from reading each case through theory from elsewhere.

Beginning from the epistemological and methodological innovations of relational analysis, the book opens up multiple struggles over meanings of poverty and diverse forms of poverty politics while not assuming that these are stable across times and places. The contributors' relational analyses of poverty politics work against reductive, economistic framings of poverty and instead interrogate multiple interlocking explanations for impoverishment. Inspired by critical race and feminist theorists around the globe, they take seriously the interoperation of class, race, gender, caste, religion, sexuality, citizenship, and other systems of social (de)valuation in framing subjects and poverty politics. They learn from the voices and actions of those who are impoverished and build relational epistemologies of ethnographic, humble collaborative engagement that disrupt Northern hegemony in the geopolitics of poverty knowledge and practice. And furthermore, these cases expand theory by revealing new subjects, sites, and practices that imagine and build antipoverty politics in new and disruptive ways.

The theoretical and political insights we draw out in the pages of this conclusion reflect our own positions in academic, social, and geopolitical knowledge hierarchies, as well as our ongoing learning through relational knowledge making as editors of this collection. Our positions as white women, as middle-class people, as rich country citizens, as academics in Northern universities have circumscribed our political imaginaries and modes of theorizing and the forms of power-knowledge they reproduce. To name but a few of the boundaries we are reflecting on now, our reading of feminist theory has often tilted toward white feminists, our "go-to" theorists have often been Anglophone rich-country-based, our political imaginaries have been oriented more toward inclusion than refusal. Even our embrace of a politics of hope, possibility, and alliance has been steeped in forms of privilege that make these yearnings seem achievable. In editing this book, we mirror our contributors' humble collaborative engagements and have worked to remake our own horizons of thought and action. Our coauthors, our graduate students, and our close colleagues have led us toward deeper engagements with critical race feminism, postcolonial thought, and black geographies as these articulate to hierarchies of power from different ontological positions.[1] Our concluding reflections explore the lessons of this book for thinkable and unthinkable poverty politics and alliance building from our ongoing reflexive learning.

Learning from (Un)Thinkable Poverty Politics

We engage thinkable and unthinkable politics as dialectically related analytics for theorizing poverty politics, subject framings, and the relations and material worlds they produce. Thinkable politics refer to projects of existing knowledge and governmental orders that stabilize hegemonic forms of political, economic, and cultural power (Roy 2016; Rose and Miller 1992; Hall and Massey 2010). Unthinkable politics are enacted by excluded, illegible, and/or forgettable subjects who build rebellious uprisings, create cultural forms that transform meanings, and challenge hegemonic systems of social (de)valuation (McKittrick 2016; Cacho 2012). Thinkable and unthinkable politics are contradictory, are theoretically incommensurable, and yet coexist, offering creative insights into other lifeworlds, tangled up with this one, but nonetheless offering creative openings and possibilities (McKittrick 2016, 79). This volume traces how thinkable and unthinkable poverty politics exist in dynamic dialectical relations with each other, reinscribing dominant orders or refusing to conform to their hegemonic power and revealing alternative subject framings and actions. Some chapters foreground thinkable politics of differential incorporation that enroll impoverished people in fighting for survival on dominant terms, and here we consider their practices, subject framings, possibilities, and limits (Pittman, Negrón-Gonzales, Ye, Maskovsky). Others explore when, where, and how unthinkable poverty politics emerge or are crushed (Glassman, Magalhães). In some cases, unthinkable politics entail refusals of, and disidentifications with, dominant racial capitalist regimes of production, consumption, and governance (Giles, Borges, Da Costa and Nagar). Other unthinkable political acts such as direct protest provoke governments, elites, and countermovements to reestablish authority by unleashing state-sponsored violence (Glassman, Magalhães). We argue for more attention to unruly unthinkable acts that refuse incorporation, even incite violent repression, and threaten existing knowledge and political-economic orders because they are the creative edges of poverty knowledge and action where we have much to learn.

THINKABLE POVERTY POLITICS

Thinkable politics, enacted by elites, bureaucrats, volunteers for charitable and/ or religious organizations, and the like, produce "poor subjects" that solidify and reproduce existing power-knowledge hierarchies. Framed through bodily comportment, behavior, speech, morality, and conformity, impoverished and racialized people are governed, disciplined, and differentially incorporated into existing projects of nation-state and economy. Impoverished subjects are made thinkable (and potentially reformable) through relational material and discursive processes that "explain" their vulnerability in terms of flaws and deficiencies of character, race, class, sexuality, caste, and/or religion. This marginal framing of Other subjects sets the terms for who can be incorporated (reformed, employed, etc.), and under what conditions, and who is to be excluded. For instance, Da Costa and Nagar (this volume) trace how criminalization of the Chhara in colonial India continues to establish them as Other in the present, with material consequences that ensure they are "held captive to modes of survival that reproduce their stigma." Framed as strangers to the postcolonial state and as low caste, they are de facto excluded from legal economic activities, and even as illegal activities are their only option, these practices reinforce discourses of their criminality. They are constructed as criminals, and their impoverishment is framed as unrelated to exclusions produced by the Indian state's projects of modernity. Negrón-Gonzales reveals thinkable poverty politics at work in the DREAM Act's supposed assistance to undocumented students in the United States. This highly selective program identifies those who are "educable" and "young" for incorporation, but simultaneously leaves unchallenged the criminalization of their undocumented loved ones. In continuing the vulnerability of immigrant families, the DREAM Act selectively incorporates and disciplines vulnerable low-wage workers who bolster the profitability of agrarian capital in California's Central Valley. The DREAM Act entails a double move, drawing on a supposedly progressive politics of inclusion and improvement through which young immigrants are incorporated into the nation, and yet their cooperation is secured through continuing to exclude and reproduce the vulnerability of their other family members through deportation and loss of livelihood, family, and residency. Across very different contexts, a poverty politics of differential incorporation produces Other subjects and reinscribes existing power hierarchies of race, class, citizenship, and/or caste that define "proper" (thinkable, governable) subjects and those who are to be excluded through criminalization. In both India and the United States thinkable poverty politics stabilize hegemonic systems of social (de)valuation and capital accumulation.

Thinkable politics also stabilize ideals of middle classes and elites as whitened, entrepreneurial, benevolent, and respectable through framings of "poor Others" as flawed and in need of reform (Adamovsky 2009; Elwood, Lawson, and Nowak 2015; Roy 2012; Fernandes and Heller 2011). Because the middle classes are aspirational subjects in many contemporary capitalist states, they play a crucial role in framing dominant understandings of who is poor, why they are poor, and what should be done about poverty (Lawson et al., 2015). For example, Ye's analysis of middle-class volunteers in social assistance programs in Singapore uncovers how middle-class actors enact a thinkable poverty politics that incorporates migrants through uneven modes of governance, ordering, and management. Low-waged, noncitizen migrants are excluded from state-provided assistance and instead are incorporated through community-based aid programs that deploy race and behavior as criteria for deeming certain people deserving of help. Social support programs for vulnerable migrants in Singapore are rationed along the lines of citizenship and race, by migration and labor policies, as well as cross-class encounters in social assistance organizations. These relational poverty politics incorporate thousands of transnational migrant low-wage workers who service and support the needs of the rising middle classes. Meanwhile middle-class volunteers secure their own position as respectable, benevolent citizen-subjects even as they benefit materially from low-wage immigrant labor.

Thinkable poverty politics are enacted not only by powerful actors but also by impoverished people themselves, pointing to crucial forms of agency by those who are often understood primarily as victims of structural violence. However, our book also points to the limits of agency within thinkable poverty politics because operating within the realm of thinkability produces tactics not transgressions, as people survive in a system stacked against them. For instance, Pittman's study of African American custodial grandmothers explores their survival strategies in the face of a social assistance system that denies them benefits as caregivers. Grandmothers creatively devise strategies to allow for the fluidity and complexity of grandparent-headed households, including resisting the devaluation of their caring labor and brokering deals with birth parents to continue claiming (and sharing) cash benefits in the absence of living wage work and high rates of African American incarceration. In other strategies, grandmothers sidestep parental authority by becoming legal guardians or keeping grandchildren off their lease to avoid losing subsidized housing. These tactics allow grandmothers to secure vitally needed resources of housing and income, but in ways that do not challenge or disrupt rules based on white, middle-class, nuclear family ideals, and the inaccurate claim that welfare recipients can always find living wage work and affordable housing. Rather, grandmothers engage in thinkable poverty politics by making themselves legible as eligible for age-related benefits and by making invisible family arrangements that lie outside these terms. But these modes of survival produce only the barest forms of life and cannot challenge racist and classist exclusions of vulnerable populations that benefit the private sector, which profits from cheap labor, government contracts granted to manage families involved in the child welfare system, and coerced prison labor.

Reading across these cases underscores, among other things, the economism undergirding thinkable poverty politics and the diversity of ways this manifests in different spacetimes, such as the overt claims of insufficient public funds by Philadelphia's local government as it rejects activists' calls for affordable housing

(Maskovsky); the air of finitude that infuses complex systems for rationing out social assistance in Singapore (Ye); and the governance of subjects by systematically devaluing care work (Pittman). The chapters remind us that bolstering capitalist economies is a central terrain of thinkable poverty politics as they normalize scarcity and inequality in ways that are foundational to racialized capitalist accumulation and dispossession. Even on the left, economism has limited our critical engagements with impoverishment. These and other insights emerge from transnational relational analysis across the cases—but in ways that are creatively open, not determinate or theoretically prescriptive. Collaborative discussions among our contributors led us to trouble economistic analyses of impoverishment and to engage the complex and unpredictable interrelation of multiple causal material and discursive processes of Othering and marginalization along axes of economy, race, criminalization, caste, gender, sexuality, citizenship, and constructions of family and home. The dynamic ways that these processes come together and apart in different spacetimes underscore the essential importance of analyzing poverty relationally, realizing the theoretical potential of transnational circulations of ideas by constantly posing new theoretical questions of the places where each of us works.

UNTHINKABLE POVERTY POLITICS

Unthinkable poverty politics are transgressive, rebellious, and illegible to racial capitalist regimes of production, consumption, and governance. For Cacho (2012, 32) unthinkable politics involves "entertaining counter-intuitive thoughts and practice[ing] imagining otherwise." These poverty politics are unthinkable because (1) they involve actions by people whose lives, theory, and politics have been framed as unimportant and powerless; (2) they arouse the threat (or promise) of state-sponsored violence; (3) they often take place in spaces deemed irrelevant such as homes, low-income neighborhoods, theaters, dumpsters, alleys, and streets; and (4) they involve collectivities forged across difference. Our contributors identify unthinkable politics that refuse existing orders of social (de)valuation (that rely on the categorization, exclusion, repression, and criminalization of difference) through practices of illiberal embodiment and disidentification that rehumanize people outside of racial capitalist orders. Unthinkable politics often elicit law enforcement and violence upon vulnerable subjects, or entail cultural productions that reframe the terms on which life is made meaningful. In short, unthinkable poverty politics bring to light complex personhoods, ideas, and politically creative practices expressed by subjects historically framed as nonpersons and their allies (Cacho 2012; McKittrick 2016). This book takes seriously the ideas and politics they enact.

Illiberal embodiments (Giles, this volume), produced by unthinkable subjects, refuse assimilation and instead create disruptive modes of personification "that confound liberal recognition and differential incorporation." They refuse thinkable politics that distribute entitlements and differentially incorporate people through disciplining categorizations and material oppressions of persons along power lines of class, race, gender, sexuality, religious difference, caste, and more. Illiberal embodiments create unthinkable politics by making lives and worlds outside the terms of liberal legibility. For example, Giles's analysis of Food Not Bombs (FNB) reveals the coming together of heterogeneous people whose practices of reappropriating, consuming, and redistributing the "waste" of capitalist food markets refuse hegemonic norms of cooking and eating. FNB activists repudiate legible (singular) identities that are subject to assimilation or exclusion within existing orders of power (Muñoz 1999; Giles, this volume). These disidentificatory practices are not about demanding recognition nor rights, but rather about performatively renegotiating multifaceted identities and cultivating new social worlds and ways of living outside normative discipline. FNB activists creatively reconfigure power lines of liberal hegemony to produce meaningful social worlds in which life is organized outside of market ideologies and systems of social (de)valuation. Da Costa and Nagar (this volume) explore the ways in which theater produces unthinkable poverty politics through "flights from captivity" by prioritizing involvement in theater over earning of money. Poignantly, Budhan Theatre performances bring together Muslims and Chhara people around shared experiences of stigma and exclusion, despite murderous violence between these communities. In the wake of a shared performance, "the suspected Muslim and the Chhara facing an intractable ordinary reality . . . hunger for this kind of unanticipated epiphany and creative revolt that conjures new modes of belonging that refuse the reproduction of their stigma as an inevitable condition of social reproduction."

Each of these cases reveals intense cultural creations, involving hunger for theater and hunger for food, that generate spaces of relational recognition full of political potential because they refuse dominant scripts of class, commodity, caste, criminality, and/or religious difference. They underscore the capacity of micropolitics, queer affects, and illiberal embodiments to catalyze ruptures in the normative "common sense" that prop up modernist development's singular obsession with bodily hunger and income, or capitalist food systems' relentless reproduction of waste. Both of these examples of poverty politics rework political discourse and hegemonic common sense about "poor people" and poverty and they build alliances that reveal the links between capital accumulation and the deployment of difference in order to drive wedges between people experiencing impoverishment.

Some political acts are unthinkable because they make visible the role of violence in sustaining racial capitalist systems of production, consumption, and governance. These are risky politics, where struggles for dignified lives lead people to incite and/or endure both physical and representational violence. We learn from Cacho (2012), who points to unthinkable politics by undocumented activists in the United States who are always already outside state protections and whose political acts incite state-sponsored violence because they are pre-configured by racial capitalist constructions as criminalized subjects. Glassman's work (this volume) in Thailand traces how unequal class relations and capital accumulation are secured through ideological and militarized violence. Despite his central focus on how militarized violence secures existing (thinkable) projects of government by stabilizing capitalist profitability and elite privilege and power, his account of the Red Shirt protests of 2010 by workers, farmers, and provincial leaders also reveals unthinkable politics. Red Shirt activists' protests of inequality and impoverishment are unthinkable in that they deliberately expose themselves to state violence with full knowledge of inevitable suffering and both social and actual death. Glassman traces brutal repression by the military and state police and the military coup of 2014 to secure the continuing power of Thai elites and to silence claims of deepening impoverishment and demands for redistributive policies. In Brazil, Magalhães traces social protests and counterprotests as impoverished people and their allies mobilized for redistribution and transparent democratic spaces in June 2013. This gave rise to violent counterprotests by "yellow shirt" nationalists involving white, older, wealthier middle-class actors seeking to reinstate neoliberal governance. Fearing deep and radical disruption of established orders, right-wing activists, closely allied with media conglomerates and powerful actors in the national congress and judiciary, engaged in extreme right-wing, openly racist, and anti-LGBT politics and demanded military intervention against the Rousseff government. Despite a leftist president in Brazil, urban social movements engaged in unthinkable politics by organizing for yet more robust antipoverty actions that were sufficiently threatening to powerful groups that they incited violent responses to secure racial capitalist class relations and forms of accumulation. Reading across these cases, we see that elites and capital enlist very different kinds of states (more rightist, more leftist, greater/lesser levels of authoritarianism, different histories and structures of civil society) in violent action to secure their collective interests, suggesting the forms that consequential challenges to impoverishment must take. The persistence of struggle in both cases also reveals the kinds of social, material, and ideological resources that sustain unthinkable politics in the face of violence.

Creative cultural productions are also unthinkable politics in their making of meanings that refuse white supremacy, class and caste hierarchies, religious discrimination, criminalization, and racialized impoverishment. While often not read as poverty politics, these cultural inventions are unthinkable politics that disrupt normative orders and reclaim the complex humanity of those constructed as Other. McKittrick (2016, 90) argues that U.S. black culture and music "are relational creative acts that unfold as reparative possibilities rooted in black intellectual activities." Da Costa and Nagar identify similar possibilities in India, tracing the ways in which discriminatory representations of Chhara and dalit people are renegotiated in creative experiences of theater. The relational connections produced through performance "combine into a politics . . . characterized as a dance between survival, reproducing normative belonging, and creating novel modes of relationality" (Da Costa and Nagar, this volume). Performance enacts complex mutual identifications and recognitions that unlearn hegemonic orders and open up alternative worlds of meaning, alliance, and hope. The disruptive importance of hunger for political theater also challenges narrowly materialist understandings of poverty as a need for income, food, and shelter. The performers, who are impoverished people, hunger for collective creativity through theater, prioritizing this over bodily hunger. Theater offers avenues for disidentification with violent and oppressive divisions along lines of caste and class and opens new opportunities to make meaning, community, and formerly unthinkable politics.

Borges (this volume) learns about unthinkable poverty politics from creative meaning making by her South African hosts in the field. Their actions and meaning making refuse to engage with economistic meanings of poverty and development. Rather, they build a combative epistemology that refuses dominant ontologies of "poor people" and "development." The family fought for a farmhouse under land reform but not merely as a place of material shelter and production/income. Rather, their struggle for home is a struggle for creative cultural recuperation of forms of belonging that are illegible to the postcolonial South African state and social order. They reclaim ancestral worlds and make visible injustices of dispossession and family relations, refusing to let them be forgotten or disappeared into state projects of modernization. For instance, racist prohibitions on civil marriages and traditional wedding customs during the apartheid era outside of the "reserves" meant that their grandparents were unable to complete their wedding ceremonies during their lifetimes. But their daughter's completion of their marriage challenges the segregation and violence of apartheid and refuses to conform to state repression or to its economistic promises of "solutions" to impoverishment. From these creative meaning-making acts, Borges's research partners produce knowledge that challenges power structures and thinkable discourses about poverty and development.

Both Borges and Da Costa and Nagar recognize unthinkable political acts that retheorize the meanings and subjects of impoverishment: as racist histories of dehumanization, wealth as the problem to be addressed (e.g., by insisting on valuing living well with little), hunger as cultural and political voice, and insistence on a politics focused on how privilege and power are always bound up with impoverishment. The authors also explicitly address what can be (re)learned about poverty and poverty politics through relational epistemologies that seek to listen and learn in ways that trouble the limits of thinkability.

Da Costa relates her struggle to apprehend hunger for theater as more than metaphoric, while Nagar lays out profound questions about how to learn in alliance across differences of power and privilege. Borges details close interpersonal relationships through which she comes to see scarcity as a "whole" that constitutes knowledge and freedom. She adopts a poetic mode of theorizing that fights the "double dispossession" of conventional ethnographic accounts that subtract and reduce by theorizing through abstraction. Across different sites, these chapters demonstrate a key lesson: epistemological projects that make knowledge about poverty that is unthinkable for normative poverty knowledge apparatuses are themselves a counterhegemonic poverty politics.

Attending to the realms of unthinkability makes visible a range of transgressive and creative poverty politics that refuse existing structures of social (de)valuation and that struggle to make life meaningful outside of hegemonic norms, identities, and practices that secure liberal democracies. Unthinkable poverty politics are a way of seeking other possible worlds, even as they always also take shape in the shadow of thinkable worlds. And this raises vital questions: How do other worlds, other politics come to be enacted out of these alternative imaginings and practices? How might we arrive at political solidarities that can challenge impoverishment from these diverse sites and insights? These questions led us to feminist alliance theory, which pushes beyond solidarity projects rooted in class logics that are too often exclusionary. Our discussion of thinkable poverty politics exposes the diverse power lines along which difference has been exploited to divide social groups. We close by exploring how feminist alliance practices create new pathways for building political solidarities by paying careful attention to how differences in power work across race, class, gender, sexuality, and other lines, how they have hindered, and how they are (might be) overcome, in the building of antipoverty politics.

(Un)Thinkable Poverty Politics and Alliances

In prior work, we have turned to alliance as a site for advancing progressive politics, speculating that unprecedented and creative challenges to impoverishment might emerge from alliances across race, class, gender, ability, sexuality, and other axes of difference (Jakobsen 1998). Scholars have flagged the mobilization of diverse coalitions within contemporary social justice movements, calling for critical analyses of how power circulates in alliance and with what implications for the politics that emerge (Leitner, Peck, and Sheppard 2006; Wainwright and Kim 2008; Koopman 2015). Feminist and postcolonial scholars have insisted on theorizing alliance as a relational process of subject formation along intersectional power lines (Rowe 2008; Nagar and Geiger 2014; Walia 2013). These lines of thought have informed our prior work on how cross-class encounters might produce more collective social subjects and inclusive poverty politics (Lawson et al. 2015; Elwood, Lawson, and Nowak 2015). From these origins, we initially conceived this collection as focused on the kinds of poverty politics that emerge from alliance across differences in power and privilege, asking when, where, and how cross-power/privilege alliances challenge thinkable poverty politics.

Our focus on alliance began as a hopeful epistemological project. We took seriously feminist and postcolonial thinking on the asymmetrical power lines of alliance making, but nonetheless centered alliance, as if it were a stable onto-logical object, as a site for a politics of possibility (Gibson-Graham 2008). We imagined sites of alliance (rather than complex relational practices of allying) that challenge existing social and knowledge orders and open up the ontological possibility of as-yet-unseen counterhegemonic poverty politics. However, an on-going process of collaborative reading and thinking with contributing authors, students in our graduate seminars, and other close colleagues has reworked our theorizations of alliance, alliance politics, and their potentials and limits. A deeper engagement with critical race feminism and black geographies on thinkable and unthinkable politics (McKittrick 2016; Cacho 2012; Rowe 2008; Walia 2013) has underscored the extent to which our initial centering of alliance as a site for building progressive poverty politics bespeaks our own privileged position in thinkable politics. Our experiences as middle-class white people, as citizens of rich countries, as minority world Anglophone academics are legible to, and advantaged in, systems of thinkability. Class, race, and other forms of privilege prefigure our theoretical and political imaginaries to see alliance as a hopeful project, overlooking the incorporative force of thinkability, forgetting the always-present outsides of democratic politics, and failing to fully appre-hend the social and material violence and pain that accompany unthinkability. In short, many of the theoretical insights that flow from this collection were for us, at the outset of the project, wholly unthinkable.

Our continuing work toward "imagining otherwise" (Cacho 2012, 32) has altered the way we theorize alliance and the connections between alliance and robust solidarity politics. We push our own tendency, and that of much work on counterhegemonic politics, to treat alliance as a stable ontological object that is created, and then from which particular kinds of politics can be expected to flow. Instead, we theorize alliance as a restless process of being in relation that can fail by reproducing thinkable modes of hierarchy and differential incor-poration. Or, processes of alliance building can be open to building affective ties of trust, accountability, and commitment that allow allies to grapple with power differences by recognizing that subjects and embodiments articulate dif-ferently within hierarchies of power. This orientation decenters alliance as a stable object, focusing instead on alliance practices and the kinds of relational subjects and poverty politics that are possible (or not) within the myriad ways that alliance work takes shape in relation to thinkability and unthinkability. The chapters discuss alliances that reproduce thinkable politics and subjects as well as those operating in realms of unthinkability. In both cases, our contributors theorize what sorts of alliance politics can take place and whether they constrain or open possibilities for radical challenges to poverty.

Sampat's and Maskovsky's chapters reveal alliance politics that bring together diverse subjects in common cause, yet the resultant political outcomes remain situated in terrains of thinkability. They theorize how alliance politics may be incorporative, reproducing relational subjects and articulating claims inscribed within existing frames of social (de)valuation. Maskovsky shows how radical activism by ACT UP/Philadelphia mobilizes people with HIV/AIDS (PWAs) across race and class differences on the basis of a shared "biological citizenship," and how they grapple with differences in power and privilege to build creative tactics that result in increased housing access for homeless PWAs. In one sense, the Philadelphia ACT UP chapter tells a story of unthinkable alliance making as challenges from low-income African American activists shifted radical democratic practices to reduce the disproportionate influence of white, middle-class activists. As other ACT UP chapters across the country were dwindling, impoverished people of color became majority members in Philadelphia, building a combined antipoverty, pro–racial justice and biological citizenship movement. Their alliance politics mobilized a diverse coalition of people and created materially significant victories. However, despite this alliance work, their political claims ultimately referred to thinkable modes of incorporation. Specifically, they sought an end to the ranking of housing applicants based on degree of ill health, arguing that homelessness has catastrophic health consequences for all PWAs. Yet by arguing that some poor subjects are in greater need than others (homeless PWAs over other homeless people) and that granting these resources is economically efficient, these alliance politics stabilize normative economic subjects in competition for limited state resources and economic rationales for their allocation: key dimensions of thinkable poverty politics.

Closely related, Sampat shows how differential incorporation in alliance politics systematically circumscribes political imaginaries to the realms of thinkability, precluding more radical refusals. She traces how allied movements in India coalesce class-, caste-, and gender-diverse groups to fight land dispossession, rentier economies, and developmentalist infrastructure projects. Across power lines, these groups articulate a common vision of more egalitarian futures, yet their political imaginary for more inclusive development from below remains bound to the existing (unequal) terms of recognition and privilege of India's historical land impasse. They resist infrastructure development by positioning the agricultural economy as a more egalitarian alternative and arguing for grounded investments in it, such as building a long-delayed irrigation canal. These positions remain firmly steeped in thinkable social and political imaginaries and leave intersecting cultural and political economic processes of differential incorporation uninterrupted. Should the movement "win" the canal, its benefits will accrue unequally to differently privileged allies, India's historical land impasse will be reaffirmed, and more radical antipoverty/land politics circumvented. Maskovsky and Sampat extend theorizations of alliance politics to illustrate how collective visions of more inclusive futures and even meaningful moments of refusal become reincorporated into thinkable poverty politics. Some of the Indian farmers refuse compensation processes that make dispossession inevitable but limit their political struggle to negotiating the terms on which it will happen. The ACT UP members reject the state's austerity logic that resources are insufficient to meet needs and so must "naturally" be rationed via ranking and prioritization systems. Yet in both cases, these are momentary ruptures that fail to destabilize normative subjects and relations, political imaginaries, and material processes of exclusion and/or differential incorporation. Such alliance politics may produce materially significant wins, but because these victories are predicated upon subjects and politics framed in dominant economic terms, they reproduce the incorporative power of thinkability and foreclose more radical possibilities.

In contrast, other chapters trace alliance politics that destabilize normative subject positions, loosen (some) limits of thinkability, and invite actions in support of unthinkable politics and those who do them. Swerts's analysis of boundary bridging in the DREAM movement shows how discursive strategies of equalization and differentiation center undocumented activists as privileged speakers/agenda setters, and prompt citizen allies to "step back," engage in critical learning about their race, class, and citizenship privilege, and deploy this privilege in support of the movement. Boundary bridging is a micropolitics of repositioning normative/Other subjects as "unequal equals" in their allied activism. Swerts traces how processes of intersubjective exchange and critical relearning open new sites of contestation and draw privileged actors into different relation with unthinkable politics. Privileged allies cannot by definition do the unthinkable politics of risking deportation by coming out as undocumented. But they can refuse some material consequences of their privilege (e.g., opting out of cross-border travel), deploy their un-vulnerability in support of the movement (e.g., transporting allies whose race and citizenship make driving a site of vulnerability), and make visible the social and material violence to which their colleagues are subjected. As Cacho (2012), McKittrick and Woods (2007), and others have argued, the stability of systems of (un)thinkability depends not just on violence but on their unseeability from privileged positions. Swerts extends these insights to illustrate how critically reflexive ally subjects can challenge the unseeingness of other privileged people. Reading across Swerts's and Negrón-Gonzales's analyses illuminates the limits to boundary bridging as an alliance politics across power lines. Outside the movement's internal micropolitics, citizen supporters and DREAMers remain subject to larger systems of social (de)valuation and differential incorporation. Negrón-Gonzales shows that for many undocumented youth, labor exploitation renders the DREAM Act a bad joke and DREAM activism unimaginable because of its far-reaching risks for (already racialized, criminalized, precarious) extended families. Her analysis lays plain that we cannot fully grapple with the limits of alliance work across difference, nor the most durable and devastating structural processes of impoverishment, without confronting racialization as a multivalent technology of division within capitalism. Nonetheless, Swerts opens the question of the potential for political work that reveals privilege and situates it in histories of oppression as a tool for change.

Theorizing alliance as relational work across power lines makes visible sites, practices, and embodiments through which privileged people's refusal of normative forms of legibility and social value can engage them in unthinkable politics. Echoing Butler's (2004) framing of the body as a site for politics across privilege and power because of the fundamental vulnerability of all life to injury and death, Magalhães's case involves middle-class Brazilians taking to the streets with impoverished people in the June 2013 protests. They deliberately expose their bodies to police violence routinely experienced by their racialized and criminalized coprotesters—for a moment vacating the bodily security that their privilege affords them. Giles's analysis of waste food recovery and consumption by FNB highlights other kinds of bodily practices of unthinkability enacted across lines of power and privilege. Concepts like illiberal embodiment and abject hexis reveal dumpster diving and consumption of waste food as an alliance politics of disidentification in which privileged *and* marginalized people make themselves illegible to normative personhood and reject its forms of bodily governance and public consumption. But, as we theorize the stakes and consequences of alliance politics constituted through embodiment, Giles reminds us crucially that bodies are always interpolated into thinkable poverty politics on asymmetrical terms: white, homeless, and/or racialized bodies of dumpster divers are very differently positioned in relation to abjection, criminality, and other constructs of social value. These accounts of alliance politics break down assumptions of a fixed or determinant relationship between subjectivity and politics, paving the way toward new transgressions and flights of political imagination that transgress lines of power and privilege. This said, thinking across these instances of alliance politics raises questions about the kinds of unthinkable politics that are possible at different sites and scales. Collective recovery and consumption of waste food is a refusal that may remain unseen, whereas mass street protest much more clearly courts violent repression. This suggests that broad public protests are more threatening to existing orders and are vital tactics for change, but that micropolitics can provide creative resources about the kinds of larger structural changes that are necessary.

The alliance politics traced in this collection underscore the urgency and ongoingness of creative struggles to break out of thinkable political imaginaries, to fight for relational subjects, queer affects and embodiments, and counterhegemonic claims that call forth other possible worlds. A broader lesson we draw from critical race feminism and black geographies theory on unthinkable politics, from the chapters in this collection, and from our own critical learning in editing it, is that alliance politics among (differently) illegible subjects are generative openings for these worlds. The limits of thinkability are pushed in unique ways by collective imagining and doing among people whose lives, theory, and politics are situated in the terrain of unthinkability. There are fewer examples of alliance politics coproduced by marginalized groups within this volume, and this reflects the limits of our own imagination in conceiving it. Yet we find suggestive windows onto the potential of unthinkable alliance politics. In Budhan Theatre (Da Costa and Nagar, this volume) members of one criminalized social group risk everyday persecution by publicly expressing solidarity with members of a differently stigmatized group. Performers and audience members together create a dual space of performing and witnessing that opens new political possibilities by making visible and speakable forms of intersubjective relation—solidarity—that had been unthinkable. While it is crucial not to be naïve about histories of suffering and death that challenge the making of these sorts of alliances, it is clear that they hold great transformative potential. For those who refuse hegemonic frames of normative subjecthood, their very presence defies the hegemonic constructions of an "ideal" subject. When unthinkable subjects insist on their own (illegible) personhood and ally with other Others, they articulate experiences of marginalization that have pitted them against each other. This leads to enactments of a politics of collective countersubjectivity that destabilize systems of social (de)valuation that interpolate some marginalized groups as subjects of (limited) social value only through devaluation of Others. Such alliance politics constitute a significant challenge to the forms of thoroughgoing outsiderness that are fundamental to liberal democratic life, and we have much to learn about the poverty politics they engender.

Full Circle: Repoliticizing Poverty

We return now to where we began: the urgent need to creatively and insistently repoliticize poverty. *Relational Poverty Politics* advances this agenda in multiple ways: bringing back into (theoretical and political) view what must be hidden to sustain hegemonic neoliberal common sense about the causes of impoverishment, identifying and taking seriously previously unseen poverty politics, and engaging in relational knowledge making as a transformational poverty politics. We join with Roy (2016), Goode and Maskovsky (2001), O'Connor (2001), and Schram (2001), among others, in insisting that repoliticizing poverty should be the central focus of critical poverty studies. This collection extends the field in key ways.

First, we argue that projects of poverty government are themselves poverty politics that stabilize hegemonic common sense about the causes of impoverishment and that differentially incorporate marginalized persons. Theorizing poverty governance through thinkability illuminates multidimensional systems of dominance that frame structural causes of impoverishment as "individual choices" and that circulate normative "common sense" that makes racialized, classed, gendered, bordered, econo-centric rationalities appear natural, necessary, and unquestionable. Theorizing thinkable poverty politics makes plain that these rationalities, and when necessary violence to reinforce them, work to maintain elite power, a hegemonic consensus that marginalizes impoverished, racialized, and other nonnormative persons and that renders alternative poverty politics invisible, intractable, and seemingly hopeless.

Second, by theorizing unthinkable poverty politics of refusal, hope, alliance, and possibility, the book reveals a range of meanings, embodiments, dis(identifications), and rebellious practices that open new possibilities for acting on impoverishment and makes visible new possibilities for transgression and transformation. This collection foregrounds the theoretical importance of multiple sites and scales (heretofore considered unimportant) to struggles against impoverishment including dumpsters, families, theaters, schools, homes, and embodiments. Struggles emanating from these sites challenge power hierarchies far beyond merely tweaking poverty policies. Rather, persons engaged in relational poverty politics struggle against multifaceted modes of incorporation into the current conjuncture by challenging their discursive production as "poor individuals" or "deviant persons," their economic exclusion, their political misrepresentation, and/or their racialization and criminalization.

The poverty politics traced in this volume are complex, and we do not frame thinkable and unthinkable as a binary. Rather, we employ them as dialectically related analytics that reveal the range of ways in which poverty is always being politicized. Frameworks of thinkability and unthinkability allow us to understand projects of poverty government, discipline, and control as well as projects of resistance, reframing, and antiestablishment refusal. Critical analyses of thinkable poverty politics call out the projects, discourses, and norms that maintain hegemonic forms of subjectivity and reinvigorate economistic and individualizing framings of poverty. Clearly, the frame of unthinkability does not render subjects voiceless and without agency; rather, unthinkable poverty politics explored by our authors offer creative lessons for building solidarities that negotiate difference rather than negating it. Contributing authors reveal that in particular times and places, poverty politics incorporate framings and tactics from rebellious, outsider politics that we have identified as unthinkable in service of progressive forms of antipoverty solidarity to fight for recognition and resources.

Third, *Relational Poverty Politics* demonstrates that making poverty knowledge differently through a variety epistemological interventions—modest theorizing, antiessentialist modes of explanation, transnational theorizing, learning from subjects, scales, spaces of unthinkable politics — is central to repoliticizing poverty. The contributors' commitments to learning from impoverished people, learning from unthinkable politics, learning from scholars rooted outside of Northern theory's hegemony all allow them to build innovative theoretical insights. They are attentive to moments when actors refuse normative framings of subjects and causes of impoverishment and take these seriously as theory and politics. For instance, Borges describes how her research partners disagree with the modernist claim that poverty is a lack that can be filled, leading her to engage concepts of scarcity instead. Da Costa and Nagar start from situated solidarities (Nagar and Geiger 2014) that attend to how the potentials of political theater are shaped by geographical and socioinstitutional locations in order to recognize their collaborators' hunger for theater as theory and as politics. In these ways, the collection is in common cause with black geographies scholars' efforts to develop a full accounting of the historical making of subordinated lives and attention to their own place making and politics that are not deferential or referential to hegemons. Our book expands the repertoire of poverty politics by learning across spacetimes to expand concepts and to use what is visible in one place to see that which has been unthinkable in another. For instance, chapters from India, South Africa, Brazil, and Singapore trace diverse ways that racialization is bound to caste, religion, class, citizenship, gender, and more, creating intersectional processes of impoverishment. At the same time, reading from these chapters to the U.S. cases underscores the overwhelming centrality and power of race as a pervasive dimension of devaluation and invisibility, bound to all other elements of outsiderness that circulate in them: citizenship, gender, family structure, care, worker/student, position as homed/homeless, and criminalization. All the chapters illustrate how domination is exercised through multidimensional processes of incorporation and/or unthinkability, but together they collectively open a space of transnational analysis rich with insights into how these elements are assembled differently in different spacetimes, with implications for the kinds of transgressions that are possible and most urgent. We have traced some of these insights in the previous pages, and readers' own situated transnational theorizing across the chapters will yield still greater learning and build new relationalities of theory.

Relational Poverty Politics charts diverse ways to theorize vast and violent injustices of the current neoliberal conjuncture and its expressions in particular places. Theorizing thinkable poverty politics brings into view the interplay between structural forces producing impoverishment and the subjectivities, relations, and meanings through which the current consensus about poverty is secured. Theorizing unthinkable poverty politics opens alternatives to reductive "commonsense" understandings of poverty as well as strategies for disrupting racial capitalist hegemonies. Making poverty knowledge through relational epistemologies remakes the limits of hegemonic political and theoretical imaginaries and is itself a poverty politics. These interrelated lines of thought that have traveled through and guided this collection offer concrete, consequential, and vital ways to repoliticize poverty. Join us!

NOTE

1. In particular we are grateful to Edgar Sandoval, Elizabeth Shoffner, Magie Ramirez, Monica Farias, Emma Slager, Austin Crane, Yolanda Valencia, Megan Ybarra, Katie Gillespie, Michelle Daigle, Tish Lopez, Lucy Jarosz, Ananya Roy, Ruthie Wilson Gilmore, Laura Pulido, Eric Sheppard, Doreen Massey, and all members of our 2014 and 2016 relational poverty seminars.

REFERENCES

Adamovsky, Ezequiel. 2009. "Historia De la Clase Media Argentina: apogeo y decadencia de una ilusión, 1919–2003." Buenos Aires: Planeta.
Butler, Judith. 2004. *Precarious Life*. London: Verso Books.
Cacho, Lisa Marie. 2012. *Social Death: Racialized Rightlessness and the Criminalization of the Unprotected*. New York: New York University Press.
Elwood, Sarah, Victoria Lawson, and Samuel Nowak. 2015. "Middle-Class Poverty Politics: Making Place, Making People." *Annals of the Association of American Geographers* 105, no. 1: 123–43. doi:10.1080/00045608.2014.968945.
Fernandes, Leela, and Patrick Heller. 2011. "Hegemonic Aspirations: New Middle Class Politics and India's Democracy in Comparative Perspective." *Critical Asian Studies* 38, no. 4: 495–522.
Gibson-Graham, J. K. 2008. "Diverse Economies: Performative Practices for Other Worlds." *Progress in Human Geography* 32, no. 5: 613–32. doi:10.1177/0309132508090821.
Goode, Judith, and Jeff Maskovsky. 2001. *The New Poverty Studies: The Ethnography of Power, Politics and Impoverished People in the United States*. New York: New York University Press.
Hall, Stuart, and Doreen Massey. 2010. "Interpreting the Crisis." *Soundings* 44, no. 1: 57–71. doi:10.3898/136266210791036791.
Jakobsen, Janet R. 1998. *Working Alliances and the Politics of Difference: Diversity and Feminist Ethics*. Bloomington: Indiana University Press.
Koopman, Sarah. 2015. "Social Movements." In *The Blackwell Companion to Political Geography*, edited by Virginie Mamadouh and Anna Secor, 339–51. London: Wiley-Blackwell.
Lawson, Victoria, Sarah Elwood, Santiago Canevaro, and Nicolas Viotti. 2015. "Poverty Politics, Class Subjects and Relational Practices in Argentina and the U.S." *Environment and Planning A* 47: 1873–91.
Leitner, Helga, Jamie Peck, and Eric Sheppard. 2006. *Contesting Neoliberalism: Urban Frontiers*. New York: Guilford.
McKittrick, Katherine. 2016. "Rebellion/Invention/Groove." *Small Axe: A Caribbean Platform for Criticism* 20, no. 49: 79–91.
McKittrick, Katherine, and Clyde Adrian Woods. 2007. *Black Geographies and the Politics of Place*. Boston: South End Press.

Muñoz, José Esteban. 1999. *Disidentifications: Queers of Color and the Performance of Politics*. Minneapolis: University of Minnesota Press.

Nagar, Richa, and Susan Geiger. 2014. "Reflexivity, Positionality and Languages of Collaboration in Fieldwork." In *Muddying the Waters*, edited by Richa Nagar, 81–104. Champaign: University of Illinois Press.

O'Connor, Alice. 2001. *Poverty Knowledge: Social Science, Social Policy, and the Poor in Twentieth-Century U.S. History*. Princeton, N.J.: Princeton University Press.

Rose, Nikolas, and Peter Miller. 1992. "Political Power beyond the State: Problematics of Government." *British Journal of Sociology* 3, no. 2: 173–205. doi:10.1111/j.1468-4446.2009.01247.x.

Rowe, Aimee Carrillo. 2008. *Power Lines: On the Subject of Feminist Alliances*. Durham, N.C.: Duke University Press.

Roy, Ananya. 2012. "Why the Middle Class Matters." *Singapore Journal of Tropical Geography* 33, no. 1: 25–28. doi:10.1111/j.1467-9493.2012.00445.x.

———. 2016. "In Defense of Poverty." *Items: Insights from the Social Sciences*. http://items .ssrc.org/in-defense-of-poverty (accessed August 25, 2016).

Schram, Sanford. 2001. *After Welfare: The Culture of Postindustrial Social Policy*. New York: New York University Press.

Wainwright, Joel, and Sook-Jin Kim. 2008. "Battles in Seattle Redux: Transnational Resistance to a Neoliberal Trade Agreement." *Antipode* 40, no. 4: 513–34. doi:10.1111/j.1467-8330.2008.00622.x.

Walia, Harsha. 2013. "Transient Servitude: Migrant Labour in Canada and the Apartheid of Citizenship." *Race & Class* 52, no. 1: 71–84. doi:10.1177/0306396810371766.

CONTRIBUTORS

Antonádia Borges is Associate Professor of Anthropology at the University of Brasilia. She does research on diverging political stances from peripheral worlds and ontologies, in particular from Brazil and South Africa. She has published in *Vibrant, Mana,* and *Estudios Sociologicos* on the political surplus value extracted from beneficiaries of state social policies, on the transversal production of racism through land dispossession, and on gender imbalance along lines of modernist exclusionary projects.

Dia Da Costa is Associate Professor in the Department of Educational Policy Studies at the University of Alberta. She is the author of *Development Dramas* (Routledge, 2009) and *Politicizing Creative Economy: Activism and a Hunger called Theatre* (University of Illinois Press, 2016). Using transnational feminist, postcolonial, and Marxian approaches, she analyzes cultural politics of "development," activist pedagogies, and unrecognized spaces of creativity and knowledge to understand the intersecting histories of colonial-capitalist, nationalist, leftist, and neoliberal politics.

Sarah Elwood is Professor of Geography at the University of Washington and cofounder of the Relational Poverty Network with Victoria Lawson. Her research contributes to relational poverty, urban geography, visual politics/methods, and critical digital geographies. Her current activities include collaborative research on middle-class poverty politics in mixed-income neighborhoods in Buenos Aires and Seattle and on visual politics in poverty activism. She is coeditor of *Crowdsourcing Geographic Knowledge* (Springer, 2012) and *Qualitative GIS* (Sage, 2009), and author of journal articles in *Progress in Human Geography, Annals of the Association of American Geographers, Transactions of the Institute of British Geographers, Antipode,* and others.

David Boarder Giles is Lecturer in Anthropology at Deakin University in Melbourne, Australia. He writes about cultural economies of waste and homelessness, and the politics of urban food security and public space, particularly in "global" cities. He has done extensive ethnographic fieldwork in Seattle and other cities in the United States and Australasia with dumpster divers, urban agriculturalists, grassroots activists, homeless residents, and chapters of Food Not Bombs—a globalized movement of grassroots soup kitchens.

Jim Glassman is Professor of Geography at the University of British Columbia. His research focuses on industrial transformation, transformation of labor, urbanization, and social struggle around these processes, particularly in East and Southeast Asia. His current research examines the development of a regional economy involving firms from South Korea, Thailand, the Philippines, Taiwan, and Singapore in the context of the Cold War. He is author of *Bounding the Mekong: The Asian Development Bank, China, and Thailand* (University of Hawai'i Press, 2010) and *Thailand at the Margins: Internationalization of the State and the Transformation of Labour* (Oxford University Press, 2004).

Victoria Lawson is Professor of Geography at the University of Washington, Director of the University of Washington Honors Program, and cofounder of the Relational Poverty Network with Sarah Elwood. She teaches in the fields of human geography, critical poverty studies, and feminist care ethics. Her research focuses on relational poverty analysis and feminist theorizations of politics to explore the possibilities for inclusive alliances across differences to challenge inequality. She is the coauthor of *Progress Handbook of Human Geography* (Sage, 2014), author of *Making Development Geography* (Hodder, UK, 2007), and editor of *Care of the Body: Spaces of Practice*, a special issue of *Social and Cultural Geography* (2011). Her writing has also appeared in *Annals of the Association of American Geographers, Environment and Planning A, Economic Geography*, and others.

Felipe Magalhães is Professor of Economic Geography at the Federal University of Minas Gerais, Belo Horizonte, Brazil. He has published in Brazilian journals and edited books on themes related to urban theory and political economy, metropolitan restructuring, and urban policy. His current research focuses on the new cycle of urban social movements in Brazil, with a particular focus on their interfaces with cultural production.

Jeff Maskovsky is Associate Professor and Chair of Urban Studies at Queens College, and of Anthropology and Environmental Psychology at CUNY Graduate Center. His research and writing focus on urban poverty, grassroots activism, and political economic change in the United States. His publications include two coedited volumes, *New Poverty Studies: The Ethnography of Power, Politics and Impoverished People in the United States* (NYU Press, 2001) and *Rethinking America: The Imperial Homeland in the 21st Century* (Paradigm Press, 2009), and a forthcoming monograph, *Poverty and the Fight for Life in the New Inner City*.

Richa Nagar is Professor in the College of Liberal Arts at the University of Minnesota. Her intellectual, pedagogical, and creative labor focuses on writing lives and struggles across the borders of languages, genres, disciplines, and geographical locations. Her most recent book, *Muddying the Waters* (2014), draws on years of collaborative building of visions and worlds, chiefly with Sangtin Writers, with whom she coauthored *Sangtin Yatra* (2004) and *Playing with Fire* (2006). She has been cobuilding a multisited community theater project that brings together amateurs and professional actors to reflect on social issues through literary texts and through their own stories (http://jananatyachintan.blogspot.com/).

Genevieve Negrón-Gonzales is Assistant Professor in the School of Education, University of San Francisco. Her work connects political economy, higher education, and immigration issues, highlighting how migrant "illegality" is (re)produced through the racialized spaces of neoliberalized higher education. Her research focuses on how undocumented young people are changing the political and legislative terrain surrounding "illegality" and national belonging. Her work has been published in *Latino Studies, Aztlan: A Journal of Chicano Studies, Journal of Latinos and Education,* and *Harvard Educational Review.* She is coauthor of *Encountering Poverty: Thinking and Acting in an Unequal World* (2016).

LaShawnDa Pittman is Assistant Professor in the American Ethnic Studies Department at the University of Washington. She is currently focused on three distinct but interrelated aspects of grandparent caregiving—a book manuscript that uses historical oral narratives and qualitative data to examine the caregiving experiences of black grandmothers from slavery to the present, scholarly publications, and a project that examines and intervenes on the health disparities experienced by grandparent caregivers and uses social and biomedical science approaches. In addition to a number of edited volumes, her scholarship has been published in *The Russell Sage Foundation Journal of the Social Sciences, Social Science and Medicine,* and *Women, Gender, and Families of Color.* Her other research interests include social stratification and inequality, urban poverty, race and ethnicity, gender and families, research methods, public policy, and health disparities.

Frances Fox Piven is Distinguished Professor of Political Science and Sociology at the City University of New York. Her academic work and activism have centered on economic and racial justice, social movement politics, and labor organizing for over five decades. She is a Relational Poverty Network Steering Committee member, and author of multiple books that inform the RPN's work, from *Regulating the Poor* (1972) and *Poor People's Movements* (1977) to *Challenging Authority: How Ordinary People Change America* (2008) and *Lessons for Our Struggle* (2012).

Preeti Sampat is Assistant Professor of Sociology at the School of Liberal Studies, Ambedkar University Delhi. Her work examines conflicts over land and "resources" around large-scale infrastructure and urbanization projects in India. She is currently working on a book manuscript that combines previous and current ethnographic and archival work, to interrogate relations around nature, infrastructure, rent, and work in India.

Thomas Swerts is Postdoctoral Fellow at the Centre on Inequalities, Poverty, Social Exclusion and the City (OASeS) of the University of Antwerp. He received his Ph.D. in sociology from the University of Chicago. His ethnographic research focuses on undocumented activism and its implications for citizenship in the United States and Europe. He has previously published on noncitizen citizenship, transnational immigrant organizing, and storytelling in the DREAM movement.

Junjia Ye is an urban geographer at Massey University in New Zealand. Her research interests lie at the intersections of cultural diversity, critical cosmopolitanism, class, gender studies, and the political-economic development of urban Southeast Asia. Alongside extensive ethnographic research methods, she also uses techniques of film and photography to create visual narratives through her work. Her writings have been published in journals such as *Transactions of the Institute of British Geographers*, *Geoforum*, *Journal of Ethnic and Migration Studies*, and *Gender, Place & Culture*.

INDEX

Abe, Shinzo, 101
Abers, Rebecca, 150
abject economies, 2, 117, 120–21, 125–26
ACT UP (AIDS Coalition to Unleash Power),
13, 77–91, 92n6, 223–24, 230–31. *See also*
LGBTQ communities
Adams, Vincanne, 20n4
adivasi, 209, 214
Adoption and Safe Families Act (1997), 27
Adoption Assistance and Child Welfare Act
(1980), 27
adverse incorporation, 6, 11, 57
African National Congress (ANC), 193
Agamben, Giorgio, 87, 123–24, 126
Aid to Families with Dependent Children
(AFDC), 28
AIDS. *See* HIV/AIDS
alliance politics, 212, 216, 228–33; of DREAM
movement, 166–80
allyship, 16, 169–70, 174–75, 180
amart (Democrat Party), 138–41, 144
American Indian Movement, 144
anarchist soup kitchens. *See* Food Not Bombs
anarcho-punk bands, 118, 119
apartheid, 186, 189, 192, 197, 227
APOC (Anarchist/Autonomous People of
Color), 116
Arab Spring (2010–12), 5, 155
Asamblea Popular Horizontal (APH), 160
"austerity urbanism," 78–79, 81, 86–87
"authentic interlocutors," 184

Bag, Alice, 119, 126
Bail, Christopher, 172
Bangladeshis, in Singapore, 50–51
Baran, Paul, 134
Bariya, Meena, 213, 216n6
Bell, John, 84–86
Belo Horizonte (Brazil), 156–57, 160
Bhal Bachao Samiti (Protect Bhal Committee),
102

black geographies, 8–9, 14, 221, 226–27, 229,
233, 235
Black Lives Matter movement, 5, 118
black money, 98
Black Panthers, 127, 144
Borges, Antonádia, 15–16, 183–98, 227, 228,
235
Bourdieu, Pierre, 122–23, 171
Brazil urban policies, 149–63, 226, 232
Budhan Theatre (India), 202, 205–7, 215, 225,
233
Butler, Judith, 122, 232

Cacho, Lisa Marie, 14; on culture of punish-
ment, 46–47; *Social Death*, 20n1, 20n7; on
un/thinkable politics, 2, 224, 226, 229, 231
California, 11–12, 61–74, 222
California Special Training Institute, 135
Césaire, Aimé, 123
Chakravorty, Sanjoy, 97–98
CHAMP (Community HIV/AIDS Mobiliza-
tion Project), 88, 92n3
Chavez, Leo, 70
Cherniavsky, Eva, 123
Chhara people (India), 205–8, 215, 222, 225,
227, 233
Chicana/os, 119. *See also* Latina/os
childcare: for grandparent-headed households,
33–35; in Singapore, 52–53
Chinese, in Singapore, 47–50, 53–54
Chudasama, Pradyumna Singh, 102–3
citizenship, 12–14, 205–7, 224; alliances for,
180; "biological," 80–81, 230; economic, 80;
multiculturalism and, 48; neoliberal, 186;
race and, 3–4, 43–57, 124, 220–24, 231, 235
Clark, Dylan, 117
class, 18, 123, 229; AIDS activism and, 79,
82–86, 91; gender and, 230; race and, 3–4,
124, 220–24, 231, 235; welfare policies based
on, 29, 52–57. *See also* DACA program;
DREAM movement

243

..

GEOGRAPHIES OF JUSTICE AND SOCIAL TRANSFORMATION